AN AMAZONIAN MYTH AND ITS HISTORY

OXFORD STUDIES IN
SOCIAL AND CULTURAL ANTHROPOLOGY

Oxford Studies in Social and Cultural Anthropology represents the work of authors, new and established, that will set the criteria of excellence in ethnographic description and innovation in analysis. The series serves as an essential source of information about the world and the discipline.

In the chilly air of a dry season dawn, a man drinks the beer served by a girl at her *kigimawlo*

AN AMAZONIAN MYTH
AND ITS HISTORY

PETER GOW

OXFORD
UNIVERSITY PRESS

OXFORD
UNIVERSITY PRESS

Great Clarendon Street, Oxford OX2 6DP

Oxford University Press is a department of the University of Oxford.
It furthers the University's objective of excellence in research, scholarship,
and education by publishing worldwide in

Oxford New York

Athens Auckland Bangkok Bogotá Buenos Aires
Cape Town Chennai Dar es Salaam Delhi Florence Hong Kong Istanbul
Karachi Kolkata Kuala Lumpur Madrid Melbourne Mexico City Mumbai
Nairobi Paris São Paulo Shanghai Singapore Taipei Tokyo Toronto Warsaw

with associated companies in Berlin Ibadan

Oxford is a registered trade mark of Oxford University Press
in the UK and in certain other countries

Published in the United States
by Oxford University Press Inc., New York

British Library Cataloguing in Publication Data

Data available

Library of Congress Cataloging in Publication Data

Data applied for

ISBN 0-19-924195-3
ISBN 0-19-924196-1 (Pbk.)

1 3 5 7 9 10 8 6 4 2

Typeset in Ehrhardt
by Cambrian Typesetters, Frimley, Surrey

Printed in Great Britain
on acid-free paper by
T.J. International Ltd.
Padstow, Cornwall

For my parents,
James and Helen Gow

ACKNOWLEDGEMENTS

My fieldwork on the Bajo Urubamba between 1980 and 1999 was funded by the Social Science Research Council, the British Museum, the Nuffield Foundation, and the British Academy. The University of East Anglia provided free time for fieldwork, while a visiting professorship to the Museu Nacional/Federal University of Rio de Janeiro, leave from the University of Manchester, and the generous forbearance of the London School of Economics, gave me the time and the wherewithal to write it.

Artemio Fasabi Gordón died on the 6th of June 1991, and I tell some of his story in this book. Pablo Rodriguez Manchinari died on the 3rd March 1990, and this book is an inadequate monument to a great friend. Mauricio Fasabi and Clotilde Gordón, Artemio's parents and Pablo's parents-in-law, must have seen me coming, for they took me straight into their lives on that unforgettable day in December 1980. Their daughter Sara Fasabi, Pablo's widow, has always provided me with a place to live well. I thank Lilí Torres, Mauricio Roberto Fasabi, Antonio Urquía, Teresa Campos, Marcial Miranda, Julian Miranda, Inez González, Juan Mosombite (padre), the late Luisa Campos, Celia Mosombite, Juan Mosombite (hijo), Ramón Mosombite, Linder Melendez, Miriam Mosombite, , Lucinda Mosombite, the late Adolfina Campos, Antonio Zapata, Arminda Quiroz, Segundo Quiroz, Julia Laureano, Segundo Blanco, Manuel Zapata, Lidia Fasabi, the late Clara Flores, the late Jorge Manchinari, Cecilia Manchinari, Felix Rodriguez, Jorge Rivas, Candelaria Camaiteri, Segundo Monsín, Etelvina Cushichinari, Virgilio Gabino, José Torres, Berna Zumaeta, Julio Shahuano, Elena Pacaya, Moisés Miqueas, and the late Pedro Gordón. There are many more, particularly those swarms of children, mostly unrecognizable to me now that they have grown into men and women and have cast aside their childhood nicknames, who were always on hand to answer my questions with a total disregard for adult conventions, and to ask their own questions for the same reason. I also thank those Campa people of the Gran Pajonal, Perené, Alto Tambo and Ene areas that I met in 1978, and especially Jaanquiri, Alesandro, and the late Augusto.

This book originated in Peru in 1988, appearing to me quite suddenly one night in December of that year in Iquitos. Fernando Santos, Frederica Barclay, and Luisa Elvira Belaunde were godparents to its inception, for which I thank them heartily. I also owe much to Dilwyn and Claire Jenkins, Michael Bowles, Cecilia McCallum, Patricia Thorndike, Alberto Chirif, Lucy Trapnell, Carlos Montenegro, Maureen Llewelyn-Jones, Alonso Zarzar, Sean and Angela Hagan, and Fiona Frank. The Dominican priests, P. Ricardo Alvarez and P. Pedro Rey, and the schoolteachers of Santa Clara were consistently generous with their practical, moral, and intellectual aid. In particular, Teresa Barinesa has always been unfailing in her help and generous with the fruits of her own profound insight into the lives of people in the Santa Clara area.

This book originated in Peru, but it owes a lot to Brazil. Its hardest passages were written in Rio de Janeiro, and it got its first public hearing as a series of seminars at the Museu Nacional there. I thank Aparecida Vilaça, Marcio Goldman, Tania Stôlze Lima, Déborah Danowski, Bruna Franchetto, Carlos Fausto, Sylvia Caiuby Novaes, Cecilia McCallum, Edilson Teixeira, Claudia Rezende, Vanessa Lea, Robin Wright, and my former students and colleagues in the Museu Nacional for their manifold support. I also thank all those commentators at seminars and lectures in Rio de Janeiro, São Paulo, Campinas, Curitiba, and Salvador for their helpful comments.

Joanna Overing once set me a literary challenge, which I here take up in her honour. I also thank Marilyn Strathern, Caroline Humphrey, Stephen Hugh-Jones, Alfred Gell, Simeran Gell, Peter Rivière, Anne-Christine Taylor, Philippe Descola, Karen Jacobs, Maria Phylactou, Heather Gibson, Terence Turner, Lynnette Caicco, Maurice Bloch, Jadran Mimica, Andrew Jones, Thomas Fillitz, Andre Gingrich, Ulrike Davis-Sulikowski, Nicholas Green, John Onians, Elizabeth de Bievres, Stephanie Jones, Timothy Davies, Sheila Arup, Nikolay Zhoukov, Jonathan Meuli, Rosie Gunraj, Cesare Poppi, Joanne Pillsbury, William Rea, Melissa Medich, Andrew Holding, Heonik Kwon, Eva Castellanos, Patricia Peach, Jeannette Edwards, Paul Towell, Tim Ingold, Borut Telban, Jean Lave, Axel Koehler, Maia Green, Penny Harvey, Ben Campbell, Elizabeth Ewart, Angela Torresan, David Rodgers, and Isabella Lepri.

I thank Nancy Munn for showing me how to research Piro art forms ethnographically, and Andreas Broeckmann for teaching me historical methodology and analysis. I thank Claude Lévi-Strauss for his very kind encouragement, and Rebecca Posen, Edward Simpson, and Sam Treglown for responding with such generous attention to my first public attempt to articulate my own ideas about Lévi-Strauss's work on myth. This book could never have been written at all but for the good will and sustained efforts of my great anthropological interlocutors, Christina Toren and Eduardo Viveiros de Castro.

This book records Piro people's curiosity about the lives of Scottish people. When we first met we had, to my knowledge, only a football match to connect us. It turned out to be much more than that. I thank my family and friends in Scotland for having supported me throughout, and I dedicate it to my mother and to the memory of my father.

CONTENTS

Contents

LIST OF PLATES

LIST OF MAPS

'Pedro, tell me, is your country of Scotland here on this earth, or is it on another planet?'

Denis Fasabi, Artemio's eldest son, 1995

INTRODUCTION

Artemio Fasabi, Piro headman of Santa Clara village on the Bajo Urubamba river in Peruvian Amazonia, told me a story about a man who went under the earth and became a white-lipped peccary, a kind of wild pig, on the evening of 15 January 1982. This book is a history of that story, which I here call, 'A Man who went under the Earth'. Such a history necessarily includes a history of the conversation and of the evening on which it was told, and beyond that a history of how the world of Piro people like Artemio had been characterized by profound changes over the previous century, and of how those changes were both effected by them and made meaningful for them.

Three reasons make Artemio's story an appropriate point of departure for this kind of historical study by an anthropologist. Firstly, I heard this story in circumstances of such heightened interest to myself that I know a great deal about the context within which it was told, and that knowledge of context is vital to any successful account of such a phenomenon. Secondly, the published literature on Piro mythology contains other versions of this myth, which differ from it in remarkable ways, and which suggest that this myth was changing as rapidly as the world of which it was a part. Thirdly, Artemio's story itself was about transformation. It told of a man who, in ancient times, went into the underworld, changed his clothing, and became another kind of being, a white-lipped peccary, an important game animal for Piro people. As such, this story serves me as a route into understanding how Piro people might have thought about change in general, and hence how they might have thought about the specific changes that they have created, experienced, desired, or feared in their own lives.

This book therefore explores the possibility of uniting two of the most important projects in European anthropology. The first is Malinowski's development of methods for the collection of ethnographic data through fieldwork by participant observation, and for the analysis of such data in order to elucidate the hold which life has for the people so studied. The second is Lévi-Strauss's reassertion of the importance of historical methods in anthropology, developed in his analysis of indigenous American mythology. They have been held to stand at odds, but the importance of both projects is illustrated well by the intellectual problems raised by Artemio's story as told to me on the evening of 15 January 1982.

Within a Changing Amazonian Lived World

That evening when Artemio told me 'A Man who went under the Earth' stood out strongly from most of my experiences of Piro myth-telling. Usually when Piro people told me myths, I would listen with interest, but I never felt that

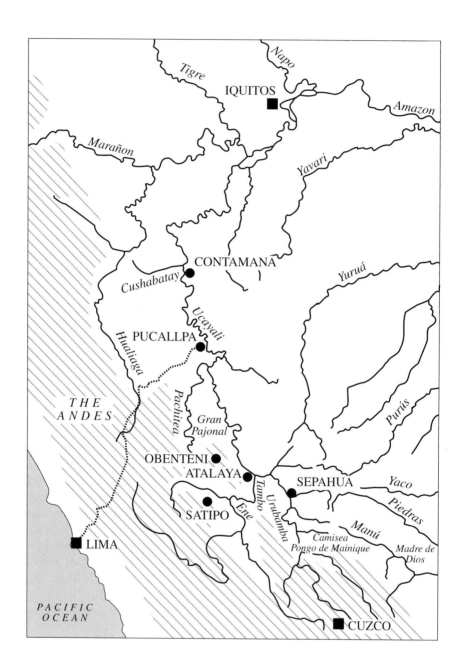

Map 1. Eastern Peru, showing places mentioned in the text

these stories meant very much to myself or to their tellers. They were riveting to hear, and they were often very intriguing, but they never seemed to have much relevance to Piro people's lives. Nor did Piro people seem to have much to say about them beyond the mere fact of telling them. They certainly never appealed to them as guides to, or justifications for, any actions. In short, Piro myths did not seem to do very much.

These stories are called *tsrunnini ginkakle* in Piro, and *cuentos de los ancianos* in the local Ucayali dialect of Spanish, and both terms can be translated as 'ancient people's stories'. The 'ancient people' were those long dead generations of Piro people whose world, so living Piro people told me, had ended with their enslavement by the rubber bosses. The ancient people had been very different, I was constantly told, from contemporary Piro people: they had no villages and lived in the forest, in small in-marrying groups which fought each other; they wore hand-woven and painted cotton robes and skirts, unlike the true clothing of today; they pierced their noses and lips to wear silver ornaments; they were powerful shamans; they were ignorant and uncivilized; they spoke no Spanish. The list could continue, with more and more attributions of salient differences to contemporary Piro people. When talking of the ancient people, Piro people always stressed the temporal distance and difference of their world, even as they would affirm that that world had been lived out here, along the Urubamba river. Similarly, when I heard 'ancient people's stories' being told, the actions described were often explicitly located in known places in the local area, but in a remote and misty past age. The talk of the 'ancient people', like the recitation of their stories, seemed like muted and fragmented echoes of a world that had been shattered by history.

Even though I found the Piro myths interesting, my failure to try to think through what these stories meant for the people who told them rested on the assumption that I already knew what they meant, and that was, 'not a great deal'. And I assumed this because I imagined that the way Piro people talked about the past was familiar and unproblematic. I imagined that Piro people were simply telling me their version of the well-known story by which an isolated indigenous Amazonian society is invaded, disrupted and altered by the forces of colonial expansion. Piro people had survived this process, which had indeed begun in earnest in the late nineteenth century as the rubber extraction industry moved into the Alto Ucayali area and as the Piro people living along the Bajo Urubamba river were transformed into debt slaves. I thought that, even if the people had survived, their culture had collapsed in the face of this massive challenge, and the newly enslaved Piro people and their descendants had had to borrow new cultural forms from the rubber bosses and other outsiders in order to endure in their new and violent world. It is a well known story, and oft-told by anthropologists, missionaries, government officials, film-makers, travellers and the like.

Confirmation for my impression came from the way Piro people talked to me about the 'ancient people' and their stories. Often my questions would lead them to say, 'I don't know, ask the old people, they know these things.' I seemed therefore truly to be in the presence of a dying tradition, which was only surviving in that most precarious of media, the memories of a few old people. This too is a story familiar enough from accounts of indigenous Amazonian societies, and from elsewhere in the Americas and beyond. A whole genre of anthropological method, rescue anthropology, had been developed to deal with this issue, and some impressive reconstructions of defunct societies had been done through interviewing a few old people about their younger lives.[1]

I had no taste for that kind of thing then. My concern was for the immediate and recent lives of Piro people. I had gone to the Bajo Urubamba precisely to study an indigenous Amazonian people who had extensive contacts with alien dominators, such as bosses in the industrial extraction of tropical hardwoods, and Catholic and Protestant missionaries. I did not, at the time, see any value in reconstructing a dead culture, for the pressing task was to study how Piro people survived in the world in which they lived, as it was constituted at the time of my fieldwork.

In doing this, I was following the project of the Peruvian anthropologist Stefano Varese, whose work has rightly been seen by Fernando Santos Granero as marking a rupture in the historical understanding of the indigenous peoples of Peruvian Amazonia (Santos 1988). In his book *La Sal de los Cerros* (1973 [1968]), about the Campa people who live to the west of the Bajo Urubamba, and in the article, 'Inter-Ethnic Relations in the Selva of Peru' (1972), Varese set out the conditions of a historical vision of the indigenous peoples of Peruvian Amazonia, or 'the selva' as it is known in Peru. He wrote 'By calling for the introduction of the historical perspective into our analysis we are not, of course, thinking of an historical narrative of events but of a general delineation of the conditions which in the course of centuries have made possible a certain social and economic structure in the Peruvian selva' (1972: 117). The call, therefore, was to analyse indigenous societies in Marxist terms, and the historical perspective was to be understood as the articulation of these societies with the development of capitalism and its attendant forms of colonialism.

The position of someone like Varese was attractive to someone like me for many reasons. I was young and left-wing, having grown up in the tail-end of a dying empire. And I was formulating my project in a world marked by the revolutionary struggles of Zimbabwe, Angola, Mozambique, South Africa, and Nicaragua. These struggles, and others elsewhere, were following the heroic efforts of the Marxist revolutionaries who had finally liberated Vietnam. People like me saw this victory, and those ongoing struggles, not simply as the 'end of imperialism', but the possibility of a new order of things in a world we perceived of as common to humanity. If the older world order had unified

---

[1] See, for example, Weltfish (1971) on the Pawnee, or Chapman (1982) on the Selk'nam.

humanity through capitalist insertion and its attendant imperialist expansion, this world order in the making would unify humanity through general emancipation from exploitation and the consequent social justice. Central to this new order was the assertion that all human histories were, in fact, our single common history.

For many of us who were studying anthropology at the time, this assertion of our one, common history chimed with our dissatisfaction with what we understood to be the existing project of anthropology. Many students of my generation felt the older methods and aims of anthropology, especially in its British form, to be both colonialist in inspiration and distancing in effect. The Marxist call for an anthropology that was dialectical, that asserted that anthropological analysis was concretely linked to the object analysed through our common history, seemed like a liberation in itself from the stultifying imperialist survey and control which we imagined had compromised an older anthropological tradition. More importantly, we found this older tradition of anthropology to be boring. That was no small point, for this was the heyday of punk music, and punk music had taught us that boredom was a very reliable guide in the identification of all forms of knowledge that were irrelevant to understanding the world we saw around us and our places within it.

That is how my project had been conceived, and that is how I set about getting to know Piro people. Inevitably, my intentions suffered a few knocks when brought into actual contact with those of Piro people. Because I was a Marxist and concerned with consciousness-raising, I made free with my analyses of the inadequacies of the laws for titling indigenous people's lands and the shortcomings of the local educational system. This was my duty towards the common history that linked Piro people and myself. My attempts at radical political engagement were brought to an abrupt halt when an important Piro leader told me quietly but sternly, 'We are happy for you to live here among us, learning how we live. That's fine. But we don't want you to tell us what we should do.'

After that, I learned to keep my views on the justice of land titling and the quality of local education provision to myself. I was living with Piro people on their sufferance, and they were perfectly capable of throwing me out of their villages. And because I undoubtedly irritated and offended them in so many ways that I was not aware of, I was determined not to do it consciously too.

But the biggest blow of all to my intentions came from the way Piro people talked about their lives and the past. Piro people had experienced most of the modes of ill-usage that have been the common lot of indigenous Amazonian peoples. They had experienced debt-slavery to violent and abusive bosses; they had experienced extensive missionization by Catholic priests and North American Protestant missionaries with scant regard for their values and ideas; they had experienced the theft of their traditional territory masquerading as the granting of land titles; and the younger people had experienced years of schooling that seemed designed solely to teach them that they were stupid. But despite these experiences, Piro people seemed to me to have a remarkable optimism about their historical circumstances, and indeed to describe it in essentially progressive terms. Instead of recounting their past and present circumstances as a litany of exploitation, brutality and injustice, they seemed to talk about it as an onwards-and-upwards tale of progress from the historic low-point of the world of the ancient people to the sunny futures beckoning to their children and grandchildren. Their history was, as they said, the long and difficult process of how they had come to be 'civilized people'. It seemed that history in Varese's sense, which I considered an unmitigated disaster for Piro people, was thought of by them as a process of learning that, rough as it had been, was well worth it.

I was totally dumbfounded by this. Because I actually liked many Piro people, I was unwilling to draw the necessary conclusion. This was that these kind and friendly people were not simply the victims of progress, to borrow Bodley's term (1982), but the stooges of progress too. History had taken away most of what had once belonged to them, and had even taken away their memories of a time when they had been the undisputed masters of an autonomous world. They had lost everything, even the willingness to resist the mental slavery that all of their defeats had brought them. It was such a depressing conclusion, and I disliked even considering it. Piro people seemed to me be but shadows of their half-forgotten ancestors.

But my hard case turned out to be the common lot of ethnographers, for I simply did not know what Piro people were talking about. When they talked about the past, I assumed they were talking about history in the sense of our common history. For me, history was what united us, and was to be the common ground of our conversations, and of my dialectical analysis of their situation. But Piro people were totally indifferent to what I thought about history. They never asked me about it, and were by turns bemused or irritated when I did offer them my historical analyses. In retrospect, I realize that they must have wondered at my strange talk, for how could I know anything worth knowing about the past of Piro people, when I was manifestly a very young man who had arrived but yesterday?

When Piro people talked about the past, they were primarily interested in the genesis of the relations of kinship which were of central importance in their everyday lives. For example, when they told me of the enslavement of the ancient people, it was I who was troubled by the brutality of that process. They were not. They were interested in how this enslavement had allowed the ancient people to escape the social enclosure that had characterized their lives. As slaves of the rubber bosses, the ancient people began to intermarry with each other, and to thus establish the ramifying ties of kinship that link together all contemporary Piro people. And these kin ties mattered to Piro people, for it was through them that they made a living, and it was within these relations that they lived. To live surrounded by generous kinspeople is the joy of Piro people.

It is not that Piro people did not see all of the exploitation, brutality, and injustice to which they have been subjected. They saw it very clearly indeed, and they had a perfectly simple explanation of it. *Kajine*, 'white people', are dangerous to deal with, and exploitation, brutality and injustice were fairly predictable consequences of any interactions with them. The potential of such consequences must be carefully managed in all interactions with white people. It has not escaped Piro people's attention that living surrounded by generous kinspeople is not a value shared by white people, and hence that white people are a very different kind of people to themselves. For Piro people, white people possess many desirable things, but the acquisition of these things requires a subtle politics to minimize the malign potential of relations with white people as far as possible.

As I came to understand what life meant to Piro people, their accounts of the past began to make more sense. In my earlier book, *Of Mixed Blood* (1991), I showed how ties between kinspeople are crucial to the subsistence economy of Piro people, for it is through such ties that labour is mobilized for the collective work of making plantain and manioc gardens, and it is along such kin ties that women circulate the game that men catch in the river or in the forest. Piro people conceive kin ties as the memories of food and care received from others, especially memories of such generosity in childhood. People are generous to kinspeople because they remember that they, too, received the fruits of such generosity when they were too young to feed or care for themselves. Given the centrality of memory in the constitution of kin ties, I argued in that book that when Piro people talk about the past they are primarily talking about kinship.

This was why, when Piro people talked about their ancestors, the 'ancient people', they stressed temporal distance and cultural differences. By maximizing these differences, Piro people could maximize the extent of the kinship ties that ordered their lives as a ramifying network of social relations. That was why they talked so much about the 'ancient people': these apparently half-forgotten ancestors were constantly evoked to affirm how much had changed, and in changing, how much had been made. The recurrent claim that the 'ancient people' did not live in villages was simply another way of affirming that contemporary people did live in villages, and of marking the scale of that fact as an achievement. Piro people had made these kinship ties precisely through their successive relationships with different forms of *kajine*, 'white people'. For these people and the other indigenous people of the Bajo Urubamba, I concluded that kinship *is* history.

This conclusion radically shifted my understanding of Piro people's history, and of my own. If Piro people can take the events and processes by which capitalism inserted itself among them, and by which colonial hierarchies came to order their lives, as the very process by which they generate kinship ties, then clearly this history was no longer, in any meaningful sense, our common history. And because this was so, it could no longer serve as our common ground, nor could it function as the object and location of my dialectical analysis of their situation and my own. The result was that *Of Mixed Blood*, for all that it remained materialist in rooting the analysis in how Piro people live through their practical engagement with the world, ended up with *two* chapters on history. The first presented an account of the recent history of the Bajo Urubamba area as reconstructed by myself from the written documentary archive, with minimal recourse to what Piro people told me. The second reproduced the first, but now as told to me by Piro people as they went about their lives, and it necessarily looked both very similar to, and very different from, the first chapter.

This division seemed analytically necessary to me, in order to prevent my ethnographic descriptions being constantly bogged down in historical arguments. In *Of Mixed Blood*, I was concerned to describe and analyse that feature of Piro people's lives that had most surprised me, their remarkable coherence. Far from being a chaotic mass of historical fragments, Piro people's lives seemed to make a great deal of sense to them. For example, it was obvious to me that the constant reference by Piro people to the importance of the legally recognized *Comunidad Nativa*, 'Native Community', could not have pre-dated land registration in the mid-1970s. Clearly, this was a recent historical phenomenon. But rather than ask, 'What idioms of village organization did Piro people use before the *Comunidad Nativa*?', I was far more concerned to show the meaningfulness of this concept for Piro people in my field experience. I wanted to show how this concept informed and was informed by other aspects of Piro people's action and experience. The mere fact that it looked novel, and was novel, did not seem to be a good enough reason to subordinate ethnographic exposition to historical reasoning. After all, I had very little idea how old anything that Piro people did actually was, and presumption in this area can be dangerous.

This partition of history seemed a relatively low price to pay for an accurate portrayal of the sheer coherence of Piro people's lives as I had experienced them. But it always disquieted me, because I still held that different histories can potentially be unified, and I hold this to be true to this day. I signalled my disquiet in the following ironic comment in the Introduction to *Of Mixed Blood*, that the first chapter on history stood, 'in splendid isolation from the main body of the book, for in its historical analysis it is methodologically quite distinct from the rest of the study' (1991: 20). The problem was not thereby solved, it was just shimmed with fine words.

If I could come to understand history in Piro people's sense, in terms of how they lived and spoke about their world in general, could I then understand how this way of living had come into being in history in my sense? I concluded in that book that we did not know enough about Amazonian history in order to do so, and in particular, we knew next to nothing about indigenous Amazonian people's agency within that history (1991: 296). But one thing was clear from the analysis in *Of Mixed Blood*: indigenous Amazonian people can do more things with history, and in history, than we have been used to imagining. I quoted a remarkable passage by Lévi-Strauss, from an essay originally published in 1942, where he wrote that, 'primitive institutions are not only capable of conserving what exists, or of retaining briefly a crumbling past, but also of elaborating audacious innovations, even though traditional structures are thus profoundly transformed' (1976b: 339). An 'audacious innovation' seemed to me to be the best description of what Piro people had done with the historical circumstances they had endured. They had not simply submitted, or survived, or resisted. They had turned around and invented a new way of living which rendered their recent historical experiences coherent to them-selves, and which they seemed to find both intellectually and emotionally satis-fying.

But how on earth, I wondered, could Piro people have made this 'audacious innovation'? Was the manner in which Piro people spoke to me about the past simply a *post-hoc* rationalization of historical experiences that had actually been lived out very differently? This seemed entirely possible, for it was hard to imagine that Piro people in the late nineteenth century experienced their tran-sition from independence to debt-slavery as a positive move towards an expanded social world rather than as a total disaster. But if they did experience this transition as disastrous, why was that memory not transmitted to their descendants? After all, my oldest informants had grown up among those same people, who were their grandparents or parents. The old people, however, told me no stories that their grandparents had told them of a golden age shattered by enslavement. Like everyone else, these old people told the same story, 'The ancient people had no villages, they lived fighting and hating each other in the forest. Then the rubber bosses enslaved them and they started to intermarry and become civilized.' Memory is selective, but this looked like collective amnesia of a startling kind.

I began, therefore, to suspect that there was something very important that I did not know about the way in which Piro people inhabit time. I reasoned that Piro people could only act in this way if they experienced their being in the world as inherently transformational, as intrinsically subject to change. This feature could not be recent, but must have already been there before any of their contacts with the agents of colonialism and capitalism. I must have over-looked some key feature of their world. The answer was obvious when I found it, but it was a long time coming to me. I had forgotten the 'ancient people's stories'. I had ignored them because I had imagined them to be irrelevant to the contemporary Piro people's situation. But if they were irrelevant, why did Piro people tell them to each other, and to me? And if they were important enough to tell and to be listened to, what might they mean?

This question brought me back to the one Piro myth I knew very well, Artemio's story, 'A Man who went under the Earth'. What had it meant for Artemio to tell me this story? I knew what the story and its telling meant to me, but what had they meant to Artemio? It occurred to me that 'A Man who went under the Earth' was an excellent route into the problems that I was facing, for I knew a lot about the situation of its telling, I knew quite a lot about its teller, and enough other versions of this story were known to me from the literature to attempt an account of what the myth meant, and hence what the telling of this myth might have meant to Artemio. Further, the conversation in which this myth was told had all the hallmarks of a historical event: however insignif-icant when viewed from our common history, that evening of conversation had known and specifiable properties, and revealed certain features of its historical conditioning. It had, from my point of view, the virtue of extreme historical concreteness.

The importance of myth in my thinking about Piro people's history and accounts of that history was stimulated by a flurry of interest in the late 1980s and early 1990s in the relation between myth and history in indigenous South American societies. Hill had edited the volume *Rethinking Myth and History* (1988), whose contributors had sought to challenge and revise Lévi-Strauss's structuralist approach to myth in the context of a historically-oriented anthro-pology. To be able to connect myth and historical methodology seemed to represent an important advance. But in reading that volume, I did not recog-nize in these critiques the Lévi-Strauss I was familiar with from reading his own work. It seemed to me that the contributors to the *Rethinking Myth and History* volume had, on the whole, simply misread Lévi-Strauss. Why this should be so is an interesting question, and I return to it later, but first we must consider what exactly Lévi-Strauss had to say about myth and history.

Reading Lévi-Strauss's Mythologiques

That myths are historical objects is central to Lévi-Strauss's analysis in the four volumes of the monumental *Mythologiques*, and in the three studies on myth which follow it, *The Way of Masks*, *The Jealous Potter* and *The Story of Lynx* (Lévi-Strauss 1970; 1973; 1978; 1981; 1983; 1988; 1995). It is well known that the *Mythologiques* is concerned with the nature of human thought, and how this thought necessary occurs in the world which it takes as its content. Lévi-Strauss's concern for myths as historical objects has received far less comment.

The relationship between myth and history forms the subject of the final chapter of *The Naked Man*, itself the final volume of the *Mythologiques*, as if to signal the centrality of this issue to that project. The Weightmans translated the title of that chapter into English as 'One Myth Only', presumably with the author's consent. Lévi-Strauss there states, looking back over the 800-odd myths that he has analysed, 'all the Indian peoples of both North and South America seem to have conceived their myths for one purpose only: to come to terms with history, and on the level of the system, to re-establish a state of equilibrium capable of acting as a shock absorber for the disturbances caused by real life events' (1981: 607). The myths are not, in Lévi-Strauss's view, intrinsically stable until they are disturbed by history. Quite the opposite, they exist because of history, they exist to dampen down the effects of disturbances in order to maintain the coherence of meaningfulness. The myths generate the appearance of stability, an illusion of timelessness that cannot be affected by changes in the world, but they do so by means of their ceaseless transformations, which marks their very historicity as objects from the analyst's point of view.

Mythic narratives are therefore historical objects for Lévi-Strauss, albeit of a curious kind: they are historical objects whose purpose is to deny history. As he states, myths, like music, 'are instruments for the obliteration of time' (1970: 16), and time is here clearly to be understood both as the phenomenal time by which we experience our existence and as historical enacted time. After all, 'One Myth Only' starts with a epigraph from Proust on the meaning of music. And the claim that myths are instruments for the obliteration of time is no mere aside, for it is clearly intended by Lévi-Strauss to be a strong one. He writes,

there is no contradiction in recognising that each American community had its own independent and extremely complicated history, whose dramatic events it constantly tried to neutralise by reshaping the myths, insofar as this was compatible with the constraints of the traditional moulds into which they always had to fit. A story already altered by such internal developments reacts externally on similar productions; adjustments are made or fresh oppositions are brought into being, transposing the constant pattern of similarities and contrasts on to different levels. During intertribal encounters, such as marriages, commercial transactions, or the taking of prisoners, all these rectifications are sparked off in sequence, and spread in a counter direction much more rapidly than those major occurrences which seal the destiny of peoples. The system has only to be disturbed at one particular point for it immediately to seek to re-establish its equilibrium by reacting in its totality, and it does so by means of a mythology which may be causally linked to history in each of its parts, but which, taken in its entirety, resists the course of history and constantly readjusts its own mythological grid so that this grid offers the least resistance to the flow of events which, as experience proves, is rarely strong enough to break it up and sweep it away. (1981: 610)

It is through this strong claim for myths as historical objects which specifically operate to suppress the threats posed by the passage of time that Lévi-Strauss is able to propose a genuine historical explanation for the vast set of transformations he has found in the myths he has analysed in the *Mythologiques*. He writes, 'The unity and solidity of the system would seem totally inexplicable, if we did not take a more sophisticated view of the peopling of America and of the historical and geographical relationships between the different population groups, than that to which our position as so-called civilised communities would incline' (1981: 607). The analysis of the *Mythologiques* therefore leads up to a new way of thinking about a long and complex historical process which is still very poorly understood, the rapid peopling of a whole continent by the ancestors of contemporary indigenous American people.

Lévi-Strauss's concern for long-range historical hypothesis formation did not start with the *Mythologiques*: it is apparent in such early writings as his essay on war and commerce first published in 1942 (1976b), and is quite overt in the essays on history and anthropology from 1949 (1963: 1–27), and on the concept of archaism in anthropology from 1952 (1963: 101–19). Indeed, his work in general, and the *Mythologiques* in particular, can be read as the mature realization of his account, in *Tristes Tropiques*, published in 1955, of his youthful enthusiasm for geology, Freudian psychoanalysis, and Marxism, three eminently historical disciplines. He remarks of his own project, 'Between Marxism and psychoanalysis, which are social sciences—one oriented towards society, the other oriented towards the individual—and geology, which is a physical science—but which has fostered and nurtured history both by its method and its aim—anthropology spontaneously sets up its domain' (1976a: 71).

If the concerns with Marxism and psychoanalysis are fairly obvious in Lévi-Strauss's work, geology is there too, in the potential for historical analysis. It resurfaces in 'One Myth Only', in his explicit comparison of a problem in the relationship between the two major myth sets dealt with throughout the *Mythologiques* to the geological concepts of anticline and syncline.

In 'One Myth Only', immediately after his discussion of the historical implications of his analysis, Lévi-Strauss makes the following comment,

It is high time anthropology freed itself from the illusion gratuitously invented by the functionalists, who mistake the practical limitations imposed upon them by the studies they advocate for the absolute properties of the objects with which they are dealing. An anthropologist may confine himself for a one or more years within a small social unit, group or village, and endeavour to grasp it as a totality, but this is no reason for imagining that the unit, at levels other than the one at which convenience or necessity has placed him, does not merge in varying degrees into larger entities, the existence of which remains, more often than not, unsuspected. (1981: 609)

Here Lévi-Strauss is making clear the implications of his work for anthropology in general, and in particular, how his approach can liberate the discipline from the anti-historical bias given to it by the functionalists.

Both Malinowski and Radcliffe-Brown ejected historical analysis from anthropological thinking for a simple reason: it was unscientific. By unscientific they meant that it raised questions that were inherently unanswerable. They were writing in a milieu where anthropological thinking was characterized by audacious historical speculations, sweeping narratives of an evolutionist or a diffusionist cast. These narratives were compelling then, and Malinowski wrote in his diary, 'Yesterday I understood the charm of 'survey study' à la Rivers, the encompassing of broad areas as a single whole. But this projection of space onto time (two-dimensional or rather multi-dimensional entity) is very dangerous' (1968: 229–30). More tersely, Radcliffe-Brown wrote, 'My objection to conjectural history is not that it is historical, but that it is conjectural' (1952: 50). Any fool could think up a plausible story of how Trobriand or Andamanese societies came into being, but the task of describing them and showing the dense meaningfulness of these societies for the people who inhabit them and make them is a much harder task. For both Malinowski and Radcliffe-Brown, historical analysis had to be sacrificed as a necessary condition of the anthropological endeavour. It must have seemed a very small price to pay for the intellectual rewards it brought.

If functionalism and structural-functionalism had ejected a certain kind of history from anthropology as a necessary condition for establishing it as a serious science, the next step was to develop a specifically anthropological conceptualization of history. And this, as far as I can see, is what Lévi-Strauss has done. We can think of Lévi-Strauss as taking seriously all the intellectual dangers Malinowski saw in Rivers's work, and that Radcliffe-Brown found in conjectural history, and then finding a method that would allay those dangers. This would not involve a return to Rivers's historical explanations as such (although see Lévi-Strauss (1963: 161–3). Instead, following the work of de Saussure in linguistics, the methodological solution was to render very explicit the difference between synchronic and diachronic modes of analysis. For Lévi-Strauss, the functionalist rejection of historical interpretations as unscientific in anthropology was ridiculous precisely because it assimilated synchrony to science, and rendered any attempts at diachronic analysis unscientific by definition. Worse still, it came perilously close to treating the timelessness of its key heuristic device, synchronic functionalist analysis, as a genuine feature of its object, tribal societies.

As I discussed above, the *Mythologiques* is the full account of this problem and of Lévi-Strauss's solution to it. In the meticulous synchronic comparison of one myth with the next, repeated over and over again, and spreading outwards from one myth told by the Bororo people of Central Brazil to eventually span many myths told by many peoples across the entire continent, Lévi-Strauss delineates a system of surprising complexity and coherence, which itself is a historical phenomenon, and must make us rethink our basic attitudes to the human history of the Americas and of the status of the monographic tradition in anthropology. Synchronic analysis must lead to diachronic analysis.

In the next section, I discuss some of the reasons why this account of Lévi-Strauss's project, which I have tried as far a possible to present in his own words, should be so unfamiliar to an anglophone anthropological audience. But it should be noted that, while many anthropologists persist in accusing Lévi-Strauss of ignoring history, or being unable to account for it, at least one historian has recognized what Lévi-Strauss was doing, and adapted his methods to produce some very long-range historical hypotheses indeed. I refer to the Italian historian Carlo Ginzburg, who has followed where Lévi-Strauss led, and has produced a wide-ranging analysis that sets historical events and processes in early modern Europe within a much greater temporal and spatial frame, that of the history of the Eurasian continent from the late Stone Age onwards (1992a). Such greater frames, long abandoned to discredited cultural and social evolutionisms and to a discredited diffusionism, can through the work of Lévi-Strauss re-enter serious debate in the disciplines of anthropology and history.

One History Only?

If the *Mythologiques* and its companion volumes are an attempt to reintroduce historical analysis into anthropological thinking in the face of the excessive parochialism of functionalist method and theory, there is another argument about history there too. Reintroducing historical analysis into anthropology runs the real risk of losing the very battle that the functionalists, among others, had won: the acceptance that human social and cultural worlds are many, and that tribal societies are not precursors of, nor irrelevant backwaters to, the supposedly genuine human history that is played out by the great civilizations, and especially by Western societies. The risk here is that the use of historical methods in anthropology will be co-opted anew by the dominant Western narratives of history, which insist on seeing Western history as the true human history, or at least insist on viewing human history in general as merely preparing the stage for its ultimate expression in Western history.

This argument is relatively muted in the *Mythologiques*, for its major points had already been made by Lévi-Strauss in his debate with Sartre in *The Savage Mind*.[2] There, Lévi-Strauss is resolutely hostile to Sartre's attempt to unite existential philosophy to the Marxist theory of history, for the simple reason that existential philosophy uses, as its privileged model of humanity, the Western philosopher and his experiences of the world. The Marxist analysis of the historical development of capitalism and other modes of production, when wedded to existential philosophy, becomes a general theory of humanity which totally excludes human diversity, the subject matter of anthropology. As Lévi-Strauss remarked,

We need only recognise that history is a method with no distinct object corresponding to it to reject the equivalence between the notion of history and the notion of human-

---

[2] Although see Lévi-Strauss's ascerbic comparison of Mandan political philosophy to existentialism in *The Origin of Table Manners* (1978: 507–8).

ity that some have tried to foist on us with the unavowed aim of making historicity the last refuge of a transcendental humanism: as if men could regain the illusion of liberty on the plane of the 'we' merely by giving up the 'I's that are too obviously wanting in consistency. (1966: 262)

The argument here is between anthropology and philosophy, for anthropology is one of the founding challenges to such a transcendental humanism (see Foucault 1970).

Unfortunately, it is precisely here that so many of Lévi-Strauss's Anglo-phone critics have become confused, leading to the systematic misreading of Lévi-Strauss's work on mythology. Partly this is due to the sheer scale and subject matter of the *Mythologiques*, which is not an easy read, as Lévi-Strauss himself has admitted (1995: xv). And partly, as Scholte pointed out (1970), it is due to genuine differences between continental European intellectual traditions and those of Britain and the USA. But it also derives, I think, from a failure to appreciate the complexity of the debates in which Lévi-Strauss is engaged. Lévi-Strauss's strictures on the ahistoricism of functionalist methods and theory, discussed before, are no more a project for a Marxist existentialist anthropology than his critique of existential philosophy is a project for an anthropology hostile to historical method. This latter, sadly, is how he has too often been read.

The misreadings of Lévi-Strauss's work in this regard are legion, and would require more space to enumerate than I have here, even if I thought the project worthwhile (see S. Hugh-Jones 1988; Overing 1995; and Lévi-Strauss 1998). Here I address one example germane to the problem at hand, and one where the author cannot be ignorant of Lévi-Strauss's work. Hill writes, in his introduction to *Rethinking Myth and History* (1988: 4), of the success of his volume, 'Here we add fresh support to the global shadow of doubt that recent research has cast on the theoretical myth that there are, or were, "cold" societies without history or "hot" ones that have "progressed" beyond myth.' On the same page, Hill makes it clear that this criticism refers to Lévi-Strauss's distinction between 'hot societies' and 'cold societies', through a reference to *The Savage Mind* (1966: 234). Leaving aside the clearly pejorative use of the term 'theoretical myth', which sits so ill in a volume devoted to mythology, I am at a total loss to know how Hill's claim is to be squared with what Lévi-Strauss says in *The Savage Mind* and in the *Mythologiques*. Even if we turn to the passage Hill cites, the problem is not further elucidated, for there Lévi-Strauss writes,

I have suggested elsewhere that the clumsy distinction between 'peoples with history' and others could with advantage be replaced by a distinction between what for convenience I called 'cold' and 'hot' societies: the former seeking, by the institutions they give themselves, to annul the possible effects of historical factors on their equilibrium and continuity in a quasi-automatic fashion; the latter resolutely internalising the historical process and making it the moving power of their development. (1966: 233–4)

This is perfectly consistent with the argument of *The Naked Man*, and there is no hint here of Hill's 'societies without history' or any suggestion of an implied progress from myth to history.

Hill's reading of Lévi-Strauss, and his consequent misinterpretation of latter's work, rest on two assumptions that are clearly articulated in the introduction to *Rethinking History and Myth*. Firstly, the history of indigenous South American peoples is there taken as primarily, if not exclusively, the history of their invasion and domination by European colonial forces. Secondly, Lévi-Strauss, by arguing that myths obliterate time, is held to have denied that indigenous South American peoples could be conscious of that colonial history. The possibility that the myths might be functioning to annul the effects of these societies' *own* histories, a series of events and processes that may have nothing to do with European colonial penetration, is not even considered. Lévi-Strauss's concern with an autonomous indigenous American history is clear enough in *The Naked Man*. Why then is such a history excluded from Hill's volume?

The answer would seem to be that Hill and many of his co-authors assume, with Sartre and against Lévi-Strauss, that historical method does indeed have a distinct object, and that this distinct object is European colonial expansion and its impact on the colonized. This is clear in the influential work of Eric Wolf, who is approvingly cited by Hill (1988: 2). Wolf, writing of the populations that have historically been most studied by anthropologists, asserts, 'The global processes set in motion by European expansion constitute *their* history as well. There are thus no 'contemporary ancestors', no people without history, no peoples—to use Lévi-Strauss's phrase—whose histories have remained cold' (1982: 385). So, if there are no 'cold societies', it is because all human societies have a history, and indeed the same history, that of 'the global processes set in motion by European expansion'. There is no room here for peoples with different histories.

As I noted above in my discussion of Varese, I once had, and continue to have, sympathy for this kind of approach, for we humans do indeed have histories in common, and these common histories explain much of importance in our world. However, the fact that humans have histories in common cannot exclude the possibility that we have separate histories too. It is absurd to claim that Amazonian history is the history of indigenous Amazonian people's colonization by European colonial expansion, as if such people were not doing things for their own reasons long before Europeans turned up, and as if they did not continue to do such things afterwards.

There is a further problem here, which is even more pernicious because it is so seldom fully recognized in calls for a historically-minded anthropology. As we saw above, the functionalists excluded historical explanations for a very good reason: it was impossible to know much about the long-term historical development of societies like those of the Trobriand islanders or the

Andamanese, because these kinds of societies did not collect archives of their pasts. This heuristic device could, and often did, slip into a stronger claim that the past of such societies was one of social enclosure and self-identical reproduction. Lévi-Strauss challenged this by saying that the mere absence of evidence did not stop such societies being historically constituted, or absolve anthropologists from the need to develop techniques for analysing them as such or from developing plausible hypotheses of long-term historical processes. Faced with the same dilemma, Wolf and Hill resolve the functionalists' problem by saying that all these societies do have histories, and that it is intrinsically knowable because it is *our* history. Why waste time on all that sifting and comparing of myths, when all that an anthropology in search of a historical method need do is rivet contemporary ethnographies to the known history of European colonial expansion?

This last solution has a strange fascination and compulsion, which must have much to do with the heady brew of narcissism, guilt, and expiation it promises many Western anthropologists. It has a fatal flaw, however. An anthropology in search of a historical method could never be founded on such a bad historical methodology. No serious historian would argue that history starts when the documentary evidence starts: the documentary archive is the available data, from which the work of historical interpretation proceeds. The shortcomings and limitations of the documentary archive must be the first thing before historians' minds. As Ginzburg commented, on the problem of studying popular culture historically, ' "Who built Thebes of the seven gates?" Bertolt Brecht's "literate worker" was already asking. The sources tell us nothing about these anonymous masons, but the question retains all its significance' (1992b: xiii).

Indeed, it was through the contemplation of what historians such as Ginzburg actually do (1992a; 1992b), and their commentaries on anthropology (see Ginzburg 1989), that I was led to question the use made of historical evidence and analysis by many anthropologists.[3] Historians live in their archives the way ethnographers live in their communities. Holidays are not enough. For all the reasons that I would never claim that all the impressions I gained during a three-week visit to a Tamang village in Nepal, however vivid they were, constitute any profound insight into the lives of Tamang people, I began to wonder about the validity of the historical methodologies which underlie much of what anthropologists say about history. I, for one, do not remember any profound discussion of historical methodology in any of my own training as an anthropologist, and I suspect this is rather general.

The unanalysed misuses of historical argument by anthropologists abound.

---

[3] I owe a great debt here to my former colleagues in the Department of Art History in the University of East Anglia, and especially to discussions with Andrew Martindale, John Onians, Nicholas Green, and Joanne Pillsbury.

Here is an empirical example of what I mean. Turner (1988) analyses a Kayapó myth which tells of the origin of white people, and he there argues, following the lines of an earlier argument by Roberto da Matta (1971), that this myth is an inversion of the Kayapó myth of the origin of fire, which had already been the subject of an impressive analysis by Turner (see Turner 1985 and [n.d.]) Turner goes on to agree with Da Matta that such inverted myths, called 'anti-myths', 'represents the first step in the opening of native culture towards the possibility of ideological and historical interpretations of its relations to the dominant national society . . .' (1988: 257). Turner's argument here is a claim about Kayapó people's history. A specific and real event, the concrete engagement of earlier generations of Kayapó people with an invasive Brazilian society, caused Kayapó people to start to tell a myth of origin of those invasive white people, and they generated this novel myth by inverting their most important myth of cultural origins. The analysis is plausible, and it looks historical enough, but is this really a historical argument?

It cannot be a historical argument for no real historical evidence is presented to back it up. For this argument to be genuinely historical, we would need genuine historical evidence of the prior states of these mythic narratives. Firstly, how do we know that when Kayapó people first came into contact with Brazilians they were already telling the myth of the origin of fire in the form recorded by ethnographers in the latter half of the twentieth century? We do not know this, and probably never will. It seems to me likely that they were, given the wide diffusion of this myth among Northern Gê-speaking peoples (Lévi-Strauss 1970), and I am willing to concede this point to Turner.[4] But secondly, what evidence is there that these same ancestral Kayapó people were not then telling these myths of origin of white people as myths about the origin of *something else*? The ancestral Kayapó people must have had many powerful and dangerous neighbours back then, and it is intellectually more plausible that myths of origin of white people would originate in small changes to existing myths rather than in the dramatic and spontaneous inversion of another myth. There is no historical evidence either way.[5] In short, Turner's account looks like historical argument, but it is not. As Ribeiro (1980) has demonstrated for a Kadiwéu case, such historical arguments about myths are possible, but precisely where there is genuine historical evidence of the myths' transformations in time.

Viewed thus, Turner's argument, like that of Da Matta, turns out to be a very weak piece of historical argumentation. If either author could produce *any* historical evidence that, at some time in the past, Northern Gê-speaking

---

[4] Its absence from one Northern Gê-speaking people, the Panará (Elizabeth Ewart, personal communication), would of course still have to be explained.

[5] Lévi-Strauss (1995) has presented an alternative, and plausible, hypothesis of the origin of this myth by diffusion from coastal Tupian-speaking peoples, which does fit with what little is known from the historical record.

peoples did not tell these 'anti-myths' in any form, and that later they did then start to tell them, we would have the basis of a genuinely historical argument. As they stand, however, Da Matta and Turner's arguments are simply excellent analyses of the relations between different myths told in the same period by the same people. That these historical arguments turn out, on closer inspection, to be fine examples of synchronic structuralist analysis does not bother me, although, in Turner's case at least, it sits strangely in the context of an overt critique of structuralist methods (Turner 1988: 195–6).

My argument here could perhaps be dismissed as unduly pessimistic about the possibilities of using historical methods in anthropology. But the problem of historical evidence is central to such a project, and wishful thinking will not make it go away. As Turner himself has demonstrated (1992; 1993), it is possible to produce a historically plausible analysis of certain major changes in Kayapó society over the past two centuries using a combination of written documentation and Kayapó oral histories. But unless the documentary archive includes recordings of Kayapó myths, we cannot do the same sort of historical analysis for Kayapó mythology. The fact that we have little or no evidence of the earlier states of Kayapó mythology does not mean that it does not have a rich and complicated history. It simply means we have no idea what that history might have been.

Is there any hope for using historical analysis within anthropology here? It seems to me that there is, and that the hope lies in taking Lévi-Strauss's analysis in the *Mythologiques* very seriously indeed. If we accept that myths are operating to obliterate time, we can look to the very myths themselves to tell us what historical events and processes they might be seeking to obliterate. If the myths are indeed seeking to come to terms with history, and seeking to re-establish equilibrium at the level of the system, it is in that equilibrium that we might begin to look for the history that we seek.

The Search for a Method

The major problem faced by the present study is that, in seeking to understand how the situation I found among Piro people in the 1980s came into being historically, data derived from fieldwork must be brought into alignment with data drawn from the available historical archive. It is only through the co-ordination of these two kinds of data that we have any chance of triangulating on the key problem: that is, how a series of historical events and processes were lived out and made meaningful by successive generations of Piro people. The use of historical methods in anthropology is of no value if all it can do is solve the limitations of ethnographic methods by recourse to an already constituted historical knowledge. An anthropology using historical methods is inevitably in search of new objects, vaguely sensed at the limits of ethnographic methods.

What might such a new object look like? My hypothesis is that what I am looking for is a system in a state of transformation, and that I have access to two features of it. Firstly, I have a good knowledge of this system as it was in the 1980s and 1990s from my fieldwork. Secondly, I have access to certain aspects of its prior states from the documentary archive. However, just as my knowledge of this system in the 1980s and 1990s must be subject to the critical anthropological analysis that attends all fieldwork, the knowledge that can be gained from the documentary archive must also be subject to critical historical analysis.

There is nothing novel about the historical analysis of the documentary archive I use in this study. In fact, I am conscious of the amateurish nature of my historical investigations, and of my ineptitude as a historian, for this work is unashamedly based on what historians would call 'secondary sources'.[6] But there is one point that must be made clearly: an anthropological analysis that uses historical methods must start from ethnography, and from the problems ethnography presents. Ethnography is to anthropological investigation what the 'primary sources' are to historians. This is the point on which Malinowski and Lévi-Strauss agree, for all the latter's strictures on the work of the former. Just as Malinowski's major works started in concrete features of life in the Trobriand Islands, the *Mythologiques* starts with a myth told by members of a society Lévi-Strauss knew personally, and about which there is a wealth of ethnographic writing.

My methodological approach here is an extension and development of a key question raised by Leach in his celebrated study of the political systems of Highland Burma (1954). He there argued that the elaborate accounts that anthropologists develop about the societies they study, and social systems they develop for those peoples, must be understood as 'as if' systems: they are accounts of Nuer, Tallensi or Tikopian societies *as if* they were historically-stable systems geared to self-identical reproduction through time (Leach 1954: 7). Such system-building is logically necessary in the process of the analysis, but the sheer beauty and coherence of the systems so built should not, Leach warns us, make us forget that they are drawn from very short periods of observation, and that nothing guarantees that they are not merely temporary states of more complex historical systems. Leach's argument was specifically directed against the then dominant structural functionalists, some of whom were willing to turn the functionalist eschewing of historical analysis into stronger claims about the manner in which tribal societies reproduce themselves over time as self-identical entities (Fortes 1958: 1).

Powerful as Leach's theoretical point against the structural-functionalists was, there is an important sense in which he was simply lucky. Leach's argu-

---

[6] Thus I have made no attempt to investigate the Summer Institute of Linguistics (SIL) sources in more depth, to contact SIL missionaries who worked with the Piro people, to work on the Franciscan archives in Ocopa, and so on.

ment was the product of a historical contingency, for the Kachin people he studied were the subject of a rich documentary archive which he was able to draw upon to build his historical analysis. The hill peoples of Highland Burma inhabited an area of strategic importance to various literate empires over the centuries. Literate people had hence long been interested in the doings of Kachin people, and generated a considerable amount of writing about them. The same was not true of the tiny island of Tikopia, or of the Tallensi people in the hills of northern Ghana. Much had probably happened in the past of these areas, but not a great deal could be easily known about that past. Therefore, the potential for successful historical analysis rests on the wealth of historical data available for the societies studied. In many cases, Leach's 'as if' constraint looks as if it is going to have to remain just that.

Above, I criticized the conflation by Hill and Wolf of history and the history of European colonial expansion. Part of the power of that conflation, and the consequent blindness to the real dangers it poses for anthropology, undoubtedly lies in the fact that, for many of the societies studied by anthropologists, the existing documentary archives were generated precisely by the processes of European colonial expansion. The significance of this for the development of anthropological thinking on history has often been missed: it is itself a historically contingent fact. That all the documentary evidence for South American history post-dates European colonization reflects the pure historical contingency that no indigenous South American people had ever spontaneously developed a writing system, or at least any writing system that has been successfully decoded. Because of this, they enter the documentary archive first and foremost as the objects of writings by European colonial agents. This may not be a genial feature of South American history for anthropologists to contemplate, but it is nonetheless true, and there is no use our bemoaning the absence of unwritten documents. Still less should we simply ignore it, as Wolf and Hill do. It is a genuine problem, and we should inhabit it.

Can we turn this lack of alternative documentation, and the manner in which the documentary archive that we do possess is totally implicated in the processes of European colonial expansion, to our advantage? I believe we can, as long as we are clear about what the written documents can and cannot tell us. Firstly, because the written documentary evidence was produced by people who were fully caught up in the processes set in train by European colonial expansion, it is dominated by the concerns of such people. The archive is not a portrait of what happened in the past, but only of a very small part of what happened in the past: those things that people who could write found sufficiently interesting to commit to paper. Secondly, the archive is only as interesting as the questions we seek to ask of it. Therefore, we must be very clear what we looking for in the archive, and what exactly it might look like if we were to find it.

It is for both of these reasons that I believe that historical analysis in anthropology must begin in ethnography.[7] Ethnographic fieldwork entails, for fieldworkers, an extreme sensitization to the nature of their assumptions about what humans are like, as these are daily brought into conflict with the corresponding assumptions of the people being studied. Ethnographers seek to find out why it is that what the people they study do and say seems to those people to be 'commonsensical, cogent, and perfectly logical', as Kulick has put it (1998: 232). It is true that, by the very nature of their work, ethnographers often choose to misrepresent this strange experience as a personal discovery, but it does in fact occur within a specific set of protocols and institutional frameworks which both guide the ethnographers' practice, and guarantee the potential validity of their knowledge. It is these protocols and institutional frameworks which make ethnography into a special kind of writing. Writing in the documentary archive which was produced within other protocols and institutional frameworks is much harder to assess as potential ethnography, however interesting it might be.

This point must always be borne in mind, because it is all too easy for an ethnographer to get carried away by what is actually in the archive. For example, when I read the French traveller Marcoy's account of how he saw a 'mission' that Piro people had spontaneously created in 1846 (Marcoy 1869), or when I read the Franciscan priest Sabaté's account of a shamanic session performed by Piro people in 1874 and which they assured him was a 'mass' (Sabaté, 1925), I feel myself in the presence of 'audacious innovations' that pre-date the rubber industry and that might help to explain why Piro people reacted to that terrible event as they did. But I am also conscious that Marcoy was a nineteenth-century French artist-cum-traveller, and that Sabaté was a nineteenth-century Franciscan priest. As such, both men were blissfully ignorant of a scientific method yet to be invented, and their observations can only be used as ethnography if we accept that they come to us respectively informed by nineteenth-century French standards of the acceptable travelogue and by nineteenth-century Franciscan standards of the acceptable report of a mission journey. We need, therefore, to ask historical questions of Marcoy's and Sabaté's accounts: why did they notice these things, and why did they record them? Before we can ask what that 'mission' and that 'mass' meant to Piro people in those years, we would first have to consider in depth what they would have meant to Marcoy and Sabaté respectively.

Ideally, to make use of these documents, I should learn much more about Marcoy and Sabaté and their worlds, in order to be able to read them critically. But I am trained as an anthropologist, and to properly apprentice myself to the discipline of history would, I think, be a misuse of my time. But minimally, I

---

[7] It is perfectly possible to treat archival materials as ethnographic data, but that requires a very different kind of methodology to the one followed here.

must be aware that there must have been much of Piro life that Marcoy and Sabaté saw and left unrecorded, and there is even more that both men could not even have imagined to be possible, and hence did not observe at all. The same point goes for all of the archive. It does indeed record earlier phases of the lives of Piro people, but it cannot be used uncritically. In order to use it for specifically anthropological purposes, we must first produce a general account, rooted in ethnographic description and analysis, of what we would expect to find within it. Only then can the archive start to speak to us of what we hope to find there.

This point can be made in a simpler and perhaps more forceful way. To my knowledge, the earliest Piro myths recorded in the documentary archive were unquestionably collected after 1947. This is a surprising fact. Why should this be so? It can hardly be that Piro people were not telling myths before that year, or never told them to someone who could have written them down. The reason is simply that 1947 was the year in which the missionary Esther Matteson arrived among Piro people, and it was Matteson, later joined by the Dominican priest Ricardo Alvarez, who was the first person ever to consider that Piro myths were worthy of recording in this fashion. And this is because Matteson was formed intellectually within American linguistics, and so saw in Piro mythic narratives exemplars of naturally occurring Piro spoken discourse, while Alvarez was formed within Dominican thought which had developed its own brand of ethnography of the peoples these priests worked among (see the journal *Misiones Dominicanas*). Nowhere in the writings of Franciscan priests about Piro people, which spans centuries, have I found any recorded myths. This is presumably not because Piro people were not telling myths, or that they never told any to Franciscan priests. The answer must be that the Franciscan priests simply never wrote them down, and we might suppose that this is because they did not think such stories mattered.

Lévi-Strauss has made this point well, in his meditation on the relationship between the disciplines of history and anthropology, where he writes, 'The anthropologist is above all interested in unwritten data, not so much because the peoples he studies are incapable of writing, but because that with which he is principally concerned differs from everything that men ordinarily think of recording on stone or on paper' (1963: 25). What motivates people to record things is a crucial constraint on historical methodology, and an interesting problem in its own right, but it cannot hold anthropological thought to ransom. In searching to use historical methods, anthropological thought must often admit defeat, not because it is intrinsically limited as an intellectual project, but because that project finds no corresponding evidence.

I offer here a salient example of what I mean. The work of Sahlins on Hawaiian history (1981; 1995) is widely held to be a historicization of structuralism, a view shared by its author (1981: 7). It looks like a progression beyond Lévi-Strauss's work, but it is questionable if it actually is. It is not even clear that Sahlins really holds this view, for references to Lévi-Strauss are sparse indeed in his work on Pacific history: Sahlins's prototype structuralist is clearly de Saussure. Sahlins's great contribution seems to me to lie not in historicizing the structuralism of Lévi-Strauss, which was an unnecessary task, but in recognizing that historical events like Cook's discovery of Hawaii are amenable to anthropological analysis of a structuralist kind.

There is, however, a severe limitation on Sahlins's work, and a very good reason for why it cannot serve as a general model of historical methods in anthropology. We can know a lot about the earliest contacts between Europeans and Hawaiians because many people on both sides were marked by a strong desire to record that contact and its effects. This not true for the Piro case: for the very meagre evidence of the earliest contacts between Piro people and Europeans, see Myers (1974) and Alvarez (1984). As a result of this purely contingent fact about the early contacts between Europeans and Hawaiians, Sahlins is able to produce his dense and fascinating analyses. Had Captain Cook and his crew been illiterate adventurers keen to keep their discoveries to themselves, and had the Hawaiians been more indifferent to the appearance of these newcomers and its significance, we would know a great deal less about all of what then happened.

Sahlins argues that we must understand history as the wagering in practice of pre-existent cultural schemes in the structure of the conjuncture. He writes, 'The great challenge to a historical anthropology is not merely to know how events are ordered by culture, but how, in that process, the culture is reordered. How does the reproduction of a structure become its transformation?' (1981: 8).

The challenge is lofty indeed, but it seems to hold anthropological thought hostage to the very thing that the functionalists liberated it from, the extreme limitations on our knowledge of those things in the past never committed to stone or paper. How can we really know if anything is the reproduction of the structure, or its transformation, when our only knowledge of it is through the structure of the conjuncture itself? After all, to my knowledge, there is precious little evidence for the orderly reproduction of the structure of Hawaiian culture before Europeans turned up. There is thus an inherent imbalance between our knowledge of the anterior states of the projects of Captain Cook and his crew and the projects of the Hawaiians *prior* to their meeting which cannot easily be resolved, and which poses extreme dangers to the endeavour. The most serious problem raised by Sahlins's work does not seem to me to be whether or not the Hawaiians thought Cook was a god (Obeyesekere 1992; Sahlins 1995), but the much more fundamental problem of how exactly we could ever come to know the answer to that question at this temporal remove.

It is precisely because of such historical imponderabilia that I think that the use of historical methods in anthropology should start with what anthropologists know best, ethnography. Great historical events such as Cook's discovery of Hawaii have a profound allure, which doubtless has much to do with how we were taught history as children, and to the inherent memorability of such events. It does not take much imagination to see them as historical problems, for they are our prototypes of historical events. It requires a lot more imagination to recognize a historical event in the Bororo myth, 'The Macaws and Their Nest', the key myth of the *Mythologiques*, and to see therein new possibilities for using historical methods in anthropology. It seems to me that it is Lévi-Strauss who has provided the essential framework for using such methods in anthropology: one grounded in ethnographic data and in the knowledge of the explicit protocols for how this data is generated. Like Malinowski, but unlike Sahlins, Lévi-Strauss starts in concrete ethnographic data.

As is well known, however, there are certain intrinsic problems in applying Lévi-Strauss's analysis to data collected by the Malinowskian method of field-work (S. Hugh-Jones 1979).[8] Malinowski's methods, which stated simply and elegantly that everything is connected to everything else, may indeed rest on a gratuitous illusion, but it has proved a very fruitful illusion over the years. For people's lives do, on the whole, tend to make sense to them, and it is that coherent meaningfulness that ethnographers working in the Malinowskian tradition pick up on, and are able to explore in all of its ramifying complexity. This coherent meaningfulness may indeed be the product of a series of secondary rationalizations (Boas [n.d.]), but it is nonetheless real, and worthy of consideration and explanation. Lévi-Strauss could not legitimately be accused of ignoring Malinowski's concern with 'the hold life has', for his interests are very different. But it is true that he does not concern himself with this problem, and it is not clear how we are to set about applying his analysis to data collected by a method that does.

Much of the recent ethnographic writing on indigenous Amazonian societies can be read as a more or less explicit attempt to link Lévi-Strauss's work to in-depth field data collected by essentially Malinowskian protocols. Some prominent examples from this burgeoning field would be Rivière (1969; 1984), Overing Kaplan (1975), S. Hugh-Jones (1979), C. Hugh-Jones (1979), Descola (1994; 1996), Santos Granero (1991), and Viveiros de Castro (1992). But on the whole, those scholars most sympathetic to Lévi-Strauss's work have been most unwilling to address the problem of myth and history, with a few notable exceptions (Hugh-Jones 1988; Overing 1995; Vilaça 1996), and this problem has been most extensively debated by those American scholars who seem less sympathetic to his work (Basso 1995; Hill 1988, 1993; Wright 1998). I suspect that the major problem here is the explicit manner in which Lévi-Strauss links his conclusions on myth and history to a condemnation of the shortcomings of

---

[8] I am aware that there are many non-Malinowskian forms of fieldwork which are perfectly valid. My reference is to my own fieldwork, and to my own data, and to the tradition within which I was formed and in which I work.

the functionalist ethnographic method. It is exceptionally difficult to know how to operationalize Lévi-Strauss insights within a method that those same insights render so intellectually disquieting.

A possible solution to the problem lies in rethinking exactly what it is that the Malinowskian methods study. We habitually imagine that we are studying a 'society' or a 'culture' when in fact we are merely studying what Radcliffe-Brown nonchalantly termed, 'any convenient locality of a suitable size' (1952: 193). Leach famously found this formulation unsatisfactory (1954: 5), but it seems to me that all Radcliffe-Brown was saying is that you have to start *somewhere*. In fact, I believe that here lies the solution to the problem set by Lévi-Strauss: the gratuitous illusion of the functionalists is resolved by constantly bearing it in mind. Therefore, I have to keep reminding myself that I was never studying 'Piro society' or 'Piro culture', for all I have ever really done was study the lives of some people in a few Piro communities over what is, historically speaking, a very short period of time. The problem therefore lies in what to call that entity that I studied and hence came to know about. I call it here the *Piro lived world*.

I use the concept of lived world, rather than society or culture, to signal a certain analytical stance.[9] The analytical concept of the lived world stresses an ethnographic project of elucidation of a found situation, over against any preconceived ideas of what form that lived world must necessarily take. It is not by that token theoretically innocent or naïve. My usage derives from Munn's important reformulation of the project of ethnography, *The Fame of Gawa* (1986), where she develops a general and synthetic account of action, space-time and value in Gawan people's lives from an exploration of how it is that actions generate the time and space in which they 'go on' (see also Munn 1977; 1983). Munn's analysis is overtly a symbolic study, and noting that *symbol* and *meaning* are to be taken as coterminous, she writes, 'A symbolic study is not substantively restricted (for example, to the examination of myth or ritual or some special, pre-defined class of objects). Rather, the practices by means of which actors construct their social world, and simultaneously their own selves and modes of being in the world, are thought to be symbolically constituted and themselves symbolic processes' (1986: 7). The search is therefore both to understand 'the hold life has', and to understand the way in which *this* life comes to have *this* hold.

A lived world is necessarily someone's lived world, and the analytical concept focuses attention on the concreteness of that other person or of those other persons. This is not the case with concepts like society or culture, which are analytically useful precisely because they transcend the specific details of

---

[9] I am grateful to my former students of the course on 'Contemporary British Anthropology' in the Postgraduate Programme in Social Anthropology at the Museu Nacional/Federal University of Rio de Janeiro for helping me to formulate this argument.

the lives of concrete individuals. They are transhistorical entities. Therein lies their danger for the current project, for it is by no means obvious to me that the object I am searching for, the system in a state of transformation, is really Piro culture or Piro society changing in time. It is obvious, however, that it is not a lived world either, and is likely to be the very thing that generates the specific Piro lived world I came to know in the 1980s. Therefore, my use of the concept of lived world signals that my search for the system in a state of transformation is overt.

The concept of the lived world allows me further to avoid another hidden danger of concepts like society or culture as transhistorical phenomena. Here I make no assumptions about the temporal effects of any actions, and instead focus first on what Piro people consider to be the temporal effects of their actions, and on what we can gather of those effects from the archive. Most importantly, I do not presuppose that the Piro lived world is necessarily marked by a concern to transmit tradition or reproduce itself in self-identical form over time. As Ingold has noted, a concern with transmitting tradition was imposed by anthropologists on many of the peoples they studied without their ever bothering to find out if the latter cared about it, or even if it actually happened (1986). And as I noted above, ethnographic fieldwork is peculiarly ill-suited to answering such questions, even if they were justifiable.

This point is important, for if Lévi-Strauss is correct to argue that myths are instruments for the obliteration of time, and that they do this by ceaselessly transforming, then the very last thing we would expect of them is self-identical reproduction over time. Instead, we would expect them to be marked by extreme openness and lability. And this brings us back to a forgotten feature of Malinowski's work on myth. Malinowski is most widely remembered for having proposed a crude functionalist approach to myth as social charter, which indeed he did, but he went on to write, of myths about death and life, 'When we examine the subjects which are thus spun into stories we find that they all refer to what might be called the specially unpleasant or negative truths; the loss of rejuvenation, the onset of disease, the loss of life by sorcery, the withdrawal of the spirits from permanent contact with humans, and finally the partial communication established with them' (Malinowaki 1948: 113). This brings Malinowski much closer to Lévi-Strauss than is usually imagined, for it is clear that the time which myths obliterate is taken by Lévi-Strauss to be just such a negative truth (Lévi-Strauss 1981: 606–7).

In the writing of this book, I have started where my ethnographic knowledge, in the Malinowskian sense, is greatest, for I begin with a myth told to me by a Piro man I knew well, in a context where I felt myself to have finally really understood something. I have asked of this myth the questions Lévi-Strauss has asked of myths in general: is this myth a historical object, and if so, what kind of historical object is it? In this book I seek to unite the perspectives of

Malinowski and Lévi-Strauss. With the former, I look over the myth-maker's shoulder at the myth being created, and with the latter, I search out all the other myth-makers who came before, and in this process, discern the evidences of an unknown past and the possibility of its delineation.

Some limits of this book

The following are some statements of what I think this book does not do, and where certain silences might be misconstrued. For example, my attempt to hybridize the approaches of Malinowski and Lévi-Strauss could be read as reactionary within the recent history of anthropology, with either negative or positive valorization. I talk little of post-structuralist or post-modern theories here, but this should not be taken as a general lack of respect for such theories or for their theorists. It is a pure effect of the problem I set myself in trying to understand Artemio's story, 'A Man who went under the Earth'. Given such a problem, Malinowski and Lévi-Strauss were bound to be far more interesting to me than, say, Foucault or Derrida. These latter writers have taught me much about my world, but very little about why Artemio told me that story.

This book may strike some readers as curiously silent about one of the most well-known features of recent Peruvian history, the civil war. Part of the explanation for this is that, even though my fieldwork in the 1980s was taking place during the gradual descent of the Bajo Urubamba area into that war, I did not really see it, and consequently know little about it as yet. My return to the area in 1995 and again in 1999 told me about some aspects of it, but not enough really to integrate it here. Besides, the key historical event I am concerned with here, that is, my conversation with Artemio, occurred in 1982, some six years before the war really got going on the Bajo Urubamba. I hope, however, that my descriptions of events on the Bajo Urubamba are sufficiently accurate to allow those who are specifically interested in that civil war to see some aspects of its local development in the present work.

I concentrate in this book on the relationships of Piro people to North American missionaries of the Summer Institute of Linguistics, and I have relatively little to say about the important role of the Dominicans in recent Piro history. I am conscious of this lacuna, for the Dominican priests and school-teachers of the Bajo Urubamba have been of immense help to me, and the village in which I spent most of my time had a Dominican mission centre. I would therefore be pained if I thought the present work could be construed as a slight against their work and its historical significance. I am, by historical contingency, much more interested in Piro people's relations to the SIL missionaries, because Piro people put us together in a single category, because I shared their awe at the power of Americans, and because I once believed that having being raised in a Scottish Presbyterian milieu gave me a privileged access to the motivations and actions of American Evangelical Protestant missionaries. I accept this shortcoming, and luckily the Dominican priest and anthropologist P. Ricardo Alvarez has published an account of the some of the same issues seen from his point of view (Alvarez 1984), which the interested reader could profitably compare with my account here.

All the Piro people I know are multilingual, active speakers of at least two languages and passive 'understanders' of more. This is common on the Bajo Urubamba, and leads to a basic assumption that people gradually assimilate knowledge of other languages over periods of co-residence. For reasons I have discussed in *Of Mixed Blood* (1991: 18–20), I did not speak Piro in the field, although I was latterly assumed to understand it. Piro people dislike hearing incompetently spoken Piro, which they consistently hyper-correct, and learners are expected to develop a very high level of passive competence before actually speaking. While I did develop a fairly good understanding of Piro, I spoke only Ucayali Spanish, and with the exception of old people and some younger women, most of my informants spoke directly in that language to me. I never spoke or very competently understood Campa, which is also widely spoken on the Bajo Urubamba.

Piro is a highly verbal language, insofar as its speakers prefer verbal to nominal constructions (Matteson 1965). This feature is also marked in Campa and Ucayali Spanish. It is therefore very difficult to translate into such a nominal language as English, especially in its most nominalist genre of academic English. For example, I have never to my knowledge heard a Piro speaker actually say *tsrunnini ginkakle*, 'ancient people's stories', although I have often heard *wane ginkaka wa tsrunni* or its variants. However, 'thus the ancient people told' does not work well as a noun in English, and such a usage would, I believe, be irritating to the reader. Equally, to translate silently 'thus the ancient people told', as 'myth' would mislead the reader, by failing to signal the difference between Piro people's articulated categories and the technical language of anthropology. At best, I can defend my practice in this book by claiming that it points to key categories of Piro people's thoughts, but not in the precise linguistic forms that would occur first to Piro people themselves.

Lilí Torres, Artemio's wife, told me early on in my fieldwork, 'You should carry a notebook, and write down all the things we say to you. That's what the SIL missionaries did.' For reasons which will become obvious, I never wrote down what people said in front of them. Instead, I trained myself to try to remember exactly what people told me each day, and wrote it down at night, or if it was especially likely that I would forget it, in quiet moments during the day. I was very young when I did the original fieldwork, which doubtless helped a great deal, and I seem to be blessed with a good memory for these kinds of things. Virtually the only use made of my tape-recorder was one Piro people themselves suggested, recording songs, and mostly the recordings were made for me by Pablo Rodriguez, who enjoyed doing so.[10] My own techniques had obvious disadvantages, since there was an unknown amount of subjective editing between the speech and the notation. In particular, it must be noted that the mythic narratives and other speech quoted here are not, when recorded by myself, verbatim texts, whatever that might mean.

On reflection, my technique had the peculiar virtues of something invented in youth and on the spot. Throughout my fieldwork, I tried to act within the canons of local politeness as far as I knew them. I asked questions, but I tried never to pursue any topic beyond the interest of my interlocutors. I think that this method, for all its manifold shortcomings, may have made me more sensitive to certain important aspects of things that actually interested Piro people, for no machines or notebooks governed the progress of our conversations, nor were their rhythms marked by fading batteries, scribbling pens or turning pages.

In my quotations of Piro texts published either by Matteson or under the auspices of the SIL, I have in most cases used the original English or Spanish translations, in deference to the undoubtedly greater competence in Piro of the SIL missionaries, not to mention their Piro informants.[11] However, reference to the original Piro texts has led to me to make a number of changes. These either reflect places where I feel that the original English or Spanish translations can be improved, or where I felt the wording was ambiguous. To avoid cluttering my own text with notification of these changes, I have on the whole left them silent. However, page references for published Piro materials always include the original text and its Spanish or English translation, and my quotations of these translations are not to be understood as direct. Readers interested in such problems should therefore always refer back to the originals. All other translations from texts in other original languages are my own responsibility.

A Piro man once said to me, with reference to Ricardo Alvarez's book about their lives, *Hijos de dioses* (1970), 'He tells lies about my people there, it's not true. He just tells lies about my people in his books to make money.'

I doubt if any of my own writings would fare better in Piro people's estimations, although I have tried here to do as a good Piro person would do, and rigorously separate out that which I know from personal experience from my interpretations, or from what I was told by others, or have read in the literature. I admit here to one direct form of lying. While most of the people referred to

---

[10] Another use of my tape-recorder was rather more problematic, although approved by local people. This was the recording of shamanic sessions. The little red power light on my recorder proved a serious irritant to people who were hallucinating strongly, as did the chunking and clicking sounds of the tape running out and being changed. On one occasion I could not even find my tape-recorder in order to start it when the shamans began to sing, for, hallucinating strongly myself, each time I looked for it, all I could see was a huge iridescent butterfly.

[11] In written Piro, most vowels approximate to Spanish pronunciation, and most consonants to English. The exceptions are: *u*: a mid unrounded vowel; *g*: as English 'h', but nasalized; *j*: as the 'ch' in Scottish 'loch'; *x*: as a palatalized 't'.

in the text are given their true names, I use pseudonyms in a few cases. Authors have little control over the potential uses of their writings as these enter the world, and so, where I think that information contained here could be potentially hurtful or damaging were it to be relayed back to the Bajo Urubamba, I have changed their names. It would be easy for local people to guess who these individuals might have been, but at least I have not actually named them here.

In this book, I use a number of nominals which seem currently to be falling from favour in the literature on south-eastern Peru, such as 'Piro' and 'Campa'. These are increasingly being replaced by the supposedly more authentic designations of 'Yine' and 'Ashaninca' respectively. While I am cognizant of the political importance of such changes, I am also aware of the false nature of such authenticity, as it seeks to impose an alien logic of 'true identity' on to the lived complexities of indigenous people's ideas. Many Campa people do, indeed, call themselves *ashaninca*, but it is not their name: it is a deictic which I could use quite justifiably to mean 'Scottish people'. Similarly, many of my Piro informants explained to me at length that the Piro word *yine* does not mean 'Piro', because it can also mean 'Campa', 'Amahuaca', and so on. When speaking Piro, I was assured, Piro people properly refer to themselves as *wumolene*, 'our kinspeople', a designation I would be as reluctant to adopt into English as I am the Campa term *ashaninca*. In these circumstances, I fall back here on such nicknames as 'Piro' and 'Campa', which have the twin virtues of being common to the ethnographic literature and of being actually used by the people they designate here to refer to each other and to themselves in the Bajo Urubamba area. In parallel, my translation of the Piro term *kajine* as 'white people' is equally laden with problems, for it is far from clear that the people so designated would care for either the Piro original or for my translation.

In this book, my concern is with the elucidation of the Piro lived world and its transformations, and I have kept comparison, regional or otherwise, to a minimum. In the body of the text, I make no attempts to link this analysis to well-trodden themes in the literature, whether regional or general. This raises an important problem, referring directly to another dimension of Lévi-Strauss's critique of the gratuitous illusion of the functionalists. I here make little effort to set the present study in a wider regional context, except briefly in the Conclusion. This is a serious gap, which I can only justify by lack of space, that is, the aesthetic constraints we place on ourselves in the form of the acceptable length for a book. For example, were the space allowed larger, I would have attempted a regional comparison of Piro, Campa-Machiguenga, and Shipibo-Conibo mythologies. Equally, the recent historical transformations I describe here for Piro people would gain greatly from an understanding of parallel developments among their neighbours, such as the messianic movement inspired by the Conibo woman Wasamea in the 1950s (Lathrap 1976; Roe 1988), which led to the transformation and intensification of design-production among those people, or the continuing importance of Seventh Day Adventism for many Campa people

(Bodley 1970, Jacobs [personal communication]). Were we but to integrate the study of such issues, I am sure we would find out many important things about the regional aspects of indigenous Amazonian lived worlds, and their wider spatio-temporal horizons, but I have not done so here. These, then, are things this book does not do. I now turn to the story Artemio told me on that evening.

PART I

Myths

1

A Piro Myth in its Context

On the evening of 15 January 1982, Artemio Fasabi Gordón, Piro headman of the village of Santa Clara, told me a story about a man who went under the earth and turned into a white-lipped peccary, a kind of wild pig and an important game animal for Piro people. His story went as follows:

The old people told a story about a man who went under the earth. They say that there was a man who was tired of living with his kinspeople.[1] He set off into the forest. He followed a long straight path, far into the forest, he did not know where he was.

Finally he came to a huge hole in the ground. He went into it and found a drum. He began to beat it, *'tan, tan, tan!'*. Suddenly a great number of white-lipped peccaries emerged from the hole, and started to chase the man. He climbed up a tree that had vines hanging from it and took the drum up with him. The tree was surrounded with white-lipped peccaries wanting to kill him. He let the drum drop and the white-lipped peccaries took it and went back into the hole. The man went away.

Later he returned and went into the hole, he travelled through it and came to the land on the other side, there was light, rivers, forest, just like here. He saw the people, and they had immense pigs in corrals.[2] He didn't know whether to show himself, but the owner of the pigs saw him, and let loose his pigs. They rushed at him and started to bite him, until he was covered in their bites and was almost dead.

Then the owner called off his pigs, and blew on the crown of the man's head and brought him back to life. He asked the man if he wanted to live there, and man said he did. So the owner took off the man's clothes, his clothing of this world, and dressed him in clothes of animal skins, feathers and bristles, the clothing worn in that world. There they drank manioc beer, fished, hunted, and so on, everything was just as in this world.

Finally the man got homesick, and asked if he could go and bring his wife and children. The owner agreed, and so he went back through the hole.

The other world was red, all red, like the sun as it is just rising, he didn't recognize anything and didn't know the path to his house. Finally he found it and arrived there, still dressed in his clothes made of bristles. His wife said, 'I don't want you anymore', and only his oldest son agreed to come to the other world, where life was better.

They went back and lived there, the man found a wife, perhaps a little female white-lipped peccary! The son became homesick and wanted to go back, but he could not find the hole, it had closed.

So they had to stay there. That is all there is to this story.

---

[1] The Ucayali Spanish term in the original was *familia*. See Gow (1991: 162–72) for discussion of this term.

[2] At this point, Artemio shifted to the word *chancho*, Ucayali Spanish for 'domestic pig' (Piro *kochi*).

Artemio's story was a myth, a story made to be retold. But when I look at my version here, I see that I have retold it badly. It lacks most of the features of Artemio's story that interested me so much when he told it to me. And this is not a new problem, for Malinowski once wrote that myths 'must be lifted from their flat existence on paper, and placed in the three-dimensional reality of full life' (1948: 122). Whatever we might do, myths tend to end up looking flat when written down on paper, having been stripped of most of what made their original tellings so interesting.

'That is all there is to this story': Artemio's laconic sign-off was typical of events of Piro myth telling. No moral was made, and no wider conclusion was drawn. Artemio simply signalled to his listeners that *this* story was finished. The story was over, and the conversation could return to its earlier form of an exchange of ideas. Perhaps this is a first clue for a solution to Malinowski's literary problem, and hence to my own. Piro mythic narratives are necessarily part of a stream of talk between people, and part of their third dimension lies in knowing more about the conversations in which they are told. Artemio told this story to me. To understand it, therefore, requires more knowledge about Artemio, about myself, about that conversation, and about that night.

The Setting of the Myth

Artemio told me this story while we were sitting together in the open plat-form area of his large house, and as part of a much longer conversation. His wife and children had already retreated to the enclosed part of their house, overcome by sleep. It was still early evening, and despite being the height of the rainy season here in southern Amazonia, it was a clear night. The waning moon, three-quarters full, had not yet risen, and I gazed out at the stars. I was contemplating the Southern Cross, clear then in the night sky, and so strange to one raised under the stars over Scotland. I asked Artemio what his people called this constellation. He said, 'I don't know anything about those things, *compadre*. Why are you so interested in the stars?' His tone was inquiring, but it put me on my guard. Usually perfectly happy to answer my many questions, sometimes Artemio would surprise me with such comments. After more than a year of fieldwork, I was still capable of stumbling, quite unexpectedly, into difficult areas. My interest in the stars was general, since I felt it to be one of the issues I should explore in Piro culture. I had thus far met with little success, for everyone else had replied with the same comment, 'I don't know anything about those things.' However, this was the first time anyone had openly suggested that there might be something unusual in my interest in the stars.

I replied in some fashion to Artemio, and our conversation continued in a desultory way. The moon rose, and the evening's darkness gave way to its light.

Artemio, who was obviously feeling slightly uncomfortable too, then asked me if it was true that Americans had been to the moon. I told him that, yes, this was true. He asked me, 'What was it like, then, what did those Americans find there?' That moment had filled me with wonder when I was eleven years old, and I tried to tell Artemio what I knew of it from television and magazine photographs, groping for metaphors appropriate to a man who had lived his entire life in the luxuriant tropical rainforest of Western Amazonia. I told him, 'There is nothing there, just stones and sand, there are no rivers and no forest, just sand, like the beaches of the Urubamba river in the dry season.' Artemio smiled and said, 'Ahhh! So it is not true what my mother told me! She told me that the ancient people said that the moon is a man with no home, who is always wandering about. But if men have gone there, and seen that it is just stone, what of that belief? Is it just a lie?'

I was mortified, and bitterly regretted my bald account of what the moon was like. Most immediately embarrassing was the suggestion that my story had thoughtlessly exposed Artemio's mother Clotilde Gordón, an old woman of great dignity who had always looked out for me, as a liar. Beyond that, there was the implied slur against all old Piro people, living and dead. And further, I had unwittingly transformed from being an ethnographer, a humble student of an indigenous Amazonian people, into being a missionary of modernist rationalism, bent on stamping out the illusion that the universe has a meaning. This arid philosophy had claimed yet another victim, and at my own hands.

While I was lost to such self-recrimination, we were joined by Julian, our mutual Campa *compadre*, who had been attracted by the sound of our voices in the growing moonlight. People on the Bajo Urubamba enjoy moonlit evenings, and often take advantage of them to go visiting. Artemio greeted him, then commented, 'This, *compadre*, would be a good night to take *ayahuasca.*' *Ayahuasca* (Piro, *kamalampi*) is the hallucinogenic drug most commonly taken, at this time of the night, by local shamans when they are curing, and Julian was the apprentice of Artemio's father, Don Mauricio, a shaman of some repute. Artemio began to tell us of his experiences with *ayahuasca*. He said that as a youth he had taken *ayahuasca* often, but had never seen anything. All he had ever seen were, he told us, 'those little glittering lights that the night makes'. I had never heard that experience, so common for me, described before by anyone else. My attention was drawn away from my broodings, and I again became absorbed in the conversation.

Artemio's experiences of hallucinogens, however, were changing, for he said, 'But recently, I took *ayahuasca* again, with my father, and I did have a vision. I saw a snake wrap itself around my waist and put its head into my mouth. I wanted to vomit but I couldn't.' Julian replied with a story about a Campa woman he knew, who lived on the Tambo river to the west of Santa Clara, and who drank *ayahuasca* mixed with manioc beer. Artemio was incredulous and laughed, but Julian assured him that this was the best way to take the drug.[3] Julian went on to criticize the local *ayahuasca*, and to praise the higher quality of the drug used by the people from the Tambo river, his kinspeople.

Pleased that the conversation was turning away from my ignorant story and its unforeseen consequences, I told them that some years before, taking *ayahuasca* in a tiny Campa village in the Gran Pajonal area, far to the west beyond the Tambo river, I had the experience of flying under the earth and seeing great cities lit up in the darkness below me. I asked, 'What are these cities, *compadre*? Are there people down there, under the earth?' They smiled, and seemed to be surprised both by my account of the vision and by my question. Artemio told me that the old people, like Old Shantako and his own father, say that this is so, that the *cajunchis*, 'shamans',[4] visit the underworld and see people down there. These, they say, are the white-lipped peccaries, who are people in the underworld. Then he told me the story about the man tired of living who went off under the earth to become a white-lipped peccary. Both he and Julian were particularly amused by the episode of the man's marriage to a '*huanganita*', 'a little female white-lipped peccary'. He concluded the story with the comments, 'My grandfather, Old Shantako, says the white-lipped peccaries used to be very abundant, they used to just let the meat rot, there was so much. But also, it is said, the white-lipped peccaries are people. They are demons, it said, they know how to cause illness.' I asked him if this is also true of the other local species of peccaries, the collared peccary (Ucayali Spanish, *sajino*; Piro, *mrixi*). Artemio told me that the collared peccary is not human, 'It's just an animal from the forest.' He continued, 'The *cajunchis*, the shamans, when they take drugs, see the white-lipped peccaries as people in the other world.'

I remembered one of the first things I had been told by Artemio's father, Don Mauricio, shortly after my first arrival in Santa Clara a year before. He had said that in earlier times there were many white-lipped peccaries on the Bajo Urubamba, but the *cajunchis* had stopped that. When I had asked for clarification, he had said that when the *cajunchis* take *ayahuasca*, they find the hole in the forest through which the white-lipped peccaries enter this world, and hide it.[5] Remembering this, I then said to Artemio and Julian, in jest, 'Perhaps we should take *toé* (another hallucinogen)[6] and go and look for the hole in the forest. Then we would have white-lipped peccary to eat!' Julian burst out

---

[3] Piro people consistently told me that it was dangerous to mix any form of alcohol with hallucinogens, while Campa people on the Ene river often drank *ayahuasca* after a day of drinking manioc beer, in my observation in 1978.

[4] From Piro, *kagonchi*, 'shaman'. This Piro word is sometimes used in Ucayali Spanish discourse on the Bajo Urubamba. The Piro plural is *kagonchine*, so I have written it here as *cajunchis* to mark its use as a loanword in Ucayali Spanish.

[5] About the same time, Don Mauricio had also offered the explanation that too many people now had guns, and hence had persecuted the white-lipped peccaries too much.

[6] *Toé* (Piro, *gayapa*) is the other main hallucinogen used on the Bajo Urubamba (see Ch. 5).

laughing and said, 'If we went down there, we would end up in Scotland!' Artemio and Julian both laughed heartily at this joke. I laughed less, since I was not sure I understood it, nor that I liked its implications. However, Artemio continued on his theme, for he had obviously not lost interest in the white-lipped peccaries yet. He said, 'My mother says that the white-lipped peccaries have a chief, an owner. This owner, it is said, is a *fraile*, a "monk" '.[7] This Julian could not resist, and quipped, 'Perhaps it's Padre Pedro!'. The reference was to the Dominican priest in charge of the mission centre of Santa Clara. Much liked by most people in the village, he was also the target of many of their jokes.

Despite Julian's levity, Artemio was serious. He continued to talk, asking me what I thought of shamanry. He asked, 'Do you think it is bad, *compadre?*'. He continued,

In the Bible we are told that sorcery is wrong, and that sorcerers are sinners and will not get to Heaven. What do you think? I say this: there are illnesses sent by God to punish us for our sins, things like whooping cough, measles, tuberculosis. But there are other illnesses which cannot be cured by doctors or the medicines you buy—these are illnesses sent by demons. Some people are bad, and cause harm, and for these illnesses the hallucinogens are good. Such sick people will not be cured in a hospital, they need shamans.

I did not record my reply, although doubtless it was some anodyne statement to the effect that both Christianity and shamanry have their place. It was growing late, and I walked off to my house across the village, to write all of this down.

A Man who was Tired of Living

During and after this conversation, and especially through the telling of the myth, I was very happy to have heard all this. This myth, as told to me by Artemio, seemed to me to be the solution to a serious problem I had: what Artemio and other people in Santa Clara thought that I was doing living in their village.

There is no doubt that my presence in the community of Santa Clara was an intellectual problem for its residents. For them, I was a member of a specific category of beings, a specific 'kind of people' as they would say: I was a *gringo* (Piro, *krigko*). On the Bajo Urubamba, *gringos* are those people, tall and very light-skinned, who come from very far away, places like the United States of America, Germany, and Russia, and in my case, Scotland.[8] The lands of the *gringos* are seen, by local people, as the essence of remoteness, for they are both

---

[7] The reference is probably to the Franciscan monks of Atalaya and Puerto Ocopa, on the Perené river, rather than to the Dominicans.

[8] The USA, Russia and Germany were, for reasons I do not understand, the most consistently named as 'lands of the *gringos*'. I suspect this was a Piro refraction of the Cold War.

far away and *afuera*, 'outside', outside both the known world of *la selva*, Amazonian Peru, and beyond even the Andean and coastal regions of the nation itself.[9] *Gringos* are a kind of 'white people' (Piro, *kajitu, wirakocha*; Ucayali Spanish, *gente blanca, huiracocha*), but they are considered to be very different from the local white people, who are well known to the indigenous people of villages like Santa Clara.

In the early 1980s, local people's personal experience of *gringos* had become slight. Intrepid travellers and tourists occasionally passed through the area, descending the Urubamba river from the Andes, and there had been an irregular flow of the *gringo* employees of diverse oil companies through the mission town of Sepahua up-river. Just as I began my fieldwork, the German film director Werner Herzog and his crew began filming *Fitzcarraldo* on the Camisea river, upstream from Sepahua. However, such personal contacts as local people had with such passing strangers were fleeting, and often hampered by linguistic difficulties and a lack of interest in the association on the part of the *gringos*.

There were two exceptions to this pattern of contacts. On the one hand, there were the missionaries of the Summer Institute of Linguistics and Swiss Mission (*Misión Suiza*) organizations (based in the United States and Switzerland respectively). And on the other hand, there was myself. In both cases, we were *gringos* who had come to stay, and our purposes seemed to include a heightened interest in local people, and especially Piro people. Since at the time I was the first *gringo* anthropologist the people of Santa Clara had met, and since my interests seemed to be in the ways of Piro people, I was initially assumed to be a *lingüista*, a 'linguist', that is, a missionary of the Summer Institute of Linguistics.[10] I had very little idea at the time of what being a *lingüista* cum *gringo*-missionary meant to the people of Santa Clara. I assumed, on anthropological first principles, that it must be bad, and that I did not want to be one. So, I went out of my way to show that I was not a missionary. Unfortunately, since I was too callow and too ignorant of how local people thought about the world, I was incapable of explaining what exactly I was doing, day after day, week after week, in their village, if I was not a 'linguist'.[11] This merely exacerbated the problem.

In early 1981, while I was living in Santa Clara, my position became increasingly difficult. I was aware of a growing hostility, as people became less friendly, and began to avoid me. Children, more friendly and forthcoming than

[9] The local Franciscan and Dominican priests were not classified as *gringos*. Instead, they were defined as *españoles*, 'Spanish people', a category of people closely associated with white Peruvians from the coast.

[10] Also called *lingüísticos* on the Bajo Urubamba, from their Spanish name, *Instituto Lingüístico del Verano*.

[11] My claim to be an anthropologist (*antropólogo*) met with little success, for local people's model of an anthropologist was the Dominican priest and anthropologist P. Ricardo Alvarez of Sepahua, whom I resembled not at all.

the adults, explained that a *sacacara* or *pishtaco* was operating in the area, and asked me openly if I was one. *Sacacara* literally means, 'taker of faces', and I was told by my young informants that this being cuts off its victim's face and cuts out the heart. I had no idea what they were talking about, and explained, with a naïvety that came back to haunt me, 'No, I am not a *sacacara*, I am a *gringo*.' The term *pishtaco* I did recognize, from previous travel in Peru and my reading of the literature, the figure of a foreign white man who comes to murder local people and steal their body fat for export to the exterior, where it is used for a variety of nefarious technological purposes. At the time, I assumed that the children were confusing the *pishtaco* image with another idea about some kind of forest spirit. Adults met my questions on the topic with evasion or nervous assertions of ignorance. It slowly dawned on me that the children had innocently been repeating what the adults were saying about me.

Being a *sacacara* was even worse, I discovered, than being a 'linguist'. I found myself being sucked into a complex network of rumours circulating about the activities of *sacacaras* in the Bajo Urubamba area. These had their main focus on the film camp of Herzog on the Camisea, but extended outwards to include other shadowy *gringos*, including myself. I was later told by the head of the mission centre in Santa Clara that Artemio had told her that people in Santa Clara had decided that if I started to kill people and kidnap their children (an extra fear, new to me), they were going to tie me up and throw me into the river.

I never did start killing people in Santa Clara, or kidnapping their children. Instead, dissatisfied and alarmed with what I had found in Santa Clara, I tried to do fieldwork in the large up-river community of Sepahua. There the fear of *sacacaras* was even more palpable in the general hostility I met with everywhere. I cut my losses and returned to Santa Clara. The hostility from local people was still there, but I just went on living among them, day after day, week after week. As time passed, things improved gradually. People were friendlier, and it undoubtedly helped that the dry season of 1981 brought the expected abundance of food, thus easing the strain of feeding me.[12] But also, I must have changed as I got to know people better, and to understand what was and what was not acceptable behaviour to them. I slowly began to learn a key local value: *gwashata*, 'to live well, to live quietly' (Ucayali Spanish, *vivir bién, vivir tranquilo*).

Perhaps this is not quite the correct formulation. From my point of view, I learned 'to live well', but from the point of view of local people, I began 'to live

---

[12] Initially I tried to pay for my keep, conscious that I should not be a drain on local resources. This was not acceptable: on the Bajo Urubamba, one can only pay for 'white people's food' (food which costs money). 'Real food' is axiomatically free. People in Santa Clara insisted on feeding me, to demonstrate the abundance of local resources and their own ability to transform this abundance into food. As a result, they managed to project their own worries about hunger on to me, such that I became constantly 'anxious' about food (see Gow 1989).

well'. In short, I began to act as if I shared this value. For the people of Santa Clara, 'living well' is the ideal of everyday life. It means living without malicious gossip, living without fighting, living in a peaceful village surrounded by helpful and generous kinspeople, living in good health, and especially eating abundant quantities of what Piro people call 'real food', plantains from the gardens and game animals from the river and forest, and drinking a lot of manioc beer.

To 'live well' in such a village is the collective product of each inhabitant's *nshinikanchi*, 'mind, memory, love, respect, thoughts with regard to others'. Living well is possible because people are *kshinikanu*,[13] 'mindful, loving, respectful of each other', and because they 'remember, think about each other'. By living well, I was demonstrating to people that I was possessed of *nshinikanchi*, or at least its rudiments. My residence in Santa Clara, initially so problematic, slowly turned into 'living well'. The Piro term *gwashata* means literally 'to reside continuously, to reside and do nothing else'. Rather than living in Santa Clara for some secret and nefarious purpose of my own, I slowly came to be seen as someone who lived in this village for the same reasons that everyone else did, because there you can live well.[14]

A key moment of transition in my position came when I became *compadre* to three men and their wives all at once. As I have said, the value of 'living well' depends on living with kinspeople. For Piro and other indigenous people on the Bajo Urubamba, the reverse is also true: those with whom one lives well are kinspeople. The most expedient way of making me into a kinsperson was to have me act as godfather at the baptism of a baby. Three men, in the late dry season of 1981, asked me to do so: Artemio, Julian, and Antonio Zapata. When, the following year, I was about to become the *compadre* of Pablo Rodriguez the next day, he told me, with his characteristic good-humoured empathy for what I did not know about local convention, 'Tonight we must say all the bad things about each other, Pedro, because from tomorrow we will never be able to joke with each other again. Tomorrow we will be *compadres*, and we must respect each other and not say bad things about each other.' Those who respect each other, and do not say bad things about each other, is a working definition of what it means to be a kinsperson for Piro people.

By becoming *compadre* to Artemio, Julian, and Antonio Zapata, and hence to their wives, I now had in their eyes a perfectly valid reason for living with them. As Artemio told me much later, talking about his own travels, 'With a *compadre*, you always have a place to go. A *compadre* is like a kinsperson, you don't have to be invited to stay in his house.' I might not actually be a

---

[13] This is the masculine adjective, the feminine form is *kshinikano*.

[14] The possible exceptions here would have been the mission schoolteachers, although, at least in the case of the mission head, it was believed that her continued residence demonstrated a similar conviction that only in Santa Clara was it possible to live well. The priest, while possessing a house in Santa Clara, mainly lived in Sepa Penal Colony.

kinsperson to anyone in Santa Clara, but I was now 'like a kinsperson'. As Artemio told the head of the mission centre, who then told me, as a supplement to the story about local people's intention of killing me if I proved to be a *sacacara*, 'But now he is a *compadre*, so he is like a kinsperson, and we're not afraid of him any more.' In short, I now had every right to be living in Santa Clara.

At the time, I understood very little of this. As my fieldwork progressed, I got to know what the people of Santa Clara thought about things much better, but it took years of thinking to understand much of it. It was only later, in the writing of my doctoral thesis and its conversion into a book, and in the prolonged and intense reflection on social life in Santa Clara that this involved, that I began to really understand what 'living well', being a *compadre*, and indeed, being kin, meant to these people. In retrospect, it seems as if I could do it, more or less, but I had no idea of how exactly I did it. I continued to be worried by other problems. Not knowing that social relationships for local people were a matter of time and familiarity, I remained concerned by the *sacacara* rumours. Still an essentialist with regards to identities, I assumed that local people must be essentialists too. Was I still, at some level, a *sacacara* in the eyes of the people of Santa Clara? What did they think I was doing there? Thus, when some months after becoming my *compadre*, Artemio told me the myth, 'A Man who went under the Earth', I experienced it as a resolution of my problem: I was not a *sacacara*, I was 'a man who was tired of living with his kinspeople'.

When Artemio told me that story, I took this phrase to mean some kind of generalized dissatisfaction with one's home. It seemed to be an excellent description of why people become anthropologists, and why they do fieldwork in the Malinowskian tradition of participant observation. And I further thought that Artemio had intended his story as a reflection on my condition, and that he recognized that it was possible, out of pure interest, to go to the far end of the earth or beyond to live with other people. As with the man in the story, I 'drank manioc beer, fished, hunted, and so on . . .'. Such, at least, were my thoughts at the time.

Some years later, I discovered that the phrase 'a man who is tired of living', has a quite different meaning for Piro people. It refers to the journey of a man who has lost a beloved kinsperson. In 1988, Etelvina Cushichinari of Pucani village, told me of her husband Monsín's journey far to the east, to the Purús river, and thence downriver to Brazil, which had led him to abandon their children and herself for many months. She told me,

He was tired of living. His father had died. He could not bear to live here anymore. Everything made him sad. He was sad when he saw the river where his father used to bathe, he was sad when he saw the village, when he saw his gardens. He was tired of living. To get rid of his sadness, he went far away, to see other things, other people. Then he remembered his children here, he felt sorry for them, and came back here to them.

Monsín listened without comment to his wife's account of his changing emotions. I later heard similar accounts told by other people. It turned out that such journeys, by men who were tired of living, were not uncommon.

Thinking about this issue later on still, it dawned on me that I myself must have been 'a man who was tired of living' in the eyes of Artemio and others in the early days of my fieldwork. They had often asked me about my family, about my parents. I had explained that my mother was alive, but that my father had died not so long before. At the time, it was not something I liked to think or talk about, since it was painful. I am sure now that Piro people like Artemio listened closely to this information, and eventually decided that the main motive for my presence among them was precisely this desire to see other people and other places, and thus to forget my own people and my own place.

From that point of view, it was not Artemio and his kinspeople that I was interested in when I turned up in their village, but the fact of them *not* being my own kinspeople. I had, from this point of view, no particular interest in the inhabitants of Santa Clara, unlike the *lingüistas* and the *sacacaras*. My interest in being with them lay in their pure difference from other people I cared about. Such an explanation, however unflattering to the ethnographer in me, probably made much more sense, I think now, to Piro people like Artemio.

So, in a certain way, 'A Man who went under the Earth' was a metaphor for my condition, but not a metaphor that I understood at the time. A few days later, having reflected on the same themes perhaps, Artemio said to me, 'I could never go far away from here to live. It would be like death. What is death if not that you never again see your kin, your father and your mother?' He was referring to my residence in his village, and to the differences between his life circumstances and my own.

Artemio's Life

At the time that he told me 'A Man who went under the Earth', Artemio was thirty-four years old, and the father of eight children. His major preoccupation was how to feed and clothe these children, and how to provide for their education, and he often asked me if I knew of other ways of making money. He was currently trying to work as an independent lumberer, extracting hardwoods from the upper Huau river with his own team, financed by a neighbouring white boss. It was a project fraught with difficulties and uncertainties. Earlier, in his young adulthood, he had pursued other plans, attempting by turns to become a bilingual schoolteacher and then a preacher. These plans, which had failed, had brought him into considerable contact with *gringos*. By 1982, however, he seemed to be changing his ideas about them.

Artemio was headman (Ucayali Spanish, *jefe*) of the *Comunidad Nativa* of Santa Clara. In Piro, the term is *gitsrukaachi*, 'the big one, the important one',

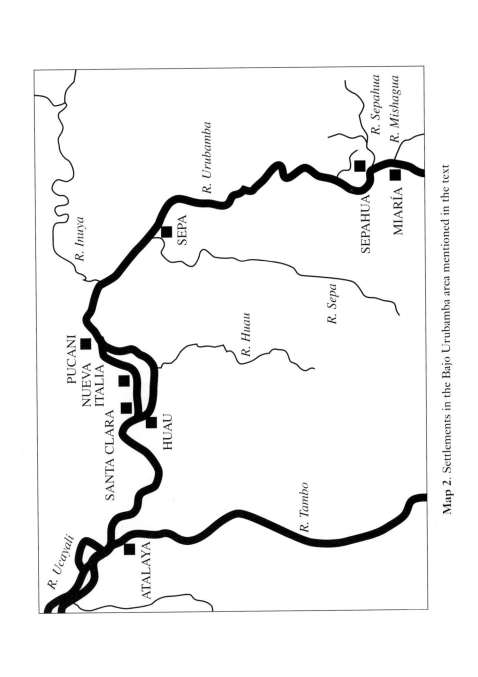

Map 2. Settlements in the Bajo Urubamba area mentioned in the text

of a group of people.[15] Piro headmen are the makers of villages. They do this by 'knowing how to speak': the headman is the one who gives collective expression, through speech, to the value of 'living well'. Of all the people who live in a village, the headman is the one who really lives there. Such is the connection between villages and headmen for the Piro and other indigenous people in the area that one could say that Artemio was headman of Santa Clara because Santa Clara existed because of him. This village was, to a great extent, the product of his actions, and while it might survive were he to die or to leave, it would be a very different village. Indeed, people in other communities often referred to Santa Clara as, *'donde los Fasabis'*, 'where the Fasabis live', despite the fact that only three out of the twenty-five to thirty adults in the village carried this surname. Artemio did, along with his father and his sister, and that was enough.

Artemio was born in 1947, in the village of Pucani, located two bends of the river above Santa Clara, as they say on the Urubamba. This was the village where his parents lived at the time, and his grandfather, Maximiliano Gordón, was then *Pokani gajene gitsrukate*, 'the important man of the the Pucani people'. Maximiliano's eldest daughter, Clotilde Gordón Manchinari, was Artemio's mother, and Artemio was her first surviving child by her second husband, Mauricio Fasabi Apuela, a Lamista Quechua man from the Huallaga river in northern Peruvian Amazonia.

Clotilde Gordón, like the rest of her kinspeople, had been a debt-slave of Francisco 'Pancho' Vargas, *el gran patrón de los piros*, 'the big boss of the Piros', until his death in 1940. I was told that Vargas had been the boss of all the Piro people, and many other indigenous people on the Bajo Urubamba and Tambo rivers, from the time when he had inherited them from his own boss, the *cauchero* (rubber boss) Carlos Scharf, who was killed by Amahuaca people on the Manú river before Clotilde was born. The historical archive tells us that Scharf had inherited his Piro slaves in turn from 'The King of Rubber', Carlos Fermín Fitzcarrald, the subject of Herzog's film, but Clotilde had heard little about Fitzcarrald, who died in 1897, beyond his name. She had been born in 1915, I guessed, and so what she remembered was Piro people's lives on Vargas's *haciendas*, up-river in Sepa and down-river in La Huaira, and at La Colonia on the Tambo river.

Aside from being the 'big boss of the Piros', Pancho Vargas was also *rutsrukatna*, 'their important one', their chief. He made them work hard in the projects he assigned them, in return for the goods he imported on the big river-boats from Iquitos, down-river on the Amazon. He also ran their political and social lives, organizing raids against their enemies, deciding who could marry,

---

[15] It would be more natural to say in Piro that Artemio was, *'santa klara gajene gitsrukate'*, 'the important man of the people from Santa Clara', and hence, for Santa Clara people, *'wutsrukate'*, 'our important man, our leader'.

and arranging and officiating at the *kigimawlo* (girl's initiation rituals) of his slaves. His slaves depended on him because, as they and their descendants told me in the 1980s, they were ignorant: they could not speak Spanish and they were afraid of other white people.[16] Vargas, who spoke Piro and Campa, was their white man, and all contacts with other white people went through him.

Vargas died in 1940, just as the region was about to experience a major change. First, the price of rubber shot up again, collapsed again, and was followed by a rapid and continued increase in the price of tropical hardwoods.[17] Vargas's ex-slaves began to work lumber, in some cases as minor bosses in their own right, and moved off the *haciendas* to found new independent villages. Such was the case of Maximiliano Gordón and Pucani village. The new economic opportunities also brought in immigrants from other areas of Amazonia, such as Artemio's father, Mauricio Fasabi.

Other new people began to appear in these newly independent communities, missionaries. Following Vargas's death, the *adventistas* (Peruvian Seventh-Day Adventists) had been operating a mission and school in the place called Huau (Piro, *Wawo*: 'little star-apple'), across the river from Santa Clara. In 1947, Esther Matteson of the SIL turned up in the midst of the Piro people to begin one of the first SIL projects in South America, and replaced the Adventists in Huau. The next year, the Dominicans opened a mission at the mouth of the Sepahua river, and named it *El Rosario del Sepahua*. All these missionaries opened schools, and Piro and other indigenous people began to move to these communities so that they and their children might take advantage of this new potential. At the same time, these communities had a heightened religious atmosphere, for the missionaries, being missionaries, were there to spread the Good News.

Artemio's parents moved to Huau, where the SIL had supplanted the Adventists, and it was there that young Artemio entered school. In the 1980s, people told me of Huau at this period, the early 1950s, 'Everyone lived there, all the Piro and Campa people.' And Artemio remembered, 'Huau was a big village when the *gringas* were there, as big as Atalaya [the nearest town]. It had everything, even electric lights.' His father, Don Mauricio, also reminisced about this village, and told me that, 'It was beautiful when the *gringas* held their religious services there, and the people sang.' However, its residents also got drunk and fought a lot, and after some years people began to abandon the village to move to new sites, making new villages along the Urubamba. Clotilde

---

[16] Undoubtedly, many could understand and speak Spanish, but were afraid of so speaking to unknown whites. Vargas also seems to have actively prevented their contact with other white people (see Gow 1991: 47–8).

[17] The rise in value of rubber was due to the Japanese capture of the Malayan plantations during the Second Wold War, and it collapsed again as they were retaken. The opening of the Lima–Pucallpa highway in 1943, with US financing for obvious strategic reasons, made Ucayali valley lumber easier to export, and therefore cheaper.

Gordón's close kinspeople moved to the other side of the river, to establish Mapchirja village (Piro, *Mapchirga*, 'Anaconda River'), and Don Mauricio and Clotilde later moved near to them because of the constant fighting in Huau, fights which Don Mauricio usually lost. Huau, as Artemio put it, was left 'small and ugly'.

Artemio was sent up-river, to the school in Sepahua, where his older sister Teresa was also studying. Why they were sent so far off, I do not know. I suspect that it reflected a general prejudice against the new generation of Piro bilingual teachers, and in favour of the Spanish priests and nuns of Sepahua, who, as white people like the *gringas*, could be expected to know more. At all events, at the age of seventeen Artemio married Lilí Torres Zumaeta, who presented him with the first beer at her *kigimawlo* (girl's initiation ritual). As a married man, he was no longer welcome in the boarding school in Sepahua. So, along with his brother-in-law Manuel Zapata, he resolved to go off down-river to the SIL base in Yarinacocha, near the city of Pucallpa on the Ucayali. There he learned to read and to write in the Piro language. Artemio and Manuel became bilingual schoolteachers, and returned to the Urubamba.

Together, Artemio told me, he and Manuel refounded Huau. Apart from Manuel's family, nobody was living there anymore, and there was no school. The two of them got together a list of families, of people from Huau, Mapchirga, and Nueva Italia, where Lilí's kinspeople lived. Artemio's mother went down-river to call her Campa kinspeople to move to the new village. Eventually, they collected the names of twenty-two school-age children, and asked the *lingüistas* to allow them to open a school. The SIL gave their permission. Together, the people of the new village cleared the football pitch, and the village was formed. Artemio taught in Huau for a year and received a salary of 100 Peruvian *soles*, which, he told me, was a good salary at the time.

It was not to last. Artemio told me that Enrique Cobos, the bilingual teacher in Nueva Italia, made a complaint against him to the SIL. There was, Cobos said, a lot of drinking going on in Huau, and Artemio was at the head of it, a serious fault in the eyes of the *lingüistas*. Artemio admitted to me that they did indeed drink manioc beer in their houses, but said that the real motive for the complaint was different. Artemio was to be appointed as successor to Cobos in Nueva Italia, but Cobos wanted his adopted son, Luciano Rodriguez, to follow him. Artemio told me,

The *lingüista* wanted me to continue, but then they held a big meeting in Yarinacocha, with all the Piro teachers from here on the Urubamba. They said they didn't want me to be a teacher, because I wasn't a pure Piro, that I was mixed with another race.[18] So,

---

[18] For the SIL, Artemio's lack of 'cultural purity' was probably a powerful argument against him. In Piro terms, this argument was not directed at Artemio's cultural inauthenticity but against his father, the 'other race' referred to (see Gow 1991: 85–9), and the notorious 'trouble maker' of Huau. There is an irony here too, for Enrique Cobos, Artemio's original accuser, was not Piro at all but *kajitu potu*, a 'real white man' (see Gow 1991: 301 and D'Ans 1982 for the remarkable history of this man).

they threw me out. But the *lingüista* liked me, and suggested that I become a preacher instead. She told me to take a Bible-study course in Quilometro 15. So I went there to study.

The course, with the *Misión Suiza* (Swiss Mission) at Cashibococha (at 'Kilometre 15' on the Pucallpa–Lima road)[19] was to last for three years, but Artemio had to give it up after only two because his house and gardens had been destroyed by the Urubamba river in flood. He now had children of his own to feed.

In Huau, it was clearly difficult to 'live well', and the same was true of Nueva Italia. There was too much jealousy and gossip. Artemio had moved across the Urubamba to the present site of Santa Clara, and there he returned to build his house. His oldest sister Lucha, now separated from Manuel Zapata and living with her new husband Juan Mosombite, lived there too. Artemio's sister Teresa and her husband Antonio, from Sepahua, soon joined them, and then his parents moved in. Over time, more people moved to the site, following one or another kinsperson. Slowly a new village was forming, with people among whom it was possible to 'live well'.

The only problem with the new village was that it had no school. The children either had to walk to Nueva Italia or cross the river by canoe to Huau. This soon changed. The Dominican priest of Sepa, Padre Elías, stopped by to investigate this new community forming on the riverbank, and there met Artemio and his brother-in-law Antonio, whom he knew from Sepahua. They asked him to open a school for their children. In 1973, the Dominicans opened the mission centre of Santa Clara and started a school taught by a secular missionary teacher from Lima. Initially, Antonio was recognized as headman, but he was soon replaced by Artemio. The new village of Santa Clara slowly grew into the community where I turned up, unexpectedly, in December 1980, and in which I then began to live.

When I arrived there, I knew something of the general history of Piro people in the Bajo Urubamba and many aspects of what I saw were not, therefore, unexpected. Indeed, I went there planning to study the effects on Piro social organization of more than a century of engagement with capitalist commodity production in extractivist industries, and of over thirty years of intensive evangelization by North American Protestant and Dominican missionaries. I was not, therefore, very surprised to discover that *gringos* like myself loomed large in local people's lives. However, nothing in my training or imagination had prepared me for the importance of *gringos* in Piro people's thoughts, or how alien such thoughts were to be. I assumed that, insofar as I was called a *gringo* by them, I knew what it was like to be one. In fact, things

[19] *La Misión Suiza* is an evangelical mission that is formally separate from the SIL, given that the latter does not engage in evangelical activity in Peru. Artemio's story, and those of other Piro people, shows just how separate they actually are.

were far more complicated than that, and being accused of being a *sacacara* was just the start of it.

Telling Piro People about My Country

After the brief attempt to do fieldwork in the up-river community of Sepahua, I decided to return to Santa Clara because, on parting, Artemio's mother Clotilde had asked to me to come back. She had said to me, 'Come back here, and tell us more about your country.' This was the only spontaneous suggestion anyone had made that I might be genuinely useful to them.[20] Being a source of ethnographic data about my own culture for my informants was not really what I thought I should be doing, but it was better than being ignored. I went back to become the resident *gringo* of the Santa Clara people.

It turned out to be something they were genuinely interested in, and people like Artemio asked me many, many questions over the months of my residence in Santa Clara. I was constantly asked to describe my own country of Scotland (Ucayali Spanish, *mi tierra de Escosia*; Piro, *Giskosya nochiji*), and I tried to do so as carefully as possible. Place of origin matters to Piro people, for it is in such a 'land' (Ucayali Spanish, *tierra*; Piro, *chiji*) that a person's *nshinikanchi*, 'mind, memory, love', is formed through intimate childhood contacts with others. It refers to a set of people united by their co-residence in a particular place at a particular time in the past. Local people had actually heard of Scotland, for our national team had lost to Peru in the 1978 World Cup: this national tragedy was to my personal advantage for, throughout Peru, I was received with much compassion.

Beyond this important fact, people in Santa Clara had only the vaguest notions of what Scotland might be like. Following the lead of their questions, and in the face of their scrutiny, I tried to specify exactly how my people differed from other distant foreigners they had heard more about, such as the Americans, the English, and the Swiss. Warming to my task in response to their evident interest, I tried to show where my country lay in relation to Santa Clara, and the relative positions of England, Germany, the United States, and so on. Piro people, like the other indigenous peoples on the Bajo Urubamba, are pernickety about such details, for they can point to any place they have travelled to with uncanny accuracy. Indeed, it was my own attempts at extreme

---

[20] Contrary to the experience of many ethnographers of indigenous Amazonian peoples, I found it was impossible to make relationships with Piro people with presents. They initially asked me for very little, fearing that any gift would make them financially indebted to me, on the model of the local boss/worker relations. They began to ask me for things only when they began to trust me, and their demands were always small and carefully thought out. They frequently offered to buy things they wanted from me, and usually asked me how much they owed me when I gave them things. I soon learned to think before I gave, ensuring that any present showed that I had thought carefully about the receiver. In an unexpected reciprocity, I later discovered that they could remember the exact identity of every present given many years before, when I had completely forgotten about them.

geographical accuracy which may have led to Julian's joke: to correctly indicate the position of Scotland in Santa Clara, I was obliged to point *under* the earth.

In this process, there occurred an unexpected transformation of my status in the eyes of local people. Learning more about my country and my compatriots in this way,[21] local people began to identify me less often as a *gringo* and more often as an *escocino* or *Giskosya gajeru*, respectively Ucayali Spanish and Piro for a 'Scottish man'. Initially flattered by such recognition, as are the members of all small nations, I soon discovered it had a deeper meaning. My relative poverty and my ignorance of how to work or repair foreign technology, which occasioned unfavourable comparison with the other *gringos* they had known, was taken as evidence that I was not a *gringo legítimo*, a 'real white foreigner' (Piro, *krigko potu*).[22] Neither American nor Swiss, bereft of an aeroplane or an outboard motor, and quite ignorant of how to work either, I was clearly not in the same league as the missionaries of the SIL or the Swiss Mission. As such, people in Santa Clara became less afraid to ask me for information about these awesome beings, and to discuss their own ideas about them. And undoubtedly, through being taken less as a *gringo*, a role for which I was in all truth but poorly equipped, and more as just a very young and confused Scottish man, I felt more at home, and hence more able to treat the people of Santa Clara as 'my own folks', as my people would say.

The conversation on the night of 15 January 1982 began with me asking for Piro knowledge of the stars, and led Artemio to ask me if it were true that Americans had been to the moon. This was, as far as I remember, the only time anyone asked me that specific question, but the association of *gringos* with mechanized flight was pervasive in Piro people's interest. I was often asked if they could travel to the countries of *gringos* by canoe or boat, or if the journey must be made by aeroplane. They were slightly disappointed by my affirmation of the technical feasibility of travel by water, and far more interested in my descriptions of the size and speed of craft used in intercontinental flights. They would say of my descriptions of Boeing 747s and the like, 'Ahh, so they are as big as this village! Not like the little planes we see here.' The Bajo Urubamba during the early eighties was the scene of intense small plane traffic, as a consequence of the nascent cocaine trade. Larger planes, like the Peruvian Air Force Buffaloes, flew over Santa Clara more or less weekly. Local people were pleased to hear that these local aeroplanes were but a pale reflection of the ones habitually used by *gringos*.

Local people were also intrigued by how such machines, the largest and

---

[21] In Piro, as in Campa, 'my compatriot' and 'my kinsperson' is designated by the same word (respectively, *nomole* and *noshaninca*). The Ucayali Spanish term, *paisano*, can also be used in both senses.

[22] In the same vein, Artemio once said, with considerable prescience, that the local Dominican priests were, 'not real Spanish people, they're just the native people of the real Spanish', because most of them are Andalucian or Basque.

most impressive known to them, were made. Never having thought about it, I was unable to enlighten them. I did not even know then in which country planes were made: I wondered to myself if Boeing might be a German or an American company. Perhaps as a consequence of this shared ignorance, Artemio told me the following, with regard to the new *peque-peque* outboard motor he had bought, 'Here, on the Urubamba, we say that the *gringos*, off there in the USA, make these things in school, as handicrafts. You know, the way our children make little bows and arrows and little clay pots. We say that the little *gringos* must make the *peque-peque* motors as a practice for making aeroplanes when they are grown up. Then they sell these things to us here.'

I do not know how seriously Artemio took this story. *Peque-peque* motors, named for their put-putting sound, are low horse-power, Briggs-Stratton motors mounted on a regionally manufactured frame.[23] They are beautifully adapted to the log-filled and opaque waters of the large local rivers, but in speed and elegance they fall far short of the powerful *Johnson* motors, as the outboard motors familiar in Europe and North America are called on the Bajo Urubamba, and far, far short of the smallest aeroplane. Artemio's story here elegantly encapsulated the difference between the lives of Piro people and the *gringos* in the registers of knowledge and access to technological advances. His story, even if invented on the spot as a joke, was consistent with the pervasive association of *gringos* with factories (Ucayali Spanish, *fábrica*) and machines (*máquina*). One man, pondering the mystery of aeroplanes, said, 'What must those *gringos* know to make such things?' Another commented on one of my stories about *gringos*, 'How might it be, then, do they live just from machines?'

This awesome technical knowledge of the *gringos* had a poignant meaning for Piro people. They felt acutely their dependence on the local *patrones*, 'white bosses', for the things they needed but did not know how to make: salt, soap, clothes, kerosene, petrol, shotguns, radios, cassette-players, and so on. To get these things, the *cosas finas*, the 'fine things' (Piro, *gejnu*), they had to enter into oppressive debt relations with their white bosses. More poignant yet was their oft-voiced knowledge that the 'fine things' they did have access to were not 'real fine things', like motorbikes or aeroplanes, but rather, as they said in Ucayali Spanish, *basura no más*, 'just rubbish'.[24] People often bemoaned their poverty, and attributed it to their ignorance, saying things like the following,

---

[23] The truth may be stranger yet, for most of the *peque-peque* motors were designed primarily for the North American lawnmower market. Their adaptation to river transport seems to be an Amazonian innovation of unknown history.

[24] The campaign against foreign imports by the revolutionary military government (from 1968 to 1980), and the aggressive assertion of nationally manufactured goods as *produtos peruanos* undoubtedly did much to reinforce this local opinion: self-professed 'Peruvian products' were both cheaper and shoddier. But the pattern is a much older one in Amazonia, and older people reminisced about a much higher quality of imports in the past. This even included money, for some people could remember the use of gold sterling, to my great surprise: Don Mauricio once told me, 'This *sol* (the national currency) is just worthless trash! The pound sterling, that was real money!'

'We are ignorant, we know how to work, but we don't know how to make the fine things!'[25]

Knowledge (Piro, *gimatkalchi*; Ucayali Spanish, *saber*) is an important aspect of Piro thought and action. Unlike *nshinikanchi*, 'mind, memory, love', which develops through the constant sharing of food in 'living well', *gimatkalchi* must be acquired by seeing that knowledge demonstrated by one who knows. Cut off by distance and poverty from where such knowledge is demonstrated, in the lands of the *gringos*, the Piro and other indigenous peoples were condemned to remain ignorant of the powerful knowledge of 'factories' and 'machines'. Artemio had personal reason to feel this predicament strongly, for he had tried and failed twice to acquire knowledge that would have freed him from the arduous and dangerous work of lumbering.

If my stories about the *gringos* confronted people in Santa Clara with a stark portrait of their own poverty and ignorance, as they understood those conditions, there was also a consistent sense that they believed their own lives to be, in many ways, better than those of the *gringos*. One of the questions about the 'lands of the *gringos*' that they most frequently asked me, and one to which they always heard my reply with a mixture of fascinated horror and satisfaction, was, 'Is there forest in your country, are there any trees?' When, in the interests of accuracy, I tried to answer by asserting that there was forest, but not that much, they would keep asking me, until I said, 'No, there is no forest there.' Then on to the next question, 'So, how do you make gardens, what do you eat?' My technical discussions of European agriculture bored them, and they were much more interested in trying to imagine an unforested world. This was the force of the man's comment quoted above, 'How might it be, then, do they live just from machines?'

In part, the idea that the 'lands of the *gringos*' were unforested simply made sense to local people. Most men worked seasonally as lumberers, and the rainy season was always marked by huge flotillas of logs going down to the sawmills and road-head in the distant city of Pucallpa. Obviously, these trees were going off to places which did not have them. But in a more profound sense, for local people, life in an unforested world would have to be a very different kind of life to their own. For them, the forest was the source of much of their food, through the making of gardens. Out of the forest they made their villages, both by clearing it, and literally by using forest products to build their houses. Apart from the 'fine things', and what they could get from the river, the forest provided them with everything else they needed and, through garden foods, with the strength necessary to get them. In fact, indirectly, it provided them with the 'fine things' too, for it was mainly through lumbering that local men obtained money, and through it, what they wanted from the stores of the white bosses in Atalaya.

---

[25] See Gow (1991: 90–115) for a far more detailed account of the local economy, and native people's place within it.

Seen from this angle, the world of the *gringos* becomes deeply unattractive. With no forest, *gringos* cannot grow plantains and manioc, and hence cannot eat food that builds the body and makes one strong. Certainly, they were impressed by my pallor and physical weakness in comparison to themselves, and noted with approval how my strength and robustness grew as I ate their food. Equally, I began to notice more the ambivalent nature of local people's notions about 'machines' and the 'fine things'. On the few occasions when local people were willing to speculate at length on what goes on in factories, there was a strong presumption that 'machines' transform raw materials by a process of weakening, by the extraction of the native potency and its replacement with delicacy. Artemio's older sister Lucha Campos told me of how she and her husband had once decided to find out if it were possible to get drunk on bottled beer 'from the factory'. They wondered at how factory beer had no strength, and drank an entire case between them. She commented, 'Nothing happened, we just got a little drunk. So we finished up drinking *cashasa*, and then got really drunk!' *Cashasa*, cane alcohol, was produced in the Ucayali area from locally grown sugar cane and retained the potency of its origin. Bottled beer, by contrast, had had its strength removed in its factory transformation.

Local people's ambivalence about 'factory products' was most marked in regard to one specific kind of 'fine thing': *medicina de la fábrica*, 'factory medicines'. On the one hand, Piro people had a keen interest in the sorts of 'factory medicines' they obtained from doctors and stores in Atalaya, or locally from the missionaries or medical posts in the villages. They were also willing to travel long distances to obtain hospital treatment. On the other hand, however, they were also convinced that many illnesses were untreatable by such means, and scornful of those white people who placed all their faith in such medicines. In particular, illnesses emanating from sorcery could never be treated thus. For these illnesses, only shamans and forest medicines could work, as Artemio pointed out to me. Only shamans, using forest-derived hallucinogens and other herbs, could cure illnesses caused either by the sorcery of forest and river demons or by human shamans.

Artemio, along with most local people, was surprised by the ignorance shown by *gringos* of the forest in general, and of shamanry in particular. This feature of *gringos*, shared with other newcomers to the region, was frequently commented upon to me. Don Mauricio, Artemio's father, once told me darkly, 'White people come here to the Ucayali, and they don't believe that animals cause sickness. When they fall ill and are cured by shamans, only then do they see and understand these things. The animals send illness to us.'[26]

In particular, the obtuseness of *gringos* in the face of demonic illness, their

---

[26] Don Mauricio told me this in the context of curing me of an illness sent by dolphins. This was caused by my European notions of the intrinsic goodness of these animals: Urubamba people fear their potent sorcery. Admittedly, the sight of the pale river dolphins surfacing from the Urubamba's turbid yellow waters is an unnerving experience, as is the sudden sound of their blowing.

refusal to take hallucinogens, and their disdain for shamans, amazed local people. However ambivalent local people felt about the activities of any given shaman, they are unanimous in asserting that certain animals and plants, most shamans, and all demons, send illnesses to people, and that 'factory medicines' avail nothing in the face of them. Only shamans and hallucinogens could cure such conditions.

Piro people's amazement in the face of the *gringos'* ignorance seemed to derive from its wilfulness. How could *gringos* deny an obvious feature of the immediate Piro lived world of the river and forest, an object about which they plainly knew virtually nothing? People in Santa Clara were clearly pleased by the interest that I showed in shamanry, and by my willingness to take hallucinogens and to heed their advice about how to avoid and to cure illnesses. Indeed, many encouraged me to train seriously as a shaman and to take the more powerful hallucinogen, *toé*. Other *gringos* they had known, along with the Dominican priests, were scornful of such things, when not actively hostile.[27]

So, on that night in January 1982, as my conversation with Artemio and Julian turned to shamanry, it was clearly straying on to this interesting terrain, for my account of taking *ayahuasca* affirmed our shared experience of the power of shamanry and of the forest medicines. Their reaction to the description of my vision was a mix of wonder, interest, and relief. If I, a *gringo*, albeit not a 'real *gringo*', had seen this underground world in hallucinatory state, and had had no idea what it was, then Artemio could safely tell me about it, and about what the shamans and the old people had said. And it allowed him to tell me that myth, 'A Man who went under the Earth'.

As I came to be part of *gwashata*, 'living well', in Santa Clara, new questions could be asked of me. I was clearly becoming more like a 'real human' (Piro, *yineru potu*; Ucayali Spanish, *gente legítima*). The story, 'A Man who went under the Earth', tells of just such a 'real human' who becomes a white-lipped peccary, and who comes to 'live well' with them in the subterranean city. I have here discussed some of my initial and later reflections on this myth, and what it meant to me. In this book, I seek to analyse what it meant to Artemio when he told it to me. In Chapter 9, I return again to the evening of 15 January 1982, to explain how this event of mythic narration was linked to a wider series of events of that period, particularly the rumours about *sacacaras*. In the intervening chapters, I analyse a series of aspects of the lived world of Piro people like Artemio, and of the changes in that world, following the trail of connections initiated by 'A Man who went under the Earth'. I begin, in the next chapter, with a consideration of what this myth means.

---

[27] By contrast, the local white people, like the indigenous people, had in general a profound respect for, and confidence in, shamanry.

2

The Meaning of the Myth

Why did Artemio tell me the myth, 'A Man who went under the Earth' on that night, and what did it mean to him to tell it to me? In my experience, this story is not a frequently told Piro myth, and the only time I have ever heard it was on that one memorable occasion. And as long as I was under the impression that it was a metaphor for my presence in Santa Clara, I did not ask Artemio or anyone else to tell it to me again. My full sense of the significance of Artemio's story developed only later, after 1988, by which time the civil war in Peru made travel to the Bajo Urubamba impossible. Over those years, I thought long and hard about this strange story and about the conversation of which it was a part, as I began to see how it helped to shed light on the lived world of Piro people and on its transformations. By then, I was fully under its spell. When at last I was planning to return in 1995, one of my priorities was to discuss these issues again with Artemio, and if possible record other versions of this mythic narrative. But, unbeknownst to me, Artemio had died in 1991, one of the first victims of the cholera epidemic on the Bajo Urubamba: true to himself to the end, he had caught the disease by taking the lead in burying another victim.

In the previous chapter, I suggested that this myth probably does not mean what I thought it meant at the time, but I am sure I was right to think it had some connection to Artemio's thoughts on my presence in his village. In this chapter, I explore this myth through comparison to other versions known from the published literature, following Lévi-Strauss's advice that since, 'a myth is made up of all its variants, structural analysis should take all of them into account' (1963: 217). My argument is that Artemio's story is a myth about human mortality, and the relationship between the living and the dead, seen metaphorically in the relationship between humans and white-lipped peccaries. It also contains, hidden within it, a visit to the sky, which connects it to the discussion on that night about the moon. Finally, I argue that this myth is demonstrably changing in significant ways, and that it is a privileged point at which certain aspects of 'ancient people's knowledge' can be brought into relationship with the potent knowledge of *gringos*.

The Sources in the Documentary Archive

As I noted in the Introduction, the relatively voluminous documentary archive on Piro people is notably deficient in recording anything that Piro people may ever have actually said. The published literature on Piro mythic narratives is

slight, but luckily it does contain a few other versions of the story Artemio told
me. In Ricardo Alvarez's important collection, *Los Piros*, there is a myth he
calls, 'The Mother of the White-Lipped Peccaries' (1960: 152–3), which was
presumably collected sometime in the 1950s. The Piro school reader *Gwacha
Ginkakle* ('The History of the Piro People'[1]) contains a version told by Juan
Sebastián Pérez, one of the first Piro bilingual schoolteachers, entitled 'The
Shallow River' (Sebastián, Zumaeta, and Nies 1974: 90–7). Concluding
Gwacha Ginkakle, Sebastián says he is telling these stories in 1968 (ibid.:
179–85). Of particular interest is a version recorded by the SIL linguist Esther
Matteson from this same Sebastián, entitled 'The Sun', published in her study
The Piro (Arawakan) Language (1965: 164–9). In this version, the main char-
acter's journey through the hole of the peccaries into the underworld continues with a journey into the sky. This version links the myth I was told by
Artemio to an apparently quite separate myth about the canoe journey of the
sun, of which other versions are known (see Appendix for full texts of all these
myths).

In contrast to the case of Artemio's story, I know little of the original
contexts in which these other versions were told. In some cases, their published
forms are likely to be quite far from their original tellings: Alvarez presents his
texts in a literary Spanish quite unlike anything spoken by any Piro person I
have ever met, which would suggest that they are not verbatim texts. Further,
Alvarez does not name the tellers, other than to state that they were, 'older and
respected people, men and women who expressed themselves in the Piro
language' (1960: 10). Presumably they were also residents of the mission of El
Rosario de Sepahua. Similarly, Sebastián's 'The Shallow River' probably
underwent unknown changes during its transformation into a chapter of a
school reader.

The case of Sebastián's 'The Sun' is somewhat different. This narrative was
published by Matteson (1965), in a study devoted to the analysis of the Piro
language from the perspective of structural linguistics which also contains a
series of Piro texts (including mythic narratives) as examples of Piro discourse.
'The Sun' is clearly a transcription of an originally oral narrative subjected to
relatively little editing, for Matteson has included the narrator's verbal hesita-
tions and spontaneous corrections. The context in which it was originally
narrated is not recorded, and it is not even clear when it was told, for Matteson only states that she worked with Sebastián between 1949 and 1961 (1965:
2). However, Sebastián was Matteson's most important male informant, and an
important leader in the bilingual school movement.[2] Close attention to the text

---

[1] The title, literally translated, would be something like 'stories of different generations'. The Piro
gwa-, and its derivatives, always point to a connection between 'living' and a time and a place in which
this living goes on. See Gow (1991).
[2] I met Sebastián in Miaría in 1988, but the tense circumstances of the visit (my companions were
very anxious to leave) prevented any long discussion with him.

itself, and to what can reasonably be guessed about its telling, provides important information for a deeper understanding of Artemio's story. It is for that reason that I start this comparative analysis with Sebastián's version of 'The Sun'.

Juan Sebastián tells Esther Matteson 'The Sun'

The following is the text of Sebastián's story, as recorded by Matteson.

Now I will tell you about the sun, and what were the ancient people's ideas about it.

This is what happened to one of the ancient people. He was weeding a manioc garden.[3] He used to go to sleep there day after day. He used to get tired, and it is said that he would go to sleep right there.

One day a deer came. It came wandering by where he was, and ran right close by him. It went, *'nikch, nikch, nikch'*.[4] The man woke up in a great fright and fled.

He slipped in a big hole. ¡*Tperoyy!*[5] He went down into that hole. When he came out again, he was in another world by a shallow river. There he met the woman who is called Kmaklewakleto, 'She who is always youthful'.[6]

She put drops of herb juice in his eyes. Immediately he was able to see. What a shallow rippled river! How the sand showed through the water, and what a beautiful beach! And there were swarms of fish there, every kind of fish, *patlu, kapiripa, gamjiru, charawa*,[7] all with beautiful designs.

But Kmaklewakleto took him, and put him in her house. There she gave him food, and showed him her pets. Kmaklewakleto raised white-lipped peccaries. Kmaklewakleto showed him other things too. In one pen, she had her fat pets. They were sleek and round.

Then she showed him her thin animals and those with sores. 'Look at my poor pets. That's why I don't take them out. If I take them out just once, they keep returning to the place where they have been, When they come back from there, they have sores.'

Then it is said that Kmaklewakleto told him, 'Father will be here soon.'

While they waited there, he saw a big canoe moving along. It was all by itself in a wide expanse of water. That was the evening star (*goprik-sagi*). He saw it coming and would have detained it, but asked in vain, 'Take me aboard!'

---

[3] Matteson translates Sebastián's, *'yonakyegisanatgimata'* as, 'he was engaged in clearing land to plant a garden.' The verb, *yonaka*, means 'to weed', rather than 'to fell'.

[4] This is an onomatopoeia of the deer's call.

[5] Onomatopoeia for the sound of a person or heavy object slipping into a hole.

[6] From the root, *maklo-*, 'young woman', and postpositional, *-waka*, which indicates a characteristic way of being. Matteson (1965) consistently analyses the suffix, *-tu/-to* as a privative, linked to the privative prefix, *m-*. She ignores that class of words where this suffix occurs with the attributive prefix *k-*. This class is made up of names of mythic or other powerful beings: *Kmaklewakleto, Kochmaloto*, mythical women who survived the flood, *Kajpomyolutu*, 'Hand-whistling Demon', *kajitu*, 'white person'. Bruna Franchetto (personal communication) has suggested to me that in these names, the suffix, *-tu/-to*, may be quite unrelated to the privative one.

[7] *Patlu* (Ucayali Spanish, *palometa*), 'Lat.: *Mylossoma, Myloplus, Metynnis spp.*'; *kapiripa* (Ucayali Spanish, *boquichico*), 'Lat.: *Prochilodus nigricans*'; *gamjiru* (Ucayali Spanish, *paco*), 'Lat.: *Colossoma bidens*'; and *charawa* (Ucayali Spanish, *hachacubo*), 'Lat.: *Sorubimichthys sp.*' (identifications from Villarejo 1979).

She said, 'Father is coming later. He'll take you aboard,' she said. After a while he saw another canoe all alone. When it dawns, this is called aurora,[8] the morning star (*gon-sagi*). He saw it there again, a canoe all by itself.

Again he would have detained it, and asked in vain, 'Take me aboard!' But that one also said, 'Father is coming later on. He will take you aboard.' It passed and went on.

After a while, it came into view. The poles were thumping on the edge of the canoe, *tloj, tloj, tloj*.[9] He stood then on the bank. There he stood. The polers said as they worked, 'Ha! There's a human being. He is one who has thrown his clothing away.'

The canoe came in close to the bank, and the man flung himself into it. He landed on the middle of the arched canoe cover. *Plejj*.[10] So he went, and they took him aboard. The canoe polers were pitch black. Inside the canoe cover sat the sun. What a terrific heat his was! His slaves were pitch black. He had enslaved the what-do-you-call-them?—the *ksajmejirune*, the wood storks (Lat. *Mycteria americana*). They were his slaves. 'They went on and on. When it was time to eat they caused him to become exceedingly sleepy. 'Sleep as you go along,' they said. So the man went to sleep.

He slept as they went along, and they eviscerated him. They took out his intestines, and hung them over the sides of the canoe. What a brightly painted heap! Then when it was time to eat, they woke him up. That is just when he ate, when the sun arrived at midday.[11] The canoe stopped for just a short while. So when it was late morning the sun stayed there a little while. It stood still.

So the slaves, who had no intestines, ate. They always drank a whole jarful of water at once, and they ate in great quantities. They could go a whole day without eating. So he also drank up a whole jarful of water, and still he was not satisfied. He wondered at himself.

But they said to him, 'What are those intestines?' He looked at them. 'Oh. I don't know,' he said.

'Throw them out,' they said. He threw them out, and then after a while they told him, 'What you threw away were your own intestines.'

So they boarded the canoe, and went out into the river, away from the place where they had eaten. They went away again, and paddled all day—it is said that they did not stop at all. Then they came again to where Kmaklewakleto was. There they left him again.

He had not thrown his clothing into the water; those who throw their clothing into the water when they go aboard are sent off to the place where the dead go, wherever that is. But he had not thrown his clothing in the water. For that reason they left him there.

Kmaklewakleto received him well again, and returned him from there. She went with him along that trail, which she knew. It is said that he arrived again where his wife and children were.

That is finished. That is all. The story ends here. (Matteson (1965: 164–9)

---

[8] '*Gawrora*', from Spanish, *aurora*, in the original text.
[9] Onomatopoeia for the sound of poles knocking against the sides of a canoe.
[10] Onomatopoeia for the sound of a person or other heavy object falling on to thatch.
[11] Original *tumananu*, '11.00 am to 2.00 pm' (Matteson 1965: 364).

Artemio's and Sebastián's Versions Compared

The most obvious difference between Artemio's and Sebastián's versions of this myth is the presence of the journey in the canoe of the sun in the latter. This journey is absent from Artemio's version, but it should be remembered that a somewhat similar journey was narrated in the context in which Artemio told me his story, to whit, my own story of the Americans going to the moon. And that, of course, was in response to my interest in the night stars, and Artemio's profession of complete ignorance.

As I have said, Piro people told me little of their ideas about the sky, so it will come as no great surprise to learn that I heard nothing about a river which circles the world, and along which the sun travels in a canoe.[12] The only suggestion of such a river and of such a canoe journey occurs in Sebastián's story and in two others in the published literature: one told to Ricardo Alvarez and published by him as 'The Canoe of the Sun' (1960: 50–1), and a version told by Roselia Pacaya, 'The King Vultures who carry the Sun', published in the Piro school reader, *Muchikawa Kewenni Pirana ga wa Pimri Ginkaklukaka* ('About Long Ago Dogs and Other Stories') (Nies 1972: 108–13). All three versions agree that the sun is carried each day in a canoe poled by birds (wood storks in Sebastián's and Alvarez's informant's version, king vultures in Pacaya's[13]), and that at midday they stop to eat, which is why the sun seems to stop in the sky around the middle of the day.

A significant difference between Sebastián's version and these other two is that the former initiates the journey through the sky in the underworld, and identifies the river along which the sun travels as the 'Shallow River' that runs through the underworld. The versions by Alvarez's informant and by Pacaya do not detail the underground journey, and hence make no reference to the peccaries whatsoever. Indeed, Alvarez's informant's version explicitly stops where the canoe of the sun enters the hole which leads into the underworld.

In Artemio's version, the theme of the canoe journey of the sun is apparently absent. Closer inspection, however, shows that this is not quite so, for a detail suggests that something similar occurs. When the central character returns through the hole of the peccaries to the world above to see his wife and

---

[12] Such a celestial river features in the cosmology of the neighbouring Campa and Machiguenga peoples to the west and south (Weiss 1970), of the Shipibo–Conibo people to the north (Heath 1980) and in the cosmology of the inhabitants of the Upper Urubamba valley in the Andes (Urton 1988), where it is identified with the Milky Way. In 1999, when specifically asked for the name of the Milky Way in Piro, Clotilde Gordón identified it as *tengognewaka gatnu gapo*, 'the sky road', rather than as a river.

[13] I have changed the original species definitions. Alvarez translates the Piro word *ksajmejiru*, which he transcribes as *shajmegiri*, by the Ucayali Spanish *tuyuyo* (also *tuyuyu*). However, the latter term in fact refers to the larger jabirú stork (Lat. *Jabirou mycteria*), called *yawuro* in Piro. Similarly, Pacaya's *klatatalu* is translated in the original as *condor* (Lat. *Vultur gryphus*). However, Andean condors are rarely if ever seen on the Bajo Urubamba, and my informants always translated the Piro term by the Ucayali Spanish *buitre*, 'king vulture' (Lat. *Sarcoramphus papa*), a much more common bird.

children, it is no longer his formerly familiar world. As Artemio told me, 'The other world was red, all red, like the sun as it is just rising, he didn't recognize anything and didn't know the path to his house.'[14] The presence of the sun ascending into the morning sky, now a metaphor for the central character's experience of a transformed world, suggests that Sebastián's and Artemio's versions are rather closer to each other than might at first appear. As I discuss further below, the journey of the main character in Artemio's version is indeed a journey into the sky, but viewed from the white-lipped peccaries' point of view.

Artemio's and Sebastián's versions can be compared, element by element, as I do in the following table. I claim no particular rigour to the method of dividing up these narratives into smaller sections. I am not convinced that Lévi-Strauss's notion of the 'mytheme', generated by analogy to the phoneme, is actually defensible. However, the tabular style of presentation of mythic narratives followed by Lévi-Strauss does reveal structural properties that might otherwise remain hidden, even when the 'minimal units' are chosen on a largely intuitive basis.

Stage 1: *The Descent into the Underworld*

Artemio's Version	*Sebastián's Version*
A man, who is tired of living, wanders far into the forest, and becomes lost.	A man, who is always tired, is weeding a manioc garden,[15] and falls asleep there.
He finds a hole, containing a drum. He beats the drum, *tan, tan, tan,* and is attacked by peccaries. He throws the drum down, the peccaries take it and flee into the hole. He follows them.	A deer passes the sleeping man, saying *nikch, nikch, nikch.* The man wakes in fright, runs off, and falls into a hole.
In the underworld, the man sees people, pigs, and pigsties. He is attacked by the pigs and almost killed. He is resuscitated by their owner, who gives him peccary clothing to wear.	In the underworld, the man is greeted by Kmaklewakleto, the owner of the peccaries, who puts medicine in his eyes, so that he can see the new world, with its shallow river, its beaches, and its brightly painted fish.
The man lives with the peccaries, just as humans do in this world.	Kmaklewakleto shows the man her pets, and complains of how they are injured when they escape and run off.

[14] On the wider meanings of this experience, see Sebastián's 'The Red Sunset' (Matteson 1965: 146–7), and descriptions of *toé* hallucinatory state in Chapter 5.

[15] Because manioc is very intolerant of flooding, it must be planted in high forest away from the old river beaches which Piro people prefer for their villages and which are prone to seasonal flooding.

Stage 2: *The Journey within the Journey*

Artemio's Version	*Sebastián's Version*
The man misses his wife and children, and asks to be allowed to return to the upper world to fetch them.	Kmaklewakleto tells the man her father is coming, and will take him in his canoe. The man mistakes the canoes of two stars for the father.
The man goes back up through the hole of the peccaries.	The man enters the canoe of the sun.
The man has changed his human clothing for peccary clothing.	The wood stork say 'Here is one who has thrown his clothing away.'
The man has trouble seeing in the upper world, and difficulty in finding the path to his house.	The man has trouble staying awake, and falls asleep as the storks pole the canoe up into the sky.
The man finds his house and is rejected by his wife and children, except for his oldest son.	The man is gutted by the storks. They give him water to drink, but it does not satisfy him. Then they trick him into throwing his own guts into the river.

Stage 3: *The Return*

Artemio's Version	*Sebastián's Version*
The man takes his oldest son back into the underworld, where they live happily as peccaries.	The canoe arrives back at Kmaklewakleto's house, where the storks leave him because he has kept his clothing, rather than throwing it away.
The man's son attempts to return to the upperworld, but cannot find the hole because it has been closed up.	Kmaklewakleto takes him back along the path through the hole of the peccaries, where he arrives back with his wife and children.

Viewed in this way, it is clear that the two versions are at once very similar and systematically different. They are transformations of each other in the sense given to this term by Lévi-Strauss, following D'Arcy Wentworth Thompson (1942). As such, they help focus attention on certain themes which, were each version to be considered separately, might perhaps escape notice. Here I attend to a number of themes that the two versions have in common, but which are as systematically different as are the fates of the two central characters.

Tiredness, Death, and Other-becoming

The man in Artemio's version is marked by a recurrent condition of being 'tired of living': it causes him to set out in the first place, then causes him to return to fetch his wife and children, then makes him return to the underworld. He apparently transmits this condition to his son, for it causes the latter's abortive attempt to return to the upper world. As I have discussed in the preceding chapter, this 'tiredness of living' is caused by thinking too much about absent kinspeople. In each case, 'living well' is disrupted by missing people who are literally in other worlds.

The man in Sebastián's version is also marked by 'tiredness', but of an apparently simpler kind: he cannot stay awake. He cannot stay awake in his garden, and hence sleeps instead of working. In Piro terms, he is both lazy and foolish. People should work, and not sleep, in their gardens. If people must sleep during the day, they should not do so alone, and far from the village:[16] the forest, like the gardens located in it, is full of dangerous things, and one should maintain vigilance there. Further, the man falls asleep in the canoe of the sun, and hence falls victim to the sun's slaves' nefarious activities and deception: vigilance is also advisable when one is in the company of strangers, however apparently well-disposed.

There is a deeper element to this 'tiredness' which links these two meanings. Piro people regularly wonder about any unusual and recurrent feelings of tiredness they experience: it is taken as evidence of sickness or old age. In both cases, tiredness is evidence of approaching death. In sickness and old age, people become tired of living, and want to die (see Gow 1991: 180–3). This same condition is not restricted to humans, for it also occurs with animals. Pablo Rodriguez told me once,

The *isula* (a large solitary ant) becomes *tamshi* (a bromeliad with long vine-like roots), *compadre*. I didn't used to believe this, but an old man on the Inuya river showed it to me. When the *isula* dies, it transforms into *tamshi*. Its legs become the vines, and flowers grow from its body. How might this be? Maybe when the *isula* becomes tired of being an *isula*, it transforms into a *tamshi*. I have seen this happen.

He continued with a list of such transformations caused by such a state of 'being tired of being oneself'. He described these transformations in Ucayali Spanish as *se hace*, 'it becomes', and *se transforma*, 'it transforms itself': in Piro, this would be *gemaneta*, 'to metamorphose, to be transformed, to be renewed in body' (Matteson 1965: 261). He told me that collared peccaries become *paco* fish, *paco* fish become collared peccaries, *cunchi* fish become doves, tortoises become bushmaster snakes, and pacas also become bushmasters. This suggests that this 'tiredness with living' is not a search for nothingness, non-being, but a desire for another ontological condition. The Piro word, *gemaneta*, is a combination of two roots: *ge-*, 'new, for the first time', and *mane-*, 'body, corporeal

---

[16] Piro people try to avoid sleeping during the day anywhere since it invites questions from others about their health, or adverse comment about their laziness. One young man told me, 'Sleeping during the day makes our eyes rot.' For these reasons, those who are sleepy tend to hide in the walled-off sections of their houses, and to doze lightly, in order to respond to any visitor's question.

form'. Dying, in Piro thought, is not the negation of life, but a further mode of ontogenesis.

The theme of death is crucial to both myths. In Sebastián's version, the wood storks initially assume the man is dead, specified by them as 'one who has thrown his clothing away', but they then leave him with Kmaklewakleto again because they decide he has not done so. The reference here seems to be to Piro funerals: the body is buried in its best clothing, while all other clothes (along with other personal possessions) are thrown away into the river or burned. In Artemio's version, the man does change his clothing, as an alternative to being killed by the peccaries. But the man's return to his wife and children raises a peculiarly poignant problem for Piro people: the continued solicitude of the dead for the living. The souls of dead people (Piro, *samenchi*; Ucayali Spanish, *alma*) continually try to interact with their living kinspeople, appearing before them and eliciting their sympathy. The strong violently reject such appeals, while the weak succumb. In such encounters, the dead must be reminded that they are dead, for any solicitude shown towards them leads to death (see Gow 1991: 183–7). In Piro thinking, it seems, the dead do not know that they are dead, and must be made aware of their condition through active rejection.

There is another aspect of death for the Piro, for the dead exist in two primary experiential forms. The *samenchi* is one. The other is the *gipnachri*, 'the corpse, bone demon'. The flesh having rotted away, the *gipnachri* bears no resemblance to the living person, and is described as an animate skeleton with flashing eyes. Far from solicitous of the living, it is actively predatory upon them. The words *gipnachri*, 'corpse, bone demon', *gipna*, 'to die, to faint', and *kapna*, 'hole', share the common root *-pna*, which Matteson translates as, 'hole, anus' (1965: 322). In this sense, a man who falls into or goes down into a hole is, by definition, a dead man.[17]

In both versions, the man is significantly transformed by the owner of the white-lipped peccaries on his arrival in the underworld. In Artemio's version, he has his clothing changed from human clothing into the peccary robe of 'bristles, skin, and feathers'. In Sebastián's version, it is the man's sight which is changed, when the owner of the peccaries puts herbs in his eyes. But these two transformations seem to correspond to each other, for the man in Artemio's version has clearly changed his visual apparatus too: he will see the upperworld differently when he returns there, wearing the peccary clothing. And, on seeing him, the wood storks in Sebastián's version clearly think the man has 'thrown his clothing away'. In Chapter 5, I explore how these transformations in the main character correspond to another modality in Piro experience, the hallucinatory state of *toé* (Piro, *gayapa*).

---

[17] In Piro, a 'grave' is *yomlechi*, and the related verb, *yomleta*, means 'to jump at an enclosure in an attempt to escape': an activity attributed to the white-lipped peccaries in Ricardo Alvarez's informant's version. I cannot elucidate this detail further.

The complex transformations of the main character correspond to the condition of the white-lipped peccaries. As Artemio told me, these peccaries are human, unlike the collared peccaries and, he said, 'in the underworld, the shamans see the white-lipped peccaries as people.' But what does this mean? Judging from Artemio's version, it means the white-lipped peccaries see *each other* as humans. Before he changes his clothing, the peccaries make two attempts to kill the man, with the organized aggression for which they are feared by Piro people. Once he has changed into the peccary clothing, however, the man and the peccaries 'drank manioc beer, fished, hunted, and so on, everything was just as in this world.' That is, everything was just as it is for *humans*, Piro people, in this world. Clearly, from the point of view of humans, white-lipped peccaries do none of those things up here. Indeed, in this world, they are assiduously desired as food, and so hunted by people. In these mythic narratives, the peccaries seem to stand for the mutability of the central character's point of view and ontological condition (see Lima 1999 and Viveiros de Castro 1998).

A further sense of this relationship between ontological condition and point of view can be gained from a consideration of the episode of the deer in Sebastián's version. The deer frightens the man by saying, as he passes, '*nikch, nikch, nikch*'. This strange sound resembles the rapid repetition of the Piro word, *nikchi*, 'meat, game animal'. Deer, like white-lipped peccaries, are important prey for Piro hunters, but quite a few people are reluctant to eat them, because they are said to be 'human'.[18] This is, on the surface, a little odd, for the same affirmation about white-lipped peccaries does not make them inedible. However, deer can be 'human' for a completely different reason to white-lipped peccaries: deer are sometimes demons disguised as deer (see Ch. 5). Demons (Piro, *kamchi*; Ucayali Spanish, *diablo*) are 'human' because they have 'knowledge', the knowledge of sorcery. Sorcery is thought of as a mode of predation, with the victim becoming the 'game animal' of the sorcerer. Demonic deer only look like deer, for they are actually demons, and, as such, inedible. Don Mauricio once told me that ever since he had seen a grey brocket deer dancing in the forest, 'just like a human', he had stopped eating them. He commented, 'That one isn't an animal, it's a demon'; then, referring to the larger red brocket deer, he said, 'the other kind of deer, the big red one, that is good game.' A deer which says 'Game, game, game' would assuredly be such a dead person in deer-guise. The white-lipped peccaries, by contrast, see themselves as people, and can be so seen by shamans in the underworld, but here humans see them as peccaries, that is, as prey, as game animals.

The deer's *nikch, nikch, nikch* in Sebastián's version corresponds to the *tan, tan, tan* rhythm that the man beats on the peccaries' drum in Artemio's. The

[18] See Sebastián's stories 'The Demon's Mouth' and 'The Deer' in Matteson (1965: 170–5 and 202–5).

drum, found in the mouth of the hole, marks the beginning of the change in their identity from peccaries to humans.[19] Where the man in Sebastián's version is frightened by the deer calling him a game animal, the man in Artemio's version actively beats the drum he finds. As I discuss further in Chapter 6, drumming is a feature of Piro ritual life, and of the transformation of identities of hosts and guests through ritual action. The man's beating of the drum therefore asserts a desire for contact with other people, whereas in Sebastián's version, the man is merely fleeing from being treated as a game animal by a demonic deer.

This leads to an important difference between the two versions: in Artemio's version, the man becomes a white-lipped peccary, while in Sebastián's, he does not. This may help explain the major difference: the absence of the canoe journey of the sun in Artemio's version. The man in Sebastián's version travels into the sky as a living man, albeit one is assumed to be dead by the wood storks. By contrast, the man in Artemio's version travels to the upperworld as a white-lipped peccary. Logically, if the peccaries in the underworld are humans just like Piro people, then they must consider this world to be the sky. In that sense, the main character in Artemio's version does travel into the sky, but critically, now seen from a white-lipped peccary's point of view.

The World of the White-lipped Peccaries

The clothing of the white-lipped peccaries, in Artemio's version, is specified as 'skin, feathers, bristles'. By putting on this clothing the man becomes human in the eyes of the white-lipped peccaries, and they in his. By contrast, the man in Sebastián's 'The Sun' retains his clothing, and hence remains a living human rather than a dead man in the eyes of the wood storks. What is the meaning of clothing here? Clearly, the man in Sebastián's 'The Sun' is wearing a *cushma*, a cotton robe, the ordinary clothing of the 'ancient people'. The man in Artemio's version, however, exchanges this garment for one made of 'skin, feathers, bristles'.

In Piro terms, a man dressed in a robe of such materials would be a very good description of a game animal. There is a Piro word *popowalu* (or *popowlu*) which is defined by the *Diccionario Piro* as 'a dressed person; an animal before it has been skinned or plucked of its feathers' (Nies 1986: 176–7). In its possessive form, *gipowa*, it means, 'a rolled bundle, a man wearing a cushma, a corpse' (Nies 1986: 57). There is, therefore, a basic analogy drawn between animal body coverings and human clothing. My feeling, without being able fully to justify it, is that the analogy is most closely drawn between human clothing and animal fur or feathers, rather than the animal skin itself. At least, a standard

---

[19] Piro drums are covered in animal skins, usually monkey or collared peccary. Nothing, to my knowledge, would prevent the use of white-lipped peccary skin, were it available.

feature of the preparation of game for food involves the burning off of fur or feathers (Piro, *yoxjeta*; Ucayali Spanish, *chamuscar*), rather than skinning.[20]

This analogy between the clothing of humans and the surfaces of game animals does not, however, explain why the man in Artemio's version, after changing his clothing, should experience the white-lipped peccaries as fellow humans. To normal human visual experience, a robe of 'skin, feathers, bristles' would hardly define its wearer as human. But we are not on familiar, self-evident ground here. Following Viveiros de Castro (1998), we can think of this clothing as the body, as long as the body of the animal is thought of as 'distinctive capacities' (see Overing and Kaplan 1987). Wearing the clothing of the white-lipped peccaries, the man would look like this animal, and hence see them, and be seen by them, as 'human'.

For Piro people, the statement that some non-human entity is 'human' is the mark of a specific discourse, shamanry. As Artemio told me, 'But also, it is said, the white-lipped peccaries are people. They are demons, it is said, they know how to cause illness.' This, as I discuss at greater length in later chapters, is a specifically shamanic discourse, where 'humanity' is attributed to those who 'know', those who are shamans. Artemio also specifically contrasted this 'humanity' of the white-lipped peccaries to the ontological condition of the other species of peccary: the collared peccary is, as he told me, 'just an animal in the forest'. That white-lipped peccaries are demons, and sorcerers, raises a problem, for, as I argued above, it is this same feature which renders some deer inedible to some people. Artemio's statement should suggest that white-lipped peccaries are inedible for the same reason, but it does not. My only suggestion is that Artemio here elided a distinction between white-lipped peccaries in general and the *giyalutna*, the 'jaguars of the white-lipped peccaries', discussed further below.[21]

Why are the white-lipped peccaries special? While both species of peccaries live in herds, the herds of the white-lipped peccaries are much larger and much more wide-ranging. Collared peccaries live in small herds, associated with small, stable, home ranges, while the white-lipped peccaries live in herds of up to 400 individuals, and travel over very large areas (Emmons 1997: 175–7). It is this heightened sociality of the white-lipped peccaries which makes them appropriate 'humans', for, like Piro people, they too live in large groups and, indeed, in villages or cities.[22]

---

[20] The Piro word *-pixi*, is used for body hair, fur, small feathers, and down (contrasted to *-meji*, 'wing, wing feathers'). It is possible that Artemio's initial statement that the clothing was made of 'animal skins, feathers and bristles' represented his search for the Ucayali Spanish equivalent of *-pixi*, which then stabilized later in the story as 'bristles'.

[21] I have certainly never heard of anyone being ensorcelled by a white-lipped peccary, or refusing to eat this animal because it is a 'demon'. Those Piro and Campa people who continue to follow Seventh-Day Adventism (see Ch. 8) do not eat white-lipped peccary, but for other reasons.

[22] See Lévi-Strauss (1970: 83–7); Lima (1999); Viveiros de Castro (1992: 58–91); and Baer (1994: 73) for other Amazonian variants of this theme.

There is another factor here. The very large home ranges of the white-lipped peccaries lead to their periodic disappearance from the immediate local world of Piro hunters and allow them to be imagined in a different world. They are thought to live in the underworld, in their cities. It is in this underworld that they are humans, but they seem to be humans of a specific kind. The other known versions of the peccaries myth, those by Alvarez's informant and Sebastián's later version, do not explicitly state that the peccaries are human. Instead, they identify them as *koshichineru* and *manxineru*, which are names of two of the *neru*, 'endogamous groups', into which contemporary Piro people say the ancient-times people were divided, and which still operate as family names among Piro people (in their Hispanicized versions, Cushichinari and Manchinari[23]). Since such group names are only ever used of Piro people and of white-lipped peccaries, the peccaries would seem to be *yine*, 'humans', in the strongest possible sense of the term, Piro humans. Alvarez's informant's version mentions other peccary group names which are not Piro group names (several of them are derived from the names of cultivated plants[24]). In this version, these other groups of peccaries were previously unknown, and are hence distinguished from the destructive and dangerous 'Piro' peccaries.

The humanity of the white-lipped peccaries is, therefore, the humanity of the ancestral Piro people. Under the earth, where they live as people, the white-lipped peccaries are divided up into 'endogamous groups' which corre-spond to the multiple enclosures or corrals in which they live. There is no suggestion that they actually are the dead ancestral Piro people, but they corre-spond to them.[25] This introduces an important dimension of temporality to the stories about the white-lipped peccaries, for as I showed in *Of Mixed Blood*, Piro people narrate their own history as the history of intermarriages and mixing between the ancestral endogamous groups, and with other kinds of people. It would seem that the white-lipped peccaries have maintained a form of social organization that Piro people gave up as the condition of their present social lives.

There is another aspect to Piro people's ideas about the white-lipped pecca-ries. The Swiss anthropologist Gerhard Baer, investigating *pagotko* masks in Bufeo Pozo in 1968, was told by a man called Morán, who was very probably the Morán Zumaeta to be discussed further in Chapter 7, that 'the mask was called hyalo, hyalotko and hayo' (Baer 1974: 7). The 'hyalo' is simply *giyalu*, 'white-lipped peccary', in another orthography. Baer, in a footnote, records the

---

[23] See Gow (1991: 62–6) for further discussion of these groups.

[24] These are 'Payoneri', *payoneru*, 'ashipa people' (*ashipa* is a kind of cultivated root); 'Kakoalineri', *kakwaluneru*, 'peanut people'; 'Gimekaneri', *jimekaneru*, 'sweet manioc people'; and finally 'Haham-lineru', which I cannot translate, although it may derive from either *gagalu* ('club'), or *gamluta* ('to kiss, to smell').

[25] See Vilaça (1992; 1997) on the Wari' and Pollock (1992) on the Culina, where the identification of dead humans and white-lipped peccaries is explicit.

response of the Swiss Mission missionary Ernst Hauser to this information. The latter informed him that, 'the terms hyalo and hyalotko are not used by the Piro. He [Hauser] points out, however, that the terms hyalu/hiyalu ('peccary') and hyalutko/hyalutna exist. According to him hyalutko/hyalutna are beings that live underground and do not show themselves; if they did it would be considered dangerous. They are also said to grunt like peccaries' (ibid.: 7, n. 6).

The 'hyalutna', or *giyalutna*, is a more interesting entity. It would be the largest and fiercest member of a species, which Matteson was told would be the 'jaguar' of the species (1965: 361), as was I. In the light of Hauser's information, this would suggest that the *giyalutna* is the owner of the white-lipped peccaries in his or her peccary form: it is possible that Artemio was thinking of the *giyalutna* when he called white-lipped peccaries demons and sorcerers. I do not, however, agree with Hauser's dismissal of Morán's spontaneous association of white-lipped peccaries and *pagotko* masks, which Baer himself shows to have some deeper foundation. The problems raised by the *pagotko* are very interesting (Baer 1974; 1976–7), but I have been unable to elucidate the connection with white-lipped peccaries further.

The Owner of the White-lipped Peccaries

If the *giyalutna* is the owner of the white-lipped peccaries in peccary form, this is not how this personage appears in the myths. There, he or she, depending on the version, is clearly not a peccary in these myths, but human. Further, this personage refers to the peccaries as his or her 'pets' (Ucayali Spanish, *sus animales*;[26] Piro *toprane*, 'her pets'). The Piro word, from the root, *pura-*, 'to raise as a pet' refers to a specific relationship. Any animal (whether wild or domesticated) becomes the *prachi*, 'pet', of its owner if he or she raises and looks after it. The relationship is one between beings of different ontological conditions, for the same type of relationship between humans generates kinship relationships (see Gow 1991, and discussion in Erikson 1987 and Descola 1998). In that sense, the owner and his or her pets in this mythic narrative are ontologically different, while, at least initially, the owner and the man are ontologically the same. This ontological similarity is emphasized by the good welcome and treatment the man receives from the owner.

This owner is also clearly a shaman, *kagonchi*. In Alvarez's informant's version, the mother of the peccaries is specified as a shaman of lesser power than the Piro shaman, while in the other versions, the owner acts to transform the man in shamanic ways. This feature is absent in Sebastián's later version, but this emphasizes much more strongly another aspect of the owner's shamanry. Here, the man sees the owner of peccaries pulling out the splinters

---

[26] In Ucayali Spanish, possessives are only used of domestic animals or dead game animals.

of the arrows he himself has shot into the peccaries and crying, 'Ay! What has happened to you this time? You have been shot at again! That's why I don't like letting my pets out, because people mistreat them.' In Sebastián's earlier version, she is reported as saying, as she shows the man the thin peccaries and those with sores, 'Look at my poor pets! That's why I don't let them out. If I let them out, they keep returning to the place where they have been. When they come back from there, they are wounded. That's why I don't let my pets out.'

In the former version, the word used for 'shot' is *yotsnaka*, 'to wound slightly'. This same verb, in repetitive mode, *yotsnata*, means 'to ensorcell' (reference is to the repeated firing of small arrows into the victim). The owner must cure her pets, removing the splinters of arrows, just as human shamans cure sick humans by sucking out the sorcery objects, which take the form of invisible little arrows or darts (see Ch. 5). This suggests that the peccaries experience human hunters as sorcerers or demons, who shoot little invisible arrows at them. In Alvarez's informant's version, the peccaries are originally immune to this 'sorcery', and it is only after the shaman has stolen the trumpets which control the peccaries that they become 'killable' game animals.

If, as I have argued, this is a myth about mortality, then it is also a myth about the mystery of mortality seen from the point of view of the peccaries. When the peccaries go up through the hole into this world, they are assailed by sorcery (the arrows of the human hunters). Some are killed and eaten, while others escape with minor injuries to be cured by their owner in the underworld. But we have also seen that from the point of view of the peccaries, they are attacked when they go into the sky. Some just stay there and do not come back.

From the point of view of humans, the ideal destination of dead peccaries is the guts of humans. Dead peccaries are eaten, to satisfy the intense human desire to eat game animals, and, by satisfying that desire, to create kinship ties (see Gow 1989; 1991). This would seem to be the significance of the bizarre episode of the gutting of the man in Sebastián's 'The Sun': without his guts, the man can, like the wood storks, eat and drink vast quantities without ever being satisfied.[27] This food, because it never satisfies, can never lead the man to 'remember' the storks, in the way of kinship. By contrast, the man in Artemio's version, who has changed his clothing, remembers the 'better life' with the peccaries, and returns there.

There is a further aspect to this. For Piro people, game animals are eaten to satisfy hunger, but they do not provide human bodily substance. This is, instead, provided by the vegetable staples of plantains and manioc.[28] Game is

---

[27] The episode of the eating without guts refers to a peculiar characteristic of wood storks. These birds are noted for urohydrosis: they cool themselves in intense heat by excreting constantly down their legs. They therefore literally appear 'gutless'. This behaviour is shared by Neotropical vultures (Sick 1993).

[28] See Gregor (1985) for similar ideas among the Central Brazilian Mehinaku, speakers of a Maipuran Arawakan language closely related to Piro.

digested in the guts and then excreted: residues that remain in the stomach over long periods cause illness and ultimately death. Therefore, the final passage of the dead white-lipped peccaries is through the human anus, which links together the various meanings derivative from the Piro word root, *-pna*, discussed above. By contrast, human flesh is destined to rot in the hole of the grave (Piro, *yomlechi*), which is a hole dug in the ground.

The Temporality of the Versions

Human mortality is a mode of temporality, and one close to the thoughts of Piro people. These mythic narratives link the temporality of human life to the temporality of the white-lipped peccaries' lives when they see themselves as people, but also to the chancy temporality of white-lipped peccaries when viewed by humans. This latter temporality is manifested by the sudden appearance of white-lipped peccaries in huge numbers, and their equally inexplicable sudden disappearances. The various versions of the myths under discussion here link these forms of temporality to others and, as I show, reveal an interesting temporal dimension in themselves.

Sebastián's narrative, 'The Sun', locates the action in a period a little longer than twenty four hours: that is, one full journey of the canoe of the sun, plus the time it took the central character to go to and from the underworld. In temporal terms, the focus is clearly on the daily cycle of the sun. This is, of course, necessarily also true of the two other versions that tell of the canoe of the sun: those of Pacaya and of Alvarez's informant. However, Alvarez's informant's version of 'The Canoe of the Sun' evokes another temporal cycle: the duration of the sun's life, and of the alteration between day and night. That version states that should the polers fail to pass through the hole into the underworld, the sun will be killed and darkness descend. Here the daily round is linked to the temporal span of the world in general.

The peccaries-only versions place little or no stress on the daily cycle. Artemio's version makes a brief reference to the dawn, but otherwise the stress is on the length of the journey and on the long time during which the man, and then the man and his son, reside with the peccaries. Further, the story ends with a marking of a radical change: the hole is closed, preventing further communication between the two worlds. In Sebastián's later version, 'The Shallow River', there is also no reference to daily cycles, and only a reference to the short time during which one of the men lived in the underworld. More generally, this version hints that, in the past, journeys into the underworld were made on more than one occasion, suggesting repeated contacts between humans and the subterranean home of the peccaries. Ricardo Alvarez's informant's version, while specifying that the man spent less than twenty-four hours in the company of the 'mother of the peccaries', also stresses that it took him five days to get there. This version, however, introduces another temporal

possibility, the shift from an originary state of the world to a later state: originally the white-lipped peccaries were dangerous and unhuntable, now they are
easy to hunt. Similarly, Artemio's version ends with the closure of the hole of
the white-lipped peccaries. Therefore the peccaries versions all deal, at some
level, with such changes from a 'before' to an 'after'.

The daily cycle, the longevity of the celestial body that produces light each
day, changes from an original state to a later state, and, above all, the mortality
(life cycle) of humans and peccaries—all these versions seem to revel in such
temporal cycles. There is more, however, for some of the versions specify
seasonal cycles too. Thus, in Sebastián's 'The Sun', the underworld is experienced by the man as a specifically seasonal phenomenon: it is clearly the height
of the dry season. The shallow waters and the beaches and the pools of this
river evoke the Urubamba at the height of the dry season (Piro, *walapu*; Ucayali Spanish, *verano*). The man sees fish which are distinctive to that season, the
schools of fish which ascend the Ucayali and Urubamba rivers at the height of
the dry season (Piro, *paligatachro*, 'that which comes up-river'; Ucayali Spanish, *mijano*). One of the species mentioned, *gamjiru* (Ucayali Spanish, *paco*), is
only known on the Urubamba in this season. Similarly, the *ksajmejiru*, wood
storks, come to the Urubamba river during this period of the year, following
the migrating fish. I was often told that, when they appear, it is because they
'see the migrating shoals of fish', and that they 'see the big dry season'. Such
seeing is a form of augury, an occult ability of these birds.

By contrast, certain versions make no mention of such seasonality.
Sebastián's later version mentions the shallow river, but names only one fish
species, *kolyo* (Ucayali Spanish, *cunchi*, a small catfish), which does appear in
migration, but is also common throughout the year: indeed, it is actively
sought after during certain periods of the rainy season. Similarly, in Pacaya's
version of the canoe of the sun, the wood storks are replaced by king vultures,
a non-migratory resident species. There is no reference to seasonality in
Artemio's version, except in the implication of an annual cycling of seasons in
'living well'. It might be remembered, however, that such a seasonal reference
occurred in the conversation of 15 January 1982: my own description of the
moon was explicitly couched in terms of the Urubamba in the dry season, and
quite fortuitously corresponded to the accounts of the subterranean river (see
Ch. 5).

The versions where seasonality is marked are Sebastián's and Alvarez's
informant's accounts of the canoe journey of the sun. This correlates with
another feature of these versions: they explicitly link the sun's journey through
the sky to that below the earth, such that the sun circulates over and then under
the world. Pacaya's version makes no mention of such a subterranean journey,
which can be connected to another change in this version: while the wood
storks are clearly servants of the sun in the other versions (Sebastián describes
them as *tkachi maknane*, 'the sun's slaves'), Pacaya stresses that the king

vultures do as they please, and that, '*wa maylune gitsrukatni wa klatatalu*', 'the king vulture is the important one/chief of the vultures.'

What is most interesting about the presence or absence of marked seasonality is that it seems to be correlated with the date when the versions were told: the early versions mark seasonality (Alvarez's informants' versions, and Sebastián's 'The Sun'), while the later versions (Sebastián's 'The Shallow River', Pacaya's and Artemio's versions) do not. Why should seasonality have dropped out of these versions? What has changed? Following Lévi-Strauss (1981), myths change in order to keep pace with changes in the world, in order to preserve the illusion of their stability. It is not obvious from the versions of the myth what that change might be, but this feature of the myth does, at least, raise a new form of temporality, that of historical change.

This entry of historical change on to the scene is marked by an important feature. Here historical change has been found inside the myth, rather than outside of it. This feature has a number of important consequences. Firstly, it is precious from a methodological point of view, for the documentary archive of Piro myths is so temporally shallow that we would not necessarily expect to find such a change within it, or at least such a salient change. Secondly, the change in the myth, from a concern with seasonality to an absence of seasonality, may initially seem trivial, but it is highly concrete. To what change in the exterior conditions of this myth in the Piro lived world might such a loss of seasonality correspond? The rest of this book is devoted to the specification of that change. To conclude this chapter, I turn to another aspect of these stories, the contexts in which they were told.

Narrators and Listeners

The differences between the versions of this myth about the white-lipped peccaries are as remarkable as their similarities. They are, as I have shown here, transformations of each other. What can we make of such transformations? I here leave to one side Alvarez's informant's version. As I noted in the Introduction, I am here concentrating on the relations between Piro people and *gringos*, and as I show, this myth seems to be of intrinsic significance for that relationship. Alvarez, as a Spanish man and a Dominican priest, would have been a very different person to tell this myth to, and I have little information on Alvarez's informant and the context of his or her version. I therefore concentrate on Artemio's version and Sebastián's two versions.

On the face of it, one might argue that Sebastián, in his first narration, had spontaneously nested a separate myth, about the canoe of the sun, into a myth about the world of the white-lipped peccaries under the earth. Alternatively, one might suppose that this myth is splitting into two: originally perhaps, Sebastián's first version was most common, and it has subsequently divided into two separate versions. We have no evidence either way, since Matteson's and Alvarez's collections of Piro texts represent the earliest documentary evidence of Piro mythology. Here, history, supposedly capable of rescuing anthropology from its plight, cannot help us through a lack of data. But in fact we do have the potential for a sort of historical analysis here, albeit of the most minimal kind, for we know the chronological order of Sebastián's versions, that one was told earlier in Sebastián's life than the other, and that Artemio's version was told later yet.

One of the most fascinating aspects of this myth lies in the radical differences between Sebastián's two versions. In 'The Shallow River', he makes no mention at all of the episode of the canoe journey of the sun. In that sense, this version is much closer to Artemio's and Alvarez's informant's version. Explaining these differences is a serious problem. I think it unlikely that the differences can have been due to a contemplation by Sebastián of the actual text of the original, and hence to his conscious manipulation of the later version. It is improbable that Sebastián had any access, after his narration of 'The Sun' to Matteson, to the published text of her transcription of that original version: if he ever saw its published form, it would have aided him little, given that it is reproduced in a non-standard technical orthography. Further, given the economy of mythic knowledge among Piro people discussed in the next chapter, it seems unlikely that a Piro narrator would want to refer back to earlier attempts to narrate a myth rather than to personal memory of those narratives.

Of course, 'The Shallow River' was told in the context of a very different conversation to that of 'The Sun'. I think it is unlikely that this myth, along with the other narratives in *Gwacha Ginkakle*, was actually written down by Sebastián. It is much more likely that it was tape-recorded in conversation with the SIL missionary Joyce Nies for later transcription. However, the context of this conversation would have been the overt intention of creating the school primer about *'gwacha ginkakle'*, 'stories of different generations', the history of Piro people, to complement *Pero chijne ginkakle*, 'the story of the land of Peru', the primer on Peruvian history (Matteson 1953). While the latter part of Sebastián's narrations are historical and personal experience narratives, the bulk of the narrations are 'ancient people's stories', presumably reflecting those mythic narratives that Sebastián found interesting to tell to the 'young people', as he addresses them.[29] But the radical differences between Sebastián's earlier and later versions are unique to the myth about the white-lipped peccaries. His earlier and later versions of narratives like 'How Fire was Found' or 'The Bird People and the Hungry People' show variations, but no changes so dramatic (see Matteson 1965: 204–9 and 158–65 and Sebastián, Zumaeta, and Nies 1974: 1–18 and 104–13).

---

[29] It is of course likely that the SIL missionaries had some say in what went into this volume, and that the selection of the narratives would not have been Sebastián's alone.

Curiously, Sebastián's later version is narrated as if it were two separate versions, in which the journey is attributed to two different men. Sebastián states, 'There are two different stories.' We might speculate that, having forgotten or decided not to narrate the 'journey within the journey', Sebastián solves the resultant structural problem by duplicating both the journey and the main character. Confirmation for this hypothesis comes from Artemio's version, which conforms to Sebastián's first version by including 'the journey within the journey', but also to Sebastián's second version by duplicating the main character, for the 'man who was tired of living' is followed by his eldest son, who thus becomes another 'man who was tired of living'. This suggests that the duplication of both the journey and the main character in Sebastián's second version reflects a genuine structural feature of this myth.

This duplication of Sebastián's second version is put to a specific use by him. Sebastián exhorts his listeners/readers, 'the young people' (Piro, *maklu-jine*;[30] Ucayali Spanish, *jóvenes*) to attend carefully to discover if either of these stories are true or not. He says, 'You young people will have to listen carefully to discover if these stories are true or not.' On the face of it, we might suspect such an exhortation to doubt to be an effect of its location in a schoolbook produced by an SIL convert under SIL supervision. However, nowhere else in *Gwacha Ginkakle*, which contains many myths, does Sebastián ask his listeners/readers to consider such questions. Indeed, one of his myths is 'The Kochmaloto Women', concerning a flood, which directly conflicts with the Old Testament account, but nowhere in the story are the readers/listeners asked to reflect on the difference. Only, in the accompanying didactic questions following the text is this issue raised (Sebastián, Zumaeta, and Nies 1974: 54–89).

This overt appeal to doubt is therefore significant. It is not a general call to scepticism about myths, but a specific call to question *this* myth. Indeed, Sebastián then proceeds to answer his question in the affirmative, saying that this story accords with his own personal experience of white-lipped peccaries, for they do indeed periodically disappear and reappear again, and with the personal experience of other hunters, who have found the hole and heard the peccaries inside the earth. This kind of argument is a characteristic mode of verification in Piro discourse: a doubt is raised, only to be resolved by appeal to confirming evidence from personal experience. This suggests that, within the project of *Gwacha Ginkakle*, Sebastián wanted to raise the problem of doubt in the veracity of myth specifically in relation to this myth, and to suggest its probable truthfulness. Perhaps one could argue that this myth, in all its variants, is about doubt, figured in the form of the white-lipped peccaries and their chancy behaviour.[31]

---

[30] This word shares the same root, *maklu-/maklo-*, with the name of the owner of the peccaries in both versions, Kmaklewakleto.

[31] As Lévi-Strauss has shown, myths can also be about states of mind, as in his discussion of forgetfulness in myth (1977: 146–97).

This appeal to doubt appears also in 'The Sun', in a very significant form. At a key point, doubt is expressed about the destination of a journey. When the man is returned to Kmaklewakleto, rather than sent off as a 'dead man', Sebastián remarks, *ginakakta wa gipnachine yajetyawakgima*, 'wherever it might be that the dead go off to, it is said' (Matteson 1965: 168–9). The word, *ginakakta*, means, 'Where perhaps?' or 'Who knows where?' If we consider to whom Sebastián was telling this myth, this little detail must take on a deeper significance. The listener was Esther Matteson, a Evangelical Protestant missionary. Protestants may be uncertain of the post-mortem destinations of any given person, but they must *know* what the alternatives are: it is a straight binary choice of heaven or hell.[32] Sebastián must have known this, since he refers in *Gwacha Ginkakle* to the importance of the SIL in bringing to Piro people the word of Christ's salvation of humanity. But Sebastián's comment also echoes the words of Kmaklewakleto, as she shows the man her pets, 'If I take them out just once, they keep returning to the place where they've been.' This place, of course, is the original lived world of her interlocutor, and all Piro people know the ultimate destination of the dead white-lipped peccaries: the guts of humans. In this story, then, the existential condition of the white-lipped peccaries is likened to that of Piro people like Sebastián who, lacking in the certainty of true knowledge, hope that this question can be answered by Matteson.

There are two other hints of the great significance of this story for the relationship between Matteson and Sebastián. Firstly, in 'The Sun', he makes two references to *yonchi*, 'design' in the context of novel visual experience: the man's sight of the fish covered in designs after the owner has put herbs in his eyes, and the sight of the design-covered mass of guts when the man awakes in the sun's canoe. *Yonchi* also means 'alphabetic writing' in Piro, and Matteson taught Sebastián the much desired knowledge of reading and writing.[33] In the later version, when Sebastián is well established as an important teacher and leader, the references to design/writing are dropped.

Secondly, the name of the owner of the peccaries is *Kmaklewakleto*, 'She who is always youthful'. In *Gwacha Ginkakle*, Sebastián refers to Matteson respectfully as *Yeye Giwno*, 'Older Sister Giwno' (Giwno was Matteson's Piro name). However, I always heard her referred to as *Makloji Giwno*, 'Young Woman Giwno'. *Makloji* is the respectful term of address for unmarried white women schoolteachers generally.[34] The significance of these two points will be greatly clarified when I turn later to a discussion of design, girl's initiation ritual, and writing. Even if of the opposite sex, the owner in Artemio's version

---

[32] See Stoll (1982: 5) for the statement of doctrine that SIL missionaries are required to affirm.

[33] See reference in *Gwacha Ginkakle* (Sebastián, Zumaeta, and Nies 1974), discussed later in Chapter 8.

[34] Nies translates *giwno* as '*señorita*, a kind of bird' (1986: 70). Since *señorita* is the Ucayali Spanish equivalent of *makloji*, this might explain the nickname.

has a similar feature: he is identified as a *fraile*, a monk, an unmarried white man. And I, too, was young and alone.

My hypothesis is that Sebastián, when he first narrated this myth to Matteson, realized its complex meaning potential for their relationship, and wanted to bring it into dialogue with her own knowledge of writing, of the cosmos, and the destination of the dead. Later, as an established teacher and an Evangelical Christian, he either dropped or forgot the journey in the canoe of the sun, but emphasized more the way in which the peccaries metaphorize the human condition, and the problem of knowing whether myths are true or not.

My account here of the contexts of Sebastián's versions of this myth is obviously very tentative, due to the nature of the available data, and in later chapters I bring in further evidence to confirm it. But, if it can provisionally be taken on trust, it suggests some remarkable parallels to the situation in which Artemio told his version. Having heard my account of what the Americans found in their visit to the moon, Artemio spontaneously brought that story into dialogue with what the ancient people said about the moon, and to question the veracity of the latter. Then, on hearing of my vision of the cities in the underworld, he spontaneously brought that into dialogue with another myth, 'A Man who went under the Earth', as confirming the veracity of such knowledge.

These similarities suggest that this myth about a man who journeys to the subterranean home of the white-lipped peccaries, then up into the sky, and about the fate of the dead and different points of view, has some intrinsic significance for the way in which a specific form of knowledge, 'ancient people's stories' can be brought into dialogue with the powerful knowledge of *gringos*. I have suggested that the differences between the various versions of this myth allow us the possibility of a historical analysis of the Piro lived world. The next stage of the investigation is to ask what 'ancient people's stories' in general, rather that just this one myth, might mean to Piro people.

3

Myths And Mythopoeisis

In this chapter, I discuss Piro mythology in general, to show how the specific event when Artemio told me 'A Man who went under the Earth' fits into the general framework of how Piro people tell myths, and why they do so. I show how myths are connected to *gwashata*, 'living well', and in particular to the relationship between co-resident grandparents and grandchildren. I further show that Piro people tell and listen to myths because they are interesting. If Chapter 2 was an example of Lévi-Straussian structural analysis, here I want to explore the ethnography of mythic narratives as I experienced them during my fieldwork. It is therefore in this chapter that I really begin the work, outlined in the Introduction, of trying to unite the intellectual traditions of Malinowski and Lévi-Strauss.

Commenting on the work of Gregory Schrempp, Sahlins notes that 'grand cosmological issues can be found even in little folk tales', and that this is what Lévi-Strauss is doing (see Schrempp 1992: ix). Piro people too must be finding grand cosmological issues in their myths, but how does this connect to their motivations for listening to them and for telling them? This is of course a Malinowskian question, and has received surprisingly little attention in the literature on indigenous Amazonian peoples which has largely concentrated on the meaning of myths, or their connections to rituals. There have been some notable exceptions to this, mainly from the American tradition of discourse analysis, such as Basso (1985; 1987), Urban (1991; 1996a), Hill (1993), and Graham (1995). Impressive as these studies are, they view the activity of mythic narration as an example of the constitution of culture through language, rather than as a distinct kind of social action connected in specifiable ways to other modes of social action, which is what interests me here.[1] I only began to address this issue myself when I developed the analysis of why Sebastián told his myth to Matteson and why Artemio told his version to me. Satisfied with that argument, as detailed in the previous chapter, a far bigger question loomed, why do Piro people tell each other myths and why do they listen to them?

As I discussed in Chapter 2, one of the most intriguing features of the versions of the myth about the white-lipped peccaries is their variability, and especially the notable differences between Sebastián's two versions. It is these

---

[1] As Basso (1987) and Urban (1991) make clear, the discourse-centred approach to culture is fully within the project of Boasian culturalist anthropology, and is one of its most fertile fields. As such, it owes little to the European sociological tradition which produced the work of Malinowski and Lévi-Strauss.

variations which were so helpful to Lévi-Strauss in his work. Here I explore the telling of mythic narratives in the Piro lived world, to show how such variations come into existence. I argue that variation is a general feature of Piro mythic narratives, even over the life course, but that certain forms of such variation are linked to specific changes in the Piro lived world.

Ancient People's Stories

For Piro people, mythic narration is an activity with certain characteristic properties. Myths are *tsrunnini ginkakle*, 'ancient people's stories'. They are usually told in moments of rest by older people to younger people, in the intimate surroundings of the house. They are most often, in my experience, told on quiet evenings, after people have eaten and before they feel overwhelmed by sleep. Most often, I was told, grandparents would tell these stories to their grandchildren. For Piro people, this specific setting for the telling of 'ancient people's stories' has a pragmatic obviousness: myths are told by people who know them well to people who do not know them at all when there is little else to do.[2]

These stories are told by old people to their grandchildren because they are interesting. I was never told that children should be told them, and telling such stories is not *giykota*, 'to give advice' (Ucayali Spanish, *aconsejar*), the discursive explication of moral values overtly directed at children and younger adults. What motivates such story-telling is, as far as I am aware, simply that they are interesting: the teller wants to tell them, and the listeners want to listen. The stimulus to tell these stories often comes from the children themselves: Artemio's son Denis, when aged twelve, told me that he often went to see his grandmother, 'to see what she will tell me'. Further, the interest of the listener is crucial to the flow of the narrative. As Basso (1985) has discussed for the Central Brazilian Kalapalo, Piro narrators depend on the listener to respond constantly with interjections of the form, *'¡Gaa!'*, 'Oh!' or *'¿Gowa?'*, 'Really?', or their equivalents in the other languages spoken locally.

There are many 'ancient people's stories'. While some Piro people claim to know many of these stories, or are held to do so, no one ever claimed to me to know them all. Some are widely known and often told, while others are known to few people. There seems to be no idea of a canon of such stories, or even precise limits to what counts as an 'ancient people's story'. The criteria of definition are that someone who tells such a story claims to have heard it told before as an 'ancient people's story'.

---

[2] Matteson (1954: 68) and Ricardo Alvarez (1970: 67) mention a defunct kind of drama called *yimlu* in which old people acted out the different characters of a myth. Matteson mentions that it had not, in the 1950s, been performed for many years. My informants in the 1980s had not heard of it. The term *yimlu*, means, 'imitation'. Presumably, even when it was performed, *yimlu* was not the major form of telling myths.

There is, however, a definite sense that these stories are 'Piro' stories, and the sources from which a teller heard them was always a Piro person. Despite the extent and time-depth of intermarriages between Piro people and other ethnic groups, especially the Campa, Machiguenga, and *moza gente*,[3] and the general multilingualism of the area, my Piro informants only ever told me 'ancient Piro people's stories'. My Campa informants never told me myths, although they happily answered questions about Campa myths I had read in the literature.[4] The only non-Piro myths I heard were told to me by two men defined as 'white people': one told me myths from his home country of Juan-juí on the Huallaga river in northern Peruvian Amazonia, and the other told me stories he had learned from Machiguenga people. In both cases, they carefully specified the origins of these myths.

Tsrunnini ginkakle, the 'ancient people's stories', are stories of the *tsrunni*, the 'ancient people'. This term, which literally means 'the old people who are unfortunately now dead', refers to ancestral generations of Piro people who have been lost to living memory through the passage of time. Like contemporary people, they were *yine*, 'humans, Piro people', but they were very different to 'nowadays people'. They lived in the forest, they used stone tools, wore home-spun cotton robes and skirts, and spoke a different kind of Piro language. While all the *tsrunni* spoke the same language, they lived in geographically isolated groups (Piro, *neru*), jealously refusing to intermarry, and fighting constantly. And they told these stories.

The world of the *tsrunni* ended, people told me in the 1980s, when they were enslaved by white bosses in the times of rubber, due to their intense desire for the 'fine things' (Piro, *gejnu*) of those whites. As slaves to the white bosses, they came to intermarry with other Piro groups, and with Campa, Machiguenga, *moza gente*, and other peoples. This period was, in the 1980s, just beyond living memory, in the world of the dead parents of the oldest people alive. It was in those events of enslavement and intermarriage, as I have discussed at length elsewhere (Gow 1991), that contemporary people found the origins of their current life in the villages they inhabited, and it was from that era that they traced out the ties of kinship which connected them. Before that period was the world of the *tsrunni*, the anonymous 'ancient people'.

In the contemporary world, given that all personal possessions are destroyed on death, there are no monuments or objects surviving from 'ancient people'.

---

[3] *Moza gente*, are people identified on the Bajo Urubamba as originating from areas of northern Peruvian Amazonia, or their descendants, and usually native speakers of Quechua or Ucayali Spanish. Individual *moza gente* may be defined, or define themselves, more specifically as Lamista, Cocama, Jebero, Napo Quechua, etc. They are never considered *gente blanca*, 'white people' (see Gow 1991; 1993).

[4] Most of my Campa informants were young adults, and my only close older informant had spent most of her younger life as a domestic slave in the house of a white boss. It is also possible that these people felt constrained against telling such myths in territory which was definitely the 'land of the ancient Piro people', not of the 'ancient Campa people'.

Even such apparently obvious remains, such as the pottery or stone axe-heads found while gardening, are equivocal: my informants were more likely to identify them with forest demons or Incas than with the ancient Piro people.[5] All that remains of the 'ancient people' is what living Piro people know about them.[6] This takes three main forms. Firstly, there is 'ancient people's language', which is only heard on the Bajo Urubamba in shamanic songs,[7] and from occasional visitors from Piro-speaking communities on the Manú and Yaco rivers, to the southeast and east respectively. Especially of the Yaco people, it is said, 'They speak ancient people's language, they say *sapna* for *paranta* (plantain), and *gaxa* instead of *wixa* (we, us, our), just like the ancient people.'[8] However, the fact of these people using 'ancient people's language' does not mean that they are more 'Piro' than Urubamba Piro people. Quite the contrary, for I was also told, of these Manú or Yaco people, 'They are not real Piro people like us, they are another people. They speak differently.'

The second form of knowledge of the 'ancient people' is the telling of *tsrunni pirana*, stories 'about ancient people'. These are stories, learned from older kinspeople, about the ways of the 'ancient people'. They usually take the form of observations made in everyday life, such as, 'The ancient people would do this, but we don't do that, we do differently now' (see Gow 1991: 63–4 and Matteson 1965: 138–55 for examples). They do not name characters, and tend not to have elaborate story form. They are descriptions of generic ways of behaving.

The third form of knowledge of the 'ancient people' is the 'ancient people's stories', stories that the ancient people are said to have told. These stories tend, like the versions of the myth I have been discussing in previous chapters, to be strongly narrative, and often have named characters. The worlds described in the 'ancient people's stories' are much more radically alien than that of the stories 'about ancient people'. The world of the ancient people was a world much like this one in which people acted differently, whereas the worlds described in the stories of the ancient people were much more alien. In those worlds, humans married animals, turned into animals, travelled to the under-world and the sky, and the like.

[5] Either way, they were not very interested in them, or actively feared them. Further, while Piro women use old potsherds as tempering materials in ceramic production, they do not, to my knowledge, search for archaeological sites to find them. They only use recent broken pots for this purpose. In this, they differ from the Shipibo–Conibo (Roe 1982).

[6] Obviously, the 'ancient people' presumably still exist as dead people in the forest, but nobody ever discussed this with me.

[7] See Chapter 5 for a discussion of shamanic song words.

[8] At least with regard to *sapna*, this is true of the Brazilian Piro–Manitineri people from the Yaco river, some of whom I met in Rio Branco (Acre) in 1987 and 1990.

Piro Ways of Telling

As I described above, and have discussed at length elsewhere (Gow 1990a; 1991), Piro people place supreme value on lived personal experience. *Nshinikanchi*, 'memory, love, respect', as a core aspect of Piro personhood, is generated through personal experience of the acts of love and memory of others in everyday life, while the key value of *gwashata*, 'living well', depends on the personal experience of well-being and tranquillity in the day-to-day life of a good village. This same centrality is found in Piro people's ways of talking and telling, where great stress is placed on whether or not the speaker has personally experienced what was being described.

In Piro, any description that is not being claimed as personal experience or opinion must obligatorily carry the 'quotative' segment, *-gima*. Thus, when a person says '*Giyagni rapokatka*', 'Then he arrived', the speaker is claiming direct personal evidence of this act. If this is not the case, if for example the speaker is simply reporting what someone else saw, he or she must say, '*Giyagimni rapokatka*', or variants of this phrase, meaning 'Then, it is said, he arrived.' The quotative segment does not specify, nor need to specify, who told the speaker about the event: the focus is on whether or not the speaker personally experienced the event. In Ucayali Spanish, there is the same rule: *dice*, 'it is said', is the equivalent. When the speaker wants to emphasize that this statement was actually uttered by a specified other person, the verb, *china*, 'to say, to utter', is used. In Ucayali Spanish, the equivalent is the verb, *contar*.

Narratives of personal experience are the most certain of stories. The narrator is the living witness of the events described, and the wider ramifications of those events may be known to the listeners from their own personal experiences.[9] By contrast, myths are the least certain of all narratives, for by definition nobody witnessed the events narrated. They are even more uncertain than rumours about distant events, for at least rumours emanate from living witnesses, albeit unknown ones. Narrators frequently end a mythic narrative by rhetorically questioning its veracity, saying things like the following, 'This is what the ancient people told. Perhaps it is a lie. I do not know, but this is what they told.' I have never heard a Piro narrator of a myth declare, as if often declared of personal experience narratives, '*¡Galikakni!*', 'This is true!' (Ucayali Spanish, '*¡Verdad es!*'). The dubiety of myths is given in the careful refusal to claim any known or knowable witness to the events narrated.

It might be tempting to see this lack of certainty about myth as a product of the recent history of Piro people. Perhaps it is a result of intense ideological pressure from Catholic and Protestant missionaries and from the Peruvian state, and of over a century of close contact with white bosses. This was indeed

---

[9] Of course, a narrator may simply be lying (Piro, *gaylota*; Ucayali Spanish, *engañar*). This is an important verbal art among the Piro (cf. Basso 1987, on the Kalapalo).

my own thought on this phenomenon, as witnessed by my reaction to Artemio's question on the evening of 15 January 1982, of his mother's story about the moon, when he said, 'But if men have gone there, and seen that it is just stone, what of that belief? Is it just a lie?'

In fact, on reflection, such comments were common, even when I had offered no counter-evidence to the claims of the myth, and proving that such expressions of doubt are a recent historical product would be impossible, given the lack of historical documentation of Piro narrative convention prior to such influences.

Certain comparative evidence, however, points strongly against such a conclusion. This same hierarchy of narrative certitude is found among speakers of related languages in the Upper Xingú area of Central Brazil, the Waurá, Mehinaku, and Yawalapíti, whose experience of missionaries has been slight, and where outsiders have consistently bolstered, rather than undermined, mythic knowledge (Ireland 1988; Gregor 1977, and Viveiros de Castro 1977[10]). Further, it has been so consistently recorded throughout Amazonia, in the most diverse settings, as by Basso (1985) for the Kalapalo, Reeve (1988) for the Canelos Quichua, Roe (1988) for the Shipibo–Conibo, and Vanessa Lea (personal communication) for the Kayapó, that it is almost certainly a *sui generis* feature of indigenous Amazonian narrative style. As with these other Amazonian cases, Piro people's experience of myth conforms closely to one of the aspects of mythic form which is central to Lévi-Strauss's analysis. In a reiteration of the point, he writes, 'However far back we may go, a myth is known only as something heard and repeated' (1988: 189). For Piro people, myth refers to a set of agents and events for whom no known or knowable witness is posited, it exists only as a story told over generations, as *tsrunnini ginkakle*, an 'ancient people's story'.

Related to the quotative segment is another feature of Piro narration: the marking of authority or source, through the verb, *ginkaka*: 'to tell, narrate'. In elaborated secondhand narratives, the narrator invariably states the source of the story, whose personal experience it was. For example, one mythic narrative concludes, '*Seyoka. Najirni ginkakleni. Nyokaka*', 'It is finished. It is my late grandmother's story. I have expounded it' (Matteson 1965: 215).

The sources of such narratives are almost invariably ascendant close kin, such as parents or grandparents, for historical narratives or mythic narratives.[11] Such marking of source establishes the probable veracity of the narrative in the absence of personal experience by referring it to ties of close kin status. As I discussed in *Of Mixed Blood*, such close kin are constituted as 'real' through densely experienced interactions, and it is not surprising that

---

[10] Ireland's account of the Waurá is particularly revealing in this sense: the Waurá consider myths to be the best exemplars of all stories, but disavow asserting their veracity because, by definition, no living narrator or other known person could have been witness to the events they relate (Ireland 1988).

[11] For a discussion of Piro historical narratives, see Gow (1990a; 1991).

they are the privileged source of interesting but unverifiable stories. Where the source is marked as distant kin or even non-kin to the narrator and listeners, it is much more likely to be overtly questioned, with a listener interjecting, with reference to the source, comments of the type, '*¡Kayloklewakleru wa male!*', 'What a liar he is!'. While Piro people have no category of fictional stories, stories which rely on the credulity of listeners are an important form of entertainment, for *gaylota*, 'lying', is an important and highly developed verbal art. In the narrative of myths, the source of a particular narrator's story is never questioned, for older real kin tend not, out of respect, to be accused of lying. Here, the accusation is directed at the ancient people themselves.

Of Piro narrative forms, myth is the most insistently narrative. Often, the narrator will refer to three levels of narration in the same story: to his or her own narrative ('Now I will tell you about Tsla'), to the narrative of the source, ('My grandmother told me this . . .') and to the narrations of the ancient people ('This is what the ancient people told . . .'). This insistent reference to narration in mythic narratives has the effect both of stressing the distance of the narrated events from the teller's lived experience, but also of focusing attention on one specific sort of experience: that of hearing narratives themselves. It would be wrong to say that myths exist outside of lived experience, for they are founded on the experience of hearing them being told.

Telling 'Ancient People's Stories'

This insistently narrative nature of mythic narrative, stressing their discon-nection from all lived experience other than of having once heard them from older real kin, can be explored in the context of who does and who does not tell 'ancient people's stories'. Only certain sorts of people tell myths and only do so in certain sorts of social contexts. It is only relatively old people who tell them in a full sense, and they tell them preferentially to junior kinspeople, especially to their grandchildren.

It is difficult to find out whether or not people actually know myths, because of the extreme reluctance of most people to tell them. Roughly speaking, people under about twenty-five years old simply will not tell myths at all, and deny knowing them. People between twenty-five and early middle age will normally refuse to tell them when asked, but occasionally narrate short segments of mythic narratives if the circumstances demand. From early middle age, forty-five years and over, people narrate myths with increasing confidence. All Piro people agreed about this: if I asked about myths, they would say, 'Go and ask the old people, they know these things.'

Initially, I thought I was hearing the last notes of a dying tradition: Piro mythology seemed to be disappearing along with many of the other ways of the 'ancient people'.[12] I came to realize, during the later fieldwork in 1988, that young people's denial of knowledge of myths cannot be taken as evidence that they do not know or care about them, and hence that they will never tell them. It is, instead, a simple refusal to narrate. This is clear for those people who are beginning mythic narratives. For example, discussing a song I had recorded in a distant village, Julia, a woman in her mid-thirties spontaneously narrated the following short myth to me. The song was *Mapchiri Wgene Jeji Shikale*, 'Song of the Anaconda's Son',[13] and Julia briefly explained the song as follows,

An anaconda married a human girl. They had a baby. One day the grandmother was sleeping with the baby in a hammock. When she awoke, she looked down, and saw the child as a anaconda curled up on top of her. She pushed the baby into the fire and burned him. When his mother arrived, she said, 'Why have you burned my baby?' The grandmother said, 'That one isn't human, it's an anaconda!' Then the anaconda father came, and took away his child, because they did not look after it. The anaconda, in revenge, made the river destroy the village that these people lived in, it destroyed that village completely. That is where this song comes from.

Older informants narrated this same myth as a long story, naming the central characters, the Kochmaloto Women and others, and continuing after the flood (see discussion below and in Ch. 5). Julia simply sketched the myth for me, restricting herself to the immediately relevant part.

Although missing from Julia's narration (perhaps because she was drunk at the time), but almost invariably present in other narrations of middle-aged people, is the marking of source. Such people usually tell the story with emphasis on who told it to them, and if that person is alive, refer the listener directly to the original narrator. For example, in 1982, Artemio, in his mid-thirties, tended to tell very short versions of myths as told to him by his mother, and then suggest that I ask her. When particularly interested, however, as in the case of 'A Man who went under the Earth', Artemio could narrate 'ancient people's stories' quite fully.[14] His youngest sister Sara, in her early twenties, would deny knowing myths at all and refer me directly to her mother. By contrast, their brother-in-law Antonio, in his mid-forties, would narrate myths to me in a relatively full form, with names of the characters and localities, but still with mention of his grandmother's prior narrations, and often suggesting I ask his mother-in-law, Clotilde Gordón, for fuller accounts.

Six years later, in 1988, Sara was willing to narrate myths in the form of short segments while still referring to her mother as a better source. But by this time, Antonio was willing to narrate myths without any reference to a prior

---

[12] This is one of the worst facets of participant observation as a method: the tendency to extrapolate from an immediate situation to longer-term processes of historical transformation. Much of the literature on 'acculturation' was marked by this tendency, which gives it a tone at once melancholy and melodramatic, a true heir of certain strands of German romanticism (see Sahlins (1995).

[13] See discussion of this song in Chapter 6.

[14] See also Chapters 4 and 8, for other myths told by Artemio.

source other than the ancient people themselves. Antonio's later narratives were fuller and more coherent, filled with details previously omitted, and he did not suggest that I seek other sources. Antonio, too, was six years older, but there had been a more important shift in his life, for he had become one of the oldest active Piro people in Santa Clara. His mother-in-law was almost permanently sick, seldom doing anything. But further, in 1988 Antonio narrated to a different audience, for he had by this point several grandchildren old enough to sit and listen as he talked. Antonio had become, as his mother-in-law had been previously, an authority on myth by being the oldest active surviving hearer of prior and authoritative events of narration. He could narrate fully because he was the one who had heard such stories from long-dead people, often unknown to younger people. Younger people are usually constrained from narrating myths, and also relieved of the necessity of so doing, by the presence of older people who are presumed to know them better.[15]

I here term this shift into fully confident narration of myths *mythopoeisis*, the making of myths.[16] As people age, and become the oldest active living authorities on the ways of the ancient people, they become mythopoeic: they tell 'ancient people's stories' with reference only to their own authority and that of the ancient people. And in doing so, their tellings expand in depth and complexity, bringing in more details, and establishing more connections. Becoming more mythopoeic, they are more at ease telling these stories, and are, in short, better story-tellers.

The following is an example. The first time Antonio told me the myths, 'The Birth of Tsla' and 'The Kochmaloto Women', in 1982, the versions were much shorter and less complex than those of seven years later.[17] Antonio's second version of 'The Birth of Tsla' included a long account of Tsla and his brothers, the Muchkajine, making a canoe, a garden, and a house, totally absent in the earlier version (see Ch. 4). He also, in the second version, ran on the narrative to include 'Tsla swallowed by a Giant Catfish'. After Tsla and the Muchkajine kill their jaguar uncles to avenge their mother's death, Antonio continued,

Tsla then said, 'What shall we do now? Let's go and work for Kamayaka.' Kamayaka was Tsla's brother-in-law. He was building a dam at the Pongo de Mainique. Kamayaka made Tsla and the Muchkajine help him. All day long they worked. Tsla got tired of working. He made a *wakawa* (a giant catfish, Lat. *Paulicea lutkeni*) swallow him. He went off down-river in the *wakawa*'s belly. Kamayaka had a parrot, which cried, 'The *wakawa* swallowed Tsla! The *wakawa* swallowed Tsla!.' The Muchkajine followed the

---

[15] I planned to investigate this issue further in 1995, but circumstances prevented me. Apart from Artemio's death, Antonio had also moved away to Sepahua. Sara, by then 38-years-old, did not actually narrate any myths, but she was far more willing to tell stories 'about ancient people' than before.

[16] My use of this concept here derives from Mimica's important study of the Iqwaye people of Papua New Guinea (1988). My usage is slightly different, since I focus on the actual telling of myths, rather than the general pre-conditions of such narratives. The adaptation is justified by the extremely 'exoteric' nature of Piro mythic narratives compared with Iqwaye ones.

[17] See texts in the Myth Appendix, and discussion of these myths in Chapters 4 and 5.

wakawa down-river, trying to catch Tsla. They couldn't get him. Only when they got to the Mishagua river did they reach him. He came out. There Kamayaka lived, there is a mountain there below the mouth of the Mishagua, it has all been eroded away now, but that was Kamayaka's house. There they lived. But the *manipawro* bird called there. This is a bad omen, it foretells death. So Tsla and the Muchkajine went off, far down-river.

In his first narration, he had told me a story segment as an introduction to the 'The Birth of Tsla', and his version was then rather different. In the first version, it is Tsla who is building the dam at the Pongo; it is Kamayaka, one of Tsla's brothers, who is swallowed, it is another giant catfish, *katsalo* (Ucayali Spanish, *saltón*; Lat. *Brachyplatystoma filamentosum*) which swallows him, and it was an unspecified 'little bird' (not *manipawro*) that tells of death. Antonio's first version is the only one I know of to say that Kamayaka was swallowed, and his second version agrees with most other versions in saying Tsla was swallowed by a *wakawa*. Most of the versions I know of consistently state that it was the Incas who were building the dam at the Pongo de Mainique, and that it was the bird *maknawlo* that called ominously.

What can we make of these changes? If we start from one of Lévi-Strauss's key insights, that there is no original version of any myth, and hence that every version is a 'good version', then we can dispose of the suggestion that the differences between the two versions reflect greater or lesser fidelity to an original that Antonio heard long before from his grandmother (the authority cited for the first version). At the very least, we have no idea what that woman's version was like, since Antonio is our only authority on it. Further, Antonio's original is likely to have been multiple too, for presumably his grandmother told it as often, and changed it as much, as he did. Moreover, on both occasions on which he told this story, he clearly experienced himself as telling *the* 'ancient people's story' of 'Tsla/Kamayaka swallowed by a *wakawa/katsalo*'.

It seems to me that the only correct hypothesis is that we are looking here at an important feature of Piro myths and mythopoeisis: that is, that as people age, they tell myths in an increasing confident and complex manner by spontaneously transforming versions they have heard long ago and their own prior narrations. This suggests that the life-course process of mythopoeisis, while experienced as closer and closer fidelity to an ancient source, is in fact the ongoing genesis of new myth versions. Lévi-Strauss has noted, 'Mythic thought operates essentially through a process of transformation. A myth no sooner comes into being than it is modified through a change of narrator . . .' (1981: 675). Lévi-Strauss is referring to changes in narrators as myths move from society to society. Here, I suggest, we can see a microscopic version of the same process: the myth changes as the narrator changes with age. This is the process of mythopoeisis.[18] We have already seen an example of this in the last

---

[18] Goody reaches a very similar conclusion in his reflections on Stanner's account of an Australian Aboriginal society (1987).

chapter, with Sebastián's two versions of the myth about the white-lipped peccaries, and can now see it as a generalized feature of Piro mythic narrative.

Ageing, Mythopoeisis, and Myths

There was a major change in Antonio's life circumstances between 1982 and 1988, beyond the six years more of life. In 1988, he had several grandchildren living with him old enough to listen to his stories. He therefore had an audience made up of kinspeople who stood in the same relationship to him as he had once done to his own source of mythic narratives, his grandmother. This fact of domestic life, which Piro people consistently reported to me as the characteristic scene of telling 'ancient people's stories', has a specific resonance for Piro people: it is the maximum temporal extension of kinship relations.

Let us look at what the world looks like to the listeners (Piro children) and to the tellers (old Piro people) of myths. Children old enough to listen to myths are those who have developed *nshinikanchi*, 'mind, memory, love, etc.' As I discussed elsewhere (Gow 1991; 1996), they do this by demonstrating their attentiveness to those who feed them by addressing these people with kin terms. These terms, in Piro, are, *mama*, 'Mummy', *papa*, 'Daddy', *jiro*, 'Granny', *totu*, 'Granpa', *shapa*, 'Auntie', *koko*, 'Uncle', and *yeye*, 'Older Brother/Sister'. The use of these terms is spontaneous in the child, Piro people say, and marks the beginning of *nshinikanchi*. It is the child's first socially important use of language, and throughout life it remains important, as the assertion of kin relationships to others. Kin relationships are initiated by the giving of food by older people to children to satisfy their hunger, but they are asserted as kin relationships *by* the child. For Piro people, it is children, not adults, who make kin relationships through language.

Old Piro people are at the opposite end of this process. As death depletes the world of their older kin, they slowly give up using, perforce, all kin terms except one, *shte* or *wiwi*, 'Younger Kinsperson'. The reciprocal of all the kin terms the child uses is this one, 'Younger Kinsperson'.[19] Eventually, this becomes the only kin term of address that the old people use, and their social worlds become an undifferentiated world of 'younger kinspeople'. Their differentiated older kinspeople are now dead, and hence not spoken to. Old people become, as they themselves say, 'orphans', without parents or other older kin, and hence 'alone'.

Not only are they 'alone', they have lost their primary relationship to language. Their dead senior kinspeople can no longer be addressed. They can only be referred to, by kin terms of reference, such as *najiro*, 'my grandmother', or *naxiru*, 'my grandfather', to which the suffix, *-ni*, 'unfortunate one,

---

[19] The same relationships hold true in local usage of Ucayali Spanish, where all junior kin are addressed as *papito*, if male, or *mamita*, if female.

one who is now dead', must be affixed, to give, *najirni* and *naxirni*. Because
these people are now dead, no meaningful social relationships with them are
possible. It is this that is marked, not their non–existence. They most definitely
exist, but now in the form of dead people, filling the forest with their malign
presence. All relationships with them are assiduously avoided.

As I discussed at length in *Of Mixed Blood*, Piro people experience life as a
continual process of the making of villages in which to 'live well', and of flight
from old houses and villages where the dead lived, which return to forest. But
as people age, they become reluctant to move far, saying that they know 'where
they want to die'. Tired of living, and of moving around, they want to die were
they are living at present. As time passes, Piro villages tend to accrete around
such intransigent older people, only to be radically transformed or abandoned
when they do finally die.

It is in such villages that children grow up, and in which they begin to call
older people by kin terms. But they will never use kin terms for the dead relatives of their grandparents, for as dead people, they will never have personal
experience of them. From their point of view, the dead kinspeople of their
grandparents are not kinspeople, but 'old dead people', *tsrunni*. That is, they
are 'ancient people'. Indeed, there are no kin terms for kinspeople older than
grandparents. Great-grandparents, if known as living people, are called by the
same terms as grandparents. If not, they are called nothing but *tsrunni*. It
would be technically possible to say, for example, 'my grandmother's grandmother' (Piro, *najiro tajirni*; Ucayali Spanish, *la finada su abuela de mi abuela*),[20]
but I have never heard anyone do so. Given the importance of lived personal
experience for Piro people, such a personage would be an exceptionally
abstract figure indeed.[21]

Piro grandparents and grandchildren face each other across the span of the
life cycle in this lived world: those close to the end of the processes of
nshinikanchi, and those at its start. As they approach death, old people are 'tired
of living', and about to become something else, dead people. Their own
beloved older kinspeople, among whom their lives were spent, are now already
dead people, and *tsrunni*, 'ancient people', for their young kinspeople. As Antonio once told me, on plans for the future of Santa Clara. 'Our grandchildren's
children . . . will be a different kind of people . . . Who knows what they will
be like? We will be long dead then, we will never see them . . .'[22]

Why should this process be accompanied by mythopoeisis, an increasing
facility for telling 'ancient people's stories'? I think the key clue lies in the

---

[20] I have never heard *bisabuelo/bisabuela*, Spanish terms for 'great-grandfather/great-grandmother'
used by local people on the Bajo Urubamba.

[21] This may account for the generic description feature of stories 'about ancient people': perhaps
originally told as stories about older relatives by people now dead, they become more anonymous and
less narrative as they are repeated over time, and the original characters slip out of lived memory.

[22] I used the full form of this statement as the epigraph to *Of Mixed Blood* (1991: xii).

dropping of markers of source in previous events of narration *other* than that of the 'ancient people' themselves. From the point of view of mythopoeic narrators, there is a major difference between a dead grandmother and 'the ancient people', who were never known personally. But they are telling these stories to their grandchildren, and know that, from their little listeners' point of view, their own remembered grandparents and the 'ancient people' are the same thing. They have come to understand what it is to be a old person, a grandparent, and hence have come to a radically new formulation of what the 'ancient people' are. Having gained such an understanding of the depth of lived time, old Piro people have a vantage point from which to understand 'ancient people's stories'. By definition, these stories are the oldest things in the Piro lived world, for there is nothing older than them: even the things created in myths necessarily post-date the events narrated. They describe primordial events, *muchikawpotgimni*, 'a very long time ago, it is said'. If the 'ancient people' lie on the temporal horizon of kinship, the events of the 'ancient people's stories' lie far beyond it.

The 'ancient people's stories' are also things of direct interest to those children who are filling the world, and whose developing *nshinikanchi* is among the newest things in that world. As the oldest living people available to a Piro child, grandparents are the preferred source of knowledge about the temporal depth of the world in general. It is grandparents who know most about *muchikawpotgimni*, and their knowledge of this era is couched in 'ancient people's stories'. There is a further significance to this. The co-residence of grandchildren and grandparents is an aspect of *gwashata*, 'living well'. As I have said, it is in the relationship between these two sorts of kinspeople that the temporal extension of kinship is most marked. As such, it is in this relationship that Piro people become mythopoeic, and hence tell myths. Whatever else they might be about, the myths are definitely not about *gwashata*, 'living well', for they recount the strange and alien doings of the beings of 'very long ago'.

'Ancient people's stories' confront Piro people, as tellers and as listeners, with alternative worlds which are at once both alien and familiar. For example, 'Tsla swallowed by a Giant Catfish', refers directly to features of the immediate known world of Piro people, such as the flow of the Urubamba river and *wakawa* catfish, the activity of fishing, or the calling of birds of ill-omen. More remotely, in the figure of the Muchkajine, it refers to the *kajine*, 'white people', who play such a crucial role in Piro people's lives. But it also refers to otherwise unknown entities and actions, such as Tsla, and his miraculous ability to be swallowed by a giant catfish and survive. Such things are known to Piro people only through mythic narratives. The same is true of all the 'ancient people's stories', which always have one foot firmly placed in the immediate phenomenal world of Piro people, and the other in bizarre and alien worlds characterized by different forms of agents and actions.

This characteristic of mythic narratives perhaps explains their interest both to their aging tellers and to their young listeners, and by extension to everyone in between them in the making of kinship. They are told and heard in a house located in a village, the most intimate and known part of a known world, but they connect the concrete features of this world to the alien and unknown powers of the 'long, long ago, it is said'. Because they address the most obvious features of the immediate lived world, mythic narratives can hardly but be of interest to Piro people, young and old. But because they then present those known and obvious features of the world as radically contingent on long-distant events and agents, they generate an enduring interest for Piro people, who tire neither of hearing nor of telling them. Mythic narratives become, so to speak, radically interesting for Piro people, by connecting the concretely knowable to the concretely unknowable. The mythic narratives assert that this unknowable past can only be known through themselves: these stories are the only witnesses to the origins of the world in which Piro people live.

Mythic narratives have a kind of autonomy, of pure narrativity, which allows them to generate connections between the known and the otherwise unknowable. Key to this is their relationship to time. Myths are always told in a *xani*, 'now': 'Now I will tell you what the ancient people told about . . .'. As I have shown, narrators and listeners stand in a quite different relationship to that 'now', for it is the old age of the former and the childhood of the latter. This differential in relationship to the 'now' of narration, dependent on the time frame of the life cycle, allows the mythic narratives to assert another differential, that between the 'now' of the narrative event, and of the different relationships of its participants to that 'now', and *muchikawpotgimni*, the 'very long ago, it is said' of the events of which the myths speak. All the relationships that mythic narratives set up between the known and the unknowable, and about which they then tell, are condensed and exemplified by this specific relationship, that between knowable lived time and time beyond living people's ken. The mythic narratives generate that temporal form, the 'very long ago, it is said', at the same time as they provide it with a content, peopling it and filling it with events. They bear witness to the very events of which they tell.

A further sense of this feature of mythic narratives can be gained by consideration of two myths I told Piro children. I was asked by children to tell stories too: '¿Qué me cuentas?', 'What will you tell me?', they would ask. On one occasion, I responded by telling 'Hansel and Gretel', as the first story that came to mind. It was a total failure. I tried to redeem my reputation as a story-teller by telling the Kayapó myth of origin of fire, dimly remembered from the literature (see Lévi-Strauss 1970; Turner [n.d.] and 1985). This was much more successful. Despite all my efforts to render 'Hansel and Gretel' in local colour, it did not make much sense to Piro children: Piro children are left to fend for themselves for long hours every day, and they would never dream of responding by wandering far off into the forest. The forest is indeed full of malign beings who live in beautiful houses, but they attack children directly with sorcery, and not by complex subterfuge. The Kayapó myth made much more sense to them, despite its extreme inversions of the Piro myth of the origin of fire, and of other Piro myths. It deals with a world which was both familiar and intelligible to Piro children, a world filled with macaws, jaguars, domestic fire, and so on. It related the known to the unknowable by unfamiliar but intelligible means, and children asked to hear it several times. By contrast, my attempt at 'Hansel and Gretel', an 'ancient people's story' from the *gringos*, confusingly related the unknown to the unknowable, and did so quite unintelligibly. It was not interesting to its young listeners, and I was never asked to repeat it.

The Myths that People Tell

Why do Piro people tell specific myths in specific contexts? What are the cues that lead Piro people to tell *this* myth rather than any other? I have no access to the primary experience of Piro myth-telling, that between grandparent and grandchild: whenever I was present, adults would direct their story-telling, out of respect, to me. However, there are certain interesting features of how I was told myths, which confirm and extend my analysis here. I have already suggested certain aspects of this issue with regard to Artemio telling me, 'A Man who went under the Earth', but here I want to explore further features of this practice. As I have noted, 'A Man who went under the Earth' was only told to me that once by Artemio. Certain myths were told to me often, one very often, and certain myths were never told to me.

'Tsla swallowed by a Giant Catfish' was the first Piro myth ever told to me, and it was also the first told to me by Antonio, who told me more myths than anyone else, albeit as 'Kamayaka swallowed by a *katsalo*'. It is the first myth in Ricardo Alvarez's collection, *Los Piros* (1960) and a version appears in Matteson's first collection of Piro myths (1951). I first heard it from the Piro leader Moisés Miqueas in Sepahua. We were sitting in his sister's house, and he was telling me, in Spanish, about his work as a guide for river trips through the Pongo de Mainique, and describing the strange antics of his *gringo* charges. Meanwhile, his sister was talking in Piro to some kinswomen. When I commented to Moisés on something one of the women had said, he looked at me in wonder, and said, 'So, you now understand our language!'. He then told me the story of 'Tsla swallowed by a Giant Catfish' (see Appendix), and after telling me that Tsla and the Muchkajine had set off down-river, to an unknown destination, he finished as follows, 'After Tsla and the Muchkajine left, the white bosses came, then came the Spanish people, and then we made the *Comunidad Nativa* of Sepahua, and so that is how it came to be as it is today.' This statement is a very condensed version of Piro historical narratives. The basic temporal frames of Piro historical narratives begin, as I noted above, with the enslavement of the 'ancient people' by the white bosses in the 'times of rubber'. This period was succeeded by the 'times of the *hacienda*' (left out in

Moisés's summary), which ended with the coming of the *gringos*, or, in the specific case of Sepahua, the coming of the *padres* or 'Spanish people', the Spanish Dominican priests. Then, in these times, Piro and other indigenous people set up the *Comunidades Nativas*, the legally-recognized and land-owning 'Native Communities' (see Gow 1991 for an extended discussion of Piro historical narration).

That Moisés was able to link this history to this myth helps to explain why it was told to me so often: 'Tsla swallowed by a Giant Catfish' is the Piro 'myth of history'. As I have shown in detail in *Of Mixed Blood*, Piro and other indigenous people of the Bajo Urubamba see their history as the formation, through the cycling of generations, of their contemporary kinship relations. And they see that process as having occurred because of their transforming relations to different kinds of white people, such as the rubber bosses, their former 'big boss' Pancho Vargas, SIL and Dominican missionaries, and Peruvian state functionaries. Further, that history is thought of in terms of the Urubamba river, for it is along, and primarily up, that river that those different kinds of white people have come.[23]

This is what 'Tsla swallowed by a Giant Catfish' is about. It deals with a foiled attempt to dam the Urubamba at the Pongo de Mainique, the furthest up-river limit of what Piro people recognize as their world: the 'ancient Piro people' never lived above the Pongo, I was told. Above these great rapids is the Alto Urubamba, territory of the Machiguenga people,[24] and beyond them, the land of the *shishakone*, 'Andean people' and *Gigkane*, the Incas.[25] Similarly, Tsla and his brothers depart down-river, for an unspecified destination. They pass the down-river limits of the Piro lived world, the upper Ucayali and the villages of the Conibo people, and disappear into the 'outside', the mysterious down-river worlds of Brazil, Europe, and the United States. The 'land of death' from which Tsla and his brothers flee on hearing the bird call is the lived Piro world.

What became of Tsla and the Muchkajine, nobody knows, and no Piro person was willing to speculate on the theme for me.[26] I strongly suspect they hoped that I or other white people might be able to tell them. When I was told this myth, there was always a certain amount of nervous laughter when the Muchkajine were first mentioned. The Muchkajine are Tsla's younger brothers, born like

---

[23] The Dominicans, uniquely, 'came down-river', from their base in Cuzco, far to the south in the headwaters of the Urubamba river. The SIL missionaries 'came up-river' from their base near Pucallpa, like all the other white peoples.

[24] Piro people told me that 'the land of the Machiguenga' lay beyond the Pongo, in the Alto Urubamba, even though many of these people now live below it.

[25] Moisés explained to me that the Incas did not die, but are instead living inside mountains in the Andes. Unlike most Piro people, who dislike the Andes and are not particularly interested in the Incas, Moisés had travelled often to Cuzco.

[26] See, however, Zacarías Zumaeta's 'The World on the Other Side' (Matteson 1965: 210–15, and discussion below in Chapter 7.

him from the dismembered womb of their mother, and they act as Tsla's assistants and audience in the myths. Further, however, Muchkajine means 'long ago white people' (*muchi-* + *kajine*: 'long ago' + 'white people'). This explains the nervous laughter when these characters are mentioned: in some way which was never rendered explicit to me, the Muchkajine are the mythic origin of historical and contemporary kinds of white people. However, despite the slight embarrassment caused, this is why 'Tsla swallowed by a Giant Catfish' was so easy for me to elicit. It deals very directly with a problem evoked by my mere presence for I, like most 'white people', had come from 'down-river/outside', the destination of Tsla and the Muchkajine.

It seems clear to me that when, in a developing relationship with a white person, Piro people come to the point of beginning to introduce mythic knowledge into the conversation, 'Tsla swallowed by a Giant Catfish' comes most readily to hand. This myth, by dealing with the spatial limits of the lived world of the 'ancient Piro people', deals with the pre-conditions of Piro people's relationships to white people in general. As any given relationship between a Piro person and a white person can be thought of as the continuation and ongoing projection of Piro history (in the sense defined above), this particular myth is the most 'interesting' one to tell, since it is the most appropriate place to start telling myths to white people. Further, when I was told this myth, the situation never had any of the intense expectant quality of the conversation that led Artemio to tell me, 'A Man who went under the Earth', and which I suggested possibly marked Sebastián's telling of 'The Sun' to Matteson. When 'Tsla swallowed by a Giant Catfish' was told to me, the emotional tone was different, for this story concerns what Piro people could unproblematically know in relation to a *gringo*: an 'ancient people's story' about the river along which those people lived, as Piro people do to this day.

If 'Tsla swallowed by a Giant Catfish' was likely to be the first myth I was told, it was also very likely to be followed shortly after by 'The Birth of Tsla', and 'The Kochmaloto Women'. These were the myths most frequently told to me, and their prominence in Alvarez's and Matteson's collections, and in Matteson's descriptions of Piro culture, confirm their central place in Piro mythology, at least from the perspective of a foreign white listener (see R. Alvarez 1960, and Matteson 1951; 1954; 1955). When I asked informants whom I knew well to tell me 'ancient people's stories', it was with these that they most often started. It seems that when the cue that leads to the telling of a myth is the term 'ancient people's story', it is the myths 'The Birth of Tsla' and 'The Kochmaloto Women' which first spring to mind. As such, they would seem to be the key instantiations of myth for Piro people: they are 'ancient people's stories' *par excellence*.

These two myths, 'The Birth of Tsla' and 'The Kochmaloto Women', are remarkably similar in many ways: both begin with a human woman becoming pregnant by a powerful and feared predator (jaguar or anaconda), and recount the disastrous consequences of such affinal relationships and the subsequent adventures of a set of siblings (Tsla and the Muchkajine or the Kochmaloto sisters). I discuss these myths in detail in the following chapters, but it can hardly be fortuitous that these Piro 'myths of myth' pivot on the relationships between grandmothers and grandchildren: it is Tsla's jaguar grandmother who saves the womb containing Tsla and his younger brothers from being eaten by her sons, and it is the human grandmother who throws her anaconda grandson into the fire, provoking the flood. These stories thus directly invoke the very relationship in which such myths are characteristically told.

These 'myths of myth', like 'Tsla swallowed by a Giant Catfish', vary from teller to teller, and as I have shown, over the life-course of any given teller. However, there is remarkable consistency in all the versions I know of, whether in the documentary archive or those I have been told, and they do not show the kinds of dramatic variation we saw for the mythic narrative about the white-lipped peccaries. This suggests that there is a basic continuity in the ways in which these mythic narratives are related to the world, and that the historical changes affecting the mythic narrative about the white-lipped peccaries are not affecting them. I discuss this feature further in Part II, with reference to the 'myths of myth', and in Part III, for the 'myth of history'.

Forgotten Myths

There are a further category of myths which people cannot tell, because, as they say, they have forgotten them. For example, stimulated by the Swiss anthropologist Baer's important studies of Piro *pagotko* or *pagota* masks (1974; 1976–7), I asked Antonio, in 1988, to tell me the 'ancient people's story' about them. In the early 1980s, my informants had responded to my questions with polite boredom, but, considering Baer's materials, I believed that important connections existed between this myth and the making and use of pottery.[27] Antonio had just told me three long Piro myths, including one completely new to me. Considering the situation propitious, I asked about *pagotko*. He began hesitantly, saying, '*Pagota* is a demon, with a big nose. He lives in the forest, and is an owner of the animals . . . . I don't really know this story well . . . . it is such a long time since my mother told me about that one, I no longer remember it well.' He promptly abandoned the attempt. Similarly, when I had begun to realize the significance of Artemio's statement about the moon, I tried to get people to tell me 'ancient people's stories' about the moon, which I already knew from published versions.[28] Nobody would tell me, all professing their ignorance. On the same occasion discussed above, I asked Antonio to tell me

---

[27] I had, at this point, failed to make the connection between this mythic narrative and the theme of the white-lipped peccaries.

[28] See discussion in Chapter 6. Out of respect for what he had told me before, I did not ask Artemio himself.

about the moon. He declined, saying he did not know the story. Later, however, I discovered in my fieldnotes that, quite forgotten by myself and presumably by Antonio, he had told me a very simplified variant of the myth of the moon in 1982, in the one and only account of the origin of the stars I have ever heard from a Piro person. Antonio had told me, 'My grandparents said that the stars were people. So too was the moon. The moon used to come down to earth. A girl, who didn't sleep with men from here, slept with the moon. She painted his face with *huito*. For this reason it has black marks on it when it is full.' Antonio's inability to tell me this myth again six years later cannot be explained by sheer boredom with the question or with the telling of myths. In 1988, Antonio told me many, and was very animated in his tellings. It was the mythic narratives about the moon and about the *pagota*, not mythic narratives in general, which he could not tell, and had 'forgotten'.

We are here in the face of the temporal dynamics of mythopoeisis. Just as becoming mythopoeic leads to an expansion of mythic narratives, in the form of an apparently more profound memory of past events of narration, narrators are also conscious of the failure of memory. However, such lapses of memory do not seem to distress them, for what is at stake here is not memorization, but interest. Piro myth narrators are not moved to transmit a canon of stories, and hence have no abstract interest in re-telling all the myths they have ever heard. They tell myths that they, and their listeners, find interesting now.

There is another issue here. Just as mythopoeisis can generate more complex and elaborated versions of mythic narratives as the teller grows older, it can also cause mythic narratives to disappear and to become forgotten, as narrators and their listeners lose interest in them. We have already seen one example of such a transformation in the disappearance of the theme of the canoe journey of the sun between the first and second recorded versions of Sebastián's mythic narrative about the subterranean world of the white-lipped peccaries, while Antonio's forgetting of the mythic narrative of the moon provides another example.

The category of 'forgotten ancient people's stories' is clearly formulated by Piro people, but obviously its salience for me arose in precisely those situations in which I wanted people to tell me specific myths. I knew these myths to exist because I had read them in the literature on Piro mythology, and I was usually disappointed when people could not tell them to me. However, it is possible that this category of 'forgotten ancient people's stories' may have a more positive significance, both for Piro people and for this analysis. Could it be that the category of 'forgotten myths' also includes myths which have never been told or heard, but which make a kind of logical sense to Piro people? As such, they would be willing to postulate their existence, but assert that they have been forgotten.

I make this suggestion because, in 1995, I was told by Clotilde Gordón of the 'forgotten' nature of a myth which I am fairly certain has never existed: the

'Piro myth of origin of designs'. In analysing the data on *yonchi*, 'design', collected in the early 1980s and especially in 1988, I was frustrated by the absence, both from my data and from the literature, of a mythic narrative that would account for the origins of these designs. This was in marked contrast to the situation among their northern neighbours, the Shipibo–Conibo people (Bertrand-Rousseau 1983; Gebhart-Sayer 1984). I had become convinced, in the process of that analysis, that there was no such myth of origin of *yonchi*, but I could not be sure. It struck me as an odd gap in Piro mythology, but a real one.

In 1995, I asked Sara Fasabi about this issue, while she was making bead-work for me. She quickly recognized the problem, and told me that she did not know the answer, and that we should consult her mother. The next day, as old Clotilde taught her daughter a new design, we did so. She took a while to understand the question, and then, grasping what we wanted to know, she said with animation,

Oh, I understand now! The ancient people perhaps told stories about the beadwork designs, but I don't know anything about those things. I only make the designs I saw my grandmother make when I was a girl. Who knows what the ancient people may have told about these designs? I have no idea.

In earlier times, the big river boats used to come up here, loaded with glass beads, white ones, red ones, black ones, and the old dead white people (*kajinni*) traded these for *tsopi* fruit.[29] Then the Piros would make a *kigimawlo* (girl's initiation ritual) with lots of beadwork.

So, there was maybe, long ago, an 'ancient people's story' about the origin of design, but old Clotilde could not remember it. She had never heard it, she told us, so did not know. But then old Clotilde shifted to a personal experience narrative about a change which interested her much more, the decline in the availability of beads since her youth. Old Clotilde was, at this point, the oldest living authority on the ways of the ancient Piro people in the Santa Clara area: the ancient people probably did tell stories about design, but Clotilde had never heard her grandmother tell them to her, so she did not know. So, if there ever was such a myth about designs, it was not interesting enough to remember or to repeat. This makes me strongly suspect that my analysis was correct, and that Piro people have never told such a myth, or at least told no myth of this kind for a long time. What better definition of a non-existent myth could one have, given my account of Piro mythopoeisis, than the statement by an old woman that her grandmother had never told it to her?

A mythic narrative about the origins of designs might be of no interest to old Clotilde, or to any other Piro people, but it is necessarily of interest to analysts. It seems to me that an old Piro person could, if they had found the

---

[29] A leguminous fruit, called *guaba* in Ucayali Spanish (Lat. *Inga edulis*). It has a sweet pith surrounding the black seeds in a long hard green pod.

question interesting, have told a mythic narrative about it. And, if they found the question of sufficient interest, they might well, given the nature of mythopoeisis, have spontaneously invented such a mythic narrative through transformation of other myths: in Part II, I show how the 'myths of myth', by dealing with design, could be good candidates for such a story. This suggests that the relationship between mythic narratives and the world is governed by Piro people's interest, but that this interest is also a kind of investment. Only certain features of the world, and certain mythic narratives, are invested with the sort of interest which renders them meaningful to Piro people, whether as speakers or listeners.

There is a methodological point of some weight lying behind this problem of 'forgotten myths'. Methodologically, we are blind to the processes of mythopoeisis as they generate totally new myths through the radical transformation of other myths. Of necessity, we can never say of any given myth that it was never told before, and is hence totally new, for we can never be sure that its absence from earlier collections of mythic narratives was a mere oversight. Nor can we expect help from our informants here, for they would hardly tell a myth which they subjectively experienced as novel. But it seems to me that the category of 'forgotten myths' points towards a potential source for new myths. If the category of 'forgotten myths' arises as the world changes, and consequently as people's interests change, there must be a corresponding, albeit unmarked, category of 'potential myths' from within which new mythic narratives can arise. The best candidates would be myths or other stories told by neighbouring peoples and heard by Piro people. These could, in the right circumstances of new-found interest, be mis-remembered as 'ancient Piro people's stories'. It is possible that some of the mythic narratives in the published archive, or heard by myself, are of this order.

Clearly, such processes would be hard to identify either by fieldwork or by historical research, given the nature of the archive available to us. One possible piece of confirmatory evidence does exist, in a distinct sub-genre of Piro 'ancient people's stories': the tales about Shanirawa. This figure is a fool, and the stories about him are intentionally amusing, for they are based on Shanirawa's constant mis-identification of simple things. He mistakes tapir shit for fish poison, and his home village for that of the *Giyakleshimane*, 'Miraculous Fish People'. However, the 'stories about Shanirawa' all seem to be based on important Yaminahua myths, such as the myths of origin of fish poison and of hallucinogens. Cecilia McCallum informs me that the Piro name Shanirawa probably derives from the Panoan term *Chanidawa*, 'Lying Enemy/Foreigner' (personal communication). The tales of Shanirawa may well be a mode by which 'potential myths' are being imported from neighbouring Panoan-speaking peoples.

I raise this possibility to dispel at once a possible misreading of my analysis. The methodology I follow here inevitably means I must track changes in known mythic narratives over time, and follow already known mythic narratives in a trajectory of being forgotten (see Ch. 6 and Part III). By no means do I think that this is all that is going on among Piro people, or with Piro mythology, and I most certainly do not think that Piro mythology is following a one-way trip to oblivion. It is a pure effect of the methodology followed here. I believe that my analysis of mythopoeisis, if followed in another direction, could potentially unveil the historical creativity of Piro mythic narratives, as 'ancient people's stories' are invented, no less than they are transformed or rendered unmemorable.

Old People, Village Leaders, and Co-resident White People

As we are now in a position to understand, myths like 'A Man who went under the Earth' are a specific kind of story for Piro people, the stories said to have been told by the long dead and anonymous ancient people. They are told today because they are interesting, and because coming to know how to tell them articulates important aspects of Piro people's experience of temporal transformation within their own lives. And they evoke a key feature of such temporality, the intimate domestic contact of grandparents and their young grandchildren. As such, 'ancient people's stories' can be thought of as structures of significance, pointing outwards from these safe domestic surroundings to draw attention towards important features of their world. It is this process that makes myths interesting to Piro people, for as Sahlins has pointed out, 'Interest is the value that something has for someone' (1981: 68).

As I have said, I was obviously never told 'ancient people's stories' in the kind of setting in which Piro people most commonly tell and listen to them. However, there is an important feature of the people who, like Artemio on that night, did tell me myths, which is related to this key aspect of 'ancient people's stories' in Piro experience. I was most consistently told myths by men who were actual or potential *gitsrukaachi*, 'important, big ones', village leaders. The word shares the same root, *tsru*, 'big, old', with *tsrune*, 'old people', and *tsrunni*, 'ancient people'. The word *gitsrukaachi* is the possessive form of *tsru*, and the first-person plural form, *wutsrukatenni*, 'our old people who are unfortunately now dead', is used to refer to all those dead older Piro people who are personally remembered: in Ucayali Spanish, people say, *los finados nuestros abuelos*, 'our late grandparents'. It was precisely this category of people who were the privileged sources of myths for living adults.

Village leaders like Artemio are, in this sense, premature *tsrune*, 'old people'.[30] As I have discussed elsewhere (1991: 205–11), a key feature of being

---

[30] Artemio once told me that he should not, in truth, be headman of Santa Clara, saying, 'My father should be the headman here, being the oldest of us. But he cannot read or write, so they made me headman instead.'

a village leader is an ability to speak well. Village leaders are also the ones who take the initiative in expanding their villages by integrating newcomers. This is, in part, what Artemio was doing when he told me, 'A Man who went under the Earth' that night: he was showing himself to be a good leader by telling an 'ancient people's story', and demonstrating through an ability to tell such stories that he was, indeed, a good Piro *gitsrukaachi*.

If missionaries and anthropologists as outsiders have inevitably spoken most to such village leaders, and if such people who have been most willing to tell myths to them, then this means that the historical archive of Piro myths is likely to reflect this fact. I have already shown this to be true of the mythic narrative, 'Tsla swallowed by a Giant Catfish', and the prominence of Tsla mythology in the collections by Matteson (1951) and Ricardo Alvarez (1960) suggest that they too were specifically and preferentially told these sorts of mythic narratives by their informants. By contrast, 'A Man who went under the Earth', and the myth about the underworld home of the white-lipped peccaries, is not apparently a commonly told Piro myth. But, as I noted in Chapter 2, there are some interesting features of the relationship between teller and listener for several of the known narrations of this myth, and this mythic narrative may have an intrinsic interest for the teller when it is being told to *gringos*.

Is there a special connection between, 'Tsla swallowed by a Giant Catfish', the mythic narrative so easily told to white people, and the variants of 'A Man who went under the Earth', the mythic narrative that seems to engage with the relationship between the knowledge of the 'ancient people' and the knowledge of *gringos*? I think that there is, and that Piro people experience these two myths as complements of each other. I return to this issue in Chapter 9. In order to reach that conclusion, we must go into the interior relations of the Piro lived world, so to speak, by following those myths of myth, 'The Birth of Tsla' and 'The Kochmaloto Women'. These mythic narratives lead us deeper into some aspects of the Piro lived world that have been appearing already: design, clothing, hallucinatory experience, shamanry, and the girl's initiation ritual. This eventually brings us to that other myth of the night of 15 January 1982, the one about the moon. Once we know why Artemio was interested in the question of whether Americans had been to the moon, we are in a much better position to understand why that story his mother told should have led him to tell me, 'A Man who went under the Earth'.

PART II

Transformations

4

Design

In the preceding chapter, I argued that myths interest Piro people because of the way in which they connect the known to the unknowable. In Part II, I follow the lead of the myths out into the Piro lived world, to explore what it is that Piro people find interesting and significant about their lives, and which gives those lives their hold. I begin in this chapter with an analysis of one of the Piro 'myths of myth': 'The Birth of Tsla'. This leads us into a deeper understanding of how Piro people think of their humanity in relation to jaguars, and how this is bound up with a key feature of the Piro lived world, 'design'. This in turn allows a deeper understanding of certain features of the Piro lived world which have been appearing already, such as the meaning of clothing and of white people, and leads to a fuller account of the nature of transformation in Piro social life.

In order to remain within the Piro lived world and its complex temporal forms, over the chapters of Part II I stick close to a single evening of talking analogous to the night on which Artemio told me, 'A Man who went under the Earth'. The evening I refer to was 6 November 1988, when Artemio's brother-in-law Antonio Urquía and his wife Teresa Campos, Artemio's older sister, told me 'ancient people's stories', and about the ways of the old time Piro people, far into the night. It was an edgy time, and the Bajo Urubamba area was clearly descending into serious conflict. Later, I was to discover that this had been the 'hot year' of the Peruvian civil war. Antonio had a premonition of how bad things were going to get, for as he concluded this evening of talk, he commented, 'Listen, the *manacaracos* (chachalacas) are calling. The old people said that when the *manacaracos* call at night, they are seeing war. Perhaps war will come here, here to where we live.' The *manacaracos* sang true that night, and that war did indeed come to the Bajo Urubamba shortly thereafter. It was to bring serious consequences to the people who lived there. However, these consequences still lay up ahead, in an unknown future, on that evening I take as my reference point here.

'The Birth of Tsla'

Antonio Urquía told me the following 'ancient people's story', sitting in his house on that evening in November 1988. Also present were his wife Teresa Campos, who made occasional comments on her husband's narrative, their daughter's four children, and my godson Hermés, who had insisted on accompanying me to hear these stories, despite his parents' warning that he would fall asleep. Antonio had already that evening told us a story about the fool Shani-rawa, and the story of the Kochmaloto Women, discussed in the next chapter, when he began as follows:

Yakonero was the mother of Tsla. She married a jaguar, one of the jaguars that live in herds (*gixoluru*). Her husband's mother was Yompichgojru.

She left her husband and married a human. She was pregnant. Her husband went to a festival and left macaw feathers along the path for her to follow. She followed him.

As she went along, Tsla spoke to her, asking her to pick flowers. She picked a flower and held it to her belly. Tsla was inside her, he hadn't been born yet. The flower entered her belly, it disappeared.

Tsla kept asking for flowers, so finally Yakonero got angry and wouldn't give him any more. Tsla made her take the wrong path, he made her follow the currasow feath-ers[1] instead of the macaw feathers. Tsla was a miraculous being, he did miraculous things.

Teresa Campos here commented, '*¡Kgiyaklewakleru wa Tsla!*', 'Tsla was a miraculous being!'

The currasow feathers led her to where the jaguars lived, to where he who had once been her husband lived. She arrived and Yompichgojru greeted her. She told Yakonero to hide high up in the roof of the house, because her sons were coming back.

They arrived and said, 'We smell human meat.' Yompichgojru told them not to kill her. They lined up outside on a balsa log. Yakonero came down to delouse them. Yompichgojru gave her charcoal to chew, rather than have to bite their lice. When Yakonero came to the last jaguar, she had no coal left, and she bit the louse. '*Klaaajjj*', she retched!

Because of this, the jaguars got angry and leapt on to her and tore her apart. Yompichgojru asked for the guts to eat. She hung them up in a *achiote* bush (Piro, *gapi-jru*; Lat. *Bixa orellana*).

After three days, three birds emerged, three little *manacaraco* birds.[2] They were Tsla and his brothers, the Muchkajine. The Muchkajine grew rapidly, in a few days they were men. But Tsla was small, stunted, a cry-baby. But he did miraculous things.

He said to the Muchkajine, 'Let's avenge ourselves on those who killed our mother. Let's get arrow cane.' They called the owner of the arrow cane, *katslupejru*.[3] They went to his house. Tsla said, 'Grandfather, give us arrow cane.' *Katslupejru* gave good arrow cane to the Muchkajine, but he gave only thin arrow cane to Tsla. Tsla got angry, and touched *katslupejru*'s neck with the arrow cane. He died, just by being touched!

Then Tsla said, 'Let's make a canoe.' They called *shino*, the giant ant-eater.[4] Long ago, my kinspeople did this when they made canoes, because *shino*'s claws look like an axe. But the opossum, *goshyolu*, came instead. He said he could make a canoe just as

---

[1] Piro, *giyeka*; Ucayali Spanish, *paujil* (Lat. *Mitu mitu*).

[2] Piro, *plejnako* (Lat. *Ortalis gutata*), the speckled chachalaca.

[3] *Katslu* is Piro for 'arrow cane' (Ucayali Spanish, *isana, chicosa*). The *Diccionario Piro* gives the possibly cognate word, '*katslupeere*: a capivara of white colour' (Nies 1986: 109).

[4] Presumably Antonio's *shino*, 'pacarana' (Ucayali Spanish, *picuro mama*; Lat. *Dinomys branickii*) was here a slip of the tongue for *suwa*, the giant ant-eater (Lat. *Myrmecophaga tridactyla*). On the occa-sion of the narration, Antonio himself translated *shino* as Ucayali Spanish *oso hormiguero*.

well as *shino*. The Muchkajine chopped down the tree, and *goshyolu* was meant to catch it. But it crushed him instead. That's why it is hard work to make a canoe. Tsla said, 'Those poor people who will come in the future! They'll have to work hard to make canoes!' If *shino* had come instead of *goshyolu*, it would now be easy to make canoes.

Then they made a garden. They made it in one day, and the next day it was producing.

Then Tsla said, 'Let's avenge ourselves on those who killed our mother.' They went to a pool below a high bank. There Tsla put sharpened palmwood stakes in the water. One Muchkajitu[5] dived in, and stuck on the stakes. He died, his blood rose to the surface. Then Tsla took him from the water, and made him well again. The second Muchkajitu did the same, he died and Tsla made him live. Then Tsla did it. Tsla was miraculous.

Then the jaguars came along. They asked, 'What are you doing, nephews?' They said, 'We're playing, diving.' They got the jaguars to join in. One dived in and died. They took out his heart, they had a clay pot there, and they put the heart in there to cook. They did the same with all the jaguars.

Finally, Yompichgojru came along. They wanted her to play too, but she was suspicious. She asked, 'What are you cooking?' Tsla said, 'We're cooking pigeons,' but she knew, she was suspicious, so she ran off. She was pregnant, and her young one was male. From them came the jaguars we have today. If Tsla had killed his grandmother, there would be no jaguars about now.

Antonio concluded this myth with the story of 'Tsla swallowed by a Giant Catfish', in the version given in Chapter 3, and then he and Teresa told me a long account of girl's initiation ritual (see Ch. 6).

In the preceding chapter, I discussed the importance of the grandparent-grandchild relations to mythic narration. How might a small Piro child like Hermés Rodriguez have related this myth to what he knew about the world? As predicted, little Hermés fell sound asleep at some point of the evening,[6] as did all the other children, so I cannot be certain that any of them actually heard 'The Birth of Tsla' on this occasion. However, they would undoubtedly have heard it before, and would hear it again. Unfortunately, it never occurred to me to ask young children about myths, but this story does contain several elements which do play important roles in the worlds of small Piro children, and about which they frequently talked to me.

A major concern for a young Piro child in this story would be the jaguars, scary beings which loom large in their imaginations. Younger Piro children are frequently warned off wandering away from the open area of the village by shouts of 'Watch out, there may be jaguars about!'[7] This primary association of jaguars with the dangers of the forest certainly enters their imaginations, for

---

[5] 'Muchkajitu' is the singular of Muchkajine.

[6] I then realized that the warning about Hermés falling asleep had been directed at me, not him, for I had to heft the remarkably heavy little boy home through the darkness.

[7] The equivalent threat to keep children from playing too much in the river is, 'Watch out, there are anacondas!' (see Ch. 6).

many children, Hermés included, spoke with fear of these animals (see Gow 1995).[8] Jaguars are bad enough, but the jaguars of this myth, 'herd-living jaguars', jaguars that live in groups, would be genuinely appalling, a nightmarish vision of horror multiplied.

In stark contrast, kinspeople are the source of Piro children's security, for they are constantly surrounded by their kinspeople in the village. Grandmothers, mothers, uncles, brothers, and so on, are the benign and safe embodiments of the human mode of 'herd-living', *gwashata*, 'living well'. In particular, for Piro children, grandmothers are a constant source of relatively conflict-free aid and succour: baby-sitters from infancy, grandmothers need be treated with less respect than mothers, and can be joked with. Piro children frequently seek refuge from a fight with a parent in the house of a grandmother, where they are usually well received. Jaguars are the very antithesis of kinship, and a palpable embodiment of such antithesis for Piro children. In the myth, the curious solicitude that Yompichgojru shows for her grandchildren, and their attempted murder of her, must be a powerful image for the young listeners of the alienness of *muchikawpotgimni*, 'very long ago, it is said'.

The myth would evoke other images of the alien for a Piro child. Tsla's miraculous acts (*giyaklewata*, 'to create miraculously') resemble the actions of shamans (*kagonchiwata*, 'to do shamanry'), the strange and fearful operations to which children are often privy, whether as victims, patients or spectators (see Ch. 5). Similarly, the name of Tsla's brothers, the Muchkajine, the 'first white people', would evoke those present-day *kajine*, 'white people', who figure so importantly in their parents' lives, and in their own, and whose knowledge and power makes them at once attractive and frightening.

Birth is a salient event for Piro children, and one at which they are regularly present, whether by choice or otherwise. They invariably have a ringside view of the births of their younger siblings, and of any other new kinsperson they choose to see being born. The bizarre birth of Tsla and his younger brothers the Muchkajine, who emerged alone from the dismembered womb hanging in the *achiote* bush, would be quite different to the bustle of such known events, as the house fills up with older women to help the mother, other kinspeople, and eventually the person called to cut the umbilical cord. Similarly, this multiple birth of Tsla and his siblings would seem strange to such a child, for birth order is crucial to a Piro child's life, defining forever the solidarity of older and younger siblings. This relationship is palpable to a Piro child in the relative sizes of older and younger siblings, the product of the gaps between their births. As we shall see, no Piro child could have companions like Tsla, who emerged with him.

---

[8] Adults tend to laugh about such fears, and say that they lie about jaguars to stop children wandering away, and falling victim to more serious dangers, like snakes and demons. This does not mean, however, that they have anything but a very healthy respect for jaguars.

'The Birth of Tsla' would also seem strange to Piro children like Hermés, by its omission of key aspects of birth rituals they will have witnessed, and of the birth ritual which ushered them into the Piro lived world, and which has ongoing ramifications in their experience. Where are the placentas of Tsla and his brothers? When a Piro child is born, it is born with an umbilical cord (*giplotsa*) and placenta (*geyonchi*). The emergence of the placenta is carefully awaited before the baby can be considered born (*gishpakatka*, 'to have emerged/been born'). Tsla and his brothers apparently lacked these accompaniments. Similarly, the cutting of the cord is attended by considerable ceremony, for a non-kinsperson of the parents must be called to do this. This sets up an enduring relationship between that person and the newborn child: the cord cutter is *gistakjerchi* (Ucayali Spanish, *padrino/madrina*) to the child, who is *gistaplolchi* (Ucayali Spanish, *ahijado/ahijada*) to him or her.[9] The resultant navel, the trace left by this ritual on the child's body, is the focus of constant attention in small babies, and for older children it is continually re-emphasized by the sucking and blowing of shamans curing the children's frequent bouts of diarrhoea. Lacking all of these attributes, and having effectively given birth to themselves, Tsla and his brothers are definitely very different beings.

Births, Human and Miraculous

The birth of a Piro child is the beginning of the process of making the neonate into a human. This is initiated by the cutting of the umbilical cord, which divides the neonate into a human baby and a placenta (*geyonchi*, 'first design'): this act originates in the decision by the assembled people that the child is *yineru*, a 'human'. If the child is not human, the whole foetus is disposed of: I heard of cases where 'fish', 'tortoises' or 'things we didn't recognize' were born.[10] When the child is human, it is separated from the placenta, which is then either buried beneath a tree or thrown into the river.[11] Thus, one half of the foetus is kept in the house to become a child, while the other half is ejected into non-human space, the forest or river. The birth of a Piro child is characterized, therefore, by the separation in two of an original unity, the foetus and placenta united by the umbilical cord. This separation must be done by someone who is not going to be a close kinsperson of the child, but will rather stand in a different and special relationship to it.

Beyond its emergence and disposal, the placenta does not elicit much interest

[9] See Gow (1991: 172–8; 1997) for further details of these relationships, and their wider implication for the parents of the child. Baptism can supplement or replace the cord-cutting relationship, with the obvious proviso that many children are not baptized, but all have had their umbilical cords cut.

[10] I assume the reference here is to severe birth deformity, but I never pressed the point too strongly. Women who had given birth to such 'animals' seemed emotionally neutral when they discussed them, in contrast to the sadness which they expressed at the loss of stillborn 'human' children.

[11] See also Matteson (1954: 77–8).

from Piro people, and I never heard people discussing it outside this context.[12] Far more interest and attention is paid to the formation of the growing baby's navel. Piro people identify the placenta with the guts, and call the period of drying and falling off of the stump of the cord, 'the closing of the guts'. This is the period of most stringent post-partem prohibitions on the behaviour of the parents, for the guts can easily reopen. However, as the guts close, the child's body now has an interior stomach which can be filled with food, which, as I have discussed, is the origin of kin ties. This differentiation of interior and exterior, lacking in the foetus, is crucial for the creation and maintenance of *gwashata*, 'living well'. The loss of the placenta is thus the possibility of the neonate's entry into Piro social life.

Clearly, in the birth of Tsla and the Muchkajine from the dismembered womb of their mother, none of this takes place. This is apparently easily explained: Tsla and his brothers are birds, and hence are born without placentas. Both of Antonio's versions specify that they were birds, as does Ricardo Alvarez's informants' version (1960): Matteson's (1951) does not (though Tsla sings like a bird as he emerges). The birds vary from *maracaná* (Piro, *saweto*) to *manacaraco* (Piro, *plejnako*) to *pucacunga* (Piro, *totumta*).[13] This, however, does not really solve the problem, for Tsla and the Muchkajine are clearly also people. This is obvious for the Muchkajine, who are the 'Long Ago White People', but it is also true of Tsla, who is clearly a human throughout the myth, although, as Antonio pointed out, not a full-grown man like his younger brothers. One informant, describing Tsla, contrasted him to the Muchkajine as follows: 'he was small, but strong, like us Piro people'. Tsla would, in short, seem to be human in the full sense of a Piro human.

Following the logic of this, and especially the actual sequence of the mythic birth, it is tempting to see the Muchkajine as Tsla's placenta. Like the placenta of a Piro child, they follow him out of the womb. But unlike the Piro child, who must lose this part of itself in order to have relations with others, Tsla keeps this part of himself as his companions, his helpers and his constant audience. He is in a literal sense innately social, for he is born with his own kinspeople.

Tsla's society with the Muchkajine has an even odder feature for Piro people: he clearly has 'twins'. Piro people can be twins, but they cannot have twins. A Piro person can be a twin (*gepirutu*, 'one who is two'), but cannot have a living twin.[14] As Teresa Campos, herself the mother of a twin and grandmother of

---

[12] While travelling in Miaría, Pablo Rodriguez told me that he had dreamt that his son had been born and that it spoke to him: this, he said, was a bad sign, and meant the baby had died. When Sara shortly after showed him his healthy new daughter, and he recounted his dream to her, she said, 'It must have been her placenta you dreamt about.'

[13] The Latin names for these species are, respectively, *Ara severa, Ortalis gutata,* and *Penelope jacquacu* (from Villarejo 1979 and Sick 1993).

[14] The Piro term for 'the other twin' is *gimushpakanru*, 'that which came out with him'.

another, explained to me, 'When twins are born, one always dies. If we try to keep both alive, then both die. Only one can live.' Everyone denied this was caused by neglect, but said instead that it was an intrinsic feature of twinness: only one can live. The surviving twin is a born shaman, as I discuss further in later chapters. Tsla too is unquestionably a shaman, of miraculous powers, but he is able to keep his 'twins' as living companions.

The Muchkajine's 'twinness' with Tsla is marked by an excess: not only do they double Tsla, they are themselves multiple. In most of the versions I heard, and in Ricardo Alvarez's informants' versions (1960), there are clearly two Muchkajine, while Moisés Miqueas's version of 'Tsla swallowed by a *wakawa*' specifies three Muchkajine, as does Matteson's (1951) version of 'The Birth of Tsla' (four babies were born, though later they are specified as only three in total). But more important than the absolute number of the Muchkajine, it seems to me, are that, firstly, Tsla is clearly differentiated from them (he is never identified as a Muchkajitu himself), and secondly, the fact of the opposition between Tsla's singularity and the multiplicity of the Muchkajine (whether two or more).

This concern for number, in Tsla's twinness and in the multiplicity of the Muchkajine, can be related to another central theme of this myth: the loss of jaguars' sociality. At the outset of the myth, the pregnant Yakonero is a lone human living with a group of jaguars. These are specified as, 'group-living, herd-forming', *gixolune* (from *gixo*, 'many'). By the end of the myth, after Tsla's revenge, there was only one jaguar, the grandmother Yompichgojru. She, however, is pregnant with a male foetus, and, as Antonio said, 'From them came the jaguars we have today. If Tsla had killed his grandmother, there would be no jaguars about now.'

On another occasion, Antonio told me,

Nowadays, jaguars do not live in groups, they wander alone in the forest. It is said that *gixoluru* ('group living') jaguars still exist, but not here. Far away, it is said. It is said that such jaguars still exist far up the Huau river, far away in the centre of the forest. How might it be? Who knows? But it is good that such jaguars do not live around here!

Contemporary jaguars present a serious threat to humans, but at least they are met alone. It is now humans, and not jaguars, who live in groups.[15]

Jaguars' current solitary condition is a potent inverted image of contemporary Piro sociability. There is a very distinctive kind of Piro narrative which never fails to elicit rapt attention in its listeners, 'stories about jaguars'. These are personal experience narratives of lone encounters with jaguars. Central to these stories is the sense of horror inspired by the scene of the lone encounter between a solitary human, usually unarmed or poorly armed, and the solitary

---

[15] There is an implicit reference to incest in the myth: the jaguars must logically descend from the incestuous union of the grandmother jaguar and her own son.

jaguar, fully armed by birthright. As Don Mauricio once said to a group of
children who were laughing nervously at such a jaguar encounter narrative,
'You should never joke about the jaguar. That one is not like our mothers and
fathers, who are always saying, "Watch out, I'm going to hit you, I'll hit you,"
but they never do. No, the jaguar is not like that. That one just kills you!' It is
as if, resentful of their lost sociability, jaguars are constantly on the prowl to
find a human temporarily in this same condition, to avenge themselves.

These same narratives invariably contain a moment which apparently sits ill
with the predominant theme of terror. This is the confrontation with the
extraordinary beauty of jaguars. As Clara Flores put it, of her first sight of the
jaguar she encountered alone in the forest, *Giyagni neknoka. Netlu. ¡Kayona
tslagatayyi Ruyliylita. Ga wa kowruwrujepita,* 'Then I looked behind me. I saw
him. What a skin like a design-covered screen! His skin quaked. And he turned
around and around' (Nies 1972: 38–9, 43).[16] The reference is to the complex
shimmering of the jaguar's markings as he moves, and is considered a feature
of great beauty.

Artemio told me of how, out hunting early one morning, he saw no less than
three jaguars on a beach of the Mapchirga river, 'They could not see me, so I
just watched them. I had my gun, but I didn't shoot. They were so beautiful,
playing with each other or just lying there. Their design-covered skins were so
beautiful to see, I watched them for hours.' Given that Artemio told me that
jaguars' skins were at the time very valuable, and given just how afraid of
jaguars Piro people are, his preference for aesthetic contemplation over either
flight or assault was remarkable.

The beauty of the solitary jaguars lies in their designs. As I have noted, Piro
people must lose their placenta in order to enter the social world. This organ is
called, in Piro, *geyonchi,* 'first design'. In order to follow the 'The Birth of
Tsla', it is now necessary to consider these designs in more detail.

The Things with Design

If the beauty of jaguars lies in their designs, they are only one exemplar of
such beauty for Piro people. As Matteson remarked, 'The design on the fur of
an ocelot or the skin of a snake, the mottling of a fish, and the markings of a
leaf are noted appreciatively, and likened to the geometrical designs with which
the Piro decorate pottery, cloth, woodwork and even their own bodies' (1954:
66). My own experience fully confirms this, as I have noted, for encounters
with jaguars. It is also true of encounters with dangerous snakes like anacondas. For example, one woman told me of having almost stepped on a *soklupi*

---

[16] The word root *tslaga-*, 'screen, grate, bars (of a cage)' (Matteson 1965: 369) is presumably related
to the name 'Tsla'. Stephen Hugh-Jones (personal communication) has told me that the body of the
mythic hero from the northwest Amazon, Jurupari, is full of holes (see also Lévi-Strauss (1997: 173–4)
on the relationship of basketry and jaguars).

snake (Ucayali Spanish, *shushupe*, the bushmaster), by far the most feared of all snakes, but commented, 'It was beautiful, covered in designs, just like a bead-work bracelet.' While Piro people do note and appreciate the beauty of things without such designs, beauty (*giglenchi*) is consistently evoked in conditions of *kayona-*, 'design-covered' things.

What constitutes *yonchi* 'designs'? Firstly, in the most general terms, *yonchi* is any pattern which shows high contrast and regular repetition, and a certain level of internal complexity. Therefore, snakes' skins and spotted jaguars have designs, while the plumage of macaws, despite the colour contrasts, do not. Secondly, what sorts of things, besides jaguars and anacondas, have *yonchi*? The short answer is many things. However, for analytical purposes, we can categorize them into four basic groups: natural species with intrinsic designs, things with designs produced by humans, aspects of hallucinatory experience where designs appear, and human bodily organs.

Design-covered species are numerous. Among mammals, the following have designs: *kayonalu mgenoklu*, 'jaguar with designs (common jaguar)', as opposed to *ksajiru mgenoklu*, 'black jaguar (melanistic jaguar)', and *serolu mgenoklu*, 'red jaguar (puma)'; *yonalu*, 'male design one', the ocelot/margay; and *shyo*, the 'vampire bat'. White-lipped peccaries have design too, but only after they have been skinned, for their ribs are *kayona-* 'with design'.[17] Many snakes are 'design covered': *kayonalu mapchiri*, 'anaconda with designs' (but not *ksajiru mapchiri*, 'black anaconda'); *myamtujwe*, 'cascabel' (Ucayali Spanish, *jergón*); *mapyolu*, 'boa constrictor sp.'; and many more. There are many design-covered amphibians, like the frog species, *tolojru*, and fish, like the *kayonalo*, 'female one with designs (*Sorubim sp.*, a catfish)', and *charawa*, 'catfish sp.', as well as insects, like the *sapnapatlo* 'lacewing sp.'. Finally, there are design-covered plants, like *kayonaksuro*, 'stem with designs (Ucayali Spanish. *jergón sacha*, a small plant)', and *kayon-sureru*, 'leaf with designs'. In all these cases, all or part of the surface of the being is covered in patterns marked by high contrast, repetition, and a degree of complexity,[18] and all these designs are likely to elicit comments on their beauty.

A second major class of 'design-covered' things are certain things produced by humans such as pottery, clothing, and the human body. Of Piro ceramic forms, 'beer bowls' (*kajpapago*), 'food bowls' (*kolpeto*), and 'beer-fermenting pots' (*gashgaji*) are painted with designs; 'cooking pots', *gimatu*, are never so painted. All old-style Piro clothing is painted with designs: the man's *mkalchi*, 'cotton robe' (Ucayali Spanish, *cushma*), the woman's *mkalnamchi*, 'skirt'

---

[17] It occurs to me that infant tapirs are also striped, but this fact was never remarked on by my informants, so I have no notion whether they are 'with-design'.

[18] That there are no birds on this list can hardly be fortuitous, although I have no explanation for it. An exception to this might be the 'ugly' designs formed by the bands of black feathers on a macaw's face, likened by one Piro woman to Campa face paint. In general, bird feathers are little used for aesthetic effect in Piro material culture.

(Ucayali Spanish, *pampanilla*), the man's *tsapa*, 'bag', and the bark crown (*sagyeta*) worn by girls during initiation ritual. Similarly, all beadwork collars and bracelets (*kigimchi*) have designs woven into them, as do certain forms of basketry.[19] Finally, the human body, for certain ritual occasions, is painted with designs in the vegetable dye *nso* (also *gmu*; Ucayali Spanish, *huito*).[20] Designs are painted on the face, but during a girl's initiation ritual, the celebrant has her entire face, upper body, and lower legs painted.

The designs produced by humans, *yineru yona* ('Piro people's design'), link Piro to series of peoples living along the Urubamba–Ucayali–Amazon river system who are defined by the Piro as 'people who know designs'. The closest contact is with the immediate down-river neighbours, the Conibo, who are considered by Piro people to have more beautiful designs than they themselves know. Beyond them, the Shipibo people are also admired for their designs, as are the Cocama people even further down-river. The 'design-with' peoples form a series along the mainstream of the Urubamba–Ucayali–Amazon, and the Piro are the most 'up-river' of these peoples. They are river people, as opposed to forest people.[21] As we shall see, white people also have designs.

Finally, designs are a feature of the onset of *ayahuasca* (Piro, *kamalampi*) hallucinatory experience, as I discuss further in the next chapter, and of certain bodily organs. One of these is the placenta, *geyonchi*, the 'first design'. I have never felt it appropriate to discuss the 'design-covered' nature of this organ when one was in view, since people were busy with more urgent matters at such times. However, Sara Fasabi suggested to me that the reason for the placenta's Piro name must be because 'it is covered in designs': my own observations, for what they are worth, confirm this impression, in the shimmering tracery of blood vessels. Further, as noted in Chapter 2, the 'design-covered' nature of human guts is referred to by Sebastián in 'The Sun'. This is not surprising, given that, as I have discussed, Piro people consider the guts to be originally co-extensive with the placenta.

These are the design-covered things: Piro people when they are painted, their clothing, their pottery, Conibo and Cocama people and their pots, jaguars, vampire bats, lacewings, a small snake, a frog, a little forest plant, the placenta, disembowelled guts. The list is reminiscent of Borges's famous Chinese encyclopaedia, and one might wonder what all these things have in common. Obviously, the simple answer is that they have designs. A deeper answer is that, by virtue of that fact, they are considered beautiful by Piro people.

---

[19] In cotton-weaving, design is produced through warp-manipulation: a technique most highly developed among the Cashinahua (Kensinger *et. al.* 1975). Piro women make little use of warp-manipulation in weaving, and have never, to my knowledge, made woven-design cotton bracelets, unlike Shipibo–Conibo women. Design-covered basketry is not a particularly important activity either.

[20] See Matteson (1954: 51–2) for a discussion of painting styles.

[21] Lathrap's distinction (1970), however problematic as an analytical tool in ethnographic and archaeological analysis, reflects a genuine folk category of the Ucayali–Urubamba region, as well as other regions of Amazonia.

The relation between design and beauty leads to three points. Firstly, there are many things without design. Unless painted for rituals, Piro people themselves are without designs (at least on the outside), and their loss of the 'original design' is a pre-condition of their coming to be human among humans. Similarly, cooking pottery has no designs, nor do most articles of Piro manufacture. The closest neighbours of Piro people, with whom they frequently intermarry, the Campa and Machiguenga peoples, have no designs, or at best 'ugly' ones.[22] This does not mean these people are without good qualities, but simply means that they cannot create visual beauty. And of course, most animals and plants lack designs too, including many species of key importance to Piro people's lives.

Secondly, there are things which have qualities directly opposed to design. For example, certain things are considered *kasoliru*, 'blotchy' (Ucayali Spanish, *morocho*). On the one hand, this refers to a specific form of 'ugliness': examples people gave were of a rotting corpse, clothing spotted with fungus, or the markings of dolphins. The aversive feature of such things seems to be due to the association with rotting, the production of a randomly spotted surface, and Piro people have a general horror of all forms of skin disease which produces the same effect. On the other hand, however, this same condition, *kasoliru*, is remarked on with pleasure when it refers to the foaming of fermenting manioc beer or of collected honey.

Thirdly, part of the beauty of designs lies in their relation to *yineru yona*, 'people's designs', the designs which women make. These designs are characteristic of Piro people, but they are also the knowledge of specific women. Their production requires that a woman learns them. It is to these I turn next.

Women's Designs

The creation of *yonchi* by Piro women refers to two major techniques, each in turn subdivided into sub-techniques. The two major techniques are *yonata*, 'to paint design', and *saxpata*, 'to weave'. Design-painting is the specific technique of applying a paint with a stylus or brush to a surface of strongly contrasting colour in order to produce design, and is opposed to covering a surface generally with pigment (*sagata*). There are four forms of *yonata*: painting with black *gitawna* pigment on the white surface of a pot; painting with white *yongaji* pigment on the red surface of a pot; painting in translucent *tlipi* juice on cloth, covering it in black *ksajijpa* mud, and then washing the cloth, leaving the mud bound to the *tlipi*-painted design; and painting with the translucent *nso*, which later darkens to blue-black, on to the human skin. There are three main forms of creating design through *saxpata*: weaving beadwork; warp-manipulation in

---

[22] My aesthetic-relativist attempts to defend the striking charm of Campa face-painting were met with incredulity and scorn by Piro people.

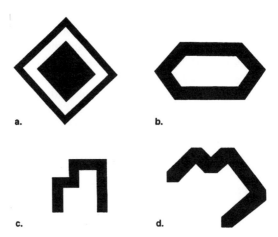

Plate 1. Examples of design templates (a) *mapyolga*, 'boa constrictor design line;
(b) *mgenoklugojistejga*, 'line on the side of the jaguar's forehead; (c) *gimnuga*, 'snake
line'; (d) *yongachi*, 'design line'

weaving cloth; and the weaving of certain forms of basketry. All of these techniques must be learned separately.

As might be suspected from its name, painting *yonata* seems to be the exemplar of all creation of design, and as I discuss below, the supreme exemplar of
all is the painting of the girl's body for initiation ritual. This painting of the
girl's body, considered the most difficult technique, is exclusively done by old
women, those who are in the grandmother generation relative to her. This, I
was told, is because only such women know enough about painting to be able
to do so. This is related to certain features of how women learn how to paint,
and of the techniques themselves.

A girl learns to paint by watching older women painting, and then practising
on her own. There is no formal teaching, other than the 'imitation' (*yimaka*) of
the actions of a knowledgeable woman who has allowed the girl to watch her paint
(also called *yimaka*). Teaching and learning are here the same thing, and a predi-
cate of learning such things is that the girl must have *nshinikanchi*, she must be
quiet, observant, and thoughtful. In order to practise *yonata*, the girl must first
learn to make the thing to be painted, and then paint it. Given that bad painting
can wreck the value of a pot or a piece of clothing, younger women often ask older
women to do the painting for them. Given that they will themselves be the object
painted, Piro people are presumably reluctant to be painted by women who do not
know what they are doing.[23] The opportunities for practising painting are therefore restricted, to put it mildly.

[23] I am grateful to a discussion with Vanessa Lea for suggesting this point, from her experience
learning Kayapó body painting.

And there are further constraints that must be mastered. Designs are generated from basic design templates, which are stereotypical forms. These template forms must be spread regularly at consistent intervals across the design field, and joined up with supplementary design lines freely invented for the occasion. These joining lines must be unique, and no copying from a present model is allowed: this is what girls do, and it demonstrates the women's ignorance of design. The aim is to create, from one of the set of templates, a design which is regular, symmetrical, complex, and which is completely original. Further, the design must be perfectly suited to the actual object painted and its unique contours. In pottery painting, the woman must know how the design is going to continue on the invisible far side of the pot, while in painting a man's robe, bag, or a woman's skirt, she must paint the same design twice, identically, but inverting it the second time. In painting the torso of a girl, the complexities multiply.

There is more still. A Piro woman preparing to paint a pot, piece of clothing, or another person must imagine the finished design in its entirety *before* she starts. All the pigments used dry quickly, and if a mistake is made it must be soon rectified. If she meets a problem half-way through, she has no choice but to abandon the attempt. Further, Piro women are harsh critics of each other's work: each piece is minutely scrutinized for faults and irregularities, and women trace the flow of the design with their fingers. No praise attends the inept but brave attempt, only ridicule. The search is for beauty, and half-measures will not do.

It need hardly be surprising, then, that Piro people hold that only old women can paint well: design-production is a style that takes a lifetime to learn. In order to acquire the knowledge that allows a woman to produce flawlessly a beautiful design, she must have spent a long time thinking about designs: she must, as Piro people say, 'hold designs in her head'. This refers to her ability to generate a design in imagination, then imagine it applied to the particular object to be painted, and then do so without any mistakes. This explains the tone of wonder in the following statement by Sara Fasabi, as she made bead-work for me,

What I ask myself is this, how come those old Piro people could make up the designs in beadwork? They couldn't read or write, but they could make these designs. It's very hard to make bracelets, but they knew how. That's why I say those old Piro people must have been very intelligent—they didn't know how to read but they could make designs. Like my mother, she can't read but she can make a design, she must be very intelligent.

Here, 'intelligence' is *nshinikanchi*. Old women, through their *nshinikanchi*, have mastered the *gimatkalchi*, 'knowledge' of design, which enables them to produce beauty. Beauty is the product of good manual art, which is the product of knowledge, which is the product of thoughtfulness, which is the Piro definition of their humanity.

I discuss the social meaning of this development of design knowledge further in Chapter 6, where I analyse *kigimawlo*, girl's initiation ritual, but certain points should be noted here. Firstly, design knowledge closely parallels, in its ontogeny, mythopoesis as discussed in Chapter 3. In both cases, knowledge is held to increase with age. Secondly, design knowledge, and hence Piro people's designs, can be thought of as the product of series of ongoing transformations in Piro women. If a Piro woman originates as such in the ritual by which she lost her 'original design', her placenta, then her ultimate aim is to have fully mastered design, to 'hold it in her head' as design-knowledge, and to produce it as beauty on other things and people. This beauty is *yineru yona*, 'human design'.

There is, however, an ambiguity here. Piro designs in general are 'human designs', and specific designs are evidence of the personal design knowledge of their specific makers, but the designs are ultimately identified with animals. This is because each of the design templates is named for the design on a specific part of specific animal species. Examples of such templates are *sapnapatloga*, 'lacewing sp. line', *kayonalga*, '*Sorubim* catfish line', *shyoga*, 'vampire bat line', *gimnuga*, 'snake line', *mgenoklugojistsejga*, 'line of side of the jaguar's forehead', and *tolojrupalga*, 'line of the leg of frog species'. For all that 'human designs' come from other women whom the painter has watched attentively as they painted, ultimately they would seem to have come from animals. I turn to this problem next.

Human and Animal Designs

Animal designs differ from 'human designs' insofar as they are intrinsic, rather than based on knowledge. The designs of, for example, *charawa* catfish or *tolojru* frogs are the spontaneous demonstrations, on their skins, of their specific identities, much as the placenta, the 'first design', is a spontaneous part of the foetus. By contrast, Piro women must painstakingly learn 'human designs' over their life-course, in a process in which many women will fail.

Despite the fact that specific design templates are named for specific species, and that people could often readily identify the specific body part on a given animal which corresponded to the design template, I never heard of any women learning designs through the contemplation of such designs. Instead, the relationship between animals' designs is one of 'resemblance' (Piro, *pixka*; Ucayali Spanish, *parecer/ser igual*). Insofar as the 'human design' templates are named for these animal designs, priority in this resemblance goes to the animal species. However, insofar as the design templates are simply the start of the design, and are never realized other than as parts of a finished design, we could not say that any realized 'human design' is a representation of the design of any given animal

Plate 2. A *gashgaji*, beer fermenting pot

species.[24] The *sui generis* nature of every realized design means that it is a 'human design', rather than the specific animal design which gave it its starting point.

The question of the origins of 'human design' in animal design can be explored from a consideration of a formal feature of design: the visual emphasis on the surface. Firstly, as I have argued at greater length elsewhere (1989; 1990), design is made on surfaces, and concerns the play between that surface and its hidden content. The stereotypic design templates, those named for animal designs, can be applied to any surface, but a great part of the skill of painting *yonata* lies in fully imagining a design which will fit *this* particular surface, be it a flat piece of cloth, a rounded pot, or the complex contours of a human face or leg. As I stated elsewhere, 'design focuses on the surface of the object, on its appearance. It enhances this appearance, and makes it visually compulsive' (1989: 28). Design is therefore in a dialectic with the content of the object covered in design. What are these contents for 'human design'? For pottery, design-covered surfaces are a property of those ceramic forms which contain manioc beer and cooked food: manioc beer pots, manioc beer serving bowls, and food bowls. Design is not applied to cooking pots, which contain food in the process of being cooked. For clothing, design covered surfaces are

---

[24] I use the term 'representation' here in the technical sense it has in art history and related disciplines, rather than in the more diffuse sense it has in the social and psychological sciences (see Gow 1995a).

Plate 3. A *gashgaji*, beer fermenting pot

a property of those clothes which contain Piro people,[25] but not of those which contain non-Piro people like the Campa and Machiguenga people. Finally, for body-painting, the design-covered surfaces are the skins of Piro people in festive state, but not in everyday states.

For pottery and clothing, the contained is either a potential body content of a person (beer or food) or a person's body. For body-painting, the contained is the person's interior. Design-painting on the body is thus the most radical of the techniques, insofar as it emphasizes that the human skin/surface is itself a container of a content. This is obviously linked to the 'first design', the placenta, in which the foetus was wrapped inside the womb, and which a baby loses as a condition of becoming human during birth ritual.

There is an important contrast here, for while human body-painting rapidly fades (*nso* lasts about a week on the skin), to be replaced on the next ritual occasion, designs painted on pottery and clothing only fade as a function of usage over time, and are never replaced. It would be a mistake to terminate the analysis of 'human design' at the point of the produced object, as if this were necessarily the endpoint of Piro women's actions, as it is in much of Western aesthetic practice.[26] None of the media of *yonchi* last very long, and part of the effect of this visual aesthetic system resides in such transience. The Piro word *gitlika* means 'to fade, to lose colour', but also 'to begin to ripen' (as said, for

[25] And also of their intimate personal property, in the case of the man's bag, *tsapa*.
[26] See Kuechler (1987) on this topic in regard to New Ireland *malanggan* sculpture.

Plate 4. A *kajpapago*, large beer serving bowl

example, of bananas). As we shall see, this combination of meanings elucidates the girl's initiation ritual, discussed in Chapter 6: the course of the ritual is accompanied by the steady fading of the girl's complex body paint, in the same process that is making her a new, adult woman.

It is significant that the human skin is the only surface which undergoes the constant renewal of 'human design': in all other cases, the design is an intrinsic and irremovable feature of the object with the painted surface. Further, Piro people, unlike their Campa and Machiguenga neighbours, seem to have a horror of any permanent skin markings: they have never practised any form of tattooing, and refer to Campa people's facial tattoos with a mixture of ridicule and pity.[27] Painted clothing, in which the designs are permanent, are marked by the fact that they are removable parts of body decoration: unlike body-painting, they can be taken off as easily as they are put on. Indeed, Alvarez remarked that, 'It is important to note that Piro clothes are and represent the persons who use them. Because of this, clothing can take the place of its owner. An article of Piro clothing can look after the house or the garden, can inform on and punish a thief, and can be the transmitter of magical powers. It is owed absolute respect' (R. Alvarez 1970: 20).[28] Clothing then, is a part of the person, but a removable part. The skin, which is painted, is not.

Why should the human skin, uniquely among objects with design, be subject to occasional renewal of design? The logic would be that the human body is unique in having lost its 'original design', the placenta, as a pre-condition of its coming to be human in the eyes of others. Everything else with 'human designs' has them added on as a feature of the material fabrication. The fabrication of a human requires, by contrast, the removal of a design. As we have seen, this fabrication is thought of as the making of the baby as a

---

[27] By contrast, no such scorn attached to Campa lower-lip and nose-piercing, which was occasionally even admired. In the past, Piro people pierced their lower lips and noses to wear silver ornaments (*seroji*), a practice now discontinued.

[28] See Viveiros de Castro (1998).

Plate 5. *Mkalnamchi*, skirts

differentiated exterior and interior. Losing the 'original design', the Piro child gains a surface, the skin, which can then be covered by clothing painted with 'human designs', and can itself on special occasions form the support for 'human designs' painted on to it by other humans. This suggests that the function of body-painting in rituals is for Piro people to share temporarily the condition of their own clothing, beadwork and pottery: that is, to have 'permanent' markings. As such, they come to share the condition of the beings from which 'human designs' themselves originate, the beautiful design-covered animals, for whom such designs are intrinsic to their specific identities. Why should this be a necessary condition of ritual life?

To look like Jaguars

When Piro people are decorated for festivals, it is not just any design-covered animal they resemble, it is jaguars. When I tried on my *cushma*, newly painted by Berna Zumaeta, Pablo Rodriguez admired it, then said laughing, 'Hey, take it off quickly, or all the dogs will start barking!' Bemused, I asked him why, and he said, 'Dressed like that, all painted, you look just like a jaguar!'

This association between painted clothing and jaguars is pervasive. To dream that one is spreading out a painted *cushma* means the dreamer will kill a

Plate 6. *Tsapa*, men's bags

jaguar, while such a dream of an unpainted *cushma* means one will kill a collared peccary. Similarly, when I dreamt of a jaguar, Pablo told me, 'That means you will buy a painted *cushma* when we go to Miaría.'[29] Just as beadwork is pervasively likened to snakes' skins, painted design is likened to the skins of jaguars.

In ritual gatherings, then, Piro people look like something we have met before, group-living jaguars. They come to look like that hypertrophy of terrible beauty that greeted Yakonero in the village of the jaguars in 'The Birth of Tsla'. As I discuss in Chapter 6, when Piro people collect in the visual appearance of group-living jaguars, they do not attempt the sort of domestic intimacy represented by Yakonero's delousing session in this myth. Instead, they drink manioc beer, fermented in design-covered pots, out of design-covered bowls, and they get drunk, sing and dance. Ultimately, as I will discuss, rituals aim at producing precisely just such domestic scenes, through the generation of sexual relations, but without the extreme ontological differences of the myth.

The bodily decorations of Piro people in ritual gatherings transform their everyday appearance into the appearance of jaguars. Everyday appearance is linked to *nshinikanchi*, the 'mind, memory, thought, love, respect' which

[29] When we got to Miaría, there were no *cushmas* for sale, but I did buy a beautiful painted skirt.

Plate 7. A girl painted for initiation ritual (photograph by Carlos Montenegro)

governs everyday relations among co-residents. Hosts and guests, however, are by definition not co-residents, and as they come together collectively, they appear towards each other in fully jaguar forms, to mark and effect the dangerous nature of their coming together. This exterior transformation is the product of *gimatkalchi*, 'knowledge', the knowledge of designs that women hold in their heads. It is the prelude to a further interior transformation, as hosts and guests begin to drink beer.

Why should hosts and guests wish to appear to each other as jaguars? The relations between hosts and guests, as residents of different villages, is necessarily marked by strain. As I have discussed in *Of Mixed Blood*, all Piro people are 'kinspeople' to each other, and all kinspeople should live together. Therefore, kinspeople who live in different villages are kinspeople with whom one by definition does not 'live well'. This is true in general, but it is also specifically true of specific people: other villages contain former co-residents, and their current residence apart is evidence of former disputes or dissatisfactions, and current ill-feeling. As the inhabitants of different villages come together in ritual gatherings, and in the consciousness of such ill-feeling, they present themselves to each other in transformed and beautified form as jaguars.

There is, however, a more powerful sense in which inhabitants of other villages can be jaguars. Shamans in other villages, because they are blamed for local cases of illness and death, are like jaguars, and may literally be jaguars. Artemio Fasabi, after commenting on how my new-painted *cushma* would make me look like a jaguar, told me the following myth,

Long ago, there was a man who was the only son of a woman with no husband. To support her, he would go into the forest, take off his *cushma*, and become a jaguar. In this form, he would wander in the forest, killing game. When he was finished he would put on his *cushma* again and become human once more, and take the game back to his mother. He brought her back collared peccary, deer, paca, everything.

The other people were envious, asking, 'How come this youth brings home so much meat?' They decided to follow him. The next time he went off to the forest, there was a group of men following and watching him.

They saw him take off his *cushma* and store it high up in a tree. They were horrified and said, 'What shall we do?' One said, 'Let's kill him,' but another man said, 'What for? We should just leave him alone.' From there, all of the sorcerers of today originate, because they did not kill that jaguar-man.

Such sorcerers, he went on to tell me, no longer exist, 'It was a thing of the old-time Piro people.' He then added,

The last was my late grandfather, Mañuco. He would become a jaguar and he had a jaguar wife, who lived in the forest. When the old man took *toé*, he would go off into the forest, paint himself with *achiote*, and wander about with his jaguar wife. Luckily, the Pentecostalist missionaries took him down to Chicosillo, where he died. If he had died in Huau, he would have killed off all the people there. As it is, there are many jaguars in Huau now.

Old Mañuco had died less than one year before Artemio told me this, and I had met him. Clearly, such things did not belong to a remote past.

What is the difference between the jaguar transformation of hosts and guests in rituals, and the jaguar transformation of shamans such as Old Mañuco? In the former case, this jaguar transformation is the product of women's knowledge of design, while the latter case is a product of self-painting: the former is necessarily a collective activity, the latter necessarily solitary. The difference is marked by the different paints involved, black *huito* in the former case, red *achiote* in the latter. Further, in the former transformation into a jaguar, the decorated people 'look like jaguars', while in the latter transformation, the person actually is a jaguar. Therefore the decoration with designs is a use of the illusion of jaguar appearance to mediate the hostility between different villages to produce ritual action, while the shaman's jaguar transformation is the use of the actual form of the jaguar to become this potent predator.

Piro women's designs have thus an apparently paradoxical quality. The knowledge of design differentiates Piro people from animals, by being a form of acquired knowledge, and one which is definitional of Piro humanity. But equally, the product of this knowledge is to transform many of the items closest to Piro people, including their own surfaces, into the appearance of animals. The resolution of the paradox lies, of course, in the temporality of design. At birth, humans lose their 'first design', the placenta, as a pre-condition of entering social life. In this, they become distinguished from the design-covered animals, which retain their intrinsic designs. However, the loss of the 'first design' becomes the possibility of 'human design' as a mode of social action; in women's ongoing acquisition of design knowledge over the life-course; in the repeated painting of the body for ritual gatherings; and in the constant 'fading' of designs over time. In the playing out of design over time, Piro people achieve what the jaguars lost in the mythic narrative, 'The Birth of Tsla', a social life.

The Transformations of Design

It would have been possible to have lived for a long time in a Piro village like Santa Clara in the 1980s without learning much about women's designs. They were relatively rarely seen: painting of the body with designs had virtually disappeared outside the rare girl's initiation rituals; old-style Piro clothing was very seldom worn; and much of the Piro-produced pottery had been replaced with imported aluminium, enamel, and plastic ware. It would have been easy to have imagined that 'human design' was disappearing totally from the Piro lived world.

Things are rather more complicated than this, for my analysis here of the importance of design in the Piro lived world is based on data collected in the 1980s and 1990s, and precisely in these villages in which so little of it was seen. My informants were happy to discuss it, and indeed to make 'design-covered' things when I expressed a desire for them. Indeed, many women asked me if I knew of any way for them to commercialize their production of such goods on a larger scale, and complained that they had so few local buyers; they contrasted their situation to that of Conibo and Shipibo women, down-river on the Ucayali, who have a large and well-organized market for their products (Lathrap 1976; Gebhart-Sayer 1984). Piro women wanted to make more, they told me, but lacked takers for their work.

Further, Piro design production in the 1980s and 1990s showed no major stylistic changes in relation to what can be told about it from photographs or objects collected early in this century or before. Significantly, of all the design-covered objects I have seen in old photographs or collections there is only one I have never seen as a recent product on the Bajo Urubamba, the design-painted paddle.[30] The range of the style is more restricted, but its internal dynamics seem to be the same. It is not becoming more 'decadent', for its formal rules do not seem to be changing.[31] We cannot, therefore, simply say that Piro design is disappearing, and mourn the loss of one more piece of human cultural diversity. Something else seems to be happening.

We can approach this problem by looking at the differential way in which design-bearing surfaces were being treated during the period of my fieldwork. The commonest design-covered objects in Piro villages in the 1980s and 1990s were painted manioc-beer fermenting pots, which were still regularly made. Painted beer-drinking bowls were made, but seldom used outside initiation ritual, and I only ever saw food bowls when Artemio's mother-in-law, Berna Zumaeta, made some at my request. Bead bracelets would undoubtedly have been more common had the beads been more available, for my gifts of beads always led to a flurry of beadwork making. Painted clothing was much rarer: painted bags were to be seen, but few men had painted robes, and only a few women had painted skirts for use in initiation ritual. As I have stated, I never saw design-painting on the body except during the one girl's initiation ritual I attended in 1981.

There is an interesting logic to this historical process: those objects most closely associated with the human bodily surface, and especially contact between surface and interior, are being replaced with non-design painted things. Thus, by the 1980s, painting the body with designs was virtually exclusively restricted to the infrequent girl's initiation rituals, and indeed to the body of the celebrant. Women's and men's painted clothing had gone the same way as had painted beer bowls. Only those design-painted forms peripheral to the human body, such as manioc-beer fermenting pots, painted bags, and bracelets, remained relatively common.[32]

The simple answer to this question is that, at the time of my fieldwork, Piro people habitually dressed in what they called *kajitu mkalu*, 'white people's clothing', or in Ucayali Spanish, *ropa legítima*, 'real clothing', and when they decorated themselves for festivals other than a girl's initiation ritual, and largely even then, they did so after the fashions of local white people. There were, therefore, far fewer opportunities for Piro women to practise their design knowledge on the bodies or clothing of other Piro people.

There is an apparent banality here, which could easily lead us astray. That indigenous Amazonian people inevitably start to wear 'Western clothes' is one of the clichés of the travel literature on the region, and of much of its ethnography

---

[30] Even in this case, however, I have seen paddles decorated with writing, which amounts to much the same thing.

[31] The Piro case seems to parallel closely the well-known Kadiwéu case (Ribeiro 1980; Lévi-Strauss 1976a; Siquiera Jr. 1992).

[32] On core–periphery relations of the human body in another indigenous Amazonian visual aesthetic system see Turner (1980; 1995).

for that matter. It is as obvious to the describers as it is unanalysed in its significance from the point of view of the indigenous people themselves. It is usually
assumed that it is to do with the fragility of the cultures of indigenous
Amazonian peoples, and their craven and pathetic desire to imitate the powerful white people who have come to live among them.[33]

Let us consider the question from the point of view of Piro people themselves, in the light of the foregoing analysis. I have argued that Piro people
originate in precisely the act by which external appearance and hidden interior
are differentiated, in the cutting of the umbilical cord. Deprived of the
placenta, the Piro neonate develops a hidden interior, which can be filled with
food by others, and a visible surface, on which the transforming *nshinikanchi*
can be registered as affect for others. That exterior surface is given to others as
the regular affability of *gwashata*, 'living well'. In certain circumstances,
however, when that external surface must be shown to those with whom one
does not 'live well', it must be beautified and transformed into something at
once terrifying and attractive: in short, into the form of a jaguar. In order to
avoid the danger of the absence of substantial intimacy with the other (as in the
scene of the delousing in 'The Birth of Tsla'), one must take on the attributes
of a beautiful and ferocious jaguar, the primordial Other of humanity.

Immanent within the myth is another possibility, for there are other Others
from whom such appearances can be borrowed. In the myth, these are Tsla's
'twins', the Muchkajine, and in the Piro lived world, the *kajine*, contemporary
'white people'. Where being painted with designs gives Piro people the appearance of beautiful jaguars, wearing *kajitu mkalu*, 'white people's clothing' gives
Piro people the appearance of 'white people'. There is a major shift in potential here, for while design-painted clothing only makes people look like jaguars,
because actual jaguar clothing is socially inimical (the jaguar shaman), 'white
people's clothing' not only makes people look like 'white people' but is also
actually made by white people. Here the appearance of the other derives from
actual peaceful contact with those others, while, in the case of jaguar appearance, it must pass through the complicated processes by which Piro women
learn and produce 'human design'.

'White people's clothing', as evidence of a peaceful exchange relationship
with white people, is informed by the myth 'Tsla swallowed by a Giant
Catfish', which, as I argued in the preceding chapter, is the Piro 'myth of
history'. Thus, wearing 'white people's clothing' locates Piro people within a
process of transforming generations via transforming relations with changing
kinds of 'white people'. It renders 'white people' and their things (*gejnu*, 'fine
things') productive in the interior of the Piro lived world.

I would not claim that my argument here is a historical one, and I would
never suggest that the reason Piro people currently wear 'white people's cloth-

[33] But see Veber (1996) and S. Hugh-Jones [1992].

ing' is because of the myth, 'Tsla swallowed by a Giant Catfish'. This argument cannot be historical for the simple reason that the earliest known versions of this myth date from the late 1940s, by which time Piro people had largely shifted to 'white people's clothing' (see Matteson 1954, and Ch. 7, below). As I have constantly reiterated, historical arguments depend on historical evidence. Here my argument is based on networks of meanings between apparently disparate practices in the Piro lived world, and largely based on data collected over a short period, from 1980 to 1995. It cannot be reliably extrapolated back to the distant past. At most, I can claim that my analysis makes sense of the way Piro people were acting and thinking in the 1980s, including about their own known past.

But the change in the clothing of the Piro must be read more as a transformation than as a profound cultural change of the kind invoked by theorists of acculturation. This is because white people also have designs. *Kajitu yona*, 'white people's design', is writing. By coming to wear 'white people's clothing', Piro people have lost an important surface for design-painting, but have developed the imperative of another order. They must learn 'white people's design', by going to school. As I have discussed in depth elsewhere, Piro people send their children to school, to learn white people's knowledge, in order to be able to 'defend themselves' from those same white people (Gow 1991: 230–325). How this came to be will be the subject of later chapters.

Even more, given the meanings of design in the Piro lived world, discussed here, this transformation is in fact the transformation of a transformation. The painting of design, and the changing of clothing, is invested with the meanings of a general transformation of visual appearance, and the mode in which people are seen by others, as we saw in Chapter 2 in relation to 'A Man who went under the Earth'. From outside the Piro lived world, the progressive abandonment of Piro design and old-style clothing looks like the abandonment of a traditional set of meanings for a new and alien set of meanings. Seen from within the Piro lived world, these changes are a new mode of transformation of a prior mode of transformation. As such, there is a meaningful relationship between the two modes of transformation, and hence meaningfulness inheres in the transformations themselves.

This meaningfulness is important, for Piro people did not share with me any apparent nostalgia for what we both considered to be a beautiful material culture. I was constantly bewildered or appalled by Piro people's lack of interest in these things, as other visitors to the area had been before me (see Gow 1991: 285; Matthiessen 1962; Huxley and Capa 1965). The casual visitor sees Piro people dressed in 'Western clothes', but cannot see how that clothing is meaningful from within the manner in which Piro people see things. The casual visitor literally cannot see all the complex relations between Piro people and jaguars, and anacondas, and white people, and so on, which alone render this appearance, in 'Western dress', both meaningful and desirable to Piro people.

This point came out in a conversation I once had with Artemio. He was again bemoaning his financial situation, the constant gap between demands on him for money, and his ability to get hold of it. He tried to elucidate his situation as follows, as much for himself as for me, 'The things we really need are these, soap and salt. Without salt, our food has no taste. And without soap to wash ourselves and our clothes, we would stink worse than dogs!' Food and shelter were not on Artemio's list, for any local person could fish in the river, make a garden for plantains and manioc, and build a house, out of materials that lay immediately to hand. Knowing how to do these things was the common knowledge of local indigenous people, and the raw materials were at their front doors. Artemio was referring strictly to necessities which Piro people could not provide for themselves, the things they required from white people. Significantly, Artemio's list contained an element for the interior of the body, salt, and one for the exterior, soap.

This was something that has taken me a long time to understand, for it seemed to me then that there were many things people like Artemio could have made, but did not. Piro people in the 1950s knew how to make soap from forest plants,[34] and their ancestors had traded salt from *Cerro de la Sal* ('The Salt Mountain') on the Perené river.[35] Piro women knew how to make beautiful pottery and weave beautiful clothing, but they did so very seldom, and expected their husbands to buy them aluminium pans and clothes for themselves and their children.

Following on from his listing of the necessary 'fine things', Artemio had added a new item: 'We also need to buy clothing, we can't live naked like the forest people.' I asked him why they could not make and wear the woven cotton robes and skirts of their ancestors, given that money was so tight and the means of acquiring it were so difficult. He said, 'Well, perhaps we could wear *cushmas*, like the old time Piro people, I suppose.' His tone was reflective, as if he had never before considered this option, and was intrigued by its possibilities. He paused, briefly lost in thought. He soon shifted mood, and continued vehemently, 'But we are not like that anymore! We have become accustomed to the fine things! We have become civilized. Our wives are now too lazy to weave, now they want us to buy them clothing!'

Artemio's attribution of laziness to contemporary Piro women is part of a general sense that the 'old time Piro people' were stronger, tougher, and harder working than their descendants. More importantly, however, the laziness of the women was here entirely justified, for it reflected a desire for store-bought clothing, a desire shared by Piro men, even if they found its satisfaction irksome. These desires were markers of contemporary Piro people's status as 'civilized people', in contrast to the forest-dwelling ancestors.

---

[34] See Matteson (1954: 48) In the crisis year of 1988, this knowledge was actively being discussed again in Santa Clara.
[35] See Tibesar (1950) and Renard-Casevitz (1993).

As I discussed at length in *Of Mixed Blood*, 'being civilized' mattered to Piro people in the 1980s because it stood for, and was the product of, a long historical process of transforming relationships to different kinds of white people. These relationships were, Piro people told me, initiated through the rubber bosses' enslavement of the 'ancient people', continuing in enslavement to the owners of the *haciendas*, through the 'liberation from slavery' when the SIL and Dominican missionaries arrived, to the creation of contemporary villages with schools and legal title to land. To be 'civilized' was to live in this kind of relationship to white people, in contrast to the prior state of ignorance and slavery. Simultaneously, the process of 'becoming civilized' generated the kin relations of contemporary Piro people, in the cycling of generations which generated new people, new kin ties and new villages. This was the force of Artemio's statement, 'But we are not like that anymore! We have become accustomed to the fine things!'

Contemporary Piro people could not wear the clothing of the 'ancient people' because they were made in different circumstances and different social relations. The 'ancient Piro people' wore locally-produced cotton robes and skirts because they did not have good exchange relations with white people, and hence relied on their own manufactures. Contemporary people, with access to money from lumbering and other activities, have both the desire for 'fine things' like white people's clothing, and the potential to satisfy those desires. The fact that they have 'become accustomed' to such things marks the temporal distance between themselves and the 'ancient people', and the ongoing transformation of relations to white people.

As I have noted, my analysis here is not properly a historical one, for I deal only with how Piro people talked about these issues in the 1980s and 1990s. In Chapter 7, I explore the historical evidence in more depth. One point, however, is clear. Piro clothing, whether the old-style, hand-woven and painted with designs or the new styles bought from white people, has dense meanings for Piro people, and the shift from old-style clothing and 'human design' to 'white people's clothing' and 'white people's design' is also meaningful to them. Indeed, these meanings are available to them from the mythic narratives about Tsla. If the role of 'human design' in Piro social life gains meaning from the mythic narrative which recounts the loss of the jaguar's social life, then the role of 'white people's design' and 'white people's clothing' gains meaning from the opposition implied in the myth between the Muchkajine, the 'Long Ago White People', and the *kajine*, the 'white people' of today. The shift in clothing, which looked to me and to other visitors like the loss of a culture and all the meanings it had contained, appears, from within the Piro lived world, as a change in the valences of relationship, rather than in the systems of meanings as such. These shifts are changes, it is true, but they are more importantly transformations, and therein lie their meaning and their meaningfulness.

5

Hallucination

In this chapter, I analyse the second of the Piro 'myths of myth' mentioned in Chapter 3: 'The Kochmaloto Women'. This continues my account of how Piro people think of their humanity, but now in relation to powerful beings and in the use of hallucinogens. Hallucinatory experience is a common and important feature of the Piro lived world, and articulates clearly the role of point of view in Piro conceptions of their condition as humans. At the end of this chapter, I discuss a recent change in Piro shamanic cosmology, which parallels the change in design discussed in the previous chapter.

'The Kochmaloto Women'

On the same evening that he told me 'The Birth of Tsla', discussed in the preceding chapter, Antonio told me the following version of 'The Kochmaloto Women'.

There were people who lived alone in the forest, a man and his wife and their two daughters. A man came there, he was an anaconda, but he looked like a man. He became the Kochmaloto's lover. She had a child. This child was a human baby, but when it slept it became an anaconda.

The grandmother was holding the baby in her skirt, swinging in her hammock, and she fell asleep, and the baby slept too. Then she awoke and saw the snake curled up on her skirt. In her fright, she let the baby fall, into the fire . . .

Teresa added, 'Long ago, my fellow tribespeople slept in hammocks with their fires underneath, just like the Amahuaca people.'[1]

. . . the baby turned back into a human and cried. Then his anaconda grandmother came and took the child to the river port, where there was a big pool. They went down into the pool. The child could be heard crying inside the pool.

He came back and gave his mother a *huito* seed, a *nso gonru* seed[2] and told her to plant it and tell him when it was big.

When it was big, a flood came, and the Kochmaloto sisters went up into the tree. The water rose and the grandfather of the anaconda child went up on to the platform of his house. The Kochmaloto sisters beat the tree with a stick, and it grew. The water rose higher, and the grandfather went up into the roof of his house. The water rose higher and higher, and he drowned.

---

[1] Contemporary Piro people sleep either on the platform floor of the house, or in beds set on that floor. Hammocks (Piro, *shechi*; Ucayali Spanish, *hamaca*) are made for babies to sleep in during the day, and may be so used by older children and adults, but many Piro houses have no hammocks.

[2] A variety of *Genipa spp.*, the fruit used in producing body paint.

The Kochmaloto sisters came down from the tree and went off in search of people. They walked through the forest. Scha, a forest spirit,[3] and his brother-in-law were hunting. From high up the brother-in-law smelt the Kochmaloto sister, and said, 'I can smell Kochmaloto!' He told Scha to grab them, but the Kochmaloto sisters put a stick in his hand. He was angry because his brother-in-law made him grab the stick.

The Kochmaloto sisters travelled on, and came to where the grey-necked wood rail[4] was fishing. The wood rail was roasting *makna* (a cultivated potato species),[5] and he said, 'I can smell Kochmaloto.' He called to the *makna*, 'Are you cooked yet?' 'Not yet,' it replied. The Kochmaloto sisters ate the *makna*. The wood rail asked, 'Are you cooked yet?', and the *makna* replied, 'They've eaten me!' The wood rail came running, and the Kochmaloto sisters ran off. But the *makna* hurt them from inside, and they threw up as they went along, vomiting it all up.

They came to the agouti's house. They were now near humans, but they didn't know. The agouti was a woman, and she was making manioc beer. The Kochmaloto sisters asked her where she got her manioc from, and she lied to them, saying, 'From where the sun goes in,' but she really got it from nearby.

Her husband the razor-billed currasow[6] came now, and said, 'A thorn got into my foot.' He asked the Kochmaloto to pull it out. But she pulled out the vein of his foot, for the foot of the currasow is just veins. He screamed and flew off, crying, '*Ko, ko, ko!*', he became the currasow as we know it today, he was no longer human.

The Kochmaloto sisters went on, and came to the village of real humans. There they lived, but they did not last long, they were very weak. One was killed when a manioc beer strainer fell on her, the other was killed by a falling *bijao* leaf.

As I have already discussed in Chapter 3, this myth bears some marked similarities to the myth analysed in the preceding chapter, 'The Birth of Tsla': in both we have an initial situation of a sexual relationship between a woman and an animal, a crucial intervention by a grandmother in the fate of a grandchild or grandchildren, and then a series of adventures involving a set of siblings. Where, in 'The Birth of Tsla', the action pivots on relations between humans and jaguars, in 'The Kochmaloto Women', the narrative revolves around human relationships with that other dangerous animal, the anaconda.

Piro people fear anacondas as much, and even perhaps more, than they fear jaguars. Contacts with anacondas necessarily occur largely in rivers, where the opacity of the waters of Urubamba mainstream obscures all visual contact with the predator. The only clue they offer of their presence is the rippling of the surface as they move in the depths. While I have never heard of anyone killed or even seriously injured by an anaconda, they represent a pervasive uncanny danger. As with jaguars, anacondas are also a handy weapon in the hands of adults for scaring children. The cry, 'Look out, anaconda!', can rapidly curtail

---

[3] Antonio said *gente de monte*. See Gow (1991) for discussion of this term.

[4] Piro, *gogru*; Ucayali Spanish, *unchala*; Lat. *Aramides cajanea*.

[5] Ucayali Spanish, *sacha papa*, lit. 'forest potato', a variety of large potato grown by Piro people.

[6] Piro, *giyeka*; Ucayali Spanish, *paujil*; Lat. *Mitu mitu*.

an over-extended play session in the river, where children can fall victims to the more impalpable river demons.

Like jaguars, as I have noted before, certain anacondas are also *kayonalu*, 'covered in designs', and hence share the potent beauty of this attribute. There is, however, a key difference between the two species: like all snakes, but unlike jaguars, anacondas are said to be immortal, 'they do not know how to die'. This is because all snakes shed their skins and become young again. In the case of anacondas, this takes on a more powerful form, for as one man told me, 'Anacondas are hard to kill! They do not know how to die. If you cut them in half, they just join up again and go on living. You have to burn them.' Don Mauricio told me the same, commenting, 'If an anaconda grabs you, there is no use cutting it with a machete. It just joins up again. No, you have to bite it. Our teeth are poisonous to anacondas, because of the salt we eat. It's hard, but it's the only way to save yourself if an anaconda attacks you. You must bite it!' Jaguars are never attributed such powers, and can be killed like other game animals. In that sense, jaguars share humans' mortal condition. Anacondas do not.

There are further connections and key differences between the two 'myths of myth'. Jaguars and anacondas are emblematic of the two major categories of non-human space in the immediate Piro lived world: the forest and river (see discussion in Gow 1991: 72–81). Tsla's mother becomes lost in the forest, and hence lives out the disastrous consequences of inappropriate contact with the forest-dwelling jaguars, while in 'The Kochmaloto Women', the grand-mother's mistreatment of her anaconda grandchild causes her and the others to live out the disastrous consequences of her daughter's inappropriate contact with the aquatic anaconda, in an extreme form of river flooding. Further, in both myths, a paint-producing plant, whether *achiote* and *huito*, plays a key mediatory role.

Having survived the flood, the Kochmaloto Women go off in search of people, and meet a series of animals and other beings who act as if they were human. When finally the Kochmaloto Women arrive in the village of real humans, they die quickly, and for trivial reasons. This inverts the ending of 'The Birth of Tsla', when Tsla and the Muchkajine murder the jaguars, in a demonstration of Tsla's miraculous powers, in his ability to die and resuscitate, and do the same for others. Here, there is an opposition between the extreme weakness and fragility of the Kochmaloto Women, and the power and durability of Tsla.[7]

The end of 'The Kochmaloto Women' also calls to mind the conclusion to the cycle of Tsla myths, in the ending of 'Tsla swallowed by a Giant Catfish'. Tsla and the Muchkajine hear the *maknawlo* bird calling, and Tsla decides that

---

[7] The Kochmaloto Women are killed by lightweight instruments of domestic life: they cannot endure even the softest of domestic implements.

they must leave the Urubamba, because this is an omen of death. As I noted in Chapter 3, this 'land of death' is the Piro lived world, which is marked by the mortality of Piro people. Further, 'The Kochmaloto Women' specifies that the Kochmaloto Women died only after they had finally arrived in the village of the 'real people', that is, of Piro people. Taking these three myths together, we find that there are three kinds of mortality here: there is the death-defying miraculousness of Tsla, the ordinary mortality of Piro people, and the extreme mortality of the Kochmaloto Women. These mythic narratives mark ordinary human mortality as, ideally, a mid-point between Tsla's immortality and the extreme mortality of the Kochmaloto Women.

I have already shown that the problem of mortality is important for an understanding of 'A Man who went under the Earth', and other versions of the peccary myth. In those myths, the problem of mortality is addressed as one of how the dead experience death as an ongoing transformation, and how this is metaphorized for humans through the point of view of the white-lipped peccaries. I suggested there that 'A Man who went under the Earth' and the other variants raise the problem of post-mortem destination as a question, by asserting that it is like the known answer to another question: where do dead white-lipped peccaries go? The answer to that question is the stomachs of living Piro people. The situation of the Kochmaloto Women is similar: they die easily when they finally find their goal, a village of real people.

To Transform

There is a further connection between the myth of the white-lipped peccaries and that of 'The Kochmaloto Women'. In 'A Man who went under the Earth', the main character survives among the white-lipped peccaries by taking on their appearance through putting on their clothing. In 'The Kochmaloto Women', the main characters survive as long as they do not meet 'real people'. This raises an issue which is emphasized by Sebastián in a version of this myth in *Gwacha Ginkakle*. He concludes with the words, *Wa satumnu koxgima manewyeginatanatkana. Wale chinangima gi shikgipukanatkana*, 'Various beings had appeared before them in human bodily form. That is why they did not live very long' (Sebastián, Zumaeta, and Nies 1974: 68 and 88).

The verb *manewyegita*, translated here as 'to appear in human bodily form in front of someone', literally means 'to come to have a body in the presence of another'.[8] The root *mane-* refers to the body as substantiality, as opposed to the invisibility or insubstantiality of powerful beings, as discussed below: I here use the term 'powerful being' (from Basso 1985) for any entity which can be

---

[8] It is related to the notion of foetal growth, *manewata*, 'to form a body'. Obviously, foetal growth is hidden, while *manewyegita* is by definition seen by another. See Gregor (1977: 321) and Viveiros de Castro (1978) for discussion of cognate terms in Maipuran languages of the Upper Xingú area.

identified as 'human' in shamanic discourse. As I noted in Chapter 2, the verb *gemaneta*, means 'to metamorphose, to be transformed, to be renewed in body', and there is a cognate term, *gimanga*, with the same meaning.

This theme is central to 'The Kochmaloto Women'. In Antonio's version, the anaconda was an anaconda, 'but he looked like a man'. In Sebastián's version, the Kochmaloto Women find a small anaconda which they decide to raise as a pet. As it grew big, '*manewyeegimatatkana*', 'it transformed, it is said', into a young man, whom they married (Sebastián, Zumaeta, and Nies 1974: 54 and 70). The same theme is central to the scene with the grandmother. Matteson's informant stated, of the grandmother's experience as she awakes to see her grandson on her lap, *Rumangagimata . . . ¡Mapchiritaa!*, 'He had changed form, it is said . . . He was really an anaconda! (1951: 54 and 57). Such transformations lie at the heart of this mythic narrative, but they do not, of themselves, seem to present any dangers. It is only when the Kochmaloto Women return to live with 'real humans' that this experience of seeing non-humans take on different bodies causes them to die. Why should this seeing of animals as human have been so dangerous for the Kochmaloto Women when they returned to humanity?

As I discussed in Chapter 2, 'transformation', in the sense of 'coming to have a new body', is not in itself considered dangerous by Piro people: the 'transformation' of an ant into a bromeliad, or a tortoise into a snake, is intriguing to see, but not dangerous. However, 'transformation' from animal into human, changing an animal body for a human body, is of a different order. As I noted in Chapter 2, the statement 'He/she/it is human' (Piro, '*Yinerni*'; Ucayali Spanish, '*Es gente*'), when made with regard to an entity which is normally either invisible or non-human, marks entry into a specifically shamanic discourse. For example, as Artemio told me, white-lipped peccaries are people, because they know how to cause illness: humans experience the 'humanity' of these animals as personal affliction. However, as Artemio also told me, shamans can, by taking drugs, actually see the white-lipped peccaries as humans in the underworld. And, of course, it is the perceptual transformation of a man into a white-lipped peccary through a change of clothing which lies at the heart of the mythic narrative, 'A Man who went under the Earth'.

In 'The Kochmaloto Women', the stress is on the transformation of animals into humans during the Kochmaloto Women's wanderings. When they finally reach 'real humans', they cannot endure, and die quickly. It would seem then that the Kochmaloto Women can withstand seeing animals in their transformed bodily form of humans, but they cannot withstand seeing real people in their normal bodily form of humans. Their sexual congress with the anaconda man, and subsequent solicitude for the anaconda child, it would seem, radically strengthen them for their subsequent contacts with supernatural beings in human bodily form, but radically weaken them for contact with real humans. Does this correspond to anything in the everyday Piro lived world? It corresponds to two sides of shamanry: shamanic action and illness. The radical strengthening of the Kochmaloto Women corresponds to the strengthening of shamans, those who see and address the powerful beings as humans. The radical weakening of the Kochmaloto Women corresponds to the weakening of humans through illness, which opens them to delusional experiences (see Gow 1991: 180–3). The Kochmaloto Women combine, in a single state, the condition of humans as shamans and as sick people.

Indeed, 'The Kochmaloto Women' would seem to be a Piro myth about shamanry, or, at least, about a key feature of shamanry, hallucinatory experience. There are three aspects to this. Firstly, hallucinatory experience is closely identified with anacondas and the aquatic realm. Secondly, seeing other beings as people is a key motivation for entry into a hallucinatory state. And thirdly, shamanry is directed to the prolongation of the life of a sick person, that is, one who is close to demonstrating the fragility of the Kochmaloto Women. It is to hallucinatory experience and shamanry that I turn next.

Illness and its Cure

The events of hallucinatory experience are powerful, even for those not participating. When people take *ayahuasca* (Piro: *kamalampi*), which they always do at night, the quiet village fills first with the sound of retching and vomiting, then with the eerily beautiful whistling and singing of the drug songs. These nights of shamanry must be a very powerful experience for Piro children, for people told me, 'When the shamans take *ayahuasca*, babies don't cry and dogs don't bark'. In my experience this was true. Even more dramatic is the taking of *toé* (Piro, *gayapa*): here the taker rambles through the forest, and occasionally enters the village to talk incoherently and behave bizarrely. Close kinspeople paint their faces with the black dye *huito*, in order that the drinker cannot recognize them. Others avoid the drinker totally.

Most use of hallucinogens is linked to specific acts of curing, for shamans take hallucinogens in order to see: to see the illness in a patient's body, and to see the track of its causes. For Piro people, illness is a subversion of *gwashata*, 'living well', and is marked by a progressive withdrawal from other people. Sick people lie all day hidden in their mosquito nets, because they are 'ugly' (Piro, *mugletu*; Ucayali Spanish, *feo*): illness renders a person unpleasant to look at, and hence unwilling to be seen. This removal from the sight of other co-residents is associated by Piro people with approaching death, which is a more radical subversion of *gwashata* and transformation of personal appearance. Sick people become, in an idiom discussed before, 'tired of living'. To prevent this, shamans must take hallucinogens in order to see the illness itself, hidden by the ordinary opacity of the human body.

The most extreme form of hallucinatory experience as a new way of seeing is in the use of *toé*. This drug, of the *Brugmansia* family and usually known in

English as 'Angel's Trumpet',[9] is used much less than *ayahuasca*, but is said to be much more powerful. It is drunk in two situations: by shamans seeking to build up or to maintain their powers, or by people on the verge of death from serious illnesses, as the medicine of extreme last resort (Gow 1991: 272–4). I was told that when shamans admit defeat in their attempt to cure a patient, they may prescribe that the patient drink *toé*, and be cured directly by the 'mother of *toé*', Ucayali Spanish, *toemama* (Piro: *gayapa-ginro*, '*toé* mother', or *nato*, an archaic term for 'mother'), who is a powerful shaman.

Toé experience is feared by Piro people, and they are as afraid of drinking this drug as they are of another person who has drunk it. However, *toé* hallucinatory experience is not, itself, characterized by fear. None of my informants described being afraid as they entered this state or during it. Instead, *toé* hallucinatory experience is described as a rapid and profound transformation of the world. The dominant affect here is perhaps best described as wonder. Pablo Rodriguez, who had taken *toé* several times, described it to me as follows, 'After you drink *toé*, you lie down. Nothing happens. Then you feel a little thirsty, your throat is dry. You ask for water. Then suddenly, everything lights up, as if the sun had risen. Then you are drunk, you see everything through *toé*.'

The metaphorization of *toé* hallucinatory experience as 'daylight' is common. Here, the rapidity of the transition between everyday perceptual experience and hallucinatory experience is likened to the speed of the transition between night and day in this tropical latitude. Other informants insistently emphasized the 'redness' of *toé* hallucinatory experience, 'just like the world at dawn', or, 'at sunset'. We have of course met this changed vision before, in Artemio's story 'A Man who went under the Earth', for this was the experience of the main character as he returned to the upper world.

When *toé* is taken for curing, the patient is cured directly by the mother spirit of the drug, for *toé* is drunk entirely alone. Nobody can or should attempt to talk to, or in any other way interact with, someone in *toé* hallucinatory experience. As one man put it, 'When you drink *toé*, you are completely alone. It is just you and the mother of *toé*.' If the drinker is weak, he or she will be locked up in the enclosed room of a house. If healthy, the drinker is allowed to roam freely. I was consistently told that the drinker would tear off all his clothes and then disappear far off into the forest for several days. Throughout the hallucinatory experience, the drinker travels with the 'mother of *toé*', who offers the drinker curing and killing powers, and shows all the things he or she wants to see. The mother spirit takes the drinker into the villages and houses of powerful beings where they eat the best of foods and drink the finest of liquors.

Pablo Rodriguez told me the following, of his own experiences, 'When you take *toé*, you do not walk on the ground like this. You walk above the ground, up here [he indicated with his hand a level about two feet in the air]. You are

---

[9] It was formerly assigned to the *Datura* family.

light, you have no body.' Clearly, Pablo was referring here to his own experience in the hallucinatory state, not that of other people looking at him. For other people, the drinker most definitely does have a body. When a person drinks *toé*, his or her close kin paint their faces black with *huito* paint, and avoid working. The face paint prevents the drinker from recognizing them.

Pablo's wife Sara explained this practice to me as follows, 'It's like this. Someone who takes *toé* knows everything, he knows when we are going to get sick and when we are going to die. He sees us like *callampa* (Ucayali Spanish: tree fungus), all rotten. In order that he does not see us like that, we paint our faces with *huito*.' I did not understand, so Pablo expanded, saying, '*Callampa* is that which grows on rotten trees, that thing you eat cooked in leaves. It's really white, and *toé* makes us see everybody like *callampa*. For that reason, perhaps, people paint their faces black with *huito*.' The taker of *toé* 'knows everything', and therefore sees Piro people's mortality, their general condition, as the ugly pallor of their faces. This sight, which evokes pity in the drinker, is actually the drinker's fault.

What the *toé* drinker is seeing is the future fatal illness which his or her gaze inflicts upon others in the transformed state of *toé* hallucinatory experience.[10] *Toé* hallucinatory experience therefore operates like a radical denial of co-residence, where mutual seeing and helping are desirable and necessary to ongoing life. A kinsperson in *toé* hallucinatory experience no longer acts like a human, but like a malign powerful being. What Pablo told me about having 'no body' refers to the world as seen by the drinker. The drinker becomes a powerful being like the mother of *toé*, and so experiences the world through the perceptual apparatus of a powerful being. As I discuss below, such powerful beings do not, in any simple sense, have bodies. What Pablo was describing was what it feels like not to be human.

This feature of *toé* hallucinatory experience has been met with before, since it is identical to the experience of the main character in 'A Man who went under the Earth', when he returns to this world after transforming into a white-lipped peccary. I argued in Chapter 2 that this man is, from the point of view of his wife and children, dead, and that the myth deals with the perceptual experiences of the dead. From the perspective of *toé* hallucinatory experience, we can refine that analysis: the visual oddness of the new experienced world is linked to the ontological marginality of the experiencer, poised between living humanity and otherness. *Toé* experience also elucidates the episode in Sebastián's 'The Sun', when the wood storks say of the man, 'Here is one who has thrown his clothing away.' This is what the drinker of *toé* does at the onset of hallucinatory experience, and marks the transition from 'having a body' (being human) and 'not having a body' (being a powerful being). As we have seen, the loss of human clothing initiated the new life of the main character in 'A Man who went under the Earth'.

---

[10] Similarly, if they do any work, the drinker will try to help them. This help is disastrous.

Toé, as I have stated, is relatively seldom taken by Piro people, and many will have had no personal experience of its hallucinatory state. By contrast, virtually all adult Piro people I met, and many children, had taken *ayahuasca*, and many had taken it often. *Ayahuasca* is said by everyone to be, 'very good for you'. The only people it is bad for are foetuses, for *ayahuasca* causes pregnant women to miscarry. *Ayahuasca* is a vine, belonging to the *Banisteriopsis* genus, and occurs in both wild and domesticated forms. Unlike *toé*, which is consumed raw, *ayahuasca* is always consumed cooked. Further, *ayahuasca* must be cooked with the leaves of the bush *chacrona* (Piro, *gorowa*) before it is ingested.[11]

Ayahuasca is taken much more frequently than *toé*, and its hallucinatory state is much less feared. However, people who would happily discuss their own or other people's experiences of *toé* were reluctant to discuss the specific content of *ayahuasca* experience except in very general terms. This may be because it is it is so much more generally experienced by Piro people: anyone who wants to know about *ayahuasca* experience has ample opportunity to do so, while *toé* experience is rare. Most of my account here is therefore based on Piro people's replies to questions I asked about my own experiences of *ayahuasca* hallucinatory state.

A *ayahuasca* session starts when a shaman announces that he (or, much less often, she) will prepare the drug and when he will take it. He asks others if they want to drink it: no pressure is applied, and anyone who wants to simply turns up at the shaman's house at nightfall. Those who want to drink it avoid eating game or drinking alcohol, and should not be either menstruating or have recently had sex. The session begins an hour or two after nightfall, as the shaman smokes his pipe, for the scent of tobacco attracts powerful beings. He begins to blow on to the *ayahuasca* pot, to 'animate' the potion. He then pours a cup for himself, blows smoke on to it, and asks the mother of *ayahuasca*, called in Ucayali Spanish, *ayahuascamama* (Piro, *kamalampi-ginro*, 'ayahuasca mother', or *nato*, an archaic Piro term of address for 'mother') to help in curing the patient, and to give 'good hallucinations' to all those drinking. He drinks the bowl, then repeats this for each other person. Having drunk, participants settle down to await the beginning of the hallucinatory state, and in the meantime chat, joke quietly, and smoke their pipes or cigarettes.

The first sign of the onset of the *ayahuasca* hallucinatory state is the sound of wind rushing through the forest, and then little lights appear, glittering in the dark. This is accompanied by a feeling of fear and nausea, and as the hallucinatory experience intensifies, these feelings are transformed and become more concrete as giant, brightly-coloured anacondas slither up from the

---

[11] Carlos Montenegro (personal communication), who conducted fieldwork in the community of Sepahua in the 1970s, was told that *ayahuasca* is the 'mother', and *chacrona* the 'father', of the resultant hallucinatory experience.

ground, wrapping themselves around the drinker, tightening their grip, and then forcing their tails into the drinker's mouth, twisting down into the stomach (see Artemio's account in Ch. 1). The nausea and fear increase exponentially, leading to violent vomiting and often diarrhoea. This experience, Piro people constantly told me, makes the drinkers want to scream out loud in terror, because they fear that they are going mad, or dying. Awful as this experience is, it is a lie, *taylota*, 'she lies' (Ucayali Spanish, '*es mentira*'). The shaman, accompanied by other people who know how, gather their courage up just as it becomes unbearable, and begin to sing. These songs tame the mother of *ayahuasca*, she calms down and reveals herself sitting in the house, a beautiful woman singing her own songs. More people arrive, powerful beings, and they sing too. These are the real hallucinations (Piro, *kayigawlu*), and with them and their songs, the drinker begins to see paths, villages, cities and distant countries. Shamans begin to see the sorcery objects glowing in the patient's bodies, and to see the sorcerers and their motives. They blow tobacco smoke and begin to suck at the sorcery objects. Intense fear gives way to state of reverie, wherein the drinkers travel and meet new people: as Julian Miranda put it, 'You feel like you can fly and go anywhere you want!' The hallucinatory experience cycles in and out of the horrific and serene phases, gradually fading into a quiet elation which continues for at least another day.

When I asked Piro people why they liked to take *ayahuasca*, they gave two characteristic replies. Firstly, they said that it was good to vomit, and that *ayahuasca* cleansed the body of the residues of game that had been eaten. These accumulate over time, causing a generalized malaise and tiredness, and eventually a desire to die. *Ayahuasca* expels these from the body, and makes the drinker feel vital and youthful again.[12] Secondly, people told me that it was good to take *ayahuasca* because it makes you see: as one man put it, 'You can see everything, everything.'

This combination of a violent transformation of the bodily interior and a transformation of perceptual experience is similar to that of Piro birth ritual, discussed in the last chapter. There, the neonate is separated into two by the cutting of the umbilical cord, which provides the baby with an interior that can be filled with food. Where, in the womb, the foetus was surrounded by the placenta, which is its own interior guts, through birth ritual it comes to be surrounded by its future co-residents, its kinspeople-to-be. *Ayahuasca* hallucinatory experience effects a similar transformation in the drinkers. *Ayahuasca* empties the bodily interior of its normal contents, and transforms the perceptual surrounding of the drinkers away from the everyday experience of this known house and these known kinspeople. Initially, the surroundings are transformed in a terrifying way: the drinkers are wrapped in brightly-coloured and design-covered anacondas which then force themselves into the bodily interior.

---

[12] See Mentore (1993) for a discussion of vomiting as 'anti-eating' among the Wai-Wai.

This horrifying experience is a prelude to the cleansing of the bodily interior, which then, in combination with the shaman's songs, leads to a transformation of the surroundings into the sight of 'everything'.

There are two points worth making about this similarity. Firstly, the anaconda phase of *ayahuasca* hallucinatory experience is an intensified experience of design, much as the foetus is surrounded by its *geyonchi*, 'first design', in the womb. In both cases, it is the disappearance of this all-encompassing design which leads to the perception of other things: the everyday world in the case of the baby, and 'everything' in the case of drinkers of *ayahuasca*. Secondly, both cases are mediated by a liquid: the mother's milk, *chochga*, in the case of the baby, and *ayahuasca* itself in the case of *ayahuasca* hallucinatory experience. Indeed, cooked *ayahuasca* is frequently called *natga* in Piro, 'mother's liquid', (in Ucayali Spanish, '*leche de la madre*').

From this perspective, we can see *ayahuasca* hallucinatory experience as bound up with the processes which, from the point of view of any given Piro person, provide the basis for his or her social world, the treatment he or she received at birth. *Ayahuasca* hallucinatory experience is the pre-condition for another kind of social life in which, instead of seeing one's own village and its inhabitants, one sees everything. To continue with the analysis, I explore further the state I have here termed 'hallucinatory experience', and which Piro people call *gimru*, 'drunkenness'.

Drunkenness

In Piro, the hallucinatory state of consciousness is called *gimru* (Ucayali Spanish, *borrachera*, *mareación*). As such, it is grouped together with other forms of sensory-motor disruption, such as the dizziness caused by ingesting tobacco, the drunkenness of beer or *gawarinti* (Spanish, *cashasa* or *aguardiente*, 'cane alcohol'), and certain effects of strong sun, illness, and other things. All these states are *gimru*. Unlike English, which in classifying altered states of consciousness separates out sensory-motor disruption from specific delusional states such as having hallucinations, and hence distinguishes the effects of alcohol from those of mescaline, Piro and Ucayali Spanish focus on the broad similarity of these relatively expansive states of altered consciousness. In this sense, Piro hallucinatory experiences might legitimately be classified as non-hallucinogenic, insofar as hallucinations are not the key feature of its classification.[13] For this reason, I here translate *gimru* as 'drunkenness', with the obvious caveat that this English term does not necessarily evoke the full meanings of the Piro term.

---

[13] A point worth making here is that *gimru* is not held, by Piro people, to have any significant qualities in common with 'dreaming' (*gipnawata*) or 'dreaming about' (*gipjeta*). Piro people do not connect 'dreaming' and 'drunkenness' as experiential states. The only exception to this is dreaming mediated by *toé*: smoking a shaman's pipe which has been cooked in *toé*, or sleeping with *toé* leaves under one's head, leads to hallucinatory dreams which are held to be experiences of reality.

A key point here is that 'drunkenness', in general, is both assigned an exterior cause and is a disruption of *nshinikanchi*, 'mind, love, respect, memory'. 'Drunkenness' subverts *nshinikanchi*, and this takes two main forms, both based on consumption. The first is the consumption of beer or *cashasa*, which leads to *meyiwlu*, 'having a good time, having fun'. The second is in the consumption of *ayahuasca* and *toé*, which leads to 'seeing everything'.

I discuss the subversion of *nshinikanchi* by manioc beer further in the next chapter, but one point can be made here. Piro ceremonial life revolves around invitations to Piro people from other villages to come and see significant changes in the host village. Such events are always mediated by beer, by the 'drunkenness' produced by the consumption of beer, and by the attendant euphoria of *meyiwlu*, 'having fun'. However, such contacts are always marked by latent hostility, for the guests and hosts clearly do not 'live well' with each other: if they did, they would live together (see discussion in Gow 1991: 215–25). Beer eases the strain of this hostility by relaxing people's unease, and making them enjoy themselves, but it can also exacerbate the hostility, which erupts into fighting. In the preceding chapter, I discussed how, when Piro people are to come into contact with people from other villages, they take on the appearance of powerful others: in the past, jaguars, and more recently, white people. When *gwashata*, as the ongoing process of 'living well', demands that Piro people be seen by those with whom they manifestly do not live well, they must transform their appearance and be seen as other than what they are in everyday life. They must, in short, look like another kind of people.

In ceremonial life, it is other known Piro people who visit or are visited in their villages. In *ayahuasca* and *toé* hallucinatory experience too, other people and other places are seen, often of exotic appearance. For example, drawing on my own experiences, the house in which *ayahuasca* is being drunk can suddenly seem to have filled up with more people than you can remember coming, and they are all singing. I once asked Don Mauricio, 'Who are these people?' He told me, 'They are the *ayahuasca* people. They come when you take *ayahuasca*. They join in, their songs are very beautiful!' As I discussed above, the claim, 'It is a human, it is a person', when used of an entity without a normally perceptible human bodily form, is a hallmark of shamanic discourse, and of the transition from everyday experiential states to drug-induced 'drunkenness'. In everyday life, this statement, 'It is a human', marks the inclusion of some being within humanity, and hence the correct relations between humans. This is the domain of *nshinikanchi*. In hallucinatory experience, and in shamanic discourse, the same statement refers to the knowledge (*gimatkalchi*) of an entity. In shamanic discourse, something is 'human' because it possesses knowledge. In hallucinatory experience, something is 'human' because it possesses human bodily form, which is evidence of its knowledge as a powerful being. To elucidate these remarks, I look at two such entities, as they reveal themselves through hallucinatory experience: the first is *ayahuasca* itself, the second is the strangler fig tree, *kachpero* (*Ficus* spp.). I choose these examples because both were regularly commented on in Santa Clara.[14]

In everyday experience, *ayahuasca* is a vine. When it is ingested as a cooked potion, *ayahuasca* initially transforms itself into an anaconda with attendant auditory hallucinations. This is the initial phase of the hallucinatory experience. When it is followed by full hallucinatory experience, *ayahuasca* reveals itself in its 'true' form, as a beautiful woman who is singing. This woman is the 'mother' of *ayahuasca*, and the vine and the anaconda hallucinations 'come from' (Ucayali Spanish, '*viene de*'; Piro, *giyakatya*) this powerful being, as Piro people express it. This same formulation is used of the relationship between human parents and children, for the latter 'come from' the bodies of their parents (Gow 1991: 152). The vine and anaconda forms of *ayahuasca* are therefore products of the potent knowledge, *gimatkalchi*, of the true human bodily form of the *ayahuasca* powerful being.

Similarly, in everyday experience the *kachpero*, the strangler fig, is a tree, of rather uncanny appearance. In the hallucinatory experience, the *kachpero* reveals itself as a person, or as house full of people. These people are singing beautiful songs. As with *ayahuasca*, these songs are the *gimatkalchi*, 'knowledge', of the *kachpero* powerful being or beings. The people are what *kachpero* really is. As Don Mauricio put it, 'We see the *kachpero* as a tree, but that is a lie, the *kachpero* is a person. We just see it as a tree. When we take *ayahuasca*, we see it as people.' This is a good definition of what powerful beings are: they are those entities which to normal sensory experience are either invisible or take non-human bodily form, but which in the hallucinatory experience reveal themselves as people and can be heard singing. I will discuss the singing further below, and here concentrate on the 'appearance in human bodily form'. Human bodily form is the 'true' form of the powerful being, while other modes of appearance are 'lies', that is, delusions.

In everyday experience, a Piro person inhabits a world full of humans and non-human others. The humans are primarily co-residents, *nomolene*, 'my kinspeople', 'my collectivity of things like me'.[15] The others are everything else. In hallucinatory experience, the nature of the humans is transformed, as kinspeople are hidden by darkness, in the case of *ayahuasca*, or by face painting, in the case of *toé*. At the same time, certain others reveal themselves in human bodily form, their 'true' forms. A condition for recognizing this humanity of powerful beings is the transformation of the humanity of the experiencer through the subversion of the everyday experience of a village full of kinspeople by the ingestion of a hallucinogen, and the consequent state of 'drunkenness'.

---

[14] *Kachpero* (Ucayali Spanish, *renaco*) was a frequent topic of conversation in Santa Clara, because of the immense *kachpero* tree (or set of interlinked trees) at the main river port of the village. This *kachpero* was regularly named as the cause of uncanny experiences in the village, and blamed for minor illnesses suffered by the village's children.

[15] See Gow (1997) for further discussion of this theme (see also Overing 1993).

A measure of the profundity of this transformation in subjective experience between everyday and hallucinatory experience can be formulated if we turn to the sight of dead people. In everyday experience, as I have often noted before, the sight of dead people is always dangerous. The soul of a dead person, *samenchi* (Ucayali Spanish, *alma del finado*), which has the visual appearance of that person, causes a lethal nostalgia in living kinspeople. This is an aspect of the *nshinikanchi* both of the living subject and the dead object of the act of seeing. Even worse is the sight of the transformed rotted corpse of a dead person, *gipnachri* (Ucayali Spanish, *difunto*), which can appear to the living as a skeleton with shining eyes. Such bone demons are demons, *kamchi* (Ucayali Spanish, *diablo*), and cause severe illness to anyone who sees them. In the 'drunkenness' of *ayahuasca* and *toé*, by contrast, the sight of the dead is a benign and, indeed, desirable experience. One old woman told me, 'When I drink *ayahuasca*, I see my dead daughter. She grabs me, and pulls me up to dance with her. We dance and dance happily. How glad I am to see her!'

Apart from the emotional tone of such encounters, the dead seen in hallucinatory experience have the qualities of the *samenchi*, insofar as they look like the living person. But they are not *samenchi*, they are the dead as fully dead, *gipnachri*. Where in everyday experience, they appear in their terrifying form of animate skeletons with burning eyes, the dead appear in hallucinatory experience as they were in life. In short, they appear as if they had never died.

This feature of 'drunkenness' initially confused me, because I was used to Piro people's generalized fear of seeing dead people in all their aspects. An intimation of clarity came through the following conversation with Don Mauricio. He had been telling me of a dream he had had about a dead kinswoman, and then said,

While we die, our spirits (*espíritos*) are eternal, they don't die. We are reborn in another life, but with new bodies. This, our body, we no longer have, this just rots, and we are born with another body. What might that new world be like? Without forest, perhaps, all cleared. This you see when you take *ayahuasca*, it is very sad to see these things.

When you take *toé*, you see dead people. I see my dead mother and talk to her. You see the living on one side, and the dead on the other. You enter a house and see the dead eating, drinking beer and dancing, just like us.

I asked him, 'Isn't that dangerous?', and he replied with surprise, 'No, why should it be? It's beautiful, you see all those who have died!' When there is complete identification with the powerful beings, the ontological gap between the one who sees and the one seen is eliminated, leading to the joy of reunion with the dead.

Such ideas do not, in any sense, reduce Piro people's fear of the deaths of close kinspeople, nor their horror of any contact with the dead. I have never heard such statements made to ameliorate anyone's grief or fear. Rather, they are statements specific to the condition of hallucinatory experience: from the point of view of humans in drug 'drunkenness', death is an illusion, and the living and the dead can come together and have a good time. That is because people in drug 'drunkenness' are not human, they are powerful beings. In everyday life, the dead most assuredly do die: from the point of view of humans in their everyday lives, death is a terrifying and unmitigated disaster. That is because people in their everyday lives are not powerful beings, but humans.

It is important here to remember the specific context in which Piro people come to experience the 'drunkenness' of *ayahuasca* or *toé*: it is invariably in the context of illness, whether their own or of a co-resident. That is, their access to the point of view of a powerful being depends on a prior crisis in *gwashata*, 'living well', caused by illness. Without illness and the threat of mortality, Piro people would have no stimulus to enter the hallucinatory state, and would consequently be unaware that, from the point of view of powerful beings, death is an illusion. This complex and paradoxical feature of hallucinatory experience is at the centre of the complex and paradoxical nature of being a shaman. I have discussed this in depth elsewhere (Gow 1991: 235–41), but here I want to explore further aspects of it through a consideration of shamanic songs, and of the specific hallucinatory experiences of shamans themselves. Shamans are in a special position, for they must constantly do what caused the Kochmaloto Women to become fragile and quickly die: that is, see others in human bodily form.

Drug Songs

The transformation of subjectivity I have identified at the core of 'drunkenness' can be explored further through a consideration of what Piro people call *gayapa shikale*, *kamalampi shikale* or *kagonchi shikale*, '*toé* songs', '*ayahuasca* songs' or 'shaman's songs'. These are the songs sung during 'drunkenness' by shamans and others. Called *ícaros* in Ucayali Spanish, I term them 'drug songs' here. These songs are the bodily-exterior manifestations of shamanic knowledge and power, and shamans are judged by the extensiveness and efficacity of their repertoire. Non-shamans may know some 'drug songs', which they sing during 'drunkenness'. Other non-shamans accompany the singing of the shamans, with '*ge ge ge*' singing.[16]

The analysis of 'drug songs' raises a particular methodological problem. I encountered no difficulties in recording such songs during shamanic sessions, and shamans and other people often asked me to record them in these and other circumstances, but I met with great resistance when I wanted to translate or discuss them. People would ask to hear my recordings, but were extremely

---

[16] '*Ge ge ge*' singing is the wordless accompaniment of the shamanic song of another person, and corresponds the '*wa wa wa*' singing of lullabies.

reluctant to talk about them. Shamans would respond to my questions by suggesting I train as a shaman, and hence diet strictly and consume *ayahuasca* frequently. 'Drinking *ayahuasca*, you will hear and understand!', they told me. People with no pretensions to shamanic knowledge disavowed any understanding of these songs, saying at most, 'These are drug songs, I don't understand them.'

My experience is in marked contrast to that of other ethnographers, such as Townsley, author of an excellent account of shamanic song language among the Yaminahua people of the Bajo Urubamba, close neighbours of Piro people (Townsley 1993). Townsley's informants were much more forthcoming in their exegesis of shamanic songs, and on the processes by which they are produced and used. Townsley describes how Yaminahua shamanic song imagery is built up by shamans through the process of *tsai yoshtoyoshto*, 'twisted language', where sung metaphors are used by the shaman in order to clarify his vision (1993: 460). It is likely that something similar occurs in the Piro case, for the corresponding Piro category would seem to be *koschepiru*, 'the words of a song', deriving from *koscheta*, 'to guess, to divine' (Matteson (1965: 346). The same word root, *-sche-*, also generates the term, *gischega*, 'a curl', which suggests a basic similarity between Yaminahua and Piro conceptualization of shamanic song imagery (see further discussion in Chs. 6 and 7).

As I have said, my informants were not willing to explain shamanic song language to me. It is possible that I did not properly press my informants for further elucidation, or seemed too diffident in response to their suggestions that I pursue shamanic training. However, it is also possible that the differences between Townsley's experience and my own may reflect real differences in the economy of shamanic knowledge on the Bajo Urubamba. Townsley was working with Yaminahua people, members of an ethnic group locally held in low regard for their shamanic knowledge (see Gow 1993), and so perhaps their elaborate exegesis reflected a desire to expand the knowledge of their technique. My own informants were working in the locally much more prestigious genre of 'down-river *ayahuasquero*' shamanry, discussed further below, and so felt no need to expand on its renown by discussing it with an outsider. At the very least, my informants were reluctant to discuss 'drug songs' outside of the context of actual shamanic practice. Such songs are intrinsically efficacious and, I was told, should neither be sung nor discussed outside of that context.[17]

The best account and exegesis I have of Piro 'drug songs' deals with one song, '*Kayonakakalura Shikale*', which Pablo Rodriguez recorded for me in 1988 from an old woman in Sepahua. When I replayed this recording in Santa

---

[17] Several of my informants criticized shamans for singing drug songs when they were only drunk on alcohol. Such songs, they told me, belong exclusively to hallucinatory experience, and should not be thus misused.

Clara, it caused considerable excitement. It was apparently unknown to local people, despite close kin ties to the singer. I was asked to play the recording over and over again, and people spontaneously answered my questions with their own interpretations of it. Two factors seem to me to have been paramount in this openness in informants: firstly, Santa Clara people were intrigued by the power of the singer's voice, the melodic line and the imagery of the song;[18] secondly, the song, while instantly identified as a 'drug song', was neither being sung in the context of a shamanic session, nor was it in active use in the Santa Clara area.

The words of '*Kayonakakalura Shikale*' are as follows:

> *Kayonakakalura*
> *Nuynumalutu*
> *Kayonakakalura*
>
> *Kigler-shini tlapawaka*
> *Wane nyapa shikalenanumta*
> *Nokowinenumta*
>
> *Kayonashtenamalo*
> *Nokowine*
> *Kayonashtenamalo*

Most people replied to my questions with the usual, 'It is a drug song.' Or, 'It is in ancient people's language, we don't understand it.' However, several people, including the original singer, did attempt to translate it, and Pablo Rodriguez, who made the original recording, went even further, and actively sought out explanations of it for me. After some difficulty, he came up with the following translation,

> One made to be painted with design,
> My partner in conversation,
> One made to be painted with design.
>
> Beautiful dry river bed,
> Thus I go along singing,
> With my horns.
>
> One with design-painted mouth rim,
> My horns,
> One with design-painted mouth rim.

---

[18] This song was rivalled in demand for playback by two recordings: another old woman's singing of *Mapchiri wgene jeji shikale*, 'Black Anaconda's Male Child's Song'; and an old blind man's playing of girl's initiation ritual flute music. All three of these 'hits' shared the quality of instant recognizability with unfamiliarity. My constant playback in all three cases was used to learn the music in question. Sheer unfamiliarity itself was not what interested people: many of my other recordings in distant villages provoked laughter when they were considered inept.

Pablo summarized the song-image as follows: 'He is covered with painted designs, he is talking to him as he goes along. He is walking in the dried-up bed of the river. He is playing his horn, it has a design-painted rim. The shaman is singing to his companion, to what he sees.'

This highly condensed image evokes powerful connections. Firstly, the reference to *kayona-*, 'painted with design', in the context of both the man walking and the horn, evokes the entire complex of *yonchi*, 'painted design', and the transformation of a surface into an intensified form of visual 'beauty'. Secondly, the dried bed of the river evokes a key image of beauty, for such a dried river bed is a feature of the height of the dry season, when people camp out on the beaches. Such clear, open beaches are considered beautiful, in contrast to the dirty and weedy forest. It is therefore an 'arena of beauty'. Further, the horn is used to call people together, for meetings or collective work, and hence the man is actively attracting the attention of another.

This song has a deeper connection to the theme of this book. Part of the reason why my attention was called to this song was Artemio's own fascination with it. In 1988, he would come to my house repeatedly, and asked me to play the recording over and over again. He told me that he wanted to learn it to sing when taking *ayahuasca*. At that time, I was not familiar with Ricardo Alvarez's informant's version of the myth about the white-lipped peccaries (1960, and see Myth Appendix). In retrospect I can see the remarkable connections between *Kayonakakalura Shikale* and the mythic narrative, 'A Man who went under the Earth', but at the time I did not. Now it seems likely to me that this song refers to the moment when the shaman in Alvarez's informant's version returns to this world with the stolen trumpets, calling the white-lipped peccaries to follow him. Unfortunately, these connections came to me too late to discuss them with Artemio.

My informants told me that this song, like all 'drug songs', came from the *kayigawlu*, the shaman's 'vision' (Ucayali Spanish, '*su visión*', 'his vision, that which he is seeing'). The *kayigawlu* is what the shaman is seeing, and we can reasonably assume that the song is a description of that vision. But it is more than that, for shamans say that the 'drug songs' come from the *kayigawlu*, and that they 'imitate/learn' (*yimaka*) them from the *kayigawlu*. This raises the question: who is the subject of '*Kayonakakalura Shikale*'? Who is the 'I' that sings this song? On one level it is the shaman who sings it who is the 'I'. But equally, it is the *kayigawlu* which is singing who is the 'I', while the shaman merely imitates him. But if the *kayigawlu* is the 'I' of the song, whom is he describing? Who is the subject of the phrase, '*nuynumalutu*', 'my partner in conversation'? And who is the object, who is that subject conversing with?

This feature, whereby it is difficult to identify the subject position of a sung discourse, has been recognized often in Amazonian musical performance. In particular, Viveiros de Castro (1992) has analysed the role of shifting subject position in Araweté song, and shown how important and revealing it is of Araweté cosmology. Similarly, Seeger (1987), drawing on Viveiros de Castro's work, has shown how the rapidly oscillating subject positions in Suyá ritual singing culminate in the identification, at the climax of ritual performance, of the supernatural animal composers of the songs and men who sing them. These same processes are at work in this Piro case.

When shamans imitate the *kayigawlu* through song, they lose the immediate evidence of their everyday humanity. They emanate the potent songs of others, and in the process become those others. Listening to the songs of the *kayigawlu*, over repeated and intensive periods of 'drunkenness', shamans come to 'hear–understand' (*gimatjema*) them. That is why shamans responded to my questions about these songs with the suggestion that I train as a shaman, and drink more *ayahuasca*. It is in 'drunkenness' that one learns what the songs mean, and their meanings are specific to the world of 'drunkenness'.

When a shaman sings the song of a *kayigawlu*, he becomes that *kayigawlu*. But, as I noted above, the state of powerful beings is intrinsically multiple. Hence the imitation of the songs of powerful beings is less a form of possession (the subsumption of one subject position within another) than the entry into another sociality. Here, the other reveals him/herself to the shaman as human, and takes on the shaman as human (from the other's point of view). The other takes the shaman on as part of its multiplicity (i.e., as part of its kinspeople). This multiplicity is of a specific sort, for the powerful beings are in the state of *meyiwlu*, 'having a good time, having a festival'. The shaman is thus accessing the intensified sociality of the powerful being, and the hallucinogens are the manioc beer of the powerful beings.

The *kayigawlu* is not, as such, singing to the shaman. *Kayigawlu* are the product of the action, *kayigawata*, 'to be made to see a vision'. The agent of the verb is *kayiglu*, 'one who causes visions to be seen'. My understanding of the relationship between *kayigawlu* and *kayiglu* is slight, but my sense is that the *kayigawlu* visions are generated by the *kayiglu* powerful being in order to allow for interactions with the shaman. But if powerful beings generate visions, what do they, in turn, look like? What is the visual form of a *kayiglu*, 'one who causes visions to be seen'? My sense here is that they do not have an intrinsic visual form, but rather an aural form. They are composed of their knowledge, and are songs (see Gow 1999b).

If intrinsically invisible song form is what characterizes the powerful beings, then this singing is not, unlike the *kayigawlu* visions, a specialized communicational activity on the part of the powerful being directed primarily at the shaman. Powerful beings sing as a primary characteristic of their state of *meyiwlu*, 'having a good time'. The shaman is thus overhearing, and then joining in with, that song. The shaman's singing of the 'drug song' is therefore simultaneously a 'learning' (*yimaka*) and a 'joining in with' (Piro, *gipxaleta*, 'to accompany, to help another'). This latter, 'joining in with', is like kinship, the multiplicity of 'other selves'. Here, the shaman is a switch-point between the experiential domains of powerful beings and humans. Nowhere is there a transcendental assimilation of the powerful being, shaman, and patient. Instead, the shaman's identification shifts back and forth between powerful beings as kin and the patient as kin.[19]

As shamans sing along with powerful beings, they attain to the subject position of those beings, and hence acquire their powers. They sing in order to see as the powerful beings see, and, having seen, to do something about it. Shamans see the bodily interior pains of the patient as 'little arrows' (Piro, *kashre*, *jrichi*; Ucayali Spanish, *virote*).[20] Such 'little arrows' imply whole unrecognized trajectories of social experience. The 'little arrows' are there in the patient's body, causing the illness the shaman is seeking to cure, because they have been shot into it by another shaman, the sorcerer causing the disease. The patient's illness is thus revealed as the specific result of another person's thwarted desires, either that of the sorcerer himself, or of the person who paid for him to ensorcell the victim. The anger caused by this thwarted desire is transformed, through shamanic action, into a sorcery object, and then 'shot' into the body of another, where it proceeds to eat the victim, causing illness. Shot into the body as 'little arrows', illness takes the form of gnawing grubs. It is the chewing actions of such grubs which cause pain. The patient is being eaten from the inside out.

The patient is the victim or game animal of a cannibal sorcerer, for such sorcerers are said to 'eat people'. Through this act of sorcery, the sorcerer asserts his or her ontological difference to the patient. The sorcerer asserts himself to be an 'eater of human flesh', like a jaguar or an anaconda, and asserts the patient to be a game animal. The curing shaman inverts this transformation of the patient, by sucking out the 'little arrows'. Sucked out, the 'little arrow' is treated as 'quasi-food' by the shaman, insofar as it is orally ingested. But it is then spat out, as 'filth' (like the game animal residues in *ayahuasca* experience). The cure inverts the processes of sorcery, by reasserting the patient as 'human', rather than 'game animal', and denying the humanity of the sorcerer, who is thereby defined as non-human, an 'eater of human flesh'. When the curing shaman reasserts the patient as human, rather than game animal, he simultaneously asserts his own co-humanity with the patient.

This feature of the curing ritual is attended by a curious paradox. The curing shaman is able to cure because he is, through the 'drug songs', in a state

---

[19] Such transcendental identification can potentially occur for Piro people, in messianic experience. It is predicated on a collective 'Other-becoming' through collective and constant dieting and ingestion of *ayahuasca* (see Ch. 8)

[20] The Ucayali Spanish word *virote* also means 'blowgun dart'. Blowguns (*pucana*) are known about on the Bajo Urubamba, but not used. For what it is worth, my own experience of these 'little arrows' came as a great surprise: they did not look like arrows or darts at all, but are rather elongated objects radiating light. They correspond well with migrainous scotomata.

of identity with the powerful beings. That is, they are human for each other. But the shaman is curing the patient because they, too, are in a state of identity, for they too are human for each other. As I have argued, this paradoxical identification simultaneously with the humanity of the patient and the radically opposed humanity of the powerful being is instantiated in the meanings of the 'drug songs', but it is also instantiated in the shamanic career itself. As I was constantly told, sorcery is easier to learn than curing,[21] such that a curing shaman is necessarily demonstrating the benign nature of his identifications with the powerful beings. A curing shaman has had to overcome his lethal urge to identify fully with the powerful beings, and so see other humans as game animals. He has gone on to see, simultaneously, both powerful beings and his patients as humans.

Becoming Double

Piro shamans are, therefore, double beings, sharing humanity with both powerful beings and their co-resident kinspeople at the same time. I have discussed certain aspects of this double identity of shamans in *Of Mixed Blood* (1991: 239–40), where I considered the role of the shaman's companion spirits, the small animate stones (Piro, *sotlutachri*, *ginkanto*; Ucayali Spanish, *incanto*) that all shamans possess. These stones are referred to by shamans as 'my children', and hence the helpful kinspeople of his co-residents. They are, however, feared by non-shamans, who are less taken with their identity as the shaman's kin, and much more by their obvious identity as powerful beings, of dubious solidarity with their co-villagers. Here I explore this duality of shamans further, from the perspective of the present analysis.

In the last chapter I noted that, for Piro people, twins are born shamans. Twins, by the nature of their births, and by the fact of their survival, are intrinsically doubled. They are a potent intensification of the human condition for Piro people: not only have they become human through the process of losing the originary other half, the placenta, but they have also lost the other twin, one who was identically human with themselves. As such, a twin is by definition *kagonchi*, a shaman. Further, Tsla was a hyper-twin, for his 'twin' was in turn a pair of twins, the Muchkajine, and hence Tsla fully merits his powers, and the epithet *kgiyaklewakleru*, 'miraculous being'.

The mythic narrative 'The Birth of Tsla', as I discussed in the preceding chapter, deals with the nature of the contemporary Piro lived world as one characterized by multiplicity: it is now Piro people, not jaguars, who live in groups, as the solitary figure of the pregnant human Yakonero at the start of the myth is replaced by the solitary figure of the pregnant jaguar Yompichgojru at the end of it. We find this same issue of solitude at the heart of the

---

[21] Compare Shuar and Achuar cases (Harner 1972; Descola 1996)

shamanry, in the figure of the patient. As I noted above, sick people remain alone in their mosquito nets all day, avoiding other people because of their 'ugliness'.

The condition of a sick kinsperson raises another poignant form of solitude, that of grief. If the sick person were to die, then the surviving kin are left *wamonuwata*, 'to grieve, to suffer, to sorrow, to be pitiable'. Those who are in this state of 'grief, sadness, sad, etc.' are incapable of ongoing social life, for their *nshinikanchi*, 'thoughts, mind, memory, love' is dominated by the absence of the dead person. They are 'alone'. The memory of the dead person, the paradoxical constant presence of one who is fully absent to immediate perception, is what generates *wamonuwata*. This condition must be fled, such that deaths lead to the abandonment of houses and villages.

In most cases, the *wamonuwata* of mourning is overcome by the mourner's surviving kinspeople. These other people experience *getwamonuta*, 'to see grief, suffering, sorrow, pitiableness', that is, compassion, and respond with an intensification of social regard and solicitude. Here, the aloneness of grief is erased in the constant assertion of the presence of others, who eventually make the griever forget the dead person, and focus back on to the living. Forgetting the lost kinsperson, they become drawn into a new condition of *gwashata*, 'living well'.

There are, however, two exceptions to this process whereby *wamonuwata* is transformed through the *getwamonuta* of others into *gwashata*. One of these is the one that lies at the heart of this book: it is the state of being 'tired of living'. This leads to travel into distant lands to live among distant peoples. The other is a shamanic career. When asked why they underwent the rigorous training and continue to undergo the discomforts of their practice, shamans gave one stereotypical response. The shamanic career originates in the unbearable grief, experienced or simply feared, of losing a child to illness. The loss of a child provokes a particularly intense *wamonuwata* in many men; since men tend to live in the villages of their wives, and hence to depend on their children as a means to relate to their co-residents, the death of a child, and the subsequent state of *wamonuwata*, tend to subvert the key value of *gwashata*, 'living well', much more radically for a man than for a woman.[22]

Inconsolable over the loss of a beloved child, certain men withdraw from social life, and remain inattentive to the solicitude of others. They fall quiet, talking little, 'thinking, loving, remembering' one who is now dead. This state, when it refers to lost adult kin, is exceptionally dangerous, for the dead soul is strong enough to kill the melancholic. The souls of young children do not

---

[22] Women also become shamans, but they do not, to my knowledge, engage in long shamanic apprenticeships. While this was never made explicit to me, I had the impression that women attain their access to shamanry through miscarried foetuses and children who died in infancy. A further condition of female shamanry is marriage to a male shaman, and the subsequent constant contact with 'drunkenness' and other shamanic activities.

possess this power, but the state is still unbearable. Contemplating his condition, the grief-stricken man conceives the project of becoming a shaman, and hence acquiring the knowledge and powers to defend his other children, and other kinspeople. To do so, however, means forsaking a large part of the pleasures of life, for shamanry means avoiding sex as much as possible, not eating many things, and especially it involves the frequent consumption of hallucinogens. A shaman begins to live much of the time in the 'drunkenness' of *ayahuasca* and *toé*. There, as we have seen, he acquires another 'social life'. He becomes, so to speak, a double being, living both 'here in the village' and simultaneously 'off there with powerful beings'.

In a fundamental sense, the existential condition of the shaman is no longer that of humanity. This is revealed at death, for unlike most Piro people, shamans enter the sky (discussed further in Ch. 8), or, as we have seen in the last chapter, they turn into jaguars. At birth humans, in order to be humans, have to forgo the primordial completeness of human and other, foetus and placenta, in order to gain access to the experience of *gwashata*, 'living well', the everyday experience of the reassuring multiplicity of humanity. Shamans, stimulated by a perhaps excessive sensitivity to their own sufferings, recover that primordial duality of human and other through prolonged and arduous immersion in hallucinatory experience and consequent contact with powerful beings. In so doing, they escape the ultimate fate of their fellow kinspeople, mortality, while being constantly involved in seeking to stave off that fate for those same kinspeople.

Returning, at last, to the mythic narrative with which I began this chapter, we can now see an additional dimension to this myth. As we saw, the Kochmaloto Women did not endure when they finally found other real humans. The reason is given by Sebastián: they had seen too many beings taking on human bodily form in front of them. This is the expertise of shamans which, as we have seen, renders them immortal. Why did this same experience render the Kochmaloto Women so radically mortal? Simply, I think, because they were never alone, there were always two of them and they were sisters. Despite the disaster of the flood, which killed all their kinspeople, the Kochmaloto Women survived as a minimal expression of *gwashata*, 'living well'. They were able to remain fully human, through all their contacts with otherness, because they always had each other. It is only when that minimal sociality is tested by re-entry to full sociality, in the village of the 'real people', that it is found wanting, and the Kochmaloto Women die quickly.

Transforming Cosmologies

Having observed Piro shamanic practices in the 1940s and 1950s, the accounts of Matteson (1954), Ricardo Alvarez (1970), and Francisco Alvarez (1951) are broadly similar to mine. Their accounts, however, suggest a dramatic change in

Piro cosmology over that same period. These earlier writers describe features of shamanic cosmology I heard nothing of in the 1980s and 1990s, and a text collected by Matteson from Sebastián refers to a series of powerful beings quite different from those I heard discussed during my fieldwork.

Judging from the accounts of Ricardo Alvarez, Matteson, and Sebastián, in the 1940s and 1950s, many Piro shamans sang in *tsrunni tokanu* 'ancient people's language' (construed as archaic Piro), and sang songs of animals and celestial beings. For example, Sebastián lists the following powerful beings: *kayjetu* (Ucayali Spanish, *tuquituqui*) 'wattled jacana'; *patutachri*, 'father'; *samenchi*, 'dead soul'; *maylu*, 'black vulture'; and he specifies that these powerful beings 'come from above' (Matteson 1965: 148–9). Matteson, in a discussion of Piro music, noted:

All Piro music and songs are supposed to have been derived from contact with the gods. Sometimes a witch-doctor in trance hears the gods sing praises to the goddesses, and answers. Sometimes the medicine man with frenzied rhythm pleads a god to embody himself and appear. (1954: 67)

Discussing Piro religion, she states,

the tribal religion is a polytheism of innumerable gods and goddesses living in heaven. The words 'heaven' and sky are synonymous, meaning 'the upper expanse'. Tsla, the creator god so prominent in the mythology, receives neither homage nor petition. Rather, invocations are addressed to the general name goyakalu (from the adjective goyaka, 'lasting') 'an eternal one'. A synonym for 'god' and for 'ghost' is kashichjeru, 'the one who seizes (us)', because the gods are conceived of as those who snatch away the life of a human being.

Any individual whose sins are comparatively few, and all powerful witchdoctors, go to heaven and become gods. They receive their 'goyaknu', which carries the added thought of splendour and majesty . . .

The ghost of any witch doctor is dreaded, because the witch doctor is supposed to go back and forth at will from heaven to earth, embodying himself in whatever form he chooses. (1954: 72)

Alvarez, too, attributes a complex vertical cosmology to Piro people, stating, 'Spiritual beings live, for the Piro, in different dwellings and are catalogued in six scales in relation to their grade and eminence' (R. Alvarez 1970: 62). He goes on to specify these as *galnachriwaka*, 'The Sky of the Birds'; *gipnachrinewaka*, 'The Dwelling of the Dead'; *kagonchiwaka*, 'The Place of the Shamans'; *goyakalunewaka*, 'The Dwelling of the Gods'; *tengogne goyakalniwaka*, 'The Sky of God'; and *klataarixawaka tengognepotni*, the uninhabited uppermost heaven. These heavens are located one atop the other.

In the 1980s, Piro people told me nothing of this celestial shamanic cosmology. During my fieldwork, shamans sang songs about powerful beings located in the river or in the forest. These included *yacuruna*, 'River People'; *lobohuahua*, 'Otter Child'; *sacha runa*, 'Forest People'; *sacha supay*, 'Forest

Demon'; *toemama*, '*Toé* Mother'; and others. As these names indicate, most shamans sang songs in Amazonian Quechua. Nobody suggested to me that shamans contacted sky beings, and the elaborated shamanic cosmologies I heard of concerned subaquatic cities, forest trees that were really towns, and the powers of the inhabitants of lakes in the forest.

There were a few exceptions to this pattern, and hints that something of the older shamanic tradition was still operative. As I recounted in Chapter 1, *cajunchis*, 'shamans', had deprived local people of an important game animal, the white-lipped peccaries, by hiding the hole by which these enter this world. This kind of activity was not the sort of thing *ayahuasquero* shamans did, and it is hence likely that the older shamanry was still practised by some old Piro people. I return to this issue in Chapter 9, but I heard little about it. By the 1980s, such shamans, like the old jaguar shaman discussed in Chapter 4, were strongly identified with sorcery, a subject no one was willing to describe to me in any great detail.

In *Of Mixed Blood*, I argued that the shamanic cosmology I was told about and which I saw in action was coherently bound up with the general symbolic structures of Piro people's lived world. Shamanic knowledge, I argued there, drew on the killing and curing powers of non-human space, the forest and river and, by focusing on the qualities of the beings that control those spaces, was able to restore life to Piro people. It stood in significant opposition to what I there termed 'civilized knowledge', which was encoded in the hierarchy of settled human space, and associated with progressive change. From the archival data discussed above, however, the situation was very different in the 1940s and 1950s. It is not clear if the accounts by Matteson and Alvarez refer to contemporary general practice, but minimally we can suppose that, in the 1940s and 1950s, some Piro shamanic practice was directed to a celestial realm, and to the powerful beings who inhabited it. Further, judging from Sebastián's account, which is a personal-experience narrative and refers presumably to his youth, before the late 1940s much more of Piro shamanic practice addressed the celestial domain.[23]

The differences between Matteson's, Sebastián's, and Ricardo Alvarez's accounts and those I heard in the 1980s have a fairly obvious source. What they described was before, and what I heard was after, decades of extended co-residence with Adventist, SIL, and Dominican missionaries, and intensive evangelization by them. As I discuss further in Chapter 8, this evangelical activity operated to transform the *goyakalune*, 'the celestial divinities' in the plural, into *Goyakalu*, 'the Celestial Divinity' in the singular, the God of the SIL and Dominican missionaries. There is a curiosity here, however, for this evangelization did not make shamanry disappear, by removing its cosmology. The

---

[23] The kind of shamanic cosmology described here resembles closely Weiss's account of Tambo river Campa cosmology in the 1960s (Weiss 1975).

practitioners and their practices persisted, and other powerful beings began to respond to their calls. Why should this be so? I suggest that there are two connected explanations, both having to do with the history of earlier missionary activity in Peruvian Amazonia.

The evangelization of Piro people by Dominican and SIL missionaries in the mid-twentieth century was not the first contact that Piro people had had with Christianity. Their ancestors had had a long history of evangelization by Jesuit and Franciscan missionaries, which ended in the late nineteenth century (see Biedma 1981; Amich 1975; Ortiz 1974; and Gow 1991). These attempts to evangelize the ancestors of contemporary Piro people had been sporadic and largely ineffectual, but they would certainly have provided Piro people with a basic vocabulary of Christian theology. Further, this knowledge would have been confirmed and expanded by contacts with the rubber bosses and *hacienda* bosses.

There is some evidence that certain aspects of Christian cosmology had already been taken up by Piro shamans. In 1874, the Franciscan missionary Sabaté observed a shamanic ritual in the village of Miaría which was explicitly termed a *misa*, 'mass' by its Piro participants (Sabaté 1925). This identification undoubtedly lay in prior knowledge of the Christian ritual gained on earlier missions in the Urubamba area, or on the mission of Buepoano, which had been founded for Piro people in Sarayacu area of the Bajo Ucayali in 1799 (see Ortiz 1974). Further, throughout the middle of the nineteenth century, Urubamba Piro people had attempted to persuade the Franciscans to establish missions for them in their own territory. Marcoy, in 1846, found many Piro people living on a 'mission' they had built in Santa Rosa, and was asked by these people to tell the Franciscans at Sarayacu to send a priest (Marcoy 1869)]. Sabaté had gone to the Bajo Urubamba in response to Piro commissions which arrived in Cuzco in 1868 and again in 1873, asking for a missionary to 'civilize them' (Sabaté 1925). From 1879 until 1881, the Franciscan P. Alemany ran a mission for Piro people at Santa Rosa, which failed because the increasing presence and power of the rubber traders led his converts to shift allegiance to them (Ortiz 1974).

The Franciscans eventually abandoned their attempts to evangelize Urubamba Piro people, citing their lack of interest in religion, and over-developed interest in material goods (see Ch. 7). However, Piro people's desire for missionaries was rather more complicated than that, for there is some evidence that Piro people, and especially Piro shamans, were open to aspects of Christian cosmology. For example, Sebastián includes in his list of entities called by shamans one called *patutachri*, 'father'. In *Gwacha Ginkakle*, he states,

Long ago the ancient people did not know much about God, although they had heard of him. But they wanted to see him. So, many took hallucinogens. They drank hallucinogens wanting to see God. They drank *ayahuasca*. They saw God, it is said, they called him 'Father'. They drank *toé* and other plants, trying to see God. But they never got there. (Sebastián, Zumaeta, and Nies 1974: 150, 152–3)

The Piro original for 'Father' here is *patutachri*, from the root *patu*, an old vocative kin term for 'father'. The *Diccionario Piro* defines this word as: '(1) a demon who appears to witchdoctors in their visions, (2) (obsolete) genii, pagan god' (Nies 1986: 164); while Matteson (1965: 316) translates the terms as a 'demon who appears to a witch doctor' under the influence of *ayahuasca*. As Matteson notes, *patutachri* is a noun derived from a verb root which does not occur (ibid.), and which could be translated as 'one who is habitually called "father" '. This strongly suggests that this 'demon' is in fact the Christian God of the missionaries and the rubber bosses. Certainly, Sebastián's identification of *patutachri* with the Christian God in *Gwacha Ginkakle* is overt, and strongly belies the SIL missionaries' identification of this being as a 'demon'.[24]

I discuss the transformations in Piro conceptualizations of divinity further in Chapter 8, but I think it is reasonable to assume that, at least by the middle of the nineteenth century, Piro people were conceiving of Christian missionaries' discourse as analogous to shamanry, and Piro shamans had assimilated some features of that discourse to their own cosmology. There was, however, another potent source for the transformation of Piro shamanic cosmology: 'down-river *ayahuasquero* shamanry'. Elsewhere (Gow 1994), I have argued that this 'down-river' form of shamanry evolved on the Jesuit and Franciscan missions of Northeastern Peru and Eastern Ecuador, and in explicit relationship to Catholicism. From that original context, it had been historically spreading throughout Western Amazonia, following the lines laid out by the expansion of the rubber industry and subsequent regional socio-economic transformations. It is very likely that this tradition of shamanry first made its appearance on the Bajo Urubamba in the late nineteenth century brought by the *moza gente* workers of the rubber bosses. The *moza gente* are the 'down-river mixed blood people', originating in the old missions along the Bajo Ucayali, Huallaga, and Amazon rivers (Gow 1991; 1993). Their mode of shamanry was fully integrated with the cosmology of folk Christianity in the region: it dealt with the powers of the river and forest and with the immediate problems of curing and sorcery, and left God, the sky and eschatology in the hands of specialists in the Christian religion.

On the Bajo Urubamba in the 1980s, the feared and respected shamans had trained and were working in this 'down-river' tradition. Indeed, many of them were in-marrying men from that area: they were Cocama, Napo Quichua or Lamista Quechua men married to local women. For local people, this tradition of shamanry had a potency derived from its 'down-river' places of origin, and its association with the large cities of Peruvian Amazonia, such as Iquitos and Pucallpa (Gow 1991; 1993). But perhaps as importantly for Piro people, as I discuss in Chapter 8, it was compatible with their recent experiences with

---

[24] Although Sebastián does include *patutachri* in the general category *kamchine*, 'demons', in his account of shamans in Matteson (1965: 148–9).

Adventist, SIL, and Dominican missionaries, in a way in which the older tradition was not. Where this older tradition asserted that Christianity was a kind of shamanry, the 'down-river' tradition asserts that Christianity is an eschatology and a cosmology with terms of reference different from, although complementary with, shamanry.

The change in Piro shamanic cosmology over that century is clearly co-ordinated with the disappearance of older formulations of the celestial from Piro cosmology in general. This is the issue with which I began this investigation, in the problems raised by the conversation on 15 January 1982, and the discussion of the stars and the moon. In the chapters in Part III, I analyse this problem in much more detail, in search of a solution to it. Here, however, I want to point out that the remarkable change in Piro shamanic cosmology over the last forty-odd years is similar to that discussed in the last chapter, the switch from *yineru yona*, 'Piro people's design' to *kajitu yona*, 'white people's design, writing', as key practices in the Piro lived world. Both changes happened over the same period. There is, however, a significant difference between them. The change from 'Piro people's design' to 'writing', which is co-ordinated with the change from 'Piro people's clothing' to 'white people's clothing', marks a shift in emphasis from jaguars towards white people, from the forest towards the down-river region. The change in shamanic cosmology, however, is a shift from a focus on the sky, to a focus on the river and forest. That is, while design practice is moving away from its referents in the immediate Piro lived world to make connections to distant places and people, shamanic cosmological practice is drawing closer to that immediate lived world.

I return to these issues in later chapters, but the point I want to emphasize here is that the changes in shamanic practice, like the changes in design practices discussed in the previous chapter, are not simply changes, they are transformations of transformations. By this, I mean that these changes are occurring in schemes of action which are already about transformation. In the next chapter, I continue this investigation with an analysis of *kigimawlo*, the 'girl's initiation ritual', which will provide a third example of the transformation of a transformation.

6

The Girl's Initiation Ritual

In the previous two chapters, I have shown how analyses of 'The Birth of Tsla' and 'The Kochmaloto Women' help to elucidate design and hallucinatory experience in the Piro lived world, but they clearly elucidate many of its other features too. In particular, both myths point towards the most important of Piro ceremonial performances, the girl's initiation ritual. On the evening on which Antonio told me so many myths, he also told me a long account of the girl's initiation ritual. His account was quite spontaneous, as if he thought that an account of this ritual logically followed on from the telling of those myths. For me, this raised the relation between myth and ritual, one of the thorniest questions in anthropology. Antonio was oblivious to such concerns, and simply following the train of his own thoughts. For him, I think, myths and the girl's initiation ritual were alike because they were all things of the 'ancient people', but with this difference, that telling myths requires much less work than holding a girl's initiation ritual: as the father of many girls, Antonio must have contemplated this problem, and may have counted himself lucky to be living in an era when the demand for this ritual was largely in abeyance. That said, Antonio's account of the girl's initiation ritual can be understood, like his mythic narratives, as a demonstration of his knowledge of the things of the 'ancient people': if seriously called upon, Antonio could have held a girl's initiation ritual for any of his daughters.

In this chapter, therefore, I analyse the Piro girl's initiation ritual (Piro, *kigimawlo* or *gishriiri*; Ucayali Spanish, *pishta*). My concern here is to analyse this ritual as a system of spatio-temporal actions, to show how it projects the general viability of the Piro lived world onwards through space and time. I then discuss the 'abandonment' of this ritual, and show how the ritual forms of Piro people in the 1980s can be seen as another example of the transformation of a transformation, co-ordinate with those described in the two previous chapters. In conclusion, I show how the *kigimawlo*, and my analysis of it, is linked to the 'forgetting' of the myth about the moon, and how these are co-ordinated with the general scheme of transformations in the Piro lived world analysed in the chapters of Part III.

Kigimawlo

The girl's initiation ritual is called in Piro, *kigimawlo*, 'bead bracelets are put on to her', or *gishriiri*, 'the tying-on' of decorations. Ethnographically reliable descriptions of *kigimawlo* can be found in Ricardo Alvarez (1962; 1963; 1970),

Matteson (1954; 1965), Baer (1974), and Román (1985). More dubious accounts include Sabaté's purported description (1925), which would seem in fact to be an account of the superficially similar Shipibo–Conibo ritual of *Ani Shreati*, which is also known locally as *pishta* (see Roe 1982; Gebhart-Sayer 1984).

As a basis for my analysis of *kigimawlo*, I use the account of this ritual given to me by Antonio Urquía in 1988. I supplement this with data drawn from my own observation of one *kigimawlo* in Santa Clara in 1981, and from the descriptions in the literature. Antonio's account misses out the event that starts the ritual process: *kigimawlo* is initiated by a girl's first menstruation (*tujre-wata*, 'she menstruates for the first time'). When this happens, she is placed in seclusion by her parents. Antonio's account starts at this point:

Thus is *pishta*. The girl is kept inside the house, hidden high up in the roof. She doesn't know men, not like today when they know men when they're still young. Inside the house, she stays. Each day she paints all over with *huito*, all of her hair and all of her body, she is very black.[1] She spends all her time spinning cotton, to make her skirt for when she emerges. When she comes out, she is painted with *huito*, all over, her legs, her trunk, everywhere . . .

Teresa Campos, Antonio's wife, interjected here for clarification, 'Painted with designs, just like your painted bag,' referring to one of the painted bags I had just bought in the up-river community of Miaría. Antonio continued:

she has necklaces with little rattles attached, '*sha, sha, sha*,' they go. She wears bead-work, a collar, and bracelets. How she resounds when she comes out!

Her lip is pierced, her nose is pierced too, she wears silver there. You see, my old kinspeople used to wear silver in their noses. Her beadwork collar has designs on it like your bag. It's really big!

She comes out and dances with the old people, just with the old people at the beginning. Her parents make a big house, surrounded with big clay pots. In the middle of the house is a really big pot, *kaplalu* they say in Piro, all painted with designs, it has a face, nose, everything, . . .

Teresa said, 'Just like a person, it looks exactly like a person.'

it looks just like a person. They make manioc beer, and they cook the mass twice. It is sweet, but very strong. When it is in the pot it foams like honey. The *kaplalu* is huge, and it is buried in the earth, only the top showing. When the girl comes out, she serves manioc beer in a big drinking bowl (*kajpapago*), then other women follow her, serving in little bowls. Sometimes three girls come out together, and each one serves beer, and then the older women serve beer. It's very strong, and in a moment you get really drunk!

The girl wears a bamboo crown, covered in designs. She dances. There are six drummers and two men playing the *piguano* flute. The *piguano* player puts on the crown of the girl, and dances. The girl is very fat when she comes out. Everyone is

---

[1] The reference here is to painting *sagata*, 'to smear with pigment', not to painting *yonata*, 'to paint with design'.

Plate 8. Girl leaving seclusion during her initiation ritual in Sepahua, 1977 (photograph by Carlos Montenegro

drunk! When someone finishes the beer in a big drinking bowl, he is given it when he leaves, as a present, to take home. The beer is taken out of the big pots with an arrow cane—a small gourd is tied to an arrow cane with two threads, and with this they take out the manioc beer.

Piro people call this *kigimawloga*, that is, *kigimawlo* is doing this *pishta*, and *kigimawloga* is the beer of the *pishta*. *Kigimchi* is the collar of beadwork she wears.

When they make *pishta*, they go to the forest, to hunt. Before there were tapir-hunting dogs, collared peccary-hunting dogs, they brought in the game. The father of the girl to be celebrated goes all along the river, inviting the people to come. If there is to be a *pishta* in Miaría, two months before, they will come here, to Santa Clara to invite us, they will even go down to Santa Rosa, on the Tambo river.

Seclusion and Revelation

The girl is secluded inside her parents' house, '*gitoko twa*', 'she stays/lives inside'. She sits on a platform built into the roof of the house, painting her entire body with *huito* and spinning cotton. This, I was told, was in order that she become fat. In Piro, this is expressed as *kamanero*, 'she has a body'. In the preceding chapter, I discussed the root of this word, *-mane*, and argued that it means 'human form'. In this context, the term seems to point towards her newly acquired substantiality. Fatness is hard to achieve for children among Piro people, and even harder to maintain for adults. Sub-adolescent children have many internal parasites, giving them a characteristic pot-belly and spindly-limbed physique, while adults' continuous labours make them muscle-bound and wiry, but seldom tubby. But, as I discussed in the preceding chapter, *kamane-*, 'with a body', has a further significance, for it emphasizes the girl's visibility. The statement can, after all, only be made of the girl when she leaves her seclusion and can be seen by others.

A deeper understanding of the significance of seclusion can be found in the following text recorded by Matteson from Sebastián:

Among the ancient people, long ago, a boy whose voice had begun to change would diet. He no longer ate everything, nor drank sweet things. He drank medicine to become a good hunter, to become strong. Thus long ago the ancient people were strong. Nowadays there are no strong people. The young men emerged fully grown and fat.

A girl too, she would lie down for a whole year. All through the dry season and the rainy season she remained lying down, hidden inside the house. When she had become fat, she came out, decorated with beadwork, she emerged.

It was the same for young men. When their voices broke, they hid. When they were fully grown and fat, they emerged.

First there was a big hunt, game was brought in, for a feast to be held. A great quantity of beadwork was prepared, and then the boys came out. As many as had become young men came out. They had become strong. They had become good hunters. They could marry.

But now we have abandoned that custom.

That is all I have to tell. That is all I remember. But there would be more. I don't remember it well now. That's it. (Matteson 1965: 142–5)

Sebastián's account raises a problem which I discuss later, but it should be noted here. Like many Piro people, Sebastián claims that there was a boy's initiation ritual corresponding to the one for girls. However, many other Piro people denied this, and there are no descriptions of such rituals in the literature. At most, I believe, boys may have left seclusion during girls' initiation rituals. Leaving that issue to one side, Sebastián's account stresses the linkage of seclusion, dieting, and bodily growth.

These features of seclusion are reiterated by Ricardo Alvarez in his accounts of a girl's initiation ritual (1962; 1963). He notes that the girl in seclusion must not eat any game animal noted for its thinness, but must instead eat tapir, birds, good fish, and consume abundant quantities of plantain drink and manioc beer, 'for these foods will make her body fatten and develop' (R. Alvarez 1962: 38). Alvarez further notes two features of the seclusion. On the first day of the seclusion, the girl's mother ties snake-skin bands around the girl's arms and on her legs above the ankle: these bracelets, 'transmit vitality to her and make her worthy of the regard of the gods' (ibid.: 37). I return to this latter detail later. Secondly, Alvarez notes that the success of seclusion, and hence the time for the ritual, is tracked by measuring the girl's arms and legs. If the snake-skin bands are tight, and the flesh spills over them, the girl has reached the time for the ritual. If not, people disapprovingly say, 'Her shins are no good' (ibid.: 38). Therefore, the snake-skin bands mark the transition of the girl from a spindly child into a mature woman. These snake-skin bands would also refer to the ability of snakes to shed their skins, and hence rejuvenate (see Ch. 5).

The condition of the secluded girl in the house corresponds to the position of the foetus in the womb: both are growing in darkness, and coming to have a 'body'. Following Alvarez's account, the similarities go further, for he records that when the girl is discovered to have first menstruated, her mother calls an old woman to carry her to the girl's house to begin her seclusion. This woman, who later assists in the *kigimawlo*, is called by the girl *nkampukjero*, 'the one who touched me, held me lightly', and in turn calls the girl, *nkampuklo*, 'the one I touched/held lightly', and Alvarez notes that the same terms are used for godparents and godchildren by baptism (R. Alvarez 1962: 36). There is a difference between the foetus and the girl, however. While the foetus is surrounded by its 'first design', the girl is explicitly not covered in design: she is totally blackened with *huito*. Only on the eve of her emergence will she be painted with designs by old women.

The secluded girl is in a state of profound self-absorption. As Antonio pointed out, 'She doesn't know men', that is, she does not have sexual relations. Further, she stereotypically engages in only two actions: painting herself and spinning cotton. Sitting in the darkness of the eaves of the house, the secluded girl constantly blackens herself with *huito*. This is an image of invisibility, as the girl renders herself coextensive with the darkness. As she spins, however, the cotton would necessarily set up a stark visual contrast, at least to her own eyes, between its whiteness and her own blackness. This idea, while never formulated by any of my informants, does not seem to be entirely alien to Piro ways of thinking, since part of the reason for her constant self-blackening is to make her 'white': when she emerges, her skin is very pale, which enhances by dramatic contrast the designs painted on her body, and the other decorations she wears. Similarly, I was told, the cotton she spins is used to make the skirt she will wear during the ritual, but she will not weave it for herself: another woman, probably her mother, will do that. The secluded girl concentrates on an earlier stage of weaving as a productive process, spinning. By analogy, her constant self-blackening is another earlier stage in a productive process, the making of her own womanly body, a task that will be concluded by the old women who paint her with designs and put the beadwork and other decorations on her.

The stillness of the secluded girl is connected to two key factors. On the one hand, as a recent producer of menstrual blood, she must remain seated in one place. Menstrual blood, *granchi* (root: *graga*) is a form of flow, which she must control through her stillness. On the other hand, while the girl is still, her condition is causing a flurry of activity of ever increasing intensity: garden-making, house-building, ceramic production, going to invite all the other Piro people, going on a big hunt, making the beer, culminating in the arrival of the guests and the decoration of the girl. *Kigimawlo* is the most elaborate and grandest of Piro ritual performances, and it has at its heart a girl quietly sitting in her parents' house, seeing nobody and seen by nobody.[2]

On the eve of the beginning of the ritual, the girl is painted by old women.[3] Ricardo Alvarez (1963: 9) states that she should, ideally, be painted by the woman who carried her into puberty seclusion, but minimally she must be painted by an old woman for, as I discussed in Chapter 4, only old women are skilful enough to paint her properly. In the early morning of the first day of the ritual, she is decorated in her finery: painted skirt, painted hat with macaw and oropendola feather decorations, a bead collar and bracelets, necklaces with bells and coins, bandoleers and anklets with little rattles, and silver nose and lip ornaments.[4] Since all of these decorations are beautiful, because her body painting is beautiful, and because she herself is beautiful, the girl is an intensi-fied image of *giglenchi*, 'beauty': her emergence elicits gasps of admiration from the assembled crowd, '¡*Kiglerpotlo!*', 'She is beautiful indeed!'

The fully beautified girl emerges at dawn on the first day of *kigimawlo*, into the gaze of the assembled guests, who are 'all of the Piro people', who are themselves all beautified. She thus reveals to all Piro people that she has successfully transformed herself into *kamanero*, 'one who has a body', one characterized by substantial human form. This moment recalls the moment of birth, when the foetus emerges from the womb with its 'first design', and the assembled spectators decide whether or not it is human. It also recalls *kamalampi* hallucinatory experience, when the *kamalampi* powerful being transforms from an anaconda covered in design into her true human form. But *kigimawlo* is different from these, for here a girl appears in a human form which she herself has enhanced through seclusion, and covered in the designs that old women painted on to her.

Kigimawlo ritual is clearly closely connected to the mythic narrative 'The Kochmaloto Women'. Indeed, this myth can be read as kind of inverted *kigi-mawlo*, and one with disastrous consequences. The Kochmaloto Women clearly

---

[2] Of particular help to my analysis here has been Viveiros de Castro's (1978) analysis of bodily fabrication through seclusion and revelation through ritual performance among the Yawalapíti of the Upper Xingú, who speak a language closely related to Piro.

[3] While unrecorded in any account, the girl must presumably have stopped painting herself with *nso* at least a week before she is painted with designs, to give time for the all-over paint to fade.

[4] At some point the girl must have had her nose and lip pierced, but I do not know when this happened.

did 'know men', and in their most dangerous form of powerful beings, such as a transformed anaconda. The mistreatment of the anaconda's child provokes a massive flood, which the child's mother and aunt escape by climbing the *huito* tree which grew from the seed the child gave them. The flood in the myth corresponds to the girl's first menstruation in the ritual, for both are novel flows of liquid. The Kochmaloto Women's ascent of the *huito* tree is like a seclusion, only instead of remaining inside the house covering themselves in *huito* juice, the Kochmaloto Women go outside and up into a *huito* tree. They do not use the fruit to make paint to paint themselves, but instead to judge the depth of the flood water.[5] Finally, far from remaining quietly sitting in the house seeing no one and being seen by no one, the Kochmaloto Women wander about in the forest, seeing and being seen by many different beings.

The most powerful connection between the myth and the ritual lies in the conclusion to the first and the stated purpose of the second. Recall that, when the Kochmaloto Women finally arrive among 'real people', they quickly die. As Antonio put it, 'They did not last long, they were very weak': they are killed by the lightest of a Piro woman's work tools, a manioc beer-strainer and a *bijao* leaf. By contrast, Piro people state that the purpose of *kigimawlo* is to make the girl 'live a long time, live to become an old woman'. It provides the girl with endurance, in the sense of 'lasting a long time'. In Chapter 5, I noted in a discussion of the mythic narratives about Tsla and the Kochmaloto Women that we find there are three kinds of mortality here: there is the death-defying miraculousness of Tsla, the ordinary mortality of Piro people, and the extreme mortality of the Kochmaloto Women. *Kigimawlo*, as a ritual action, is directed at extending the ordinary mortality of a Piro girl such that she will be able to 'live to be an old woman'. Therefore the ritual operates not to provide the girl with immortality, but to evade the extreme mortality of the Kochmaloto Women.

Elsewhere (Gow 1999a), I have argued that *kigimawlo* condenses this longevity as the progressive control, over a woman's life, of three types of liquid. Firstly, a girl controls her *granchi*, 'menstrual blood, blood liquid', in seclusion. Secondly, as a mature woman, she controls *koyga*, 'manioc beer liquid', and especially, *kigimawloga*, 'girl's initiation liquid, girl's initiation beer', in the rituals for her own daughters. Finally, as an old woman, she controls *yonga*, 'design-painting liquid', in painting girls of her granddaughters' generation for *kigimawlo*. By endowing the girl with a long life, *kigimawlo* gives her the potential to live through these phases of the life-cycle, and hence to effect the ongoing viability of the Piro lived world.

---

[5] Although not mentioned in Antonio's version, this scene occurs in others (see versions in Matteson (1951: 55; 58) and Sebastián, Zumaeta, and Nies (1974: 59–60; 76–8).

To have a Good Time

When the girl emerges, she is carrying an immense beer drinking bowl, *kajpapago*, filled with *kigimawloga*, 'girl's initiation ritual beer'. She then serves all the guests, who must drink this beer as she holds the bowl. If she so wishes, she can choose her husband at this moment, by serving her chosen man first: Artemio was the first served at his future wife Lilí's *kigimawlo*, apparently by prior arrangement. The girl then serves everyone else, and is followed by a line of older kinswomen, who serve beer in smaller bowls. As Antonio put it, 'The beer is strong, quickly people get drunk!' Unlike normal manioc beer, *kigimawloga*, 'girl's initiation ritual beer', is fermented twice, and is hence very strong.[6]

Drinking strong beer makes the guests drunk. As I discussed in the preceding chapter, drunkenness on beer is a form of *gimru*, 'drunkenness', but one very different to hallucinatory experience. Where the 'drunkenness' of hallucinogens subverts *nshinikanchi* by transforming the person into a powerful being, the 'drunkenness' of manioc beer and other forms of alcohol subvert *nshinikanchi* by making the person *mshinikatu*, 'forgetful, disrespectful'. Drunk, people can 'forget' their respect and shame, and hence enjoy themselves. When drunk, Piro people can abandon their quiet everyday demeanour, to laugh loudly, joke, flirt, and generally mess about. This is what they call *meyiwlu*, 'having fun, having a festival', and it is the product of drunkenness. As the largest Piro ritual performance, *kigimawlo* is the most intensified form of *meyiwlu*, which is in turn the product of its intensely strong beer.

As I discussed in Chapter 5, fermented manioc beer produces the transformed bodily state of 'drunkenness', in a manner analogous to the drunkenness produced by hallucinogens. In both cases, this drunkenness mediates contact with other beings, whether powerful beings, in the case of the hallucinogens, or other humans, in the case of manioc beer. There is, however, a key difference. While the drunkenness of hallucinogens is aimed at identification with and acquisition of knowledge from powerful beings, the drunkenness of manioc beer is aimed at identification with other humans. The drunkenness of manioc beer makes people ebullient and talkative, and hence 'forgetful', *mshinikatu*. In certain uses of manioc beer drunkenness, this 'forgetfulness' can be used to make people speak of things which they normally wish to keep hidden, such as specialist knowledge.[7] In the specific case of *kigimawlo*, this

---

[6] Antonio once told me that this doubly-fermented beer tastes like brandy.

[7] Sara Fasabi and her niece Victoria were once speculating about whether another woman knew an effective form of contraception, and Sara said, 'Next time I have beer, I'll get her drunk and then we'll find out!' Sebastián, in *Gwacha Ginkakle*, tells two myths in which knowledge supernaturally acquired from animals (weaving from a spider, and archery from a hawk) was made general to the Piro when other people got the acquirers drunk, and hence to talk. Both myths end on the theme that the central character, by succumbing to these invitations to drink, led to an early end to the animal's teaching. This resulted in a consequent disparity in the distribution of knowledge among living people: some people are skilled at weaving and archery, others are not (Sebastián, Zumaeta, and Nies 1974: 114–41).

Plate 9. Dancing during a girl's initiation ritual in Santa Clara, 1981

'forgetfulness' makes hosts and guests lose their 'shame' (*paachi*; Ucayali Spanish, *vergüenza*), and become animated. This animation is then manifested in
two related forms: a willingness to sing and a willingness to dance. In *kigi-*
mawlo, there is a progress from singing to dancing, and then an oscillation
between the two throughout its course, until it ends in the drinking of the last
beer and the singing of the last song.

Jorge Manchinari, describing the initiation rituals he experienced in his
youth on Vargas's *haciendas*, commented, 'How people sang, the women, when
they got drunk! Women also get drunk, drinking manioc beer. They sang beautiful songs!' I begin by looking at this women's singing, then show how this is
transformed into male instrumental music, and so into dancing.

The songs women sing during *kigimawlo* are called, appropriately enough,
suxo shikale, 'women's songs'. Women sing them in various other contexts: they
can sing them alone in their houses, or in small gatherings. To my knowledge,
they all deal with sexual desire and relationships with men. Indeed, Piro
women told me that they sing them to men, and some women told me that they
had sung specific songs in order to acquire specific men. Pablo Rodriguez,
discussing Julia Laureano's rendition of *Mgenoklo Shikale*, 'Female Jaguar
Song', which he had recorded for me, explained:

When a woman sings, she does not say straight out to the man that she wants him. No, she'll sing that she is a jaguar, that she's walking around and around. She 'puts herself as a jaguar' (Ucayali Spanish, '*se pone de tigre*'). The man hears this, and thinks about it, and if he understands, he knows she is singing to him. She doesn't say it straight out.

Therefore, 'women's songs' are overtly metaphorical, the singer 'puts herself' (*se pone de*) as something she is not. The Piro equivalent of Pablo's phrase would seem to be *koscheka*, 'to take out, to remove, to pronounce, to invoke' (Matteson 1965: 346): the verb root also means, 'to put'. It is complemented by the verb, *koscheta*, 'to guess, to divine': this would be the action of the targeted man. Women's song, therefore, must be thought about and understood, and through songs, women seek to influence the thoughts of men, and to make those men attend to their desires.

There are several aspects of these songs which are worth spelling out further. Firstly, like the 'drug songs' discussed in the last chapter, 'women's songs' are marked by a sliding of subject position. The woman sings about herself as something she is not, just as the 'drug song' is sung, initially at least, from the subject position of the powerful being, not the shaman. But, while in the 'drug song' the singer seeks an identification with the subject position of the original singer, in 'women's songs', the singer seeks no identification with the sung subject position, but rather seeks the target man's identification of her intent. What matters here is not the singer's subject position, which is clear to her, but the man's, which is not clear to himself.

The following example will clarify this argument. It is *Mapchiri Wgene Jeji Shikale*, 'The Anaconda's Male Child Song', which I mentioned in Chapter 3. This song was sung for me in 1988 by an old Piro woman named Eusebia, in Sepahua. Its words are as follows:

> *Tsergakaka chininipa*
> *Tsergakaka chininipa*
> *Niklonamtenutkano*
> *Mapchiri wgene jeji*
> *Niklonamtenutkano*
> *Mapchiri wgene jeji*
>
> *¿Pagapga ginakgetkokla*
> *Raplejkamtenutkano?*
> *¿Pagapga ginakgetkokla*
> *Raplejkamtenutkano?*

> Made to weep,
> Made to weep,
> Now that he has swallowed me,
> Anaconda's male child,
> Now that he has swallowed me,
> Anaconda's male child.

On which other river maybe,
Will he vomit me back up?
On which other river maybe,
Will he vomit me back up?

This song was a great favourite in Santa Clara, and I was asked to play Pablo's recording of it over and over.[8] People admired the singer's voice. They also told me that it made them sad, explaining, 'It is a young girl singing, she is afraid of an older man who wants her. She is afraid he will take her away with him, only to abandon her later.' The sadness it evoked was caused by the disparity between the known age of the singer and the implied age of the subject position of the song.

In what sense could *Mapchiri Wgene Jeji Shikale* express a woman's metaphorized desire for a man? How could a Piro man find this song attractive, were he to gain the insight that the singer is singing it to him? It sounds more like a complaint. However, it has hidden depths. Firstly, the singer asserts her fear of the man, who is impressive, strong and widely travelled. This would be flattering enough. But more profoundly, she is putting herself in the man's position: on the whole, it is Piro men who must move in with their wives, not Piro women who fear being taken away by men. Most Piro men live in close daily contact with their wives' kinspeople, compared to the relatively few women who live with their husband's kinspeople (see Gow, 1991). So here the singer asserts that she understands the man's fears, that her kin may, indeed, seem to be like frightening animals. But, she asserts, she will stand by him if he marries her. There is doubtless much more to this song too.

The same is true of *Mgenoklo Shikale*, 'Female Jaguar Song', discussed above. Its words, as sung by Julia Laureano, are as follows,

Mgenoklolan-gita,
Mgenoklolan-gita,
Piklewanatana,
Piklewanatana,
Mgenoklolan-gita,
Mgenoklolan-gita.

Piklewanatana,
Piklewanatana,
Gowuka nanuko,
Pyaplewanatyana,
Gowuka nanuko,
Pyaplewanatyana,
Mgenoklolan-gita,
Mgenoklolan-gita .

[8] See alternative version and translation of the words in Matteson (1954: 67).

I am a female jaguar
I am a female jaguar,
You are afraid,
You are afraid,
I am a female jaguar
I am a female jaguar

You are afraid,
You are afraid,
Far away,
As you are going along,
Far away,
As you are going along,
I am a female jaguar,
I am a female jaguar.

As noted above, Pablo Rodriguez translated this song as follows, 'she is a jaguar . . . she's walking around and around'.[9] Here again, why should this be attractive to a man? The point is that women do not actively seek out men, it is men who actively seek out women. Sometimes, however, men are a little afraid of women, and worry that their advances may be rejected. So the woman sings that she is a jaguar walking about: she asserts that she already knows the man is interested, and tells him to be more courageous.

Men have some help in interpreting the 'women's songs' sung to them. Firstly, women do not make them up, although they are allowed and encouraged to adapt standard songs to their own purposes. There is an established repertoire, and as I noted in the previous chapter, Matteson recorded that Piro people told her that these songs derived ultimately from the celestial gods. Secondly, many 'women's songs' refer to specific mythic narratives.[10] In Chapter 3, I noted how listening to a recording of *Mapchiri Wgene Jeji Shikale* led Julia Laureano spontaneously to narrate 'The Kochmaloto Women'. Similarly, *Mgenoklo Shikale* clearly refers to the end of 'The Birth of Tsla', where the jaguar grandmother Yompichgojru becomes suspicious, then frightened, and then runs away. Then there is the song, *Gayawagka Gajeru Shikale*, 'Pongo de Mainique Man Song', which refers to 'Tsla swallowed by a Giant Catfish', and *Maylo Shikale*, 'Female Black Vulture Song', which refers to the myth of how fire was found, and so on. These connections between songs and mythic narratives both help the man targeted by the song, and add depth to the feelings expressed in and through them.

In general, then, 'women's songs' are potent because, through them, women 'put themselves' as others: as animals, and especially as mythical beings. But

---

[9] Matteson (1954: 68) gives another version of this song, with alternative words.

[10] I say 'many' here because I know of certain songs which I cannot link to specific mythic narratives. However, I suspect that all 'women's songs' could ultimately be tied to Piro mythic narratives, if my knowledge of both were more extensive.

further, in asserting their own condition as other through these songs, women metaphorize the existential condition of men, who are their targeted audience. If the song works, which depends on the woman's charm and skill and the man's understanding, they produce sexual relationships.

In festivals, and especially in *kigimawlo*, women's singing of 'women's songs' takes on a new dimension. Drunk, they sing these songs in chorus. This is called 'accompanying', 'joining in with' (Piro, *gipxaleta*), as in the case of the 'drug songs' discussed in the preceding chapter. Here, rather than the specific sexual desire of this woman for that man, women's collective singing brings to the fore the generalized sexual desire of women for men. In *kigimawlo*, this leads to the men responding with instrumental music. In particular, the old men who play the *tumleji* flute (Ucayali Spanish, *piguano*) take up the women's songs, and play them back to the women as flute melodies. As flute music, the 'women's songs' are rendered wordless, and yet more generalized. In the male instrumental music, nothing need be 'guessed'.[11] They are also rendered much louder, for the playing of the *tumleji* stimulates other men to begin drumming. With this increase in loudness, *kigimawlo* is now in full swing.

With the *tumleji* and drumming filling the air, people now begin to dance. Men and women choose their partners for the special twirling dance of *kigimawlo* (Piro, *gansata*; Ucayali Spanish, *danzar*[12]). In dance, men and women come together as couples, and all the potentials of sexual conjunction are now in play: flirtation, assignation, jealousy, etc. The *kigimawlo* continues like this until the beer begins to run out. My informants varied in their estimation of how long this took: some said a week, others a month. Whichever might be true, like all Piro festivals, *kigimawlo* is about attaining and sustaining a plateau of *meyiwlu*, 'having fun': once worked up into this state by beer, music, and dancing, Piro people like to keep going until the beer runs out.

Throughout this festivity, the girl at its centre engages in two actions only. She serves the beer, and dances. But there is an important difference between her and everyone else: she does not drink herself to begin with, and she dances only with old men and women. She is not in 'drunkenness', and hence not in *meyiwlu*.[13] Further, she is obliged to be highly constrained in her behaviour, for she must not let the beer spill. This is no mean feat, for the bowl she serves from is very large and heavy, and presumably increases with difficulty as the people being served get drunker.[14] The penalty for spillage is the negation of

---

[11] Men also have a special genre called *jeji shikale*, 'men's songs'. I have never heard these sung by men, and the few examples I have heard sung by women do not allow for any generalizations. In my experience, when Piro men did sing for pleasure they invariably sang *huayno* or *cumbia* songs in Spanish.

[12] Matteson argues that the Piro verb *gansata* derives from the Spanish *danzar* (1965: 254).

[13] Compare to Shipibo–Conibo *Ani Shreati*, where the girl does get drunk (Roe 1982).

[14] This difficult task is similar to the extreme mediation of the removal of beer from the big *kaplalu* with the gourds tied to canes: everything is remote from normal practice. The 'good manners' of the girl (see Lévi-Strauss 1978) are like the prohibitions of shamanry, where nothing which has spilled over may be consumed. There is a theme here of control over flow: flow must be just right, rather than excessive.

the point of the whole ritual: rather than living a long time, if she spills the beer she will have a short life.

As the girl being initiated quietly goes about her work, two things are happening. Firstly, she jingles, from all the decorations and little rattles she wears. This is the first sound of *kigimawlo*. When I saw the ritual in Santa Clara in 1981, there was a palpable excitement in the guests, assembled sleepy and cold in the chilly dry season dawn, at the first sound of the girl's costume. This jingling sound is produced by the girl's movements. Having sat so long immobile, the girl is now on the move, setting in motion the transformations in sound that are so crucial to *kigimawlo*. As she goes about serving beer and dancing, she continues to jingle, and hence to animate the assembled multitude. Secondly, and at the same time, she is losing her decorations. Inevitably, her painted designs are fading, as discussed in Chapter 4. The girl's designs, like those of the guests, are in the process of *gitlika*, 'to fade, to ripen'. Then, as Antonio reported, the girl's crown is taken off her and put on the *tumleji* player. Finally, as the beer runs out, she is divested of all her decorations. I turn to that act next.

The Transformation of Humanity

Antonio, in his account, stressed that all the Piro people must be invited to the *kigimawlo*. All my informants stressed this, for 'all the Piro people along the river' must be invited to a *kigimawlo*. So, through this ritual, the Piro people scattered along the Urubamba in their separate villages are brought together, in the single big house of the festival. In the ritual event, all the living Piro people are brought together in one house in drunken singing and dancing. This is produced through the consumption of beer. This beer must be made by women; it is very hard work, and so, inevitably, it runs out at some point. In *kigimawlo*, as the beer begins to run out, the girl is finally and fully divested of her decorations, and her special *kigimawlo* skirt is replaced with an adult woman's skirt.

As this happens, the assembled guests sing *Konchoga Shikale*, '*Koncho* Beer Song'.[15] The following is the version sung for me by Clara Flores of Huau village, in 1988.

> *Konchoga, konchoga, konchoga*
> *Numeta, numeta, numeta*
> *Shapale, shapa*
> *Putagatanutkano*
> *Konchoga, konchoga,*

---

[15] My informants translated *konchoga* into Ucayali Spanish as *afrecho del masato*, 'dregs of the beer', but this is not the standard Piro term (*gichicha*): it would seem to be a loanword from Andean Quechua (see Zuidema 1985).

Konchoga, konchoga, numeta
Konchoga, konchoga, numeta
¿Ginakle wa koya?
Shapale, shapa
Putagatanutkano.

Koncho beer, *koncho* beer, *koncho* beer
I'm getting drunk, I'm getting drunk, I getting drunk,
Dear auntie, auntie,
You invite me to drink,
Koncho beer, *koncho* beer.

Koncho beer, *koncho* beer, I'm getting drunk,
Koncho beer, *koncho* beer, I'm getting drunk
Where is the beer?
Dear auntie, auntie,
You invite me to drink.

This song was interpreted by Lidia Fasabi, Clara Flores's daughter-in-law, as follows, '*Konchoga* is the dregs of the manioc beer. If today is a *kigimawlo*, what is left over of the beer tomorrow is the *konchoga*, and when they drink that, this is what they sing. They get drunk again on the dregs of the beer.'

With the singing of *Konchoga Shikale*, the transformations of music and of attendant subject positions reach their final point. As the assembled guests drink the dregs of the beer, which are thin, strong-smelling and potent, they sing to the mother of the girl to give them beer: '*Shapa, shapale*', which I translated above as 'Dear auntie, auntie'. An equally good translation, given Piro vocative kin terminology, would be, 'Dear mother-in-law, mother-in-law.' They thus sing from the subject-position of the prospective son-in-law of the girl's mother, and hence the prospective husband of the girl. They sing as if the whole assembly of guests were the son-in-law-to-be. In short, they sing collectively as potential affines. Further, the strong-smelling and potent beer of the dregs is a metaphor of amniotic fluid (see Gow 1989), which in this case would be the amniotic fluid of the future child of the initiand and her husband-to-be.

The music of *kigimawlo* thus proceeds from women's desire songs, which metaphorize the existential condition of their desired sexual partners as their own 'other' desire, through the wordless responding melodies of the *tumleji* and drums, to the full embodiment of the male affine's voice. But a Piro son-in-law could never say, as a son-in-law, what *Konchoga Shikale* says, for Piro men do not talk to their mothers-in-law (Matteson 1954; Gow 1991). What *Konchoga Shikale* does is to collectivize the position of the son-in-law-to-be, who can call on his 'dear auntie' to get him drunk, and in the process turn him into a son-in-law.

This transformation of subject position, whereby the assembled guests sing from the subject position of the son-in-law-to-be of the mother of the initiated girl, signals the coming end of the ritual and of the series of subject-position transformations, and focuses attention on a series of other transformations which *kigimawlo* effects. The girl for whom the ritual has been performed is now an adult woman, and a potential wife and mother. Her parents, the owners of the ritual, have become potential grandparents, while the 'old people', those who stand in a grandparent relationship to the girl and who took the lead in her decoration, in the flute music, and in the dancing, are being 'finished': of them, as of the beer, it will be said, *'Maleshatka'*, 'They are finished, there is nothing left'. Once the girl is a wife and mother, and her mother is a grandmother, there is no further place for the old people. However, the old women have done something, they have demonstrated the success of their own *kigimawlo* rituals long ago, for they, clearly, have lived a long time.

With the singing of *Konchoga Shikale*, and the complete removal of her decorations, the girl at the centre of the ritual is transformed into simply one of its participants. As Ricardo Alvarez puts it:

With this act, the girl definitively leaves her seclusion, and is admitted into society, which she enters in the dress of a Piro woman. She continues dancing, but no longer as the celebrated woman but as just as one more of the women gathered there. She can leave the dance and freely sit among the different groups of women to chat and laugh with them. (1963:11)

One might wish to demur at Alvarez's notion of 'an admission to society' here, for it smuggles an alien social logic into Piro ritual action. Closer to Piro people's ideas, I think, would be his characterization of the initiand divested of her special ornaments as just 'one more of the women gathered there'.

Finally, when even the 'beer of the dregs' has all been consumed, *kigimawlo* is over, and the guests disperse back to their villages. The Piro lived world has been temporarily condensed into a single house of *meyiwlu*, to effect the transformation of a girl into a woman. That done, the guests go home and the Piro lived world expands anew.

'All the Piro People along the River'

When *kigimawlo* is over, what has happened? The initiand has ideally been provided with a long life, and has been made marriageable. Now, as an ordinary adult woman, she will and should 'know men'. In this process, the guests who depart have been crucial, for, as my informants stressed, 'all the Piro people along the river' must be invited. *Kigimawlo* is, therefore, predicated on the opening up of the village, the place where people 'live well', to all other Piro people. Why should this be so? The answer lies, I think, in *Konchoga Shikale*: the guests are there to insert affinity into the village, in the form of the prefigured son-in-law of the girl's mother. It is not simply that the girl has been made into a woman, but that the ritual has, in the same movement, found her a husband, in the collective subject position of *Konchoga Shikale*.

From the point of view of the hosts, the guests are *yine*, 'humans', and they are, insofar as they are Piro people, by definition *wumolene*, 'our kinspeople'. But they are not *wumolene potu*, 'our real kinspeople'. Were this so, they would not have to arrive as guests: 'real kinspeople' live together in the same village. The guests have already denied being the 'real kinspeople' of the hosts by refusing to live together in the same village, and been denied as 'real kinspeople' by the hosts for the same reason (see Gow 1991: 221–5). The collapse of *gwashata*, 'living well' as mutual co-residence leads such 'real kinspeople' to become, progressively over time, 'distant kinspeople'. As such, the guests come to be potential affines, and the ideal source of the girl's husband-to-be.[16]

The logic of the guests in *kigimawlo* is one aspect of a consistent logic in the Piro lived world, whereby kin ties are denied in order for them to be recreated in another form. I have already discussed the example of birth ritual, where a co-resident is called to cut the neonate's umbilical cord. The cord-cutter, as someone who would normally be defined as a kinsperson, is through this act defined as non-kin to the child's parents. But in doing so, the cord-cutter, the child, and its parents enter immediately into new forms of relationship, as described in Chapter 4. These relationships are characterized by an increase in *kshinikanu*, 'mindful, thoughtful, respectful' behaviour, and hence become a kind of 'hyper-kinship' (see Gow 1991: 172–8). In order for a new-born baby to have the potential to become *yineru*, a 'human', a prior kin tie between the parents and a co-resident kinsperson must be temporarily denied, only to be re-created in a stronger form. However, it is these new 'hyper-kin ties' between the cord-cutter, the neonate, and its parents which allow for kin ties to develop between the child and its older kinspeople (see Gow 1997 for a fuller discussion of this point).

A similar process occurs in *kigimawlo*, for as Alvarez noted, the beginning of seclusion generates a similar 'hyper-kin tie' between an old woman and the pubescent girl in the holder/held relation. However, this relationship pales in the face of much more powerful form of 'hyper-kin tie' made by the ritual. This is the prefigured relationship between the girl's husband-to-be and her parents, especially her mother. After the marriage, this relationship, between son-in-law and parents-in-law, will be characterized by the most intensive *kshinikanu* behaviour of all: the mother-in-law and son-in-law seldom, if ever, speak to each other, but they will love each other strongly (see Matteson 1954: 79; Gow 1991: 134–7). As I noted above, in singing *Konchoga Shikale*, the assembled hosts and guests enunciate what the girl's husband-to-be will never be able to say to her mother, 'Mother-in-law, get me drunk!' This woman will then have converted from being a distant kinswoman into a real mother-in-law.

The denial of kin ties in *kigimawlo* takes an interesting and significant form.

---

[16] There is nothing to prevent a Piro girl marrying a co-resident man, but there is a general desire for sexual partners from other villages (Gow 1991: 129–46).

The hosts and guests, arrayed in their festive finery, appear to each other not as *yine*, 'humans', but as jaguars and anacondas. Their painted skins and clothing gives them the appearance of jaguars, while the abundant beadwork gives them the appearance of anacondas. The most intensively decorated person is, of course, the initiand herself. The husband-to-be has his first sight of his future wife leaving her seclusion in fully heightened jaguar and anaconda form.

This dramatic moment is, as I noted above, analogous to two other moments of novel appearance in the Piro lived world. At birth, the foetus and placenta emerge from the hidden womb into the space of the parents' house and the sight of its kinspeople-to-be. The neonate emerges with its *geyona*, 'first design', the placenta, attached to it. Similarly, in the 'drunkenness' of hallucinogens, the powerful beings become visible, first as design-covered anacondas, then as 'humans'. There is consistent logic whereby the sight of 'new people', the emergence of 'humans' from invisibility, is attended by design and its subsequent loss and transformation into fully human form.

The scene of *kigimawlo*, where hosts and guests appear to each other as jaguars and anacondas further evokes the scenes of the 'myths of myths' discussed before, 'The Birth of Tsla' and 'The Kochmaloto Women'. In the former, Tsla's mother Yakonero engages in a form of seclusion, by hiding in the eaves of her mother-in-law's house. When she leaves this seclusion, and joins the jaguars as a wife, she is undone, for she reveals her extreme difference to the jaguars by retching as she bites a jaguar's louse. The jaguars therefore treat her as a game animal, and eat her, rather than treat her as a wife. The Kochmaloto Women also engage in a kind of seclusion, this time high up in the *huito* tree. This seclusion is more successful, for it allows them to interact without danger with a succession of powerful beings and animals in human form. However, the Kochmaloto Women fail in the ultimate purpose of the seclusion, for they die quickly when they again meet 'real humans'.

If a key concern of these mythic narratives is with the disastrous consequences of marriage or sexual relations with dangerous animals like jaguars and anacondas, then the parallel concern of *kigimawlo* is with arranging the successful transformation of 'other people' (the guests) into co-resident affines. *Kigimawlo* openly asserts the collapse of *gwashata*, 'living well', by explicitly inviting people from other villages to come, as guests, to the ritual. As I discussed in *Of Mixed Blood*, host/guest relations necessarily affirm the definitive collapse of co-residence (Gow 1991: 221–5). As hosts and guests meet in the big house of the *kigimawlo*, they do so in the appearance of the dangerous others of the 'myths of myth', jaguars and anacondas.

Of course, the hosts and guests only 'look like' (*pixka*) jaguars and anacondas. They are really other people who have a history of bad relations with each other. This is revealed through the use of manioc beer. The hosts get the guests drunk, and hence get them to reveal themselves as 'humans'. Drunk, people sing the songs of desire, and effect desire in dancing. They shift from being 'distant kinspeople' in relation to each other, in the visual appearance of jaguars and anacondas, to becoming potential or real sexual partners. This transformation is only possible because hosts and guests actually *are* humans for each other, and because the beer can reveal this. Unlike neonates, with their placentas extending from their insides out, the hosts and guests have guts hidden inside their bodies which can be filled with beer. And unlike hallucinogens, beer is not itself a powerful being, and hence does not reveal itself to be human. Instead, it reveals these apparent jaguars and anacondas to be really humans, other Piro people.[17]

The transformations effected by *kigimawlo* are as much temporal as spatial. The guests at the ritual are, ideally, 'all the Piro people along the river'. As I noted in Chapter 3, the flow of the Urubamba river is the medium of Piro people's conceptions of historical processes, and this is as true of their understanding of the ongoing production of kin ties in village-making as it is of their ongoing relationships with kinds of white people (see Gow 1991). The historical making of kin ties can be seen as an ongoing dispersion of Piro people along the river as they make new villages, and move in search of places where they can 'live well'. But this river is also a maximal form of 'flow', like the 'flows' of menstrual blood, beer, and painted line which order the *kigimawlo*. The Urubamba river is *tsruru*, the 'big one', and its continued flow is the product of Tsla's actions, for it was he who frustrated the attempt to block its flow with a dam, as recounted in 'Tsla swallowed by a Giant Catfish'.

This same mythic narrative asserts that the Urubamba river is also the 'land of death', for it is the presence of mortality there that causes Tsla and the Muchkajine to leave. This 'land of death' is where Piro people live, and their lives are marked by mortality. *Kigimawlo*, by providing the girl with a 'long life', allows Piro people to effect all the changes which are required to ensure the ongoing production of their lived world despite that mortality. By celebrating the initiand's control over her menstrual blood, the ritual sets up the conditions for her future control over the flow of beer in her daughters' initiation rituals, and, further into the future, her control over the flow of design painting in rendering girls of her granddaughters' generation beautiful for their initiation rituals. Equally, the ritual sets up the transformations in kin relations which allow for sexual relations and for real affinity, by transforming 'distant kinspeople' into real husbands and wives and other affines. The ritual transforms the temporal distancing of kin ties into the genesis of future kin ties by creating new sexual relations. Coalesced in the big house of *kigimawlo*, all the Piro people along the river generate afresh the conditions for their re-dispersal along that river.

In the previous chapter, I showed how shamans seek to resolve the problem

---

[17] My analysis here has benefited greatly from discussion with Aparecida Vilaça on the comparable structure of Wari' ritual (see Vilaça 1992; 1997).

of mortality through a process of doubling, and becoming immortal. This is, from the point of view of other people, necessarily a solitary project of the shaman. *Kigimawlo* is a different, but parallel, solution to mortality, for it stresses multiplication, both in the assemblage of many people for the ritual, and in the ongoing multiplication of Piro people through marriages, impregnations, pregnancies, births, and the raising of children. The ritual seeks to achieve, through the initiand's projected 'long life', what the jaguars lost in the myth: the status of *gixolune*, 'being many', that is, a social life. But the ritual does not strive for the immortality characteristic of shamans, anacondas, or the divinities. Instead, it seeks to simply evade the fate of the Kochmaloto Women, who died too quickly. The purpose of *kigimawlo* is to effect the ongoing viability of Piro social life in a world marked by mortality, not to overcome this key condition of that world.

Changed Beyond all Recognition

In the 1980s, Piro people told me that the *kigimawlo* was no longer performed. This is a complicated issue, however. In one sense, this claim was untrue, for I had seen one myself, and other recent performances had been witnessed by others.[18] It is possible that my informants meant that it was now no longer performed as often or as elaborately as it had been in the past, which is probably true in part. Certainly, in the 1980s, almost all the oldest women I knew had undergone the ritual, while fewer middle-aged women had had it held for them, and very few young women. However, it is not clear to me that it was actually held less frequently. Given that the Urubamba Piro population has expanded rapidly since the 1940s, it is possible that the frequency of the ritual had remained the same as the population expanded, with the apparent effect that it was being held less often because relatively fewer girls underwent it. It is very difficult to know if, at any time in the past, all girls actually underwent the full *kigimawlo* ritual. My informants assured me that indeed, 'long ago', they did so.

Be that as it may, my informants in the 1980s assured me that this ritual was no longer performed. But they were able to provide detailed accounts of it, and in particular they would talk about it in the context of the past, and especially the remote past of the 'ancient people' and the more recent past of the *haciendas* and Vargas. Pancho Vargas was the main instigator of *kigimawlo* during the *hacienda* period, I was told, and was apparently an expert flute player. In my informants' accounts, he was portrayed as the collective 'old man' and 'father-in-law' of Piro people: he decided who got married and to whom.

When I asked Piro people why *kigimawlo* was no longer performed, they

---

[18] I saw a very short *kigimawlo* in Santa Clara in 1981, while Carlos Montenegro had seen a larger one in Sepahua in 1977 (personal communication) and Román (1985) reports another in 1984 in Miaría.

gave two replies. Firstly, I was told, people are 'too lazy' these days, and that *kigimawlo* is too much work. Secondly, and connected to this, they told me, 'There are too many people now, for you have to invite all the Piro people.' This would, given the population expansion, involve a quite astonishing quantity of beer and food. This explanation would seem entirely acceptable, but if we turn to the historical archive, we find that things are more complicated than contemporary people allowed. For example, Matteson noted of the situation in the late 1940s and 1950s:

Puberty rites and the accompanying festivities used to be one of the most colorful features of Piro life, so much so that whenever it was known that such a ceremony was to be held, local whites would try to be present, This intrusion, together with the general condemnation of the rite and festival by civilized neighbours, has resulted in its discontinuance in the villages nearest civilization. Recently in a town where whites prevented the usual puberty practices, a girl wearing European dress painted geometrical designs on the dress over her breast to celebrate, 'being ready' . . . Weddings in the past were much more colorful festivals than now, having been reduced for the same reason as the puberty festivals were discontinued. (1954: 79)

Matteson's evidence is a little contradictory here. Did local white people really flock to a girl's initiation ritual to condemn it? Had the ritual been generally discontinued, or only, 'in villages nearest civilization'? Which town was this where 'whites prevented the usual puberty practices'?

The first contradiction is relatively easy to clear up: clearly, local white people, on the whole, liked the ritual. That is why they attended it.[19] Who then were these 'civilized neighbours' who condemned it? A clue lies in Matteson's usage of the term 'town'. At the time, there were only three communities in the Bajo Urubamba area that could remotely merit this title, Atalaya, Sepahua, and Huau. Piro people do not seem to have lived in Atalaya in any great numbers, so the choice is between Sepahua and Huau. Since such rituals were performed in Sepahua and described by Ricardo Alvarez, it seems most likely that this 'town' was Huau itself, and that the disapproving 'whites' of Matteson's account were the Seventh-Day Adventists. I discuss this point further in Chapter 8, in the context of Adventist action among Piro people.

There is, however, more to this issue. Sebastián concludes the account of seclusion quoted earlier as follows, 'But now we don't do this. We do things differently now. Just recently we don't—we no longer diet—quickly also. There is no such practice now' (Matteson 1965: 144–5).[20] Sebastián does not place the correct performance of *kigimawlo* in an earlier period of his own life, but rather in the lifetime of *muchikawa tsrunni*, 'long ago ancient dead people'.

---

[19] I was told that when the infant-school teacher in Santa Clara announced that her pupils were to hold a play girl's initiation ritual, using ink for paint and drinking unfermented manioc beer, several local white people turned up in the village, expecting the real thing.

[20] I assume Sebastián's stifled 'quickly also', comment, refers, like Antonio's statement quoted above, to early assumption of sexual activity.

For Sebastián, Piro people of 'today' do not do this. Logically, therefore, we must suppose that the ideal performances for Piro people in the 1980s, which were located in the youth of the old people, were not so considered in the 1940s and 1950s.

What, then, is being lost? A key point here is contemporary Piro claims of 'laziness'. Many older people wanted to perform *kigimawlo*, but the others were *desanimados*, 'unwilling'. Collective action had to originate in a collective willingness to act. Lacking that collective desire, older people seemed to accept with relative equanimity the changed times: they did not seem unnecessarily burdened by tradition. In the 1980s, the collective desire for *meyiwlu*, 'having a good time', was channelled into the performance of the *fiestas de la Comunidad Nativa*, 'festivals of the Native Community', the 'Native Community' being the legally recognized land-holding unit of Peruvian law (see Gow 1991: 205–28). Apart from relatively small-scale personal parties, such as children's birthdays, or the larger San Juan and Carnival celebrations, all festivals were organized on a community basis, and all were tied to calendar dates, rather than to the developing body of a girl. As I described in *Of Mixed Blood*, the festivals are marked by a progress from fairly formal community action, with a marking of the village identities of hosts and guests in the schoolhouse, towards chaotic drunkenness throughout the host village, then spreading to other villages.

These rituals focus on the school and the formal identity of the village as a registered *Comunidad Nativa*. Both facets are closely tied to writing, and to the status of 'being civilized': the school is the place were the knowledge of writing is transmitted, and the power of the *Comunidad Nativa* status resides in its official inscription on paper in the title documents (see Gow 1995a). However, as I argued in Chapter 4, writing is experienced by Piro people as a transformation of 'design', such that the school and the *Comunidad Nativa* can be thought of as transformations, in the strictly Lévi-Straussian sense, of 'design'. That would suggest that the *fiestas de la Comunidad Nativa* might be transformations of *kigimawlo*.

It seems an audacious leap to see the 'festivals of the *Comunidad Nativa*' as *kigimawlo* transformed. Can this be sustained? Schools, and especially the secondary schools, *escuela secundaria*, operate through very similar principles to the older puberty seclusion. Piro people emphasized the importance, in the school, of their children's constant attendance day after day, and their ceaseless attention to the art of writing, much as the secluded girl devotes herself to spinning cotton. Further, Piro people showed a strong preference for sending older children to distant secondary schools, where they had to be boarders (see Artemio's experiences in Ch. 1): boarding away is therefore like puberty seclusion. There are important differences, however. With the school, the long-term viability of Piro social relations is now seen to rest with active engagement with 'white people's knowledge', rather than 'old time people's knowledge'. The school and the *Comunidad Nativa* reveal the viability of Piro sociality as an expansion of numbers, for Piro people emphasize the growth and multiplication of their villages in recent times. Therefore, the very thing that makes *kigimawlo* 'too much work', the fact that there are now so many Piro people, makes the festivals of the *Comunidad Nativa* both possible and desirable. The rituals in the 1980s were not focused on the celebration of one girl's attainment to maturity, but on the education and preparation of all children for adulthood.

Schools, in the 1980s, were a form of 'seclusion' for all children, from a young age, in the 'schoolhouse': this was to give them the knowledge to *defenderse*, 'look after themselves' (see Gow 1991: 229–51; 1990a). This 'seclusion' is regularly celebrated through the *fiestas de la Comunidad Nativa*, which preserve almost exactly the key features of *kigimawlo*, but now directed at the school and schoolchildren. Each *fiesta de la Comunidad Nativa* began with presentations by schoolchildren, which was then followed by food, football matches, manioc beer drinking, and dancing. It is even possible that this new 'seclusion' and its new rituals respond to the latent desire for a 'male *kigimawlo*', which I noted above.

The *fiestas* of the 1980s differed from *kigimawlo* in all surface characteristics, but they were also almost identical at a more profound level. Both are about *meyiwlu* and drunkenness. Both are about knowledge, whether of 'design' and '*tumleji*-flute music', or of 'civilization'. Both are about the decoration and transformation of appearance, whether as jaguars or as white people. And both are about music, be it the music of 'women's songs' or the newer music of *cumbia* records. And both are about sexual desire. This profound identity between the two forms of ritual performance was what allowed Piro people in the 1980s to see them as the same kinds of things, for both are *fiestas* and *meyiwlu*, 'festivals, ritual performances, having a good time'. But this profound identity also sustained and gave meaning to the differences between *kigimawlo* and the *fiestas de las Comunidades Nativas*. The latter drew much of their meaning for contemporary Piro people, young and old, from the fact that they were not things of the *tsrunni*, 'the ancient people'. These *fiestas* were consciously experienced as novel, and inserted into historical narratives of transforming relationships to white people. These historical narratives include the *kigimawlo*, the major ritual activity of their oldest participants, but only as a ritual that is no longer performed.

What has changed here? Apparently everything and nothing. There is, however, a deeper point to note, for *kigimawlo* was never about stability. This ritual was already about transformation: the transformation of a girl into a woman, and all the other transformations which the ritual effects in the Piro social world. Therefore to say the Piro people's festivals have changed is slightly inadequate. It would be better to say that the Piro people have changed the way they change themselves. There is one small clue in the literature which suggests that the transformation in Piro ritual performances follows a logic that is inherent in Piro people's conceptualizations of ritual performance. Ricardo Alvarez states the following:

The origins of [the initiation rituals] are not within the tribe itself, nor are they copied from other groups. Tradition asserts that they were imposed by a people who spiritually dominated the Piro, without specifying which people these were, although all Piro people agree in saying: 'The Inca taught it to us.' (1962: 35)

I never heard anything of this kind, and no mention is made of this by Matteson or other writers. Alvarez's own account is enigmatic: how can the common assertion he reports that the Inca taught this ritual to Piro people be squared with his statement that the people who taught it are never specified?[21] That said, however, it does seem that Piro people once associated this ritual with another, non-Piro, people. If their 'traditional' ritual life was held to have been of alien origin, it seems reasonable to suppose that it would have facilitated an active acquisition of a new ritual life from other peoples.

Sticking to the surer knowledge of actual descriptions of the ritual, it is clear that *kigimawlo* has always been, for as long as it has been performed and known, about 'other people'. The ritual always implicated 'white people'. This is true in two forms. Firstly, the beadwork (*kigimchi*) which gave the ritual its name was a product of relations of exchange with white people, transformed into body-decorations with Piro designs (see Clotilde Gordón's statement in Ch. 3).[22] As such, beadwork can be seen as a precursor to the *fiestas* of the 1980s, where Piro people emphasize their relations with *kajine*, 'white people' even more dramatically. Indeed, as I discussed in Chapter 4, in the 1980s, Piro people dressed for *fiestas* in their best 'white people's clothing', and it could be argued that this is an extension of the 'white people'-meaning of 'beadwork' to the total appearance of the hosts and guests (see Gow 1991: 223–4 on the role of 'being civilized' in *fiestas*). The second role of 'white people' in the *kigimawlo* is even more direct, for when Piro people lived as debt slaves on the *haciendas* of Pancho Vargas, it was he, I was told, who sponsored the *kigimawlo*, and played the *tumleji* flute. During this period, *kigimawlo* literally had a white man at its centre.

The transformation from *kigimawlo* to the *fiestas de las Comunidades Nativas* follows a consistent logic, when viewed from the place of white people within these two ritual performances. *Kigimawlo* implicates white people in its focus on beadwork, and hence the sources of the raw materials for these decorations, the glass beads. The period of residence on the *haciendas* was strongly associ-

---

[21] In marked contrast to many of their neighbours (Weiss 1975; Lathrap, Gebhart-Sayer and Mester 1985), Piro people seldom attribute importance to the Incas in their mythic or historical narratives. The major role of the Incas is their malign activities in 'Tsla Swallowed by a Giant Catfish'. This feature must, I believe, be related to the historical role of Piro people as active traders with the Inca state.

[22] The Piro word for glass bead, *tuwutu*, can be plausibly analysed as 'supernatural salt'. This suggests that glass beads replaced the meanings of salt for Piro people, as the famous trade in salt from the Cerro de la Sal on the Perené river declined (see Renard-Casevitz 1993).

ated, in the 1980s, with Vargas's exploitation of Piro people's ignorance, and they liberated themselves from that ignorance by moving out of the *haciendas* to the new villages with schools. There, a new generation of Piro people, like Artemio, learned to read and write. Thus, they learned a new form of *yonchi*, 'white people's designs', and performed new rituals, the *fiestas de las Comunidades Nativas*, focused on the schools. Therefore, *yonchi*, central to *kigimawlo*, was transformed into 'writing', and the new rituals celebrated a new mode of control over relations with white people.

My account of *kigimawlo*, therefore, presents a third example of a transformation of a transformation, to join the account of design and shamanic cosmology discussed in the previous chapters of this part. Indeed, this is hardly surprising, given the tight linkages between these three domains in the Piro lived world. In Part III, I turn towards a more historically-oriented approach, to suggest reasons why these transformations of transformation took place, in an analysis of how the modes of transformational action described here link up with the horizons of the Piro lived world. Before that, however, I want briefly to return to the evening of 15 January 1982.

On the Surface of the Moon

My formulation of a concept of transformations of transformations in the chapters of Part II contains a certain inherent problem. What is the historical meaning of these transformations, and in what temporal frames do they operate? In what ways were the regular *fiestas de la Comunidad Nativa* in the 1980s informed by the very rare performances of *kigimawlo*? In what ways did shamanic action in the down-river *ayahuasquero* style in the 1980s draw its meanings from a defunct shamanry directed at celestial beings? And in what ways did the meanings of going to school or wearing 'white people's clothing' for a Piro child in the 1980s depend on the muted presence of 'Piro people's designs' and 'Piro people's clothing'? Are these transformations of transformations purely historical phenomena, meaningful only from an external analyst's point of view, or were they meaningful to Piro people in the 1980s?

Throughout the chapters of Part II, I have based my discussions on a single evening of narration, that by Antonio Urquía and Teresa Campos in November 1988.[23] This has shown that it was possible, with a minimum of recourse to the documentary archive, but a maximum of recourse to my own field data collected in the 1980s, to produce an account of these transformations of transformations. This strongly suggests that the transformations of transformations are not merely historical features of social change, with one mode of practice replacing another over time, but could be thought of by Piro people in the 1980s in the way I have discussed them here. All the major structural

---

[23] My argument here owes much to discussions with Tânia Stôlze Lima.

coordinates of the transformations of transformations were clearly co-present in the 1980s, for all appear in Antonio and Teresa's narrations of November 1988. It must be remembered here that several young children were present on that night too, and were, indeed, the privileged listeners of those accounts.

One transformation of a transformation, however, was missing on that night: the contact between celestial beings and humans which ordered the older form of Piro shamanic practices. However, it should be recalled that, as I discussed in Chapter 3, this was the night on which Antonio could not remember the 'ancient people's story' about the moon. What was that mythic narrative? In April 1982, as I noted in Chapter 3, Antonio had told it to me as follows, 'My grandparents said that the stars were people. So too was the moon. The moon used to come down to earth. A girl, who didn't sleep with men from here, slept with the moon. She painted his face with *huito*. For this reason it has black marks on it when it is full.' Despite its brevity, this very short story connects the 'ancient people's story' about the moon, the contact between a celestial being and a human woman, to puberty seclusion. In Antonio's story, the girl 'didn't sleep with men from here', much as the girl in puberty seclusion, 'does not know men'. Further, when she sleeps with the moon, she paints his face with *huito*, much as the secluded girl constantly blackens herself with this same dye. The dark stains on the surface of the moon are, therefore, the product of an illicit union between a secluded girl and a celestial being.

A secluded girl, as I discussed above, does not 'know men': the penalty for this would be a failure to grow fat and beautiful. The girl in the myth, who does have contact with a man, renders his face darker. And darker in a specific way, for as I noted in Chapter 4, 'blotchiness' is opposed to 'with design'. 'Blotchiness' is ugly, and associated with the marks of rotting. This myth of the moon is the myth of origin of moonlight, that special light which, as we saw in Chapter 1, Piro people associate with *ayahuasca* hallucinatory experience. The rupture of a girl's seclusion leads to the ideal conditions for seeing powerful beings take on human form.

Antonio's extremely short version can be supplemented by two slightly longer versions in the literature. One was told to Matteson by Sebastián, and runs as follows:

Long ago, the moon was very bright, very white. However, one day he kept annoying Klana. She was very dark, she always painted herself with *huito*. Klana was very dark. He always said to her, 'That one is very dark! Look at me, I'm nice and white!'

Klana got tired of it. She grabbed his face with her hands covered in the dark juice of *huito*. All day long he tried to wash his face, but in vain. That is why we now see the moon with black stripes. This is because of Klana's hand, it looks like a hand there. Nowadays he is not very bright. Long ago he really shone, and at night things could be seen clearly. But because of Klana, now it is not very bright. (Matteson 1965: 168–71)

The other was told by Doris Pacaya, presumably to the SIL missionary Joyce Nies. It runs as follows:

Long ago, there was a woman called Klana. She was always making herself beautiful. She had very white skin and very long hair. One day she went to look for *huito* fruit. When she found a *huito* tree, others went up to get the fruit for her. She put them in her basket and took them home.

Cutting the skin of the fruit, she put the pulp in a clay pot. When the *huito* pulp had turned black, Klana painted her legs, face, arms and wrists.

The Moon came along and bothered her. He said, 'Paint me too.' He annoyed the one who was painting herself.

She pretended not to hear him and looked the other way. She grabbed the *huito* pulp, but the Moon did not guess what she was going to do because he was not looking at her. When he turned back to look at her and started to talk to her, Klana stained his face with *huito*.

That is why the Moon now has stains on his face. It's his own fault, because he was bothering the one who was making herself beautiful.

That is all there is to this story. (Nies 1972: 103–7)

In contrast to Antonio's story, these versions do not assert that the moon slept with Klana: in these versions, the moon is merely 'annoying' (that is, flirting with) her. However, they do what Antonio's version does not do, for they provide a motive for Klana's painting of the moon's face: the moon is flirting with Klana, and in revenge she smears his face with her *huito*-stained hands. There, however, they part company, for Sebastián's version asserts that Klana was painting herself all over with *huito*, like a girl in puberty seclusion, while Pacaya's version asserts that Klana was painting herself with designs, and she is clearly not in puberty seclusion, for she searches for *huito* trees. This connects to a further difference: in Sebastián's version, the moon is very white while Klana is black, while in Pacaya's version, Klana is very white and beautiful. Further, the valence of blame for the current state of the moon is inverted: in Sebastián's version, it is Klana who is to blame for the current darkness of the moon, while Pacaya's version lays the blame firmly on the moon himself.

Ricardo Alvarez, in his collection of Piro mythic narratives, apparently collected no versions of this story. However, his book does contain two myths about the moon (see full texts in Myth Appendix). First, and closest to the versions discussed above, there is the short myth, 'Klana, the Discontented Woman' (1960: 98–9). In this version, Klana is most assuredly not in puberty seclusion, and is noted for her active pursuit of men. But it does seem to contain a allusion to the scene of the painted face in the following passage: 'She wanted to marry the moon and she even stretched out her hand for him to grab her and take her with him. But the moon did not want her, for one of Klana's husbands was the moon's brother.' Here, rather than rejecting the moon's advances, or accepting only his, Klana is rejected by the moon because she has sex with too many men. This version, therefore, extends the inversions noted in the other versions of the myth about the moon even further.

These inversions are further extended in another myth collected by Ricardo Alvarez, 'The Moon's Festival' (1960: 76–9). This long narrative seems to be utterly different from those already mentioned, but it contains many similar elements. Here the moon descends from the sky to attend the *kigimawlo* of a Piro girl, but no mention is made of the painting of his face, or of any sexual relation between the moon and the girl. Instead, the moon arrives as the guest at the initiation ritual of the intended wife of a dead Piro man. It is this dead man whose face is obscured in the myth, by a cloth rather than by painting. And rather than being painted by a human woman, here the moon offers beer to humans: instead of a human woman covering the moon's face with painting 'flow', the moon offers people a beer 'flow', but one which has the disgusting rotting qualities which attach to the painted face of the moon in the other versions. And where Klana's marking renders the moon's face 'blotchy' like a corpse, here the moon's beer makes its drinkers 'change skin', and achieve immortality.

What is the meaning of all these inversions? We need hardly be surprised by variation among different versions of mythic narratives, as I have discussed in depth already. But here, I think, we are confronting something rather different from ordinary variation. The extreme variations and inversions we see in these versions of the story about the moon seem, to me, to be co-ordinate with its forgetting: it becomes hard to remember because it is being radically destabilized by the profound inversions to which it is subject. Lévi-Strauss, commenting on the nature of this process in an essay on how myths die, has noted:

We know that myths transform themselves. These transformations . . . bear sometimes on the framework, sometimes on the code, sometimes on the message of the myth, but without ceasing to exist as such. Thus these transformations respect a sort of principle of conservation of mythic material, by which any myth could always come from another myth. However, the integrity of the original formula may itself deteriorate in the course of this process. This formula degenerates or evolves, as you will, beyond the stage were the distinctive characteristics of the myth are still recognisable, and where myth retains what a musician might call its 'lilt'. In such cases, what does the myth become? (1977: 256)

Lévi-Strauss goes on to argue that myths finally exhaust themselves through these transformations, and transform into fictional elaborations or into history.

Lévi-Strauss's argument is couched in terms of the death of myth as it passes spatially from one people to the next. My argument here follows his, but from the perspective of time, and hence adds a new possibility. In the case of the Piro mythic narratives about the moon, we see that they can also simply become unmemorable, and as such, slip into silence. But perhaps 'slip into silence' is not the best formulation, for we already know of another possibility for this mythic narrative: it may transform into a question to a *gringo*. As we have seen, on 15 January 1982, Artemio asked me if it were true that Americans had been to the moon. On that occasion, he even provided a minimal version of the myth, in the negative, so to speak, when he reported his mother's words, 'She told me that the ancient people said that the moon is a man with no home, who is always wandering about.' This detail is absent from any of the other known versions, and suggests that Artemio's version, had I ever have been able to elicit it, would have been marked by the same level of inversion as the known ones.

On the evening of 15 January 1982, the mythic narrative of the moon did not simply die. Instead, it was transformed into a long conversation about the nature of the cosmos, and ended in another mythic narrative, 'A Man who went under the Earth'. On that evening, I was still in the grip of a common folk model of how cultural traditions like those of indigenous Amazonian peoples weaken and disappear. Lévi-Strauss's work opens up a new possibility. He suggests that as myths die, they can form a retrospective or a prospective history. While the former founds a traditional order on a distant past, the latter, makes 'this past the beginning of a future which is starting to take shape' (Lévi-Strauss 1977: 268). The Piro myth about the moon can transform itself into a conversation about the remarkable power of *gringos*.

Whatever else the Piro mythic narratives about the moon are about, they all seem to concern contacts between humans and a celestial being. As I have already discussed at length, such mythic narratives seem to be disappearing from the Piro lived world. We saw one example of this process in the transformations of the mythic narrative about the white-lipped peccaries, from Sebastián's first version to Artemio's 'A Man who went under the Earth', where the chronological sequence of the narrations is marked by the transformation of the celestial journey from that of a human to that of the white-lipped peccaries. In Chapter 5, I noted how this same feature, the loss of contact between humans and celestial beings, is occurring in Piro shamanic cosmology, where it is being replaced by a heightened concern for the powerful beings of the river and forest.

Piro shamanic cosmology provides us with a clue to what is happening here. The contemporary modes of shamanic action, focused as they are on powerful beings of the river and forest, constantly affirm for Piro people the interest of the Piro 'myths of myth', dealing as they do with relations between humans and the key predators of the river and forest domains. The mythic narratives about the moon, however, have lost their anchorage in the older mode of shamanic practice directed at the celestial divinities, and are hence fragmenting and becoming forgotten, as are other mythic narratives about contacts with celestial beings.

This point connects up with Alvarez's otherwise enigmatic comment quoted above, that the snake-skin bracelets worn by the girl in seclusion, 'transmit vitality to her and make her worthy of the gaze of the gods' (1962: 37). This brief remark suggests that part of the function of the girl's seclusion is to keep her away from contact with humans in order to render her more beautiful in the sight of the *goyakalune*, the celestial divinities, and that seclusion is a period of intense communion between the secluded girl and these divinities. No other sources on the *kigimawlo* mention this feature, but I do not think it can be easily dismissed, for it fits beautifully with the logic of the ritual itself. The girl acquires, in seclusion, a privileged relationship with the eternal celestial divinities, which must then be collectivized through the 'good times' of the ritual to provide the ongoing viability of the Piro lived world.

As we have seen, the *kigimawlo* is being replaced in this project of ongoing viability by the *fiestas de la Comunidad Nativa*, through a process of increasing engagement with 'white people's knowledge'. White people have, over the century, become increasingly central to Piro people's sense of the viability of their lived world. Is this increased centrality of white people connected to the loss of the shamanic practices of contact with celestial beings, and with the loss of mythic narratives about such contacts?

This brings us back to the themes of the conversation of 15 January 1982, when my question to Artemio about the stars led him to ask me about the Americans and the moon, and eventually led him to tell me, 'A Man who went under the Earth'. The analysis here suggests that a deeper understanding of that conversation requires a wider reflection on the meaning of Artemio's question, 'Is it true that the Americans have been to the moon?' That requires a deeper knowledge of what exactly 'Americans' could mean to Artemio, and how he was able to link them to the 'ancient people's story' about the man who turned into a white-lipped peccary in the underworld. That will require an analysis of how, over the past century, Piro people invented Americans, and *gringos*, for themselves. It is to this problem that Part III is dedicated.

PART III

The *Gringos*

7

The *Gringos* Envisioned

In Part II, through the analysis of the two Piro 'myths of myth', I explored a series of important modes of transformational action in the Piro lived world, and the manner in which these modes of action are themselves transforming. This analysis finally arrived at the other myth from the evening of conversation on 15 January 1982, the 'ancient people's story' about the moon. In the process, it became clear that very important changes had taken place for Piro people in the course of the twentieth century. Key transformations occurred in their lived world, and in the means by which that lived world was to be projected into the future. The analysis of design, clothing and the girl's initiation ritual suggested that these transformations of transformations were linked to the growing place of white people in the Piro lived world, and the analysis of shamanry and the myth of the moon suggested that this change is co-ordinated with a transformation in Piro people's ideas about celestial beings. This in turn extended and deepened the understanding of the issues raised in Part I, the problems posed by 'A Man who went under the Earth'.

In the chapters of Part III, I carry this analysis forward, in search of a solution to the puzzle of the conversation of 15 January 1982. What exactly is the connection between my story of what Americans found on the moon and Artemio's story, 'A Man who went under the Earth'? In Chapter 2, I suggested that this latter story is intrinsically meaningful for the relationships that Piro people have with *gringos*, and in Chapter 3 I noted its relationships to the 'ancient people's story', 'Tsla swallowed by a Giant Catfish', which I suggested was the Piro 'myth of history'. In one sense, the solution to this problem is simple enough, and was detailed in Chapter 1, namely that Americans, *gringos*, had played an important role in the lives of Piro people from the late 1940s onwards, in the form of SIL missionaries, and they had been a prominent feature of Artemio's own life. But, as I demonstrated in Part II, what American missionaries did in this area over that period was connected to endogenous transformations within the Piro lived world that probably had little to do with their activities, even if Piro people in the 1980s told me that they did.

In Part III, therefore, I am looking for the historical conditions of the transformations of transformations, and how these connect to the forgetting of the myth of the moon, and to the transformations in the myth about visiting the subterranean world of the white-lipped peccaries. Because this is so, I must stress again a point made in the Introduction: the historical analysis engaged in here is regressive, for it starts from a problem raised by my own fieldwork data from the 1980s. Therefore my interest here is not really with questions of the sort, 'How did Piro people react to the arrival of SIL missionaries?', although such questions are addressed here. My interest is in how the situation I found in the 1980s could have come into being as a transformation of previous states of the system. Since this system is clearly located in how Piro people think and act, and have thought and acted, it must be sought there, and not in what we might happen to know about the recent history of the Bajo Urubamba area. For this project, we need some good evidence for how Piro people were thinking and acting in the past.

Unfortunately, as I discussed in the Introduction, the nature of the documentary archive and the mode in which it was produced means that, until very recently, it does not contain much that can reliably be considered to be anything that Piro people may ever have said or thought. On the whole, Piro people's thoughts were only recorded when they intersected strongly with those of the documentarists. For example, Sabaté's account of his travels among Piro people in 1874 contains much of interest, referring as it does to the period immediately prior to the extension of the rubber industry into the Bajo Urubamba area. But Sabaté only records what Piro people said to him when it impinges directly on his own interests in his journeyings and in the potential for evangelization. Reading his account, it is clear that the Piro people he met must have had very complex motivations of their own for how they acted, but Sabaté tells us nothing of them. This pattern is general to the archive until very recently.

There is, luckily, one very significant exception to this pattern, 'The Story of Sangama' (Matteson 1965: 216–33; Sebastián, Zumaeta, and Nies 1974: 189–230; all subsequent quotations are from Matteson's text). It was told by the Piro leader Morán Zumaeta to the SIL missionary Esther Matteson, and concerns his older cousin Sangama, who was the first Piro person who claimed to know how to read. The story refers to the early decades of the twentieth century, when Piro people were living in debt-slavery to their white bosses, and long before any attempt was made to provide schooling for them. I have already published a preliminary analysis of this story (Gow 1990; 1996). I summarize here the key points of that analysis, but I also extend it to another aspect of this text: what it was that Sangama read from the papers he found thrown away by the white bosses. In particular, I am interested in Sangama's prophetic description of an aeroplane, and of the attempt by distant people, the *paneneko*, the 'very much other people', to send goods by aeroplane to Piro people to liberate them from dependence on their bosses. My argument is that 'The Story of Sangama' gives us access to how Piro people, or at least some of them, were thinking in the early decades of the twentieth century, and helps to elucidate the complex changes in design, in shamanic cosmology, and in ritual that I documented in Part II.

That 'The Story of Sangama' should be among our earliest documents to record at length Piro people's own formulations of their world, and that it should be centrally concerned with writing and with aeroplanes, is far from fortuitous. The practice of writing and reading is central to the SIL project, focused as it is on obedience to the command of Jesus, 'Go ye therefore, and teach all nations, baptising them in the name of the Father, and of the Son, and of the Holy Ghost' (Matthew 28: 19). In SIL practice, this commission is understood as an injunction to translate the Bible into all existing human languages, such that the Gospels are immediately available to everyone in the vernacular. Further, SIL missionary action was always conceived in techno-cratic terms, for they were willing to make full use of technologies like aero-planes and radios, and experienced such technologies as key to their success (see Stoll 1982). Literacy and aeroplanes were, therefore, both important prac-tical media of SIL evangelical action, and powerful symbols of that action for SIL missionaries.[1] It comes as no surprise, then, that Esther Matteson found Zumaeta's story about Sangama worth recording and publishing.

Morán Zumaeta's Story about Sangama

'The Story of Sangama' is a personal-experience narrative told by Morán Zumaeta about his older cousin Sangama, whom Zumaeta had known in his youth. It is difficult to date exactly the period during which the events related in 'The Story of Sangama' occurred. Matteson records that she worked with Morán Zumaeta in 1948 (1965: 2). She reports that he had a son about thirty years old (ibid.: 137), but does not specify to which year this fact refers. In 1982, his granddaughter Lilí Torres Zumaeta, wife of Artemio Fasabi, who was born in 1950, described him to me as old but still active, which suggests he was not more than seventy-five to eighty years old. I met Zumaeta in September 1988 in Miaría, but his ill health prevented any interview. He seemed to me by then to be in his eighties.[2] If these guesses are correct, the events referred to in Zumaeta's story cannot be placed after the mid-1920s, at the latest, for he states that it was in his childhood (before puberty) that he knew Sangama. But it is unlikely that it refers to a time earlier than 1912, the collapse of the rubber industry, for the circumstances of the story indicate a more settled existence than the upheavals and migrations that accompanied the later years of rubber production (see Gow 1991: 42–4). Taken together, these fragments of evidence suggests that the period of the story is from about 1912 to the early 1920s.

It is essential to remember that 'The Story of Sangama' is a personal-expe-rience narrative, and hence must be understood in the specific context of who

---

[1] Indigenous Amazonian peoples' wonder at aeroplanes and writing are common themes in SIL literature (see Wallis 1966 on Shapra, and 1961 on Huaorani).

[2] The continuing importance of Sangama for contemporary Piro people was indicated in the name given by Zumaeta to the organization of native communities based in Miaría, *La Federación Guillermo Sangama.*

is telling it to whom and when. It was specifically addressed to Matteson, the woman who was teaching Zumaeta to read and write in Piro, and may have been introducing him to literacy for the first time. As we shall see, however, Zumaeta clearly thought that things were more complicated than that. And it was being told during a period of dramatic enthusiasm for learning this knowledge. Matteson herself reported,

The ability of some to read Spanish . . . indicates an intense desire for learning and progress, since the advance was made in Spanish-speaking schools where the Piro appeared stupid, and were ridiculed and scolded. They persisted until many of them could sound out the words quite fluently, but in a majority of cases without very full understanding of the content . . . In 1947 under the auspices of the Summer Institute of Linguistics, a Piro orthography was prepared and primers and booklets were presented to the people. They were received enthusiastically. Well over a hundred and fifty have undertaken to learn to read, and of them about forty read well at present.[3] (1954: 65)

The enthusiasm of this response by Piro people to SIL education must be understood in the context of how writing had been experienced by Piro people before this time. Before the 1940s, writing had been both a practical and a symbolic marker of the power differential between Piro people and their white bosses. In the language of the era, *los blancos civilizados*, 'the civilized whites', could read and write, while the *indios salvajes*, 'the savage Indians, the wild Indians' could not (see Gow 1991: 42). There does not seem to have been a particular effort on the part of the bosses to stop their indigenous workers from reading and writing, and no mention is made in Zumaeta's story of any reaction from the bosses to Sangama's activities. Rather, it was simply taken as the natural condition.[4] The meaning of writing on the Bajo Urubamba at this time emerges in Ricardo Alvarez's account of Martín Saavedra, a white man who fled with his Piro affines from the abuse of white bosses during the first decade of this century. Alvarez's account is clearly based on Piro personal-experience narratives. Alvarez reports that the boss Baldomero Rodriguez, trying to find out if Saavedra was a Piro or a white man, sent him a letter in his hiding place: obviously, it was assumed, only a white man could reply (R. Alvarez 1959: 47).

To what extent the white bosses of that time made use of writing in their dealings with their Piro workers, I do not know. In other areas of Amazonia in that era, and more recently on the Bajo Urubamba, there was a ritualization of the debt relations through the careful annotation in account books of the transfer of

---

[3] Zumaeta may have been one of those Piro people who learned to read and write in Spanish from the Adventists. See also Sebastián's account of his attempts to learn to read, as discussed in Chapter 8.

[4] Later, as schools were opened, there was direct opposition to such education for indigenous people by certain white bosses. Others, with an eye to the future, came to see the potential value, to themselves, of an educated and hence skilled labour force (see Gow 1990b; 1991).

goods and the subsequent debts.[5] This was never mentioned by my older informants in their accounts of Pancho Vargas: I have the impression from these accounts that Vargas preferred to rely on memory and secrecy in these transactions, and on a careful assessment of how much he could get away with. Judging by Zumaeta's story, writing seems to have occupied a rather exalted position in the eyes of Piro people: Sangama tells Zumaeta, 'When the white man, our boss, sees a paper, he holds it up all day long . . .'. Although unnamed in the story, this boss was very probably Vargas himself. Writing was thus seen as a mysterious knowledge of the whites, connected in some way to the mystery of their leisure, wealth, and extraordinary power.

A Sky Steamboat full of Clothes

Sangama told Zumaeta and his other kinspeople that the papers he read, which had been picked up from the rubbish thrown out by the white bosses, were written by his own children living in the very distant cities of Manaos and Belem do Pará, far down-river along the Amazon in Brazil, and in Europe. I discuss Sangama's remarkable account of the mechanics of writing and reading later, but I begin my analysis of Zumaeta's story with Sangama's account of what the papers were telling him. This allows us a better understanding of the story in the specific historical conditions of Sangama's world.

In Zumaeta's story, Sangama makes it clear that the power of the white bosses over Piro people rests on their knowledge of writing, and the way in which that knowledge gave them control over the fluvial trade. Sangama constantly reiterates the chain of places on the riverine system which governed the rubber industry, 'Manaos, Pará, and Europe'. Then, however, he goes on to subvert this known geography and means of transport with the fantastic image of the *ten-gogne yapachro waporo*, the 'sky steamboat'. Zumaeta reports Sangama as saying, of a paper that his cousins have asked him to read:

It says that in Pará there is a sky steamboat [*ten-gogne yapachro waporo*, 'sky travelling steamboat'], and that it is coming here.

In its prow is a big dog, with a shining collar. It is chained and locked, it says. The dog travels in the prow of the sky steamboat.

The steamboat travels through the sky, and people travel there, those who are coming to us.

There are people who are impeding its coming, those who live midway, shooters. They keep shooting at the sky steamboat with wings. They try to shoot it down. They turn it back by shooting at it all the time. That makes it turn back.

That is what they tell, the ones who live in what's-it-called—Pará, who say, *'telenten-ten, telenten, ten, ten, ten, ten. Ten, ten, telelelelen, ten, ten, ten, ten, ten.'* That's what they say.

---

[5] See Huxley and Capa (1965) and D'Ans (1982) for the Bajo Urubamba area, and S. Hugh-Jones (1992).

You are the ones they would want to visit. They are thinking about you. Then you would have the sky steamboat, and you would wear the clothing included in the merchandise.

Then some of the others who were listening to his words said, 'That's what we'd do when the clothing came. We'd put it on.'

I also was there listening intently, and delighted with what he read from the paper. It seemed to be true that he was reading from the paper.

Then he said, 'When the merchandise comes it will all be given away. The people there told me,' he said.

'It would be wonderful if it would come. What's the matter with those who live midway? They keep shooting the sky steamboat. They keep shooting the sky steamboat and it escapes and returns. They are guilty for hindering her,' he said.

Then he announced, 'Look. That's the way we would like to be. I'm like this now. I don't wear trousers, nor shirt. I never do. You've never seen me wearing trousers, white people's trousers or shirts.

But I am immensely rich, because I have wealthy children. I always act like a poor person [*kwamonuru*, 'sufferer'] here, wearing these clothes, this *cushma*, this clothing,' he said.

Look at me, "Wide purple front."[6] All our kinspeople call me that. "Sangama, wide purple front, purple robe, like a what's-it-called, a *gonu tjiglu* [a kind of small bird[7]] or like a *koyatale*'s [a kind of hawk[8]] back," they say to me. But it doesn't hurt my feelings, because I have plenty of things with my children in Europe, European things.

They say all kinds of things to me, but I'm not hurt by the words of my kinspeople. I say, "They see me here acting like one who suffers, but I have many children in Manaos, and daughters in Pará and Europe. The people there have wealth, but I act like one who suffers here," I say.

Now they say, now, some day the thing that travels in the sky will come. It will travel on the far side where it always flies, and then some day it will come here, they say. We will see it.

There are three important and interlinked problems for elucidation here. The nature and provenance of the 'sky steamboat', its contents, and the people who are sending it.

Matteson consistently translates Sangama's 'sky steamboat' as 'airplane', but in Zumaeta's telling, the emphasis is on the outlandish imagery of the 'sky steamboat', and he plays down the aeroplane aspect until he comments on Sangama's story: 'Where did he hear about the airplane [*teno yapachro*: 'sky traveller']? We didn't know. None of the other old people knew that the plane was coming. Yes. He's the one who told about the airplane.' Zumaeta's stress

---

[6] I am unsure why this should be an insult, unless it refers to the faded condition of Sangama's old *cushma*. Painted clothing does fade from strong black to a purplish colour, at least to my eyes.

[7] Also called onomatopoeically *pushropushro* (Ucayali Spanish, *pichihuichi*), this bird lives along the banks of the river, and angrily flashes its wings at canoe travellers, in a way that Piro people find very comical.

[8] Ucayali Spanish, *gavilán lagartijero*, or *gavilán adivino*.

here is on hindsight. Sangama's 'sky steamboat' turned out to be something that Piro people were to come to know well in the late 1940s through the arrival of the SIL missionaries, but which Sangama himself can never have seen. It is clear from the text of the story that, for both Zumaeta as narrator and Matteson as listener, Sangama's 'sky steamboat' was an aeroplane: if this story was indeed told in 1948, it was told within a year of Urubamba Piro people's first direct experience of aeroplanes (see Ch. 8). But even if Sangama never saw an aeroplane himself, it is far from improbable that he was inspired by some account of those machines. Perhaps his account of the people shooting at the 'sky steamboat' was spurred by accounts of aerial fighting in Europe in the First World War.[9] But even is this is true, why should such accounts have fired his imagination so?

Sangama's image of the *ten-gogne yapachro waporo*, the 'sky travelling steamboat' is, before it is anything else, a kind of *waporo*, 'steamboat' (Ucayali Spanish, *vapor*, *lancha*). The *waporo*, 'steamboat' is a central image in all Piro people's accounts of life on the *haciendas*. The mysterious power of the bosses hinged on their ability to call these great vessels, loaded with the 'fine things', from far-away Europe, up along the Amazon to the Urubamba. Only the bosses knew how to call these steamboats up-river, and only through the bosses could Piro people gain access to the remarkable things they contained. As Clotilde Gordón told me, remembering her childhood living on Vargas's hacienda at Sepa, 'The big riverboats would arrive at Sepa, bringing lots of goods, the fine goods, and lots of cane alcohol.' The big steamboats travelled along the riverine system which links the Urubamba and Ucayali rivers to the Amazon mainstream and thence to the 'outside', to such remote and mysterious places as Europe. The flow of the Urubamba, as I noted in Chapter 3 in the context of the discussion of 'Tsla swallowed by a Giant Catfish', is central to Piro people's understanding of history, for it is from down-river, the unknown destination of Tsla and the Muchkajine, that white people and their wealth come. Sangama's sky steamboat is therefore no different, in this respect, from other steamboats.

However, unlike those known steamboats, Sangama's 'sky steamboat' does not travel along the river, but flies. Flight itself would have been no novelty to Piro people, for birds fly. Further, we have already met the mythic image of the canoe of the sun, which connects river vessels to wood storks or king vultures, both being kinds of birds notable for the size of their wings and their powers of soaring flight. Indeed, it seems very likely to me that Sangama's image of the 'sky steamboat' drew on this specific mythic image. Unlike the canoe of the sun, however, this vessel is going to come to the Urubamba, and bring with it all the wealth of the people of Manaos, Pará and Europe.

Sangama describes himself as appearing to be *kwamonuru*, 'a poor person, a

---

[9] In the text, Zumaeta states that one of the things the bosses read were newspapers.

griever, a sufferer', one who is given nothing. But this is a visual illusion, for he is in fact 'rich', with many children. As Zumaeta relates, Sangama told him:

Only for a while can our boss torment us, mock us, order us about, giving us nothing, leaving us without clothing. When the sky steamboat arrives, it will bring all the wealth that could be wanted, and then truly, we will be without bosses,' he said, 'I am always receiving paper which says this.

This is much more poignant than any simple desire for material goods. As I discussed in Chapter 5, 'suffering' is the motivating condition of one who becomes a shaman. It is a condition of tragic and irrecoverable loss, and of the search for solutions for this condition in a new relationship with the cosmos. There is, in Sangama's account, a clear messianic strain, a feature common in the history of the region (see Varese 1973). In the 1920s, the Campa people along the Perené river to the west experienced an intense messianic response to the arrival of the Adventist missionary Stahl (Bodley 1970; Brown and Fernandez 1991). It is possible that Sangama was formulating his ideas in terms of that movement, or that Zumaeta's narration was inflected by subsequent knowledge of it. As I discuss further in Chapter 8, Zumaeta was a leader of Huau village during its Adventist period.

What would it have meant to Sangama and his listeners to be 'without bosses'? The boss, *patrochi* (Ucayali Spanish, *patrón*), was a relatively new phenomenon for Piro people, and it is possible that Sangama had experienced their genesis within his own lifetime. In the 1870s and 1880s, Piro people were drawn with ever-increasing intensity into the rubber industry. Initially, they exchanged food for merchandise with Brazilian traders, but were soon drawn into active rubber production, and then into direct debt slavery to the white rubber bosses, and most famously to 'The King of Rubber', Carlos Fermín Fitzcarrald. By the 1880s, the white bosses were living in Piro territory, and Piro people were living on the stations of these new people (see Gow 1991).

Disastrous as this new dependence on the rubber bosses was to prove, there is good reason to think that at the time Piro people actively sought out these relations. Certain writers of the time, such as Fuentes, attributed Piro people's enslavement to Fitzcarrald's conquest of them by 'blood and fire' (quoted in Matteson 1954: 26), but my own informants never did so: they always insisted that the 'ancient people' were enslaved by the rubber bosses because of their desire for the white people's 'fine things'. This point is important, because what Piro people understand by 'slavery to the bosses' is not a condition of unfreedom, or domination by alien invaders. Instead, they see it as the result of the grotesque inequality in exchange relations between themselves and white people, caused by an extreme disparity in knowledge. For my informants, and very probably for the Piro people of the late nineteenth century (see Gow 1991: 64–5), slavery to the bosses was a condition voluntarily entered into, however paradoxical that formulation may seem to us, and only to be escaped by acquiring new knowledge.

There were good historical reasons for the tone of Piro people's early relationships to the rubber bosses. The rubber industry and the consequent power of the rubber bosses over their Piro slaves was a product of the transformation of an older regional trade network, in which Piro people were important traders, into a system where Piro people became fully dependent on the white bosses for all imported goods. For as long as records exist, Urubamba Piro people had been at the centre of a complex network of riverine trading in this area of Amazonia (Myers 1983; R. Alvarez 1984; Camino 1977; Roman and Zarzar 1983). From the late eighteenth century until the 1880s, they had also made many attempts to establish closer relations with Franciscan missionaries, and these priests were on many occasions invited to establish missions for Piro people in the Urubamba area. The Franciscans, who made several attempts to found such missions, were always sceptical of the Piro people's motives, suggesting that the latter were more interested in the material goods of the missionaries rather than their spiritual message (Gow 1991: 34–7). I have discussed the religious dimension of this problem in Chapter 5 and return to it in the next chapter, but it is unquestionably true that Urubamba Piro people progressively lost interest in the missionaries once they were able to achieve stable and direct contact with white traders linked to the growing rubber industry of Central Amazonia (Gow 1991: 37–8). This trade was marked by very rapid expansion in the intensity of transactions in wealth items, as the demand for rubber escalated.

As Piro people entered into direct relations with the rubber traders, initially their situation seems to have been to their advantage. Piro people's new alliance with these white people, historically important intermediaries possessed of fabulous quantities of *gejnu*, 'wealth' would have greatly expanded their potential to create ongoing relations with those other indigenous peoples without access to such goods. Visitors to the area at the time, such as Fry (1889), speak of the material wealth of Piro people in the early phase of the rubber industry, and Samanez y Ocampo reported on the situation in 1883–4:

In exchange for rubber, they obtain metal tools and clothing, not only for their own use but for trade, as well as keeping a portion in their own stores. They wear trousers and shirts, or knitted vests; they wear straw hats or caps, which the traders bring them. They also wear the robe, their primitive costume, which they find more comfortable when they work at poling canoes . . .

The women have no other clothing than the *pampanilla* (hand-woven skirt) . . . Instead of the little shawl they used to wear to cover their backs and sides, they now wear a little jacket or blouse, which only just reaches the waist above the navel. A great belt of innumerable strings of white beads and necklaces of garnets, or of valuables of various colours, combined with good taste, finish their simple dress.

The men also wear, as a tie, neckbands of fine beads of various colours, very well woven by the women. (1980: 66–7)

The trousers, shirts, vests and straw hats were clearly obtained from traders, but the same would have been true of the raw materials for making the women's blouses and necklaces, and for the beadwork.[10] Piro people of this period clearly had much wealth.

This situation was soon to change, for reasons Piro people could hardly have foreseen. As the rubber industry developed, and especially as it neared its end, the situation of the Piro workers with respect to 'wealth' and their treatment by their bosses seems to have worsened dramatically. There were several rebellions and flights from bosses (Gow 1991: 43–4). This worsening of conditions continued and intensified in the subsequent *hacienda* period. In this new condition, with Piro people living as debt-slaves on the agricultural enterprises of bosses such as Pancho Vargas, they experienced the general stagnation of the post-rubber Western Amazonian economy. There was little wealth about, and Piro people got very little of what there was. Most of my oldest informants in the 1980s complained of their situation at the time. Jorge Manchinari, Pablo Rodriguez's grandfather, who was born in Vargas's *hacienda* at Sepa, told me in 1988:

Vargas treated us very badly, we worked for him the whole time and we never had anything. When I was a youth, my father died and Vargas said that I had to pay off my father's debt. But what debt was that, if he never gave us anything?

I ran right away from there, and went down-river to the Bajo Ucayali. Down there, I came to know clothes for the first time. Working there, I became familiar with trousers and shirts. When we lived with Vargas, he never gave us anything!

Many other people seem to have fled from Vargas too, to avoid his abuse and to have better access to wealth. Particularly galling for these people must have been memories, lived or recounted, of the quantities of wealth received from white people in earlier times.

For Sangama, as later on for Jorge Manchinari, this humiliation was marked by a lack of white people's clothing. Sangama refers to other people's joking comments about his 'wide purple front', his cotton robe. What did white people's clothing mean to Piro people at this time? In earlier chapters we have seen that, for Piro people, clothing is a mode of appearance towards others, and that by wearing a new kind of clothing one can transform one's mode of appearance towards others and hence establish new modes of relationships with them. For Piro people in the late nineteenth century, the acquisition and wearing of 'white people's shirts and trousers' would have been both the material condensations of their successful new relationships with those people, and the means by which their newly acquired co-residence with the rubber bosses was rendered as bodily appearance. Dressed in 'white people's shirts and trousers', Piro people would 'look like white people', just as the central character of 'A Man who went under the Earth', by changing into the clothing of

---

[10] I know of no earlier references to Piro people wearing such imported clothing. Clothing was, however, an important trade item in the earlier indigenous trade network.

the white-lipped peccaries, came to be a human in their eyes. In both cases, the transformation of clothing establishes peaceful coexistence, as humans, between entities which had formerly been separated.

In Chapter 4 I argued, of the situation of the 1980s, that the wearing of 'white people's clothing', was inflected by the meaning of design-painted clothing, and by the mythic narrative, 'The Birth of Tsla'. New design-painted clothing renders Piro people in the appearance of jaguars, and was central to the mediation of hostile relations between distant kinspeople in the production of new affinal relations (see Ch. 6). As such, design-painted clothing engaged with the appearance of the primordial otherness of the jaguars, the affines of Tsla's mother. Ritual life temporarily made hosts and guests appear to have the social lives of the mythical 'group-living jaguars', a social life that no one but a shaman would seek to live out full time. By contrast, 'white people's clothing' was inflected with the meanings of the other Others of the Tsla myths, the Muchkajine, the 'Long Ago White People'. It pointed towards a desirable peaceful relationship with successive kinds of white people. This was the vision Piro people had of their history in the 1980s, and it linked the practice of wearing 'white people's clothing' to their current relationship to kinds of white people and to the 'myth of history', 'Tsla swallowed by a Giant Catfish'.

It would be risky to project this analysis back from the 1980s to the late nineteenth century, for there is no reason to assume that the mythic narratives on which it is based were told in this same form at that earlier period. Indeed, as I discuss below, there is reason to believe that an important transformation in Tsla mythology had occurred over that century. However, two points can be made about the situation in the late nineteenth century. Firstly, the shift in attention from the Franciscan missionaries to the traders-cum-rubber bosses was unquestionably a shift from one 'kind of white people' to another, and would probably have had a similar meaning to Piro people in the 1880s as it had for their descendants a century later. Secondly, the rubber bosses were willing to set up co-residence with Piro people on the explicit basis of exchanging local products for 'wealth', which the Franciscans had been so reluctant to do. As such, they would have seemed, from the Piro point of view, to have been a new and better 'kind of white people', at least initially. Things, of course, were to change drastically.

As the rubber industry collapsed into the stagnation of the *hacienda* system, what seems to have been particularly troubling for Piro people was the new-found meanness of their bosses, and their refusal to provide them with clothing. The white people had started to negate the relationship of co-residence based on mutual common appearance, and by denying their clothing to their Piro workers, stressed both the visual and power differences between them.[11]

---

[11] By time of the collapse of the rubber industry, Piro people seem to have had no choice but to stick with their bosses: all the other possibilities of trading had been destroyed by the conditions of the rubber industry (Gow 1991: 44–6).

This explains Sangama's concern for clothing as the key item of *gejnu*, 'wealth', being sent in the 'sky steamboat', and the apparently simple-minded response of his listeners to the prospect of this clothing arriving, 'We'd put it on.' In short, if this wealth arrived, Piro people would be a very different kind of people. Transformed visually by the new clothing of this new kind of white people, they would come to be human in a new way in the eyes of white people. They would, as Sangama put it, stop being slaves, they would be without bosses.

This redemptive possibility inhered in a feature of the world which was always implicit in the nature of the rubber industry and the *hacienda* economy: direct contact with the actual producers of the wealth Piro people had received in such abundance before, and subsequently in such miserable quantities. These are the people Sangama constantly lists as the residents of 'Manaos, Pará, Europe'. As Sangama says,

How many white people there are, more than could be told, in the place called Pará! In Manaos, how many there are! One is not known. We could get lost. It is not like the place we live now. We have only thatched houses. The houses all have metal roofs there . . . There is one called Pará, and one called Manaos, big cities, white people's cities. There is a place called Europe, with a big city, a city of miracles (*kgiyaklewaklewak-pokchi*). The big steamboat goes there all the time, and the sky steamboat flies there.

At one point, Sangama calls the people of Pará, *paneneko*, 'very much other people'. This usage is significant, for while the residents of Manaos, Pará, and Europe are identified as *kajine*, 'white people', it is clear that Sangama thought of them as a different kind of people to the local white bosses. If Piro people could shift from the stingy Franciscans to the generous rubber bosses in the late nineteenth century, then a generation later Sangama held out the possibility of switching from their stingy bosses to another new 'kind of white people', the *paneneko*.

Sangama describes the big city in Europe as '*kgiyaklewaklewak-pokchi*', 'city of miracles', from the root verb, *giyaklewata*, 'to do miracles, to create miraculously'. We have met this term before, in relation to Tsla, for he was a *kgiyaklewakleru*, 'a maker of miracles, a miraculous creator' (see Ch. 4). The verb *giyaklewata* is an intensification of *kagonchiwata*, 'to do shamanry', and refers to extraordinary powers of shamanic action. Sangama's account here is an early version of the fascination with the world of the *gringos*, with their technology and their factories, discussed in Chapter 1. The 'city of miracles' in Europe would, therefore, be the origin place of the *gejnu*, 'fine things', and its inhabitants, the *paneneko*, the makers of these things.

What did Sangama mean by the *paneneko*, the 'very much other people'? There seems to me to be little doubt that Zumaeta assumes that the SIL missionaries themselves were one variety of these 'very much other people', and that their aeroplanes were the 'sky steamboat' of which Sangama told. Or at the very least, that in telling this story, Zumaeta was trying to bring his personal experience of Sangama into dialogue with Matteson's appearance and her project. It is of course important to stress that we cannot really know what Zumaeta thought of the SIL at this time: Zumaeta's 'SIL missionaries' were presumably very different to the SIL missionaries as they experienced themselves. But what might Sangama, talking long before then, have meant by these 'very much other people'?

'The World on the Other Side'

We can think of Sangama's *paneneko*, the 'very much other people' as the inhabitants of the distant cities of Manaos, Pará, and 'Europe'. In that sense, the 'very much other people' are the originators of the wealth which Piro people had in such abundance during the early phases of the rubber industry. But what exactly did Sangama think of such people and places? Clearly, in one sense, Sangama's 'Manaos, Pará, Europe' are those cities in Brazil I have been to, and this continent of my birth. But it is equally clear that Sangama must have thought of them very differently from the way I am accustomed to do. Indeed, Sangama asserts that these places, where the sky steamboat is flying around, are *pnu sreta*, 'on the far side', as opposed to the *gewi*, 'here' from which he speaks, which he refers to as *tye sreta gogne*, 'the world on this side'. I suggest that Sangama's *pnu sreta*, 'far side', was an allusion to the unknown destination of Tsla and the Muchkajine in the mythic narrative, 'Tsla swallowed by a Giant Catfish', and that his *paneneko* were the residents of that location.

The evidence for this lies with another document in the archive which bears a remarkable set of connections to 'The Story of Sangama'. This is a myth written down by Zacarías Zumaeta, Morán's son, and then orally narrated at Matteson's request for her to record on tape (Matteson 1965: 137). The myth is entitled in its published form, *'Pa Sreta-Gogne Pirana'*, 'The World on the Other Side' (Matteson 1965: 210–15). Zacarías, the narrator, specifies that the story was told to him by his grandmother, who may, therefore, have been Sangama's paternal aunt. It reads almost like a commentary on the story of Sangama, and it may well have been produced specifically for that purpose. To my knowledge, it is unique among Piro mythic narratives in actually specifying Tsla's destination quite clearly.

Zacarías's story tells of how a group of ancient people, led by their chief Powra, set off down the Yami river. Yami is the older Piro name for the mainstream of the Piro lived world (Matteson 1965: 412), the river currently known by the separate names of the Urubamba, Ucayali, and Amazon rivers. These ancient travellers meet various *panene*, 'other peoples', on the way, with whom Powra tells them to have no contact. 'These are not the ones,' he says. Those who disobey him and have sex with the 'other peoples' rot and die. Eventually, the voyagers come to the end of the river, and passing through a hole defended by a giant eagle, they find themselves in another world. They travel along another river, up into the sky, eventually arriving at Tsla's village. There, the women and children find wealth objects scattered about, and scramble to collect them. Tsla tells them to throw such things away, for 'they have already tarnished'. He gives all of them new wealth from his storehouse. Powra is anxious to leave, and the voyagers set off back home, which they eventually reach.

The similarities between Zacarías's story and Sangama's account of the world he read about are remarkable. In Zacarías's story, the voyagers visit different peoples as they descend the river, 'Then they saw people, other people, mixed ones, *Patquina* People,[12] Plantain People, Stone People, Water People, Salt People, Alligator People.' Since no mention is made here of the known downriver neighbours of Urubamba Piro people, such as the Conibo, Shipibo, and Cocama peoples, the implication is that they are very far downriver. The evocation of these strange peoples and their villages is strongly reminiscent of Sangama's constant listing of 'Manaos, Pará, Europe'. The final destination of the travellers in the myth, Tsla's village where wealth lies about on the ground, is very similar to Sangama's own ultimate place, that big city of miracles, Europe.

In Zacarías Zumaeta's story, when Powra and his people reach the very end of the river, they then go up into the sky through the *tkachipna*, the 'hole of the sun':

Then apparently they went from this world to the sky. They came to the place where the two worlds join. There seemed to be no place to go, other than the hole of the sun. They came to the hole, where a giant eagle waited to drive people back. They turned a pot upside down over the giant eagle's head so that it could not snatch them, and so went into the hole. Emerging on the other side of the hole, they saw the dawning day. They saw no forest at all.

We have met the 'hole of the sun' before, in the discussion of the 'canoe journey of the sun' narratives in Chapter 2. The logic of Zacarías Zumaeta's story would seem to be that the Yami river (the combined Urubamba, Ucayali, and Amazon rivers) eventually ends in the sky, far to the east.[13] The river along which the voyagers travel in the sky must necessarily be the same as the one along which the sun travels in the mythic narratives of the canoe journey of the sun. This means that Zacarías Zumaeta's story unequivocally locates Tsla's

---

[12] *Patquina* (also *huitquina*; Piro, *jena*) is an aroid with giant triangular leaves. It is a virulent weed species in Piro gardens.

[13] Although the mouth of the Amazon lies some 5000 kilometres down-river from the mouth of the Urubamba, Piro people are well aware that the Ucayali flows into the Amazon, and then flows east into Brazil. This knowledge is likely to be ancient, given Piro trading expeditions to the Central Amazon area (Myers 1983); and compare Weiss (1975) on Campa knowledge of the general geography of Amazonia.

destination as a village on the banks of this celestial river. This would also answer the question of what exactly Sangama's 'sky steamboat' could be. It is a steamboat that travels on just such a celestial river.

Nowhere in 'The Story of Sangama' is there any explicit identification of the *paneneko*, the 'very much other people', or of their cities, with Tsla and his celestial village. However, if we bring Morán Zumaeta's 'Story of Sangama' and Zacarías Zumaeta's mythic narrative together, there is nowhere else that a Piro listener could have located Sangama's cities and sky steamboat. Zacarías's story describes *pa sreta gogne*, 'the world on the other side', while Sangama says the sky steamboat is on 'the far side', *pnu sreta*. Communication between *tye sreta gogne*, 'the world of this side', and that other world is in both cases rendered problematic by a hostile force. The giant eagle of Zacarías's mythic narrative corresponds to the midway 'shooters' of Sangama's story.

If my analysis of Zacarías Zumaeta's 'The World on the Other Side' is correct, and that Sangama was arguing that the *paneneko* were either Tsla or other inhabitants of Tsla's celestial village, and that the sky steamboat was a vessel from that celestial village, why does he never say this? There are two major reasons for this, I think. Firstly, Sangama is describing his own special-ist knowledge, and not telling an 'ancient people's story'. Sangama is providing a radical future alternative to the actual conditions of his lived world, rather than telling a story about a radically different past. Secondly, both of these stories must be understood in the context of their narration, and especially in relation to Matteson as listener. I take each aspect in turn.

Among the things acquired in Tsla's village by the ancient people in Zacarías's story are clothing. This is the *gejnu*, 'wealth', that Sangama complained that Piro people lacked. But in Zacarías's story, the ancient people receive 'wealth' that lasts, rather than 'tarnishing'. Obviously, if Piro people had 'wealth' that endured, they would have no need for trade relationships, and no need for white people. The story, 'The World on the Other Side' is about a heroic trading expedition into the sky, and the acquisition of 'enduring wealth'. It is an 'ancient people's story', for Zacarías Zumaeta is clear that neither he nor anyone else he knows ever experienced this, or claimed it as personal knowledge. As a mythic narrative, Zacarías's story provides a solution to the problem set by the Piro 'myth of history', 'Tsla swallowed by a Giant Catfish'. A heroic group of travellers could, if sufficiently courageous, visit the destina-tion of Tsla, and bring back his wealth.

Sangama's account of the sky steamboat suggests an inversion of this mythic solution. Instead of travelling to the house of Tsla, like Powra and his fellows in 'The World on the Other Side', Piro people can await the arrival of the *paneneko*, the 'very much other people', in their 'sky steamboat'. As such, 'The Story of Sangama' asserts that 'Tsla swallowed by a Giant Catfish' is the Piro 'myth of history', for novelty is going to appear from down-river. There is another inversion here. A pre-condition for access to Tsla's village in 'The

World on the Other Side', and the wealth it contains, is containment from other people. It is only those who do not develop social relations with 'other people' who survive and arrive in the 'place of miracles', Tsla's village with its enduring wealth items. As such, the myth inverts a key aspect of Piro experience, for it is only by having such social relations with other people that access to such wealth is possible. Morán's story about Sangama suggests an inversion of this solution too, insofar as Piro people could have direct relations with the *paneneko* if the latter should arrive here.

I think Sangama's failure to identify his 'far side' with the celestial village of Tsla can be understood in the context of Zumaeta's own narration of this story to Matteson. As I noted in Chapter 3, narrators of 'Tsla swallowed by a Giant Catfish' always leave the destination of Tsla and the Muchkajine unspecified, and I argued that this is because this mythic narrative is the Piro 'myth of history', insofar as it sets all contemporary relations with white people as part of the ongoing making of the Piro lived world. Sangama, as he spoke, would never have needed to specify the connection of his account to mythic narratives about Tsla. Insofar as he was speaking about a future event of transformation through relations with a new kind of white people, his Piro listeners would have made the connection instantly for themselves. When Morán Zumaeta told 'The Story of Sangama' to Matteson, however, he could not have been so sure of such a connection being made. Instead, I think that here he was concerned with another kind of connection to mythic narratives in the telling of this story. He was seeking to elicit from Matteson some kind of commentary on 'ancient people's stories', and in particular the question implicit in 'Tsla swallowed by a Giant Catfish': where did Tsla go, and where do white people come from?

There does, however, seem to be more to this problem, for as I noted, Zacarías Zumaeta's story is the only specification known to me of the actual destination of Tsla. Sangama's account of the 'sky steamboat' and the *paneneko* seems to be specifically in dialogue with this mythic narrative, rather than simply with 'Tsla swallowed by a Giant Catfish'. It seems to me therefore likely that, in the past, this latter mythic narrative was much more closely connected to myths of the form of 'The World on the Other Side', and that these myths, where humans contact Tsla through journeys down-river, have subsequently been forgotten. The reason for this forgetting would be a profound change in Piro people's relationship to the world since the late nineteenth century. As I noted above, before the coming of the rubber bosses to Piro territory in the 1880s, Piro men had engaged in long-distance trading down-river, often down to the Amazon mainstream. This down-river trade was transformed by the coming of the rubber bosses into debt-slavery to these men, and that trade became an almost total dependence on the rubber bosses for the wealth objects that Piro people had once gone to seek down-river. By the end of the nineteenth century, all the trade along the Ucayali was dominated by the white bosses, and by their steamboats, and the proliferation of their entrepôts. It is in these changed circumstances, I suggest, that mythic narratives about the down-river trade were forgotten, and 'Tsla swallowed by a Giant Catfish' survived to become the Piro 'myth of history'.[14] White people had no longer to be journeyed towards, but were now resident in Piro territory. It was therefore from such white people that Piro people's questions about the nature of Tsla's destination could expect answers.

If this hypothesis is correct, it is possible to interpret Sangama's account of the 'sky steamboat' and of the *paneneko* as a response to mythic narratives like 'The World on the Other Side'. In Sangama's formulation, contact with Tsla and his wealth does not depend on a heroic expedition by Piro people to the end of the earth, but instead on the arrival of the 'very much other people' here on the Urubamba. It is no longer the extreme distances and dangers of the journey to Tsla's village which is the problem, but the malignity of those 'midway' who are trying to prevent the 'sky steamboat' coming, and the ignorance of Piro people who, unable to read, do not know that this is happening. The mythic narratives of journeys to Tsla's village, as they were being forgotten, resurfaced in inverted form as Sangama's analysis of the content of writing.

If the mythic narratives about down-river trading expeditions were indeed being forgotten at the period that Sangama was formulating his account of writing, why then should Zacarías Zumaeta have told this 'forgotten' myth to Matteson? Clearly, this mythic narrative had not been totally forgotten, for Zacarías must have heard it from his grandmother after his father's experiences with Sangama. However, it seems to me very likely that Zacarías Zumaeta told this story to Matteson as an explicit commentary on the relationship of his father Morán's story about Sangama to the mythic narrative, 'Tsla swallowed by a Giant Catfish'. The son's story provides the link between these two narratives through another 'ancient Piro people's story'.

But why, then, is Zacarías Zumaeta's mythic narrative 'The World on the Other Side' the only known Piro myth to specify the destination of Tsla? I think this must be referred to the specific context in which this myth was 'told': as Matteson noted, Zacarías Zumaeta first wrote the myth down. By doing so, he demonstrated his mastery over the novel technique introduced by Matteson, and foreseen by his elder kinsman Sangama. It is therefore possible that this specific way of 'telling' the myth, in the form of a written commentary on his father's personal-experience narrative of Sangama's remarkable behaviour, may have led Zacarías to remember a myth that, in other circumstances, would have been unmemorable. On the brink of oblivion, 'The World on the Other Side' briefly regained its interest as a young Piro man wrestled

[14] Mythic narratives and other stories which refer to up-river trading expeditions to the Andes have survived this process, even though that trade also ended in the late nineteenth century (Gade 1972). I suspect the reason for their survival is that the up-river trade simply stopped, rather than being replaced with a new form.

with the problems of the novel technique of writing. Faced with the problem of a blank sheet of paper, and the question, 'What should I write down here?', Zacarías's grandmother's story, 'The World on the Other Side', sprang most easily to his mind.

Sangama's Analysis of Writing

One of the most intriguing aspects of Morán Zumaeta's story about Sangama lies in the latter's account of writing and reading. Zumaeta could himself read by the time he told this story, or was in the process of learning, and there is continual reference throughout the text to the bizarreness of Sangama's own account of reading, relative to the technique taught by Matteson. However, Sangama's account of writing is completely coherent from within Piro people's conceptions of design and shamanry. What Sangama did was to explain writing to Piro people in a manner that may be very hard for a literate Western person to understand, but which would have made complete sense to his Piro listeners. Indeed, Sangama seems to have rendered writing thinkable to Piro people, and hence to have led many of them to pursue the acquisition of this knowledge.

Throughout Zumaeta's story, virtually no reference is made to the written characters. These are mentioned only at the beginning, in Zumaeta's description of watching Sangama reading, 'When he studied, I saw his mouth move. His eyes kept moving, following spans of letters. He read it all, turning the pages, pointing at the letters.' The word used here for 'letter' is *toyonga*, 'her design line' (possession is by the grammatically female *kiruka* 'paper'). The term corresponds to the naming of design templates, discussed in Chapter 4. This is Zumaeta speaking, for Sangama is never quoted as mentioning such designs. *Yonchi*, 'design', is also the standard Piro word for 'writing', and if it is necessary to distinguish 'writing' from other forms of design, it can be specified as *kajitu yona*, 'white people's design'. Why then does Sangama himself never discuss *yonchi* in his account of reading?

The reason, I suspect, is precisely because he saw written marks as *kajitu yona*, 'white people's design'. Unlike the designs painted by Piro women, and their northern downstream neighbours the Conibo, Shipibo, and Cocama peoples, 'white people's design' probably lacked, for Piro people at that period, the aesthetic force of *giglenchi*, 'beauty'. Certainly, alphabetic writing does not conform to the underlying aesthetic principles of these real design systems. Aesthetically, it lies closer to the 'ugly' designs of the Campa, Machiguenga, and Amahuaca peoples. The mystery of reading, therefore, could not lie with the designs themselves, and must inhere in the object they cover, the *kiruka*, the paper. If paper matters so much to the white bosses, Sangama may have thought, the reason cannot lie in the ugly little designs, but must lie with the object these designs decorate, the paper.

Sangama says that the paper has a body. He says *'Kamanro wa twu kiruka'*, 'This paper has a body, a human form'. We have met this formulation often before, in the earlier discussion of shamanry and of *kigimawlo*. Here, Sangama asserts that the immediate visual identity of 'paper' is based on an ignorance of the knowledge of reading. For one who has this knowledge, one who can read, the paper appears as a human woman, rather than being this flimsy design-covered object. Reading is, therefore, the knowledge of how to see paper in its hidden human form. Sangama sees the paper in her true form of, *Tomane sernamaylo sagnamlejro*, 'Her body, with her red mouth, the one whose mouth is always smeared with red pigment.' Here, the verb for painting specifies the non-design painting of *sagata*. The red dye *gapijru* (Ucayali Spanish, *achiote*; Lat. *Bixa orellana*) is very seldom used for body-painting by Piro people, and never for painting with design, as I noted in Chapter 4.[15]

Zumaeta stresses his confusion at this point, for here the contrast to his own experience of learning with Matteson must have been greatest. Commenting on the scepticism and ridicule of other Piro people, Sangama explained reading to Zumaeta as follows:

You folks listen to me, but others belittle me. They say, 'Sangama, the ignorant, the liar. He does his lying by reading dirty paper from the outhouse.' They laugh at me, and distort my words all the time. Why should my eyes be like theirs? My eyes are not like theirs. I know how to read the paper. It speaks to me. Look at this one now.' He turned its leaves. 'See. She speaks to me. The paper has a body; I always see her, cousin,' he said to me. 'I always see this paper. She has red lips with which she speaks. She has a body with a red mouth, a painted mouth. She has a red mouth.

Zumaeta reports that he stared at the paper, but saw no woman there, but Sangama insisted and said that the paper was asking if Zumaeta wanted to know her. Zumaeta asks if this is true, and Sangama replies,

Yes. Paper does that. That's why the white converses with her every day. Haven't you seen him? Watch him do that. When the white, our patron, sees a paper, he holds it up all day long, and she talks to him. She converses with him all day. The white does that every day. Therefore I also, just a little bit, when I went down-river a long time ago to Pará. I used to go there all the time, I was taught there. I entered a what-do-you-call-it, school. I was enrolled. A teacher sent for me. That's how I know, cousin'.[16]

Sangama's claim to have learned to read in a school in Belem do Pará is not impossible: indigenous people from this area of Peru do seem to have travelled

[15] It would be fascinating to know if this image of the 'paper woman' is based on a white woman wearing lipstick: there seem to have been very few white women on the Bajo Urubamba during this period. The image would also evoke the visual appearance of a woman making manioc beer, in the chewing of red sweet potato.

[16] The terms used in the narrative for 'school', 'enrol', and 'teacher' are all Piro constructions, not Spanish loan-words.

as far during the rubber period.[17] However, Zumaeta himself did not accept this account, for it was not supported by any other witness.

If Sangama had indeed been taught to read in a school, why then does he describe the paper as having a body, and a mouth with red lips? His whole account makes sense only as a sustained analogy to the use of the hallucinogen *ayahuasca*. Sangama's account of writing would have made sense to his audience because it appeals to the use of this hallucinogen to overcome the experiential unavailability of important knowledge and events. Just as shamans justify their knowledge by appealing to personal hallucinatory experiences, Sangama justified his knowledge by reference to personal visual experience of paper in its transformed state of a woman. As he put it, 'Why should my eyes be like theirs?'

The absence of reference to *yonchi*, 'design', in Sangama's account, and the insistence on the human form of the paper, correspond to the place of design and human form in *ayahuasca* hallucinatory experience. The designs which appear in the early phases of the *ayahuasca* hallucinatory state are the prelude to full hallucination: they are the mendacious anaconda form of the *ayahuasca* powerful being, before she appears in her true human form. The design-covered paper is the mendacious everyday appearance of *kiruka*. Her true form, revealed only to those who know, like Sangama and the white bosses, is a woman who speaks.

In shamanry, the mother spirit of the *ayahuasca* allows the drinker to see powerful beings in human form, and to hear and understand their songs. As I discussed in Chapter 5, such songs are incomprehensible to non-shamans, but they are the pre-condition of the shaman's knowledge. We find the same relationship in Sangama's reading. Zumaeta tells the following of Sangama reading aloud, in response to the desire of others to hear what the paper says:

It says, '*Telente. Ten-telente. Ten-ten-ten-te telenten telelen ten ten ten, ten ten ten ten. Telelenten. Ten ten. Tentelen. Mi Yoropa. Mi Manawo. Mi Pará. Telententen. Ten ten telelen. Ten tan tan. Tan tan ten telen. Telen. Ten ten telelen. Telen, telen, telen, ten ten ten ten ten. Telelen ten ten ten ten ten.*' he read from it.

What is this strange language? As some of his listeners commented, 'We didn't understand.' In part, Sangama's words here are Ucayali Spanish adapted to Piro pronunciation: this is recognizable in the stretch, '*Mi Yoropa. Mi Manawo. Mi Pará*'. In Ucayali Spanish, this would be '*Mi Europa. Mi Manaos. Mi Pará*', 'My Europe. My Manaus. My Belem do Pará.' This would have been understood by his listeners. The rest is in another language unknown to his listeners, and to myself.[18] For Sangama,

---

[17] Lucia van Velthem (personal communication) reports that there is, to this day, a community in Belem who are recognized as descendants of Peruvian Cocama who arrived in the nineteenth century.

[18] My own guess would be that the source for Sangama's paper's language is Brazilian Portuguese: Sangama's '*ten*' resembles the frequently used '*tem*' ('there is, there are, he/she/it has') of that

reading, like sung discourse in shamanry, is access to a special language not understood by others.[19]

Sangama specifies that while the paper is talking, it is only transmitting messages from others, much as the hallucinogen *ayahuasca* is both a powerful being and a vehicle for contact with other powerful beings. The messages of the paper had the following source, Zumaeta reports,

> He would laugh, 'Hee, hee, hee, hee! One of your own granddaughters wrote to me,' he would say. 'Here are her words. She says she is coming. Your granddaughter says she is coming on the steamboat.' He told that to one whom the rest were calling 'father'.

> 'They are the ones who wrote it', he explained. 'A daughter of mine, who lives on the river bank in Manaos wrote it. She says that when the steamer crosses the water, such goods as have never been spoken of here will come. The steamer will bring the goods. She tells me the goods will come here.'

The joke that makes Sangama laugh is that the paper is bringing messages to Piro people from his own daughter, and hence from their kinswoman too. Sangama's daughter would be 'your granddaughter' to a man he called 'father'. As we have seen, Sangama specifies that he also has children in Europe.

Who are these children of Sangama? Contemporary shamans on the Bajo Urubamba have magical stones called *incantos* (Piro, *ginkanto, sotlutachri*) which they address as their 'children' (Gow 1991: 239–40). When shamans take *ayahuasca*, these stones reveal themselves as people, and they both protect the shaman from enemies and help in the curing. In that sense, Sangama's claims to understanding of the messages of the papers is based on a further dimension of the shamanic metaphor.

But there may be more to this. It is not entirely impossible that Sangama had children in Manaos and Europe, as he claimed. Many young Piro children were taken away by white bosses during those times to be sold as domestic slaves in the cities of Amazonia and beyond.[20] The practice continued until at least the 1980s, and was much feared by Piro people, as is indicated in Artemio's comment about me noted in Chapter 1. If Sangama had lost children in this way, however, it is unlikely that any of these children became wealthy or literate

---

language. In Ucayali Spanish, word-final *n* is often realized as the nasalization of the preceding vowel, in a manner similar to Brazilian Portuguese. This would also tie in with the geography of Sangama's story. He could easily have heard Portuguese spoken by Brazilians in Brazil, if he did indeed travel to Belem do Pará; on the Urubamba, for some Brazilians visited and resided in the area; or on the Purús river to the east, where most Piro people were living in the first decade of the twentieth century. Fry (1889) reports that many Piro people spoke Brazilian Portuguese in the 1880s.

[19] That Sangama's analysis was not unique to him is implied by the word *koschepiru*, 'the words of a song, content of a piece of writing' (see Chs 5 and 6), which suggests that the analytical metaphor of song words and the content of written text was general to Piro people.

[20] See R. Alvarez's account of Saavedra (1959). Piro people had been, and were to remain, active agents of this trade, stealing women and children from neighbouring peoples (see Fiedler 1951: 161; Matteson 1954: 92; and Gow 1991: 47–8).

when they grew up, nor is it probable that they became journalists. One way or another, however, such lost children would explain Sangama's strange behaviour. As I discussed in Chapter 5, it is the 'suffering' (Piro, *wamonuwata*) caused by the loss of a child that makes a man want to become a shaman in the first place. As we have seen, on several occasions, Sangama calls himself *kwamonuru*, 'a sufferer'. Indeed, the totality of his project is linked to the general 'suffering' of Piro people.

At the end of his story, Zumaeta returns to a question that has preoccupied him throughout, 'How could Sangama read?' He says, 'Maybe he was just lying; maybe not. What was the score? But it is said that he was a twin. Maybe that is why he thought up such things, and the things he told originated in his own mind.' As I have discussed in Chapter 5, a surviving twin (Piro, *gepiritu*) is, by that token, a born shaman. Unlike other people, they require no training, because they already have a double in the dead twin (Piro, *rumushpakanru*). This word means 'his one who was born with him', and also means, more generally, that which is natural or characteristic to a person. Thus, Zumaeta implies, Sangama could indeed read because he was a born shaman, and his extraordinary knowledge of reading originated within himself. The whole force of the narrative has been leading to this conclusion.

This is hinted at in the manner in which Sangama teaches Zumaeta to read. One day, Zumaeta asked Sangama to teach him how to read, and Sangama agreed. 'Perhaps he was a little drunk,' Zumaeta comments, and continues:

'If you want it, you can receive the paper,' he said. Then he said, 'Come here. I'm going to teach you.'

I went to his side. 'Come on, cousin,' he said then. 'Prepare the crown of your head.' He blew into his cupped hand and transferred the breath to the crown of my head, clearing his throat, '*Gajjjj. Gajjj.*' Again he endowed the crown of my head with his breath, and then my back. He gave it to me all over my back. '*Gjjj.* See that. It will enable you to read,' he said to me solemnly.

I thought he would teach me to read by means of my eyes, but he drew out his breath and endowed me with it, transferring it to the crown of my head, to my throat and back. He whirled me around as he blew, '*Gajj gagajj.*' He inserted it into my back. '*Gajj, gajj.*'

'Cousin, that paper you gave me, let's not damage it by failure to observe taboo,' he said to me. 'From now on you will be able to read. You will understand me. You will hear about Pará and Europe. You will be wise. There are people there. How could this be in vain?' he said.

'From now on you too observe taboos. Don't drink manioc beer all the time,' he ordered me severely.

Sangama transfers the knowledge of reading to Zumaeta by means of his breath. He does not simply 'blow' on his hands: he blows in a specifically shamanic manner. The 'throat-clearing' refers to what is currently called *yachay* on the Bajo Urubamba[21]: this is the magical phlegm of shamans, produced by their constant consumption of strong tobacco and hallucinogens. It is lodged in the stomach, but shamans raise it up into their throats in order to blow shamanically. The sound, '*Gajjjj, gajjj*', which appears in the text, is specific to this type of blowing, as the shaman's breath is forced out over the phlegm, causing it to rattle and to acquire the potency of the shaman's knowledge. Shamanic blowing is thus imbued with the knowledge of the shaman, and transfers part of that potent knowledge to the one blown upon. As Zumaeta points out, 'That's why to this day I don't forget what he said. 'Some day you also will know how to read,' he said to me. I think of him now. What he said has been exactly fulfilled. His exact words I have carried out. And I have gained it all.'

Zumaeta is therefore telling Matteson that his success in learning to read and write was due to that prior act of teaching, lodged in Sangama's magical breath. Whether or not Matteson herself understood this, I cannot tell. Like most of her SIL colleagues, she seems fairly unsympathetic to shamanry in her writings, and not to have known much about the forms or meanings of hallucinatory experience. Further, it seems unlikely to me that, had the SIL missionaries fully understood this story, they would have allowed its publication in *Gwacha Ginkakle*, a Piro language school primer.

Be that as it may, we are now in a better position to appreciate Sangama's remarkable achievement. He was able to explain reading, and hence writing, to other Piro people in a way which was intrinsically meaningful to them, given that it made sense in terms of the modes of action, in the narration of myths, in design and in shamanry, that made up their lived world. Further, Sangama was able to connect knowledge of writing to the specific problem of their lived world at that time, their oppression by their bosses, and to that which they held to be the general conditions of their historical experiences, the departure of Tsla to an unknown destination down-river. Most Piro people may not have believed him, but he must at the very least have started them thinking about the possibilities of learning to read. A few others, like Zumaeta, were spellbound by his account, and set off in active search of this knowledge.

Possible Origins for Sangama's Analysis

Where on earth did Sangama get these strange ideas from? Did they indeed 'originate in his own mind', as Zumaeta said? There is one small clue in the documentary archive which suggests that ideas like these may have been entertained by other Piro people too. In 1874, the Franciscan priest P. Luis Sabaté was travelling up the Urubamba in the company of a group of Piro men. They

---

[21] *Yachay* is from the Lowland Quechua verb, 'to know'. See also Chaumeil (1988), for a discussion of this issue.

had tried to dissuade him from going up-river, warning him that the 'Campas' (presumably Machiguenga people) were waiting to kill anyone who attempted to ascend the river. On 29 July, at Montalo, they see the 'Campas' up-river in their canoes. Sabaté reports of his Piro companions,

So great was the terror they had of meeting them, that every day on arriving at the halt on some beach, and on taking out my breviary to recite the divine office, these Piros came up to me and asked me what the book told me about the Campas: if they were close or angry, if they were waiting for us or if they would do anything to them. They believed that the book spoke to me, and it was enough to look into it for it to tell me what was going to happen, clarify any doubts, or show me what was hidden; for that reason, they asked me to read my book, not just so I might give them news about the Campas; but also that I might tell them where the tapir had passed, in which place they might fish with success, and other idiocies of the sort; for they firmly believed that the breviary was an oracle, and that it contained the secret of all things, for which reason they called me Cajunchi, which means sorcerer. So great was the superstition about this matter that had taken hold of these savages that, despite my work to disabuse them of it, they once dared to ask me for the breviary, that they might consult for themselves the fancies that they attributed to it. Naturally, I reprimanded them for such a pretension, making them see how in error they were in this; and I flatly refused to let them take it in their hands, saying at the same time, that that book was sacred, and they were forbidden to touch it.

As I had always diffused the fears that they had of meeting the Campas, and told them that the breviary had said nothing about this issue to me; now that they saw them so close, they became furious with me, they heaped abuse on me because I had tricked them, they said my book was a liar, and in great alarm they prepared to enter into combat. (Sabaté 1925 [1874]: 295–6)

Obviously, we would need to know a great deal more about Sabaté's own understanding of books and the status of his breviary, and about his attitudes to Piro people's desire for books, in order to know why he decided to report this one incident among all the many others he doubtless experienced but failed to record. It has the suspicious ring of a formulaic story of pagan ignorance about it to me, much like the stories of Inca Atahuallpa's fabled reaction to the Bible. That said, we can assume that it also records what his Piro guides actually said to him.

It is entirely possible that Sangama was a boy during this period, and heard this incident described from the point of view of those men whom Sabaté termed, 'the Piros'. Perhaps such ideas were general among Piro people in this and earlier periods, even if this is the sole reference to such ideas I have yet found in the archive. Gebhart-Sayer (1985) has demonstrated that the Shipibo–Conibo peoples, the northern neighbours along the Ucayali river of Urubamba Piro people, were fascinated with the books of the missionaries in the nineteenth century, and resented the priests for refusing to give any to them. Gebhart-Sayer further notes that Shipibo–Conibo people seem to have even produced their own books, each page covered in complex designs.

As I discussed above, the Franciscan missionaries had been an important target of Piro people's interest throughout the nineteenth century, and many Piro people had lived on the mission run by Alemany from 1879 until 1881, at Santa Rosa de los Piros on the Alto Ucayali near the mouth of the Urubamba. It is possible that, Sangama too had lived on this mission. Franciscan missionaries (Piro, *payri*; Ucayali Spanish, *padre*), as I noted above, seem to have functioned as the prototype 'white people' until the expansion of white traders into the Alto Ucayali. Books, reading, and writing were clearly central to the Franciscans' activities, but they certainly made no attempt to extend these techniques to Piro people, and it is likely that the latter shared their northern neighbours' fascination with the priests' books, and their resentment at the priests' meanness with regard to them.

If such ideas were more general to the area, what Sangama did was to take them and elaborate them into a new form. The concern of the Piro men described by Sabaté, or of the Shipibo–Conibo people described by Gebhart-Sayer, was with the books of missionaries. Sangama was living in a later era, when the missionaries had lost what little power they had had over the indigenous peoples of the region, and been replaced by the *patrones*, firstly the rubber bosses and then the *hacendados*. In this new situation, as I noted above, writing symbolized the generalized hierarchy of 'savage Indians' and 'civilized whites', or in Piro terms, between *yine*, 'humans', and *kajine*, 'white people', and the way in which that hierarchy depended on the white people's total control over the regional exchange network on which Piro people depended. Central to that problem, for Piro people, was the extraordinary knowledge of the white bosses.

This is where Sangama's dramatic re-analysis of writing was inserted. He took advantage of the new availability of 'paper', for unlike the avaricious priests, the bosses were profligate with paper, throwing it away. Hence the joke noted above, 'They say, "Sangama, the ignorant, the liar. He does his lying by reading dirty paper from the outhouse."' Using the tools that lay to hand, he formulated an account of writing as a potential form of knowledge for Piro people, and one which, if they possessed it, would transform their lives. Sangama made clear that it was not the books themselves that mattered, but the knowledge of how to read the messages they contained. In an audacious piece of cosmological speculation, Sangama formulated the knowledge of 'white people's designs' as a potential future project in the Piro lived world. He may not have been generally believed, but his audience would have easily recognized the nature of the analysis itself, as it drew on their common understanding of design and shamanry.

Contacts between the Earth and the Sky

The limitations of my analysis of Morán Zumaeta's story about Sangama for a general account of Piro people during the early part of the twentieth century should be borne in mind. At best, it is a portrait of how two Piro men, Sangama and his younger cousin Morán Zumaeta, were thinking at this time, and cannot be given the general status of 'how Piro people were thinking then'. Doubtless other Piro people had their own specific formulations of their condition, and their own cogitations on the way mythic narratives linked up with, and rendered coherent or otherwise, their experiences. However, 'The Story of Sangama' is our only detailed example of such cogitations, and, at best, we can only speculate that other Piro people's formulations at this period would have been coherent transformations of Sangama's.

'The Story of Sangama' can also be looked at in the light of the general schema of transformations of transformations in the Piro lived world that I discussed in Part II. The relevance of 'The Story of Sangama' to the transformation in design discussed in Chapter 4 is obvious enough. Indeed, in this story we see how one of the causes of the decline in design production, the switch from Piro painted clothing to 'white people's clothing', was thought through by Sangama in relation to a innovative re-analysis of 'white people's design'. The transformation in the condition of Piro people was conditional on learning the mysterious knowledge of the true identity of paper and its little designs. As I discuss further in the next chapter, this meant that Piro people, in order to change their circumstances, needed to acquire the knowledge that lay hidden behind 'white people's designs'.

Similarly, Sangama's analysis of reading was a virtuoso re-interpretation of shamanry. As a twin, and hence a 'born shaman', Sangama said that it was through paper and reading, and not through hallucinogens, that one can contact the celestial beings, the *paneneko*, the 'very much other people'. It is likely that the period during which Sangama was expounding his radical ideas was also one of crisis in Piro shamanry, as they came into increasing contact with the down-river tradition of *ayahuasquero* shamanry. Many people from northern Peruvian Amazonia had moved into the area during the rubber period, and some had remained and intermarried with Piro people (see Gow 1991; 1994). It is possible that Sangama's analysis of reading was a product of this more general questioning of existing Piro shamanry in these new conditions.

Further, Sangama was discussing his ideas about the world during a period when *kigimawlo* was transforming in its practice and meanings. As I argued in Chapter 6, this ritual generates the ongoing viability of the Piro lived world by linking a young girl's control over her interior transformation to a general manifestation of Piro people's abilities to acquire wealth from other peoples, as manifested in the *kigimchi*, 'beadwork' and other decorations. Sangama's world was one marked by an extreme lack of such wealth, and by bitter memories of an earlier period when such wealth was abundant. This was also the period in which the boss, Pancho Vargas, became central both to Piro people's access to wealth, and to the *kigimawlo* itself. Sangama's vision of the coming of the 'sky steamboat full of clothing' would dramatically restore such wealth, and be a dramatic transformation in the mode by which the Piro lived world generates its ongoing viability.

Sangama's account of the 'very much other people', insofar as it deals with contact between Piro people and celestial beings, addresses that other 'ancient people's story', the one about the moon. This mythic narrative was, as I showed in Chapter 6, about puberty seclusion, girl's initiation ritual and design. It is possible that Sangama's virtuoso re-analysis of writing was dependent on the fact that this myth was already beginning to fragment, and hence to open up the possibilities of new formulations of the relationships between humans, celestial beings, and designs.

Before leaving 'The Story of Sangama', a final question can be raised of it: did Sangama predict the arrival of the SIL missionaries? There is no reason to think that Matteson thought so, nor that she and her colleagues published this story twice because it seemed to prefigure their project. Unlike Dominican missionaries (see R. Alvarez 1984), SIL missionaries show little taste for finding such prefigurations of their project in indigenous Amazonian people's ideas. As I noted above, Matteson and her colleagues were probably more interested in the account of reading and the aeroplanes. In this story, both Sangama and Zumaeta reveal a diligent searching after knowledge of writing, a searching which is, within the SIL project, the pre-condition for the knowledge of the 'Word of God', the Bible. This story also recounts Sangama's groping attempts to describe an aeroplane, a machine that loomed as large in the practicalities of the SIL missionaries' lives as it did in their self-consequence.

Did Zumaeta think that Sangama had predicted the arrival of the SIL missionaries? It seems almost certain that Zumaeta did so, for the story, and the point of narrating it to Matteson, would otherwise make little sense. Zumaeta reports that Sangama told him, 'Some day a teacher will come here. Some day a sky steamboat will come here, and he will travel in it. That will be seen here one of these days; we will see it. Now the oppression will end.'[22] This was clearly understood by Zumaeta to be a prophetic reference to the SIL missionaries, who did indeed arrive in aeroplanes from their base down-river in Yarinacocha, and beyond there, from the USA. Sangama's prediction of the arrival of the SIL missionaries and their specific mode of transport is thus further testimony to his shamanic powers of reading, which in turn originate in his condition as a twin. Through this story, for Zumaeta at least, the SIL project was inserted into the Piro lived world as the fulfilment of an earlier shamanic vision of the future.

That Sangama should have envisioned the arrival of the SIL missionaries is, from a Piro perspective, hardly very surprising, given that shamans see the

---

[22] The word for teacher here is *yimaklewatachri*, 'one who habitually teaches, who habitually shows how to do things.'

future in their visions. There is, however, a more profound point about the nature of the Piro lived world here. Lévi-Strauss, commenting on the manner in which indigenous American peoples distant from each other integrated the arrival of Europeans into their mythologies in remarkably similar ways, notes that, 'this phenomenon would be incomprehensible unless we accept that the place of the Whites was already marked in the form of a hollow space within systems of thought based on a dichotomous principle that at each stage forces the terms to become double . . .' (1995: 220) He goes on to show how the same principle helps to explain the well known, but intellectually disquieting, friendly receptions offered by the indigenous Mexicans and Peruvians to the arrival of the Spanish *conquistadores*, whom they recognized from older revelations.

Sangama's vision of the *gringos* is obviously of a very different historical order to these earlier predictions, but I think it reflects a similar logic. As I noted above, 'The Story of Sangama' seems to be in dialogue with the Piro 'myth of history', 'Tsla swallowed by a Giant Catfish'. Sangama's world was marked by the disastrous consequences of their co-residence with *kajine*, 'white people', who had appeared from down-river, the destination of Tsla and Muchkajine, the 'First White People'. Sangama's envisioned solution to the sufferings of living with the bosses did not involve any withdrawal from such contacts, but their replacement by co-residence with *another* kind of 'white people', the *paneneko*. Kajine, 'white people' are therefore subjected to a constant process of doubling, and the solution to the troubles they bring lie in establishing contacts with new kinds of 'white people'. This was Sangama's solution, but it would be one that would have made sense to any Piro person, for the prototypical 'white people' are the Muchkajine of the mythic narratives, who are the very essence of doubling. As I argued in Chapter 4, the Muchkajine are Tsla's double, his placenta and twin, and they in turn are twins (or triplets, depending on the version) of each other. As such, ongoing doubling is hardly a surprising characteristic of the current forms of white people. We can perhaps paraphrase Sangama's logic as follows: if our white people are bad, then by the very nature of 'white people', somewhere further out there are another kind of white people, good ones.

8

The *Gringos* Arrive

In the 1980s, my informants described the period beginning in the late 1940s as the 'liberation from slavery', for it was then that Piro people ceased to live on the *haciendas* of their bosses. They moved then to new communities centred on schools, which had been established by the SIL missionaries. One of the first of these communities was Huau, where the SIL missionary Esther Matteson arrived in 1947, the year Artemio was born, and where he first attended school. In this chapter, I analyse the events of this period, to show how the arrival of the SIL allowed Piro people to transform their social world, and to begin to establish the way of life I have here called 'the audacious innovation'.

In contrast to the period discussed in the last chapter, the arrival of the SIL would seem to present less serious problems to historical analysis. It was a period that many of my older informants had lived through as adults, and hence remembered as lived experience, and we have documentary evidence from the accounts of Matteson and other missionaries, and to a lesser extent from Piro people themselves. Certain curious lacunae exist, however. In the 1980s, my informants usually described this period as a simple shift from the *haciendas* of Vargas, following his death in 1940, to the new villages established around the schools opened by the SIL missionaries, or the Dominicans in Sepahua. But these missions were not founded until at least seven years after the death of Vargas, and there is evidence that many Piro people had left the *haciendas* before the 1940s. Further, despite the fact that these new communities focused on missionaries, Protestant or Catholic, my informants seldom mentioned religious conversion in their accounts of the period, and stressed instead the founding of schools and villages. This silence is all the more remarkable given the overt intentions of the apparent agents of these changes, for clearly the SIL missionaries and Dominican priests were primarily motivated by religious conviction. In the 1980s, it was as if this religious dimension had been forgotten, submerged under the educational and land reform initiatives of the 1970s.

My argument here suggests strongly that the founding of these new, school-centred villages took place in a context of extreme crisis in the Piro lived world, and of radical messianic expectations of new relations with celestial beings of the kind we saw in Sangama's account of the 'sky steamboat'. This expectation, while endogenously generated within Piro people's life experiences of the time, was given form by the activities of an earlier missionary group, the Seventh-Day Adventists, and by the enthusiasm of many neighbouring Campa people for that message. Many Piro people seem to have taken up this enthusiasm for Adventism, responding as it did to their own questions about the nature of the world, and thereby laid the groundwork for their later enthusiasm for the SIL message. However, having lived through that prior period of radical messianic expectation predisposed Piro people to see the SIL mission as a project for a new mode of 'living well', and so progressively to abandon and ignore what those missionaries saw as its religious dimension.

As I noted in the Introduction, my focus here is on the consequences of the relations between Piro people and the SIL missionaries, and I do not consider in any depth the effects of Dominican evangelical action, or the small group of Piro people who continued to be Adventists. This is because, even though most of my fieldwork was conducted in Dominican-affiliated communities, those residents of these communities who were my main informants had spent the period discussed here in SIL-affiliated communities. My account here could not, therefore, be applied to those Piro people who had always lived in Sepahua, or to those who remained loyal to the Adventists.

'The New Life'

I begin this account of the dramatic results of the arrival of the SIL missionaries with the testimony of one of its presumptive instigators, Esther Matteson. In a description of Piro religion and of the failure of previous missionaries, Catholic or otherwise, she wrote the following with reference to the early 1950s:

Since 1949, translations of portions of the Bible without sectarian teaching have been supplied them. This has met with enthusiastic reception on the part of some 300. In fact, most of the Piro of the Urubamba relate their recent marked advance in education to this source. Without question it has had far more effect on the Piro culture than the superficial religious influences previously mentioned. (1954: 73)

Presumably, Matteson's 'without sectarian teaching' refers to a supposed contrast between SIL practice and that of the Adventists they had supplanted in Huau, and that of the Dominicans in Sepahua.[1] Her figure of some 300 people for the enthusiastic reception of the SIL message is significant, given that this is well over half of the population of Urubamba Piro by her estimate at the time, 'between four and five hundred' (1954: 27). How did Piro people interpret these events, and why did they give the SIL project this enthusiastic reception?

In 1968, in *Gwacha Ginkakle*, Sebastián describes the new lives initiated by the arrival of the SIL missionaries in a chapter entitled '*Genshinikanrewlu*', and it is there translated as the '*La Vida Nueva*', 'The New Life' (Sebastián,

---

[1] Matteson may have felt obliged to make this statement, since active proselytization conflicted with the legal basis of SIL activity in Peru (see Stoll 1982).

Zumaeta, and Nies (1974: 159–63). The root of this word is the same as *nshinikanchi*, and in the *Diccionario Piro* the term *genshinikanru* is translated as 'conversion, change in attitude' (Nies 1986: 39). *Genshinikanrewlu* means 'caused to have a new way of thinking, memory, love, respect'. This suggests that, for Sebastián, the arrival of the SIL missionaries initiated a transformation in the core faculty of the Piro person, their 'thought, mind, love, respect'. The term is nothing if not revolutionary.

I do not know what exactly Sebastián had to say about 'The New Life', for that chapter was torn out of my copy of the book by an SIL functionary before I was given it in the Ministry of Education building in Lima (I had paid for it). Apparently the Ministry of Education had strong objections to its sectarian religious bias. Despite this censorship, it is possible to gain some idea of what Sebastián may have said from the chapters that survived intact. Sebastián describes the 'present-day lives of Piro people', *Yine Gixyawakatka Pirana*, as follows:

The Piro people of my generation did not know about books; also, we didn't live in villages. We used to live scattered about in temporary shelters,[2] and after a couple of years we moved off to another place. In the dry season we lived on the beaches, and in the rainy season in the forest. We always returned to the beach when the river fell. Now we have schools and we live in villages.

In 1968 there began for us the teaching of mechanics, carpentry, and the raising of animals. Also, the teaching of health care.

In past times, we Piro people didn't wear clothes like those used by white people, but instead hand-made clothing. The men wore *cushmas* and the women wore skirts, painted just like the men's *cushmas*.

They always hunted animals, birds, and fish with arrows. In those times there were men who were naturally good hunters, and others who had learned this skill using herbs. Now in 1968, we are forgetting how to hunt with arrows. We have grown accustomed to using the implements of the white people: the cast-net and shotgun. Good archery has been lost now.

The spiritual life of the Piro people has also changed. Before, the shamans were feared and to children it was said, 'Watch out! Don't talk or laugh. Don't make fun of the shaman or he will ensorcell you, and you will die!' But now it isn't the shaman, but God who is feared and loved. Now only a few people fear shamans.

Neither are the demons feared, because we know God looks after us. He is great and made everything that exists.

Thus have our lives been changing, since we know God. We praise him and thank him, hoping that everything that we ask him for he will give to us, if that is his will.

Perhaps in the next generation there will be no one who doesn't know how to read. This is the story, as I see it, of the Piro people, from times past up until today and the way our lives have changed. That is all. (Sebastián, Zumaeta, and Nies 1974: 179–85)

---

[2] Called *tambos* in the original, these are temporary shelters, built rapidly of wild cane by travellers or people camping on beaches in the dry season.

The tight linkage, in Sebastián's account, of writing, changes in residence, clothing, subsistence, fear of shamans, and relationship to God are remarkable, and I think far from fortuitous. This total package is what the *genshinikanrewlu*, 'the new way of thinking' meant, at least to Sebastián, and probably to most Piro people, at the time.

Sebastián's account of the 'present-day life of Piro people', sounds remarkably like my own informants' accounts of 'being civilized' in the 1980s (see Gow 1991). The only major difference to 'the audacious innovation' would be in the relative place of regard for shamans and God, for by the 1980s, shamans were renascently active, and service to God was less central. However, Sebastián's account suggests strongly that the 'New Life', as an event, was a solution to a particular problem in *gwashata*, 'living well': 'The Piro people of my generation did not know about books; also, we didn't live in villages. Now we have schools and we live in villages.'

As I discussed in *Of Mixed Blood*, living in villages was central to the definition of 'being civilized' in the 1980s, and schools were definitional of 'real villages', and hence of the possibility of 'living well'. The same theme appears in Sebastián's account, but here the villages and schools are predicated on the event of the 'new life'. Sebastián's statement that the 'Piro people of my generation' did not live in villages, but rather move about on river beaches and in the forest, appeals to the strongly negative moral meaning of 'living scattered about' for Piro people: 'living well' is only possible in villages, in stable day-to-day relations with others (see Gow 1991: 226–8). As I discussed there, Piro people described their social lives to me as necessarily predicated on a centre with whom they lived, be it a 'chief', a 'boss', or the school and the *Comunidad Nativa*.

There is another dimension to Sebastián's statement about his generation 'living scattered about', which suggests that it refers to a precise historical moment, rather than to a general moral condition. Discussing the establishment of schools by the Peruvian government, Sebastián states that, in the past, 'the old dead Piro people had no gardens; they lived with their bosses and ate the food from the bosses' gardens ... they lived in the white man's places. They depended on the white man. He protected them. Whatever dangers they feared, only he helped them. (Sebastián, Zumaeta, and Nies 1974: 171–3)

In contrast, the Piro people of Sebastián's generation lived scattered about. This contrast in conditions seems to be a reference to the actual chaotic conditions of the early 1940s. My oldest informants in the 1980s assured me that they had lived as debt-slaves on Vargas's *haciendas*, before Vargas's death in 1940, when many left for the Manú river during the mini-rubber boom of the Second World War era. It seems that Vargas's death was experienced as a chaotic moment by many Piro people since they had lost the centre of their village life, the person who, in Sebastián's words, 'protected them'.

Vargas may have protected Piro people on the *haciendas*, but as we saw in the previous chapter, he also maltreated them. It was against this maltreatment that Sangama spoke in his remarkable vision of the 'sky steamboat full of clothing'. Sebastián's account of the 'present-day lives of Piro people' reads like a total fulfilment of what Sangama said would be true of the future, with regard to 'wealth' (*gejnu*). The Piro people now have clothes like white people, they have white people's shotguns, cast-nets, knowledge of mechanics, carpentry, animal husbandry, and health care. And above all, they have God. As Sebastián puts it, 'we know God looks after us'. The Piro word that Sebastián uses here is *girukotyawu*, 'he takes care of us'. This suggests that, for Sebastián, the new lives of Piro people had God at their centre. God now acted as the bosses had done before.

How could God act as a boss? For Christians like Sebastián, God could act as a boss in the sense of 'protecting' his followers: like a very powerful boss, God could help them with whatever dangers they feared. However, I think that Sebastián's formulation actually conflates two distinct kinds of relationship to God. The first is the 'New Life', the *genshinikanrewlu*, in which communities are centred on God in the sense that, as communities of believing Christians, their residents 'live well' together because each person follows God's laws. The second is a messianic notion of the community, whereby people strive literally to live with God, by entry into the sky and consequent divinization. Historically, I argue, the first formulation is a product of the second, for the 'New Life' was made out of a prior messianic moment. To understand this process, I begin by looking again at Piro conceptualizations of divinity.

Divinity and Humanity

What notions of God did Piro people have when the SIL missionaries turned up? In *Gwacha Ginkakle*, Sebastián, after discussing the period of the rubber industry, says:

The times of rubber went on for many years, and then when it ended, those who taught us about God came.

Before that, we had knowledge of God, but very little. When the *gringos* arrived,[3] then we understood that God existed in the sky, that he loved us, and that he had a son called Jesus (Piro, *Geso*) who died for us.

Long ago the ancient people did not know much about God, although they had heard of him. But they wanted to see him. So, many took hallucinogens. They drank hallucinogens wanting to see God. They drank *ayahuasca*. They saw God, it is said, they called him 'Father'. They drank *toé* and other plants, trying to see God. But they never got there.

My father told us that he had heard that God existed, but he wanted to know him and learn who he was and where he lived. Then, the shamans told him that by drinking *toé* and *ayahuasca*, he would see God.

---

[3] Sebastián's use here of the word *klatalune*, 'those who are white', for 'white people', rather than the more common *kajine*, suggests that the reference is to American missionaries.

Therefore he too wanted to see God. He drank *toé* for five days in the forest. But he told us that he did not see him and went on asking, 'Where does God live, under the earth or in the sky?'

Then one day after the time of rubber there arrived those who explained to us about God. They told us that he exists and the he had created all that can be seen and that cannot be seen. Then we also understood that Jesus lived in this world, and that he died for our sins. (Sebastián, Zumaeta, and Nies 1974: 150–3)

Sebastián's father, discussed here, was very probably of the same generation as Sangama.

Sebastián's account here contrasts rather sharply with that given by Matteson herself. As I discussed in Chapter 5, she described Piro religion in the late 1940s and early 1950s as 'a polytheism of innumerable gods and goddesses living in heaven', with 'heaven' synonymous with the sky; the culture hero Tsla received no homage or petitions; invocations were directed to a generalized *goyakalu*; divinities were characterized by their endurance, eternity; divinities were *kashichjeru*, 'the one who seizes', because they were the ultimate source of human mortality; and that people with few sins, and all-powerful shamans, enter the sky and become divinities (1954: 72). Matteson's account is broadly similar to that of Ricardo Alvarez, who adds, however:

According to tradition, Goyakalu lived with the Piro after creation through an infinity of generations. In this direct and personal contact with them, he left the precepts of life, myths and knowledge of the cosmos. The day that the Piro aggrieved him, he went back to his home, from whence he had come, to return no more. This absence caused them great distress and they will always have it. From that moment there was manifested in the cosmos the 'gochate' or failure, disequilibrium, sin. The Piro try to re-establish this lost equilibrium, the reparation of sin, in many ways. (1970: 60)

I have difficulty imagining how one might say, in either Piro or Ucayali Spanish, 'an infinity of generations', nor was it ever suggested to me that *Goyakalu* told myths to Piro people. I suspect that Alvarez is here engaged in Vatican II-inspired hyperbole, and searching for a prefiguration of Catholicism in Piro religious ideas. That said, however, his account corresponds more closely in key features to Sebastián's account than Matteson's does.

It seems likely that Matteson, as a Protestant, sought to downplay any specifically Christian elements in the older Piro ideas of divinity, and in particular she states, of the three centuries of Jesuit and Franciscan missionization, 'there is practically no apparent influence of Roman Catholicism on the beliefs and practices of the Piro' (1954: 72). However, as I discussed in Chapter 5, while Matteson was right to assert that the *goyakalune*, divinities in the plural, were the interlocutors of shamans at the time she was writing, there was clearly also an interest in the Christian God. As I discussed there, the Christian God seems to have been assimilated into Piro shamanic cosmology as the divinity *patutachri*, 'Father', and was contacted and called upon by shamans.

What was the nature of Piro people's relationships to Divinity at this period? Ricardo Alvarez's account suggests that Piro people's collective relationship to Divinity was connected to the notion of *gocha*, 'sin'.[4] Matteson also records the word root, *mukochi-* (*mukochri* is the derived noun), 'to displease a supernatural being, fail to observe a taboo' (1965: 309), which has the same range of meanings as *gocha*, and is used by Sebastián in the same way. I do not know what the meaning of these words, *gocha* and *mukochri*, were for Piro people before the period of SIL and Dominican evangelization. In the 1980s, on the very few occasions on which Piro people talked about 'sin' (Ucayali Spanish, *pecado*), they did so in basically Christian terms and, assuming I knew more about such things than they did, were unwilling to expand on their own views. However, I did have the sense, when Piro people talked about 'sin', that they identified it with the joys of social life: the manifold pleasures of sex, of drinking manioc beer, of eating game, of speaking ill of each other, and so on. It is these pleasures which make social life possible, and, as they say, ultimately kill them (see Gow 1991: 180–3). These are also the things which shamans must avoid if they are to acquire and maintain their knowledge (Gow 1991: 235–41). I discuss this issue further below, but it seems to me that, at the time of the arrival of the SIL, the Piro notions of *gocha* or *mukochri* were probably broadly similar: 'sin' was ongoing social life, and a consequent distance from Divinity.[5]

The epithet of Divinity as *kashichjeru*, 'one who seizes (us)', recorded by Matteson, can be interpreted in this light. Divinity, whether singular or plural, is characterized by *goyaknu*, 'eternity', which is the opposite of the human condition of mortality (see Ch. 5). Humanity's lack of durability is caused by 'sin' which, following Ricardo Alvarez, is due to humans' distance from Divinity. That distance is literally the distance between the earth and the sky.[6] Living on the earth, and trying to 'live well', Piro people constantly weaken themselves so that they become 'tired of living' and eventually die. This death is thought of as 'seizure' by Divinity. That such ideas were circulating in the 1980s is revealed in the following conversation between Jorge, a young Campa man from Huau, and Artemio's mother, old Clotilde. They were discussing the death of Jorge's young son, the second to die in as many years. In his desperation, Jorge asked, 'But, aunt, why did my son have to die?' Clotilde simply gestured upwards, in the local manner by pointing with her lips, and said, '*Goyakalu, Tasorentsi*', respectively Piro and Campa words for God.[7] Beyond

---

[4] As Matteson points out, *gocha* is a loanword from Quechua (1965: 278), and it probably entered Piro from the use of Quechua as a *lingua franca* in the Ucayali missions.

[5] I am grateful to Cecilia McCallum for pointing out to me (personal communication) that the implication of this is that Piro people do not see any 'kinship' between Divinity and humanity.

[6] See Weiss (1975) for Campa formulations of this problem. Weiss's Campa informants called their lived world *Kamavéni*, 'The River of Mortality'.

[7] This scene took place around the time that Jorge announced his desire to train as a shaman (see Ch. 5).

the knowledge and power of humans, even those of shamans, are the reasons of Divinity.

As Matteson noted, for some people this is not so, for those, 'whose sins are comparatively few, and all powerful witchdoctors, go to heaven and become gods' (1954: 72): for such people, death is itself a transformation into *goyakalune*, 'divinities'. For the great majority, however, death is the ongoing transformation of the person into 'dead souls' and 'bone demons' (see Ch. 5). What Piro people fear most in these ordinary transformations is not the existential prospect of such a future, for they are willing to discuss their own post-mortem destinies with great good humour. Far more frightening are the horrors of co-residence destroyed, as a beloved kinsperson transforms into a dead soul and terrifying skeletal demon, and the consequent irreparable destruction of the everyday kin relations of *gwashata*. As Artemio once told me, 'Sometimes I think it would be better if all of us, all my kin and my children and my wife and me, died at once from an epidemic illness. Then we wouldn't miss each other.' I was shocked by this sentiment, but Artemio did not seem to be in a particularly pessimistic mood when he said this. His tone was rather one of intellectual curiosity: the measure would be extreme, to be sure, but it would at least solve the intense pain caused by the one by one attrition of death. His speculations continued:

Or why can we not live forever, changing our skins like snakes and becoming young again? Snakes grow old, they shed their skins, and become young again. They are all soft then, and cannot bite. Or we could be like tortoises, who also live a long time. When you stick a pole into a tortoise, it just laughs. Even when the pole has rotted away, the tortoise is still alive. Only when it is crushed by an *uvos* tree does the tortoise cry, for the *uvos* tree does not know how to die.[8]

As we have seen throughout this study, human mortality, and the fate of the dead, is a central preoccupation of Piro cosmological speculation. It is not, however, thought of as a personal existential predicament, a fear of nothingness, but as a problem for the survivors. It is an existential problem of abandonment: it is seen from the point of view of the living, those who are abandoned, and from that of the dead, those who abandon. Its resolution lies with Divinity, knowing nothing of death, living way up overhead in the sky, and far from humanity.

There are at least three possible solutions of this problem. The first might be called the *kigimawlo* solution. Here, mortality can be sufficiently postponed, through the correct techniques, so that it does not really matter. Girls' initiation ritual, if correctly observed, allows Piro people to live long enough to undergo all of the lived transformations necessary to generate a full world of kinship, and hence to exhaust their social productivity. In so doing, they

---

[8] The *uvos* is *Spondias mombin*, and is used as a medicine. I do not know its Piro name.

become 'far too old'. Here, the solution to the human condition lies in full identification with humanity. As we have seen, some of the mythic narratives about the moon, those which tell of how Klana painted the moon's face, deal with a disruption of just such an orderly progression of full identification with humanity in seclusion: the moon's corpse-like face is the product of the inappropriate contact between a celestial being and a secluded girl.

The second solution is in shamanry. As I discussed in Chapter 5, shamans, through their constant entry into a hallucinatory state and consequent identification with powerful beings, escape the general human condition of mortality. This was, in Piro shamanry, associated with the descent of the divinities to the shaman during hallucinatory experience, and his 'post-mortem' translation to the sky as lightning. Here, the solution to the human condition lies in full identification with Divinity, in the solitary project of becoming a shaman.

The third solution of this problem would resemble the second, but take the form of a collective shaman-becoming. Here, Piro people would collectively seek to live without 'sin', and seek a full identification with Divinity. As Artemio's speculations suggest, such a collective project would imply a radical transformation in the human condition, as mortality is escaped. It would also imply a generalization to all Piro people of the condition that leads people to become shamans. This is the state of *wamonuwata*, 'to grieve, to suffer, to sorrow, to be pitiable'. Just as it is an individual man's experience of 'suffering' which stimulates him to become a shaman, it would require a generalized sense of 'suffering' to lead to a collective project of shaman-becoming. We have already seen certain aspects of such a state in Sebastián's account of the lives of the people of his generation, and in Zumaeta's story about Sangama. If living with Vargas was bad, living without him was worse. It is to evidence that Piro people responded to this condition of generalized suffering with a project of collective divinization that I turn next.

Going to the Sky to be with God

In the documentary archive, there is one direct reference to a process of collective divinization. It occurs in a personal-experience narrative of a Piro woman's first sight of an aeroplane, which she interpreted as the coming of God. The narrator of this story was Dionisia García, who was Antonio Urquía's paternal grandmother. Her story is published as '*Nato Yonisyani Ginkakle Tenyapachro Pirana*', 'Our Late Mother Dionisia's Story about the Aeroplane', in the SIL primer *Muchikawa Kewenni Pirana ga wa Pimri Ginkak-lukaka* (Nies 1972). Dionisia García's story runs as follows:

We saw the first aeroplane a long time ago. I was still a young woman and my daughter Ana María was too, while Miguel, Felipe and the other little girl were still very little.

Before that time, our boss Pancho had told us that a man with wings and shoes would come, flying through the air, and it was said that this was how God would come.[9]

And that day when it came, we were living down-river from Contamana in Inahuaya village at the mouth of the Cachiyacu river. We were alone, just sitting around, Ana María, the children and me, when we suddenly heard a noise coming from the big straight stretch of the Cachiyacu: hlalalalalalalala. Ana María said, 'Mother, what is that noise, hlalalalalalalala? Maybe it's a jaguar.' 'Who knows what it is?', I replied to her, 'A jaguar? Perhaps it is black jaguars who have come out on to the big straight stretch of the Cachiyacu.' We went to look, but we saw nothing. All we heard was the sound, hlalalalalalala.

I said, 'Take the axe to kill the jaguar!' I grabbed the machete and Ana María the axe and we ran off to find out what it was. As we looked around, Ana María looked up and saw the aeroplane. We saw it as a person with wings and shoes, just as we had heard in the stories. 'Ay! Perhaps it is truly God, for they said that he will come with wings to carry his children into heaven.' We looked up, thinking we saw his open arms, when in fact it was an aeroplane.

Then we shouted, saying, 'Father, we are here! Take us with you!' We thought the pilot was God, but he wasn't. 'Father, here we are, your children!' As we watched the aeroplane went on, and we said to each other sadly, 'It seems he didn't see us. If he had seen us, he would have come down to take us away.'

We were wrong to imagine that it was God, when it was just the pilot, a white man. This happened when we lived on the Cachiyacu river. That is the story. (Nies 1972: 21–7)

Dionisia Garcia presumably told this story to the SIL missionary Joyce Nies, but I have no evidence as to when she did so. It is easier to date the event recounted in the story from internal evidence. Ortiz (1974: 584) records that aviation began in Peruvian Amazonia in 1932. The Inahuaya–Cachiyacu area, where the events recounted took place, is far to the north of the Bajo Urubamba, down-river on the Bajo Ucayali, and hence much closer to the then important administrative and commercial centres of Iquitos and Contamana. It is therefore hardly surprising that Piro people who lived there would have had earlier experience of aeroplanes than Urubamba people. A date in the early 1930s fits with the age of Dionisia's daughter, Ana María: she was about sixty-five to seventy years old in 1980, and is called a *makloji*, 'young woman, adolescent' (i.e., thirteen to twenty years old), by the narrator, so this event is likely to have occurred in the early 1930s. Dionisia's total unfamiliarity with what she saw suggests that this must have been one of the first aeroplanes to cross the area, and possibly the very first.

Dionisia García's story is unquestionably a report of a tense personal expe-

---

[9] The detail of the shoes is puzzling. Clearly, some part of the aeroplane was so interpreted, but why as shoes? Wearing shoes is an important practice in present-day Piro formality, but I suspect that there is something more profound here, which would be elucidated by a deeper knowledge of Pancho Vargas himself. It may be significant that the Lima seat of the Franciscans, whom Vargas clearly admired, is called *Los Descalzos*, 'The Shoeless Ones'.

rience. The rapidity with which Dionisia identified the aeroplane as God shows that at least some Piro people, at this period, expected God to come directly from the sky, and were willing to interpret unusual and unforeseen events in such a messianic light. Dionisia's story corresponds closely with Sangama's account of the 'sky steamboat', and both have their origins in the shared experience of 'suffering' in Vargas's *haciendas*: while not explicitly stated in Dionisia's account, she and her kinspeople were living in the Cachiyacu area to avoid Vargas, just as Julio Manchineri was to do later, as I noted in Chapter 7.[10] According to her grandsons Antonio Urquía and Moisés Miqueas, Dionisia moved back to the Bajo Urubamba in the early 1940s, following the death of Vargas, to live in Huau.

In the preceding chapter, I discussed how difficult life seems to have been for Piro people living on the *haciendas* of Vargas. The 1920s and 1930s were a period of extreme depression in the Western Amazonian economy, which was characterized by a perpetual boom-and-bust cycle in various agricultural products (Gow 1991: 44–8). My older informants told me how much they had suffered at the hands of Vargas. For some Piro people, this suffering seems to have been seen as generalization of *wamonuwata*, 'to be sad, to grieve, to suffer'. It is likely that the perception that such suffering was being generalized to all Piro people would have led easily to a desire for collective divinization. We have already seen how Sangama interpreted this problem, and the response of his listeners.

Dionisia's story comes from the same milieu as Sangama's prophetic vision, and addresses similar elements, but there is a crucial difference. Where for Sangama, the 'sky steamboat' was to bring the 'very much other people' with their wealth to live among Piro people, Dionisia saw the aeroplane as God returning to take his children to heaven. So, where Sangama proposed a solution to the crisis of *gwashata* to lie with the arrival of the *paneneko*, 'very much other people', Dionisia, as well as other Piro people, expected a radical transformation of humanity, and their imminent translation to the sky. Sangama's vision implied that 'living well' was to be re-established by co-residence with a new kind of white people, while Dionisia's story implied that 'living well' was to be re-established on a much more dramatic basis, as co-residence with God in the sky.

In her story, Dionisia points to the boss Pancho Vargas as the source of her mistaken identification of the aeroplane with God. There is, however, an alternative and much more powerful source for these ideas: Campa enthusiasm for Seventh-Day Adventist missionaries. As Bodley (1970) and Brown and Fernandez (1991) have discussed, the North American Adventist Stahl had been evangelizing Campa people in the Perené area to the east, with considerable success,

---

[10] The Cachiyacu–Inahuaya (Cushabatay) area has long been inhabited by Piro people with kin ties to Urubamba people, and was therefore the most obvious destination for these latter when they sought to flee from Vargas.

since the early 1920s. Urubamba Piro people would have known of these developments, given the extensive network of intermarriages, kin ties and other relationships covering the area and linking Campa and Piro people together: Dionisia's grandsons Moisés Miqueas and Antonio Urquía told me that Dionisia's father was a Campa man from the Gran Pajonal area.[11] By the 1930s, the message of Adventism had been brought into the Alto Ucayali by a Campa man from the Perené, in response to local enthusiasm, and led Adventist missionaries to found a mission at Unini, on the Alto Ucayali river just below Atalaya (Pérez Marcio 1953).

What was the nature of this enthusiasm in the Alto Ucayali and Bajo Urubamba areas? Bodley conducted research in the 1960s in an Adventist mission community on the Alto Ucayali, and investigated Campa people's responses to Stahl's and later Adventist's evangelization. He noted how they developed their own account of the message:

Stahl never set a date for the great Advent, but in the minds of the Campa it was imminent. They expected Christ to appear today or tomorrow, not ten or twenty years in the future. The coming was to be an extremely cataclysmic event. One informant said that the dead were to arise, all evil would be destroyed, and the believers and risen dead would be taken to the house of God in the sky were there would be no more sickness, death or growing old. Some stressed that the earth was to be burned and the unbelievers would die like *Huangana* (the white-lipped peccary, an animal that runs in herds and may be slaughtered in large numbers). (1970: 113)

This vision corresponds closely with Dionisia García's story, and especially with her concerns with 'not being seen', and consequently being left behind on earth. While not mentioned in Dionisia's story, the detail of the white-lipped peccaries would have had profound significance for Piro people. As I discussed in Chapter 2, these peccaries are intrinsically bound up with the problem of mortality, and movements between an upper and a lower world.

There is no question that Vargas would have been hostile to the arrival of the Adventists. As Bodley (1970) and Brown and Fernandez (1991) note, the power of the bosses over their indigenous workers was profoundly threatened by the message of Adventism, and there were reprisals against converts. For the Bajo Urubamba case, possible confirmation of such hostility comes from the foundation of a mission in Atalaya in 1932 by the Franciscans. This mission was founded by priests invited by Vargas from Puerto Ocopa, and he provided the land for it (Ortiz 1974).[12] Vargas, who was well known in the region for his political astuteness, would have seen the advantage of a Franciscan presence in

---

[11] Román (1986) records that a Piro man, Ulises Díaz, went to the Perené river in 1919 to join the Campa converts to Adventism there. This date seems far too early to me, but Díaz's account shows that some Urubamba Piro people quickly showed an interest in Campa Adventism.

[12] An expedition sent by Vargas to fetch priests from the Franciscan mission of Puerto Ocopa is described by Zumaeta in 'The Story of Sangama' (Matteson 1965: 228–9), and was also described to me by Clotilde Gordón, who went on it as a young girl.

Atalaya to compete with the Adventist message. However, even though this new mission was located on the same site as previous Franciscan missions directed to Piro people, no attempt was made to evangelize Piro people. This was presumably to avoid antagonizing Vargas himself, who would have wanted no competition for control over his Piro and other workers.

Further evidence of animosity between Vargas and the Adventists is shown by the fact that when Vargas died in 1940, the Adventists rapidly opened up a new mission at Huau on the Bajo Urubamba itself (Pérez Marcio 1953). Many Piro and Campa people, who had been residents of Vargas's *haciendas* such as La Huaira and Sepa, began to move there. Piro people at that period had few alternatives to living in the Adventist community of Huau: Vargas was dead, the other bosses were poor, and the only alternative was, as Sebastián put it, to 'live scattered about'. By establishing a mission with a school, the Adventists provided a place in which Piro people could try to 'live well' again. Further, at this time, Piro people who had fled from the Bajo Urubamba to get away from Vargas began to return. Dionisia García returned to the Urubamba with her kinspeople in the early 1940s to live in Huau, undoubtedly drawn by the presence of the Adventists.

Rethinking Heaven

What was the nature of the relationship between Piro people and the Adventists in Huau in the early 1940s? In the 1980s, my informants had little to say about this period, other than to laconically note its existence. It seems, in people's memories, to have been largely supplanted by the subsequent arrival of the SIL missionaries, and the 'liberation from slavery'. Nor is there much in the available documentary literature, for both the SIL missionaries and the Dominicans are relatively silent on this period immediately before their arrival. My sense of this period, however, is that it was experienced as one of radical messianic expectation. The evidence for this lies in the abandonment of both fermented manioc beer and of *kigimawlo*, the girl's initiation ritual, at this time. My suggestion is that this was caused by a combination of two streams of ideas. Firstly, there was the active Adventist preaching against fermented manioc beer, and preaching about the imminent arrival of God. Secondly, there was a Piro formulation that the imminent coming of God would render fermented manioc beer and its attendant rituals unnecessary, for their lived world was coming to an end.

Matteson commented on the situation of manioc beer in the 1940s and 1950s as follows: 'Masato, the fermented manioc drink, is used very little by the Piro on the Urubamba now. Its use probably was commoner a few years ago. However, an unfermented or slightly fermented manioc drink is common' (1954: 46). Reading this on the Bajo Urubamba in the early 1980s, I was incredulous, for fermented manioc beer was made constantly by Piro women, and as constantly

drunk. Festivals were unthinkable without it. The idea of Piro people drinking
unfermented manioc beer at a festival was so improbable to me that I initially
dismissed Matteson's observation as abstentionist wishful-thinking. This
seemed all the more probable, given that some Piro people were, at that period,
clearly drinking large quantities of commercially acquired cane alcohol (see
Gow 1991: 52). However, Antonio Urquía told me the following, in the context
of a discussion of the return of his father's family, including Dionisia García,
to the Urubamba from the lower Ucayali after the death of Vargas:

Originally Huau was an Adventist village with an Adventist schoolteacher, who prohib-
ited the people from eating big catfish, small catfish, monkey, collared peccary, and
from drinking manioc beer. They were only allowed to eat deer. At this time Sepahua
did not yet exist. My father-in-law used to live in Huau with his children. Morán
Zumaeta was an important man there.

  Then the *lingüista* Esther arrived and told them it was all right to drink manioc beer,
and to eat whatever they wanted.

This strongly suggested that Matteson had indeed recorded a real and remarkable feature of contemporary Piro life.

  Matteson noted of the Adventist missionaries whom the SIL had ousted
from Huau:

The Seventh-Day Adventist missionaries have exerted considerably more influence
[than the Catholic priests]. Their abstinence from certain meats, and observances of a
period of inactivity, fit in well with the taboos of the Piro. The chief contributions of
this group to the tribe have been a definite decrease in drunkenness, and instruction in
Spanish in the mission schools. (1954: 72–3)

  Matteson is unquestionably correct here, but she does not explain the
underlying dynamic of Piro people's interest in Adventism at that time. The
heightened observation of 'taboos' (avoidance of *gocha/mukochri*, 'sin')
suggests that Piro people were collectively seeking to acquire a specialist
knowledge being brought by the Adventist missionaries. That knowledge was,
I believe, the ability to enter the sky and become divinities themselves. Following from my analysis of Dionisia García's story, the search for this knowledge
seems to have preceded Piro people's direct contacts with Adventist missionaries in 1937, for it was being formulated by at least one Piro woman living in
an area far to the north of the Bajo Urubamba in the early 1930s. In that sense,
the Adventist message, when brought directly to Piro people in Unini and
Huau, would have resonated strongly with Piro people's own understanding of
fermented manioc beer. Piro drunkenness is an important social state, which
allows for ongoing social life through the transformation of respectful relations
in the festive forgetting of drunkenness. As I noted above, drinking fermented
manioc beer is one of the key forms of *gocha* or *mukochri*, 'sin'. To abandon its
use implies that Piro people thought that contact with Divinity was imminent,
and hence ongoing social life was no longer necessary.

This point is confirmed by the fate of *kigimawlo*. As I noted in Chapter 6, during this same period, Piro people had stopped performing girls' initiation rituals, possibly under pressure from the Adventists. However, Adventist preaching would, at this period, have fitted with an obvious problem in performing *kigimawlo*: throughout the *hacienda* period, it had been Vargas who sponsored and led girls' initiation rituals, and he was dead. If *kigimawlo* had been important in articulating Piro people's relations with their boss Vargas in the 1920s and 1930s, their willingness to abandon it in the 1940s suggests that they no longer saw it as necessary. If the girl's initiation ritual effects the ongoing viability of the Piro lived world through the girl's control over her actions in seclusion, and through the consequent generalization of this transformation in the subsequent drunkenness, then Piro people would have had no problem in abandoning both the beer and the ritual when they felt that their lived world was becoming unviable, and new lives in the sky were possible.

My suggestion is, therefore, that in the chaotic conditions of the late 1930s and early 1940s, increasing numbers of Piro people began to take on the radical messianism of their Campa neighbours, and to believe that the arrival of Divinity on earth was imminent. In these conditions, they abandoned manioc beer and the girl's initiation ritual, because these were means to effect the ongoing temporal transformation of the Piro lived world. With the arrival of God imminent, and translation to the sky a real possibility, there was no need for such practices any more. The Adventists, preaching about 'the coming of God', had brought Piro people the necessary technical knowledge for entry into the sky, and hence for becoming divinities themselves.

Confirmation of this analysis lies in a curious feature of certain Piro people's attitudes to song and the girl's initiation ritual. When I travelled to Bufeo Pozo in 1988, women were initially reluctant to sing *suxo shikale*, 'women's songs' for Pablo Rodriguez to tape for me, saying that they were *kamchi shikale*, 'demon's songs'. When they discovered I did not disapprove of these 'women's songs', however, they enthusiastically sang them to me. When I discussed this incident later with Lucha Campos in Santa Clara, she said scornfully, 'They call them 'demon's songs' because women sing them when they drink manioc beer. That's just a lie of the *evangelistas*. They're nothing to do with demons, they are songs women sing. They are beautiful! Those people living there up-river are really ignorant!'

The same process occurred with *kigimawlo*. Julia Laureano told me, in 1995, 'I used to have all the things for doing girl's initiation ritual. I used to have the beadwork, and the painted crown and the painted skirt. But that one, my husband, he told me to throw them away. He said, 'They belong to demons, and that ritual is for getting drunk. We should not do those things, and we should live as *evangelistas*!' So I threw them into the river. But now I repent of what I did, and I wish that I had not done so.

Usually, the term *evangelista*, 'Evangelical Christian', refers to SIL missionaries or to the followers of their message. However, there is no evidence that
SIL missionaries ever attempted to ban singing or the girl's initiation ritual.
From the evidence of their writings, the SIL missionaries seem to have appre-
ciated Piro song style (see Matteson (1954: 66–8), and as I noted in Chapter 6,
Matteson seemed to be have been bemused by the abandonment of the girl's
initiation ritual. Clearly the *'evangelistas'* in Lucha's and Julia's accounts were
not the SIL missionaries. Who, then, were they?

These *evangelistas* were presumably the Piro followers of the SIL mission,
but why then did they insist on banning things that the SIL missionaries themselves did not? This, I think, reflects the way that the Piro conception of 'being
an *evangelista*' was formulated in contact with Adventist missionaries, who
unquestionably did prohibit the consumption of all alcohol. This piece of
Adventist doctrine was enduring because it allowed Piro people to reformulate
the nature of their ritual life. As I discussed in Chapter 6, the girl's initiation
ritual and 'women's songs' are about the drinking of fermented manioc beer,
and the consequent state of drunkenness. There too, I quoted Matteson's
report that all Piro musical styles except lullabies derive ultimately from the
goyakalune, the celestial divinities, and noted the fragmentary evidence from
Ricardo Alvarez which connects the girl's initiation ritual to these same divinities. If, through Adventist preaching against drinking, Piro people came to see
these things as things of the *kamchine*, 'demons', this suggests that they were
using Adventism in order to reclassify the *goyakalune* of ritual life and of
shamanry as *kamchine*, 'demons'.

What exactly is a *kamchi*, 'demon'? In Piro cosmological thought in the
1980s, and presumably back in the 1930s and 1940s too, 'demons' (Ucayali
Spanish, *diablos*) were not associated with any notion of absolute evil.[13] They
are unquestionably inimical to humans, insofar as they seek to kill and eat
people. But, as I explored in Chapter 5, they are also 'humans', and can be
contacted and tamed into helping people by shamans. Indeed, the identification of a being a *kamchi* seems to depend on one's point of view: a helpful
kamchi is no longer a *kamchi*, while anything that reveals itself to be lethally
dangerous becomes *kamchi*.[14] As such, the redefinition of the *goyakalune* as
kamchi would not have been too great a step. During the period of messianic
expectation, and faced with the crisis of their lived world, Piro people seem to
have re-identified most of the *goyakalune* as *kamchine*, 'demons'. Rather than

---

[13] Obviously, it might be better to translate *kamchi* by some other English word. However, the usage
is now well entrenched in the literature, and is consistent both with Ucayali Spanish and with Weiss's
translation of the corresponding Campa term, *kamári/camari* (1975).

[14] The notion of an intrinsic and enduring 'evil', as embodied in a Christian notion of Satan (Piro,
Satanasyo; Ucayali Spanish, *Satanás*) seems to be totally foreign to Piro people's cosmological thought.
'Endurance', as we have seen, is a quality unique to Divinity, and the notion of an 'Evil Divinity' probably does not make very much sense to Piro people: I never heard Satan mentioned outside of Christian ritual discourse.

being the source of Piro people's ability to project their lived world into the future, they came to be seen as the source of their inability to do so. Through the message of Adventism, the only true God was to be *Goyakalu*, the Christian God, and all the rest were redefined as *kamchine*, 'demons'. Thus, Piro love songs became *kamchi shikale*, 'demon's songs', and the girl's initiation ritual became a 'thing of demons'.

The basic groundwork for Piro people's response to Adventism had been laid long before. As I noted above, the Christian God had long been assimilated into the cosmology of Piro shamanry, and people like Sebastián's father had sought out knowledge of this being, *patutachri*, through the use of hallucinogens. The Adventists, when they appeared, must have seemed like a special kind of shaman, privy to the specialist and true knowledge of this God of whom Piro people had heard so much, but whom they had such difficulty finding. Further, as their relations with the white bosses worsened, the Adventist missionaries must also have appeared as a new kind of white people, leading them to a new way of living, 'going to the sky to live with God'.

There is reason to believe, however, that Adventism, and the specific historical context of its introduction, must have been somewhat troubling for Piro people. Firstly, it was institutionally tied to Campa people. For Piro people in the 1980s, Campa people stood for historical backwardness, enclosure, and a refusal of history (Gow 1991: 149), and there is no reason to believe things were very different in the 1930s and 1940s. On Vargas's *haciendas*, and before that in relations with the rubber bosses, Piro people seem to have maintained a more privileged position in the eyes of local white people than Campa people. In the 1980s Piro people saw themselves as a primarily riverine people, while they saw Campa people as primarily a forest people. To live on the big rivers was to be open to relations with new kinds of white people, and hence to be historical, while to live in the forest was to avoid white people and history (Gow 1991; 1993). Adventism, brought by Campa converts from the west, would probably have conflicted with Piro people's general sense of how history should unfold.

Secondly, despite the extent and time-depth of their interactions, Piro and Campa cosmologies conflict on certain basic points. For Campa people, there is an important opposition between those things which come by river from downstream, which are associated with white people and which are, on the whole, bad, and those things which come from the sky, which are good. The Adventists were associated with the latter, as missionaries who travel in aeroplanes continue to be (Brown and Fernandez 1991: 144; Karen Jacobs [personal communication]). In Piro cosmology, by contrast, things which come by river from downstream are strongly associated with the sky, as I discussed in the preceding chapter. Travelling by river and travelling by aeroplane are not so much opposed to each other by Piro people as thought of as lesser and greater versions of the same thing. These differences in cosmology would have made the Campa-inspired enthusiasm for Adventism harder for

Piro people to share, and would have predisposed them to shift focus were an alternative to present itself.

The alternative arrived in 1947, in the form of the SIL missionaries. From this point of view, we can better understand the meaning of Dionisia García's remarkable story about the aeroplane. Her story was probably told to the SIL missionary Joyce Nies, and asserts a shift in view between seeing the aeroplane as God himself to seeing the active agent of the aeroplane as 'just the pilot', i.e., a white man. This transformation in perspective expressed in the story asserts clearly, I think, the actual temporal transformation in Piro people's interest from a messianic expectation associated with Adventism, towards co-residence with the SIL *gringas*. I discuss the reasons for this change further below, but an important reason for it certainly lay with the SIL missionaries' greater wealth, and their ability to mobilize much more dramatic resources than the Adventists: after all, the SIL missionaries did indeed habitually travel in *tenyapachro*, 'aeroplanes', while the Adventists did not (see Pérez Marcio 1953). As such, the SIL missionaries were much better candidates for being Sangama's *paneneko*, 'very much other people', for those people who, like Zumaeta, were intrigued by his prophecy. Even for those who were not so taken, the sheer fact of the SIL's mastery of aviation would have been sufficient evidence that these were a highly desirable new kind of white people.

Living with the Gringas

The SIL missionaries arrived on the Bajo Urubamba in 1947, and rapidly established themselves among the local Piro people, eventually ousting the Adventists from Huau. The reasons for their ability to do so are obscure to me, but central to their success must have been the allegiance of Piro people. As I have shown, Adventism, a primarily Campa-led movement, would have been somewhat troubling for Piro people, but it was a solution to the extreme difficulties in which they found themselves. The SIL missionaries were able to supplant the Adventists among Piro people, I suggest, because their project provided what Piro people saw as a better solution. The greater merit of the SIL project, in the eyes of Piro people, would seem to have been its explicit direction towards them, as Piro people.

What seems to have most impressed Piro people about the SIL missionaries was their willingness to learn to speak Piro, to translate the Bible into that language, and to open schools with teaching in Piro. As Sebastián put it, following on from his account of the coming of the teaching about God:

The year in which Esther Matteson arrived among us was 1947. After she had come, they said about her, 'She wants to learn our language, and translate the Word of God into our language.' Later, she told me about the Piro language, and explained that we could have books and learn in our own language. 'It would be good and we could do it,' she said. (Sebastián, Zumaeta, and Nies 1974: 155 and 157)

In Sebastián's account, 'our language', 'the Piro language', and 'The Word of God', are very close in form: *wtokanu*, 'our language/word'; *yineru tokanu*, 'Piro people's language/word'; *Goyakalu tokanu*, 'God's language/word'. The translation of the New Testament into vernacular languages is central to the SIL project, but I think that Piro people probably understood it in a quite different sense. Language is a major marker of the difference between Piro and Campa peoples, and this is true even although many of the former and some of the latter are bilingual in both. Matteson's project, formulated as Sebastián understood it, held out the prospect of a solution to the crisis they were experiencing directed specifically at them, as Piro people, rather than received second-hand from Campa people, as with Adventism.

In the 1980s, learning the Piro language had a specific meaning for Piro people: the desire for extended coresidence with them. Since almost all Piro people are multilingual, social life can proceed without the need for the co-resident other to understand or speak Piro. However, *gwashata*, 'living well', depends on the ability of this other to understand Piro, for only then can that person be truly 'human'. For example, I remember well the astonishment of a stranger in Miaría when I replied in Spanish to something that she had said in Piro: '*¡Yinerni!*', she exclaimed to another woman. In this specific context, the best translation of the force of this statement might be, 'But it's a human being!' To understand Piro is to enter a condition of expanded moral possibilities. Vargas spoke Piro, I was told, but the Adventists had made no attempt to learn this language. By wanting to learn the Piro language, Esther Matteson signalled to Piro people her desire for a deeper and more profound relationship with them.

Matteson's project of translating the Bible into Piro would have held out to Piro people a solution to a problem inherent in Adventism and of the messianic crisis in which that message took hold. If, as the Adventists undoubtedly preached, the solution to the serious chaos in which Piro people found themselves lay in 'The Word of God', then that solution was couched in a language, Spanish, and a form, writing, which had potent meanings for Piro people at the time. Writing, as we have seen in Chapter 7, was a symbol of the power that the white bosses had over their Piro slaves, while Spanish was, and remained, *kajitu tokanu*, 'white people's language'. The Adventists had opened schools in Unini and in Huau, but instruction was exclusively in Spanish. This would have presented insuperable difficulties for Piro people learning the truth about *Goyakalu tokanu*, 'God's Words': learning a technique of which they were institutionally ignorant in a language that they felt themselves to understand and speak badly.[15] As Matteson noted, many made heroic efforts to overcome

---

[15] Obviously, many Piro people at the time would have spoken Spanish, but only the local dialect of Ucayali Spanish. Teaching, in the Adventist schools, would have been in the unfamiliar form of erudite coastal Peruvian Spanish.

these difficulties (Matteson 1954: 65, quoted in Chapter 7). To have 'God's Words' translated into Piro, and to be taught to read in Piro, would greatly reduce the effort required, but more importantly it would assert the exclusivity of the new relationship between Piro people and this new kind of white people. The centre of gravity of Adventism had been among Campa people. The SIL missionaries who set up in Huau were clearly primarily interested in Piro people.[16]

One consequence of the SIL project was the centrality of schools. Schools were there to teach children and adults to read and write in Piro, and then Spanish, in order that they might have access to the Word of God, the Bible (Piro, *Goyakalu tokanu steno*, 'The Collection of God's Words'). The sorts of community forms entailed by this project were, however, interpreted by Piro people as the primary purpose of the SIL project. Sebastián's 'conversion, new life', as we have seen, was primarily a new mode of 'living well', through a relationship with the *gringos*, this new kind of white people, and through them, with the cosmos.

The school, and its stress on reading and writing, would have had a potent meaning for Piro people. As we saw in the previous chapter, at least one Piro man, Sangama, had formulated the key to the power of the bosses as lying in their power of writing, *kajitu yona*, 'white people's designs', and *kiruka*, 'books, papers'. The identification of writing as an important attribute of white people was general to Piro people, and their illiteracy was a powerful image of their ignorance. But, as we have seen, the importance of writing for Piro people was also connected to their understandings of *yonchi*, 'designs', and to the role of design in ongoing social life. The SIL project held out the promise of inserting 'white people's designs' into the heart of Piro social life, in the specifically Piro form of the written Piro language.

The SIL project thereby solved another aspect of the dilemmas presented by messianic enthusiasm for Adventism. Most Piro people had abandoned performance of the girl's initiation ritual. As such, the centrality of *yonchi*, 'design', in controlling the process of transforming social relations had been lost. By translating the 'Word of God' into Piro, and by opening schools in which Piro people could learn to read and to write, Matteson provided a means by which Piro people could re-insert design at the centre of their social world and its ongoing transformation. Now, however, the design was to be the powerful technique of 'white people's design', writing, rather than the technique of 'human design'. The girl's initiation ritual, as I discussed in earlier chapters, united all the Piro people scattered along the Urubamba into one place to celebrate the successful seclusion of a pubescent girl, and through the ritual, to

---

[16] Piro people would not have been motivated by any desire to exclude Campa people, but by a desire to assert Piro centrality. Many Campa people remained living in SIL-affiliated Piro communities, and many Campa children first learned to read and write in Piro (see Gow 1991: 231).

project that transformation into the future. The vacuum left by the abandonment of this ritual in the messianic period of Adventism was then filled by the founding of schools. Indeed my informants, recalling this period, insisted that all Piro people lived with the *gringas* in Huau. While probably never literally true, the image of united residence in a single village is close to the uniting of 'all the Piro people from along the river', which is central to the imagery of the girl's initiation ritual.

Life in SIL-dominated communities also had its own forms of ritual, which were intimately linked to the issue of writing. These were religious services (Piro, *gapatjeru*; Ucayali Spanish, *culto*). These rituals were characterized by prayers, readings from the Bible, and song. The songs were a new musical genre invented by the SIL missionaries, *Goyakalu shikale*, 'God's songs', hymns. These were written by the SIL, and are on the whole adaptations of North American hymns, with Piro words fitted to the original melodies. When I heard them sung in Bufeo Pozo in 1988, considerable effort was made to sing them from the hymn book, rather than from memory, and it seemed that this reading was crucial to their performance. Julia Laureano, from Santa Clara, bemoaned the fact that she had lost her hymn book, even though she seemed to remember the words of these hymns well enough.[17] The collective singing of these songs was, I was told, a key feature of being *evangelista*, along with reading the Bible and praying.

My analysis in Chapters 5 and 6 of such musical genres as 'drug songs' and 'women's songs', suggests an interesting possibility for these *Goyakalu shikale*, 'God's songs'. If, as I argued there, all Piro sung discourse is characterized by a shifted subject-position, such that the singer never sings from his or her own subject-position, the same is likely to be true of hymns. It seems entirely probable that Piro people considered, and consider, themselves to be *evangelistas* only when they are actively singing *Goyakalu shikale*. That is, it is in the very act of singing these *Goyakalu shikale* that Piro people came to occupy the subject-positions referred to within them. The model here would be shamans' songs, the 'drug songs', where the singer seeks identification with a specific other subject-position. Take the following example, that of *Kigler-Pagognepa Shikale*, sung for me by Julia Laureano:

> *Kigler-pagognepa,*
> *Kigler-pagognepa,*
> *Gerotu nopji netanu wane,*
> *Gita chinanu rugletkatka.*
> *Kigler-pagognepa,*

---

[17] When Julia Laureano sang SIL hymns in Piro, I was always amazed by her exact imitation of an American Midwest vocal style reminiscent of Country and Western music and quite unlike her singing in Piro, Campa, or Andean styles. This was presumably an exact imitation of SIL missionary women's voices. It was as if this style, the way the SIL woman missionaries themselves sang, was the correct one for the genre of 'God's songs'.

Kigler-pagognepa,
Ruknokatkana wa Satanasyo
Kigler-pagognepa.

In the good world to come,
In the good world to come,
I will see my new house
I will say everything has been made good.
In the good world to come,
In the good world to come,
Satan will have been overcome,
In the good world to come.

In singing this song, I suggest, the singers come to be the people for whom the proposition it contains is true. Rather than merely celebrating the faith of an *evangelista*, this is the moment of being an *evangelista*. Just as the singer of 'drug songs' seeks an identification with a powerful being, so too the singers of 'God's songs' seek such an identification. Certainly, singing was mentioned far more often to me than prayer in accounts of *evangelismo*. As Don Mauricio remembered Huau, 'it was beautiful when the *gringas* held their religious services there, and the people sang.'

The 'New Life' lived out

The activities of the SIL missionaries would have had, from the perspective of Piro people, a certain ambiguity. If my analysis of Adventism is correct, the nature of the SIL project must have struck Piro people as slightly odd: why establish the whole extended project of schools and so on simply to teach knowledge which would render social life unnecessary? Piro people would have been faced with a choice between the educational dimension of the SIL project, and its specifically religious aspect, as two radically opposed solutions to the problem of how to 'live well'.

For the SIL missionaries themselves, these two projects were the same: schooling gave access to reading skills, which in turn gave access to the Bible, which in turn would lead Piro people to be Christians. And there is good evidence that the SIL missionaries were bemused by the reactions of Piro people to their work over the years. Stoll has pithily summarized SIL accounts of their impact on Piro people, basing himself on a critical reading of mainly SIL-friendly documentary sources. He writes:

Matteson found the Piro sunk in such an appalling moral condition that she could not include their folk tales in her primers for Piro children. Yet within a few years Piro headmen were asking her to reform their *patron*-dominated villages in a burst of enthusiasm for the Protestant Ethic. A government official was amazed by the sudden change. He needed food supplies for the penal colony at Sepa, but the Piro never had anything to sell because they were usually drunk. Soon he was shocked to see sobriety, new houses and gardens. The Piro had surplus food to sell and wanted to produce more. They were going to school and reading the Bible.

In only eight years Matteson finished the New Testament and 'witnessed the complete transformation' of the tribe. After 15 years, in 1962, the *Peruvian Times* reported that 'the Linguists expect to be able to withdraw soon, leaving observers to keep the tribe on the right lines for a few years.' In the 20th year of the Piro work, Matteson reported that, despite many weaknesses which seemed overwhelming, the Piro church was prospering and God's Word prevailing against fear of evil spirits. And as the Piro work approached its 30th year, Matteson's successors faced the same problems she had: except perhaps when a missionary was in the village, congregations and Christian leaders carried on as they had prior to salvation. (1982: 125–6)

Stoll captures well this strange mixture of radical transformation and of futility, but he is wrong to say that Piro people 'carried on as they had prior to salvation'. This may be true with regard to certain aspects of religious life, but it was certainly not true with regard to ongoing social life. Piro people had radically transformed the basis of community organization over this period.

By the 1980s, at least in the communities I knew best, there was relatively little interest in the specifically religious dimension of SIL activities. Artemio's village of Santa Clara was, of course, by then a formally Catholic community, but even in the nominally Protestant communities of Huau, Nueva Italia or Pucani, there was some collective religious activity, but not very much.[18] There were sporadic revivals of enthusiasm, such that people would occasionally seek to live, temporarily, without drinking, and two brothers-in-law from Nueva Italia suddenly set off for the Swiss Mission base at Cashibococha to learn, it was said, 'to be preachers'. In general, however, there was little interest in following what Sebastián had called the 'New Life'. Indeed, many Piro people were openly defiant of Evangelical missionaries. In 1988, I was attending a festival in the new Campa community of Centro Pucani, when the Swiss Mission preacher turned up and ordered the people to throw away their manioc beer. Many did so, but Celia Mosombite, the Piro schoolteacher, refused, and led a substantial portion of the population in a beer-drinking festival that competed with the missionary's service throughout the afternoon. As she said, 'What right have the *gringos* to tell us what to do?'

What Piro people did not give up as time passed, however, was the centrality of schools and of school education in their social lives. It seems that they chose subsequently to de-emphasize the specifically religious aspects of the SIL work, while concentrating on its educational aspects. The reason for this undoubtedly lies in the manner in which school education is a transformation of the older systems of *yonchi* and *kigimawlo*: both provide a means by which social life can be projected into the future. This was not true of the period of messianic enthusiasm for Adventism, or for Sebastián's 'New Life': those were

---

[18] I saw more such activity in the large up-river communities of Miaría and Bufeo Pozo in 1988.

short-term solutions to periods of extreme crisis in 'living well'. Within Sebastián's own narrative of 1968, discussed above, we see a shift from the 'New Life' to the 'present-day lives of Piro people', as a solution was found to the problem of 'living well'. By the 1980s, my informants, such as Artemio, had reformulated the nature of those transformations, eliding the 'New Life' and its religious dimensions, and stressing the importance of schools and the consequent 'liberation from slavery'.

Of major significance in the decline and forgetting of the religious dimension to the transformations of the 1940s and 1950s must have been the return to the use of fermented manioc beer. Abandoned in the face of an extreme crisis, and with the sanction of Adventist missionaries, fermented manioc beer returned to the scene, to collectivize and generalize the new knowledge being acquired. As I discussed in Chapter 6, by the 1980s, Piro people had developed new forms of ritual life, the *fiestas de la Comunidad Nativa*, which focused on the collective appropriation of acquired knowledge for the generation of communal viability. As in the case of the *fiesta* in Centro Pucani, described above, many Piro people were now openly hostile to missionaries' attempts to prevent the consumption of fermented manioc beer.

Some confirmation of this analysis can be drawn from Sebastián's term for the 'New Life', *genshinikanrewlu*. The term, translated as 'conversion, new life', clearly implies a profound change in ways of thinking, but not necessarily of the highly interiorized kind valued by the SIL missionaries themselves (see Vilaça 1996; 1997), on missionary work among the Wari' people, Rondonia, Western Brazil). As I have discussed, the root word, *nshinikanchi*, 'mind, thinking, love, memory, respect', is profoundly relational, and depends on other people towards whom it is manifested. As such, *genshinikanrewlu*, 'new mind, new thinking, new love, etc.' would require a collective transformation in ways of thinking. It would, therefore, have been extremely vulnerable to any mass defections from it. This point may also explain the forgetting of the period of messianic enthusiasm in the 1980s. *Genshinikanrewlu*, 'The New Life' was important while it lasted, as a 'new way of thinking, living with other people', but it became unmemorable as Piro people achieved what they would later term, 'the liberation from slavery': villages centred on schools, rather than on the bosses.

Remaining on the Earth

The period of messianic expectation, and its subsequent transformation, can be further interpreted through the Piro mythic narrative, 'The Ancient People Who Tried to Enter the Sky', told to me by Artemio in the context of a longer conversation about Evangelical Christianity. This 'ancient people's story' deals with an attempt by a group of ancient Piro people to enter the sky and become divinities. It was certainly being told in the late 1940s and 1950s, in substantially the same form as Artemio told it to me, for Matteson recorded a version from Sebastián (1965: 156–9), and Ricardo Alvarez published a version in his collection (1960: 28–31). I here focus on an analysis of Artemio's version, since the context of the specific conversation during which it was told reveals much about its interest for Piro people.

In June 1982, Artemio was discussing with me the problem of what to do about Ulises Díaz. This man, I was told, was the last Piro Adventist living on the Urubamba, and he was attempting to move into Santa Clara at the time. Díaz was apparently unpopular all along the Urubamba,[19] and was trying to find somewhere to live. Artemio agreed that he and his children could live in the territory of Santa Clara, but encouraged them to move into the little Campa community hidden up the Mapchirga river within Santa Clara's territory. Nobody wanted him in the village itself. Part of Díaz's unpopularity stemmed from his refusal to drink manioc beer or cane alcohol, which, in a healthy adult, was tantamount to a refusal of social life. Artemio commented, 'It is easier for old men like Díaz to not drink. They aren't interested in dancing and drinking and women anymore, so they can follow the precepts. For young men who like having fun, it's much harder.' He went on to tell me that he liked Evangelical Christianity, but that it was impossible to follow it in a community like Santa Clara:

To be an *evangelista*, you have to live in a village of Piro *evangelista* people. When I lived in Quilometro 15, I liked the way of life, having services every day, praising the Lord, and everyone preaching. But here it is impossible, there are too many distractions. The people in Nueva Italia say that it is an *evangelista* village, but it isn't, because they're always drunk. The chainsaw operator there is a very mistaken man. He wants to be a preacher, but he also likes drinking. Cobos is better, he doesn't dance or get drunk, but he has other faults.

We should remember here that it was Cobos's allegations of backsliding, perhaps rooted in favouritism, which put an end to Artemio's career as a teacher. Artemio went on to criticize the local priest and Catholicism generally for setting up divisions for, 'after all, it's all about God and Jesus, isn't it?' Then, even-handedly, he criticized the Nueva Italia people for refusing to come to mass in Santa Clara.

I then asked Artemio if the ancient time Piro people had had an idea of God, and he said, 'Yes. My mother told me that long ago when the old people took *ayahuasca*, they said it was their God who sent them visions. Those who took a lot of *ayahuasca* knew a lot about God, they were good and went to heaven. Those who knew nothing did not.' He then told me the following myth:

---

[19] Presumably he must also have had problems with the people of the still nominally Adventist communities of Unini and Ramon Castillo on the Alto Ucayali river, just below Atalaya. See Román (1986) for an account of Díaz's life from his own point of view.

There was once a group of Piro people who took a lot of *ayahuasca* and so knew a lot, so that they could go to heaven. They were led by a great drinker of *ayahuasca*, a doctor of *ayahuasca* you might say,[20] who had drunk a lot and knew how to cure the sick. They were taking *ayahuasca* and preparing to go to heaven. God sent down a rope, a chain on which to ascend. It was like a plate on the rope.[21] The chain came down, and the people got on to the plate. They began to ascend.

Along with the good people, an adulterous woman got on board too. When they got halfway up, half of the chain broke. The good people were taken up into the sky, but the bad people fell a long way off, into a lake. They are still there, it is said, and the lake in which they live is very wild, nobody can get near it. But now nobody knows where this lake is.

He continued:

Long ago, my Piro kinspeople drank *ayahuasca* all the time, day and night. That was their work. They were great drinkers of *ayahuasca*, and so went to live in the sky. Now there is nobody who knows how to do this, nobody knows how to travel into the sky. The old-time people did not worship the moon or the sun or the stars, but instead they worshipped God whom they saw in their visions.[22]

He went on to ask me if I thought there was life after death, and then expressed his desire to take the powerful hallucinogen *toé*, because, 'My father told me that when you take *toé*, you see the dead people, all of your dead relatives. For this reason, I now want to take *toé*.'

Reviewing this conversation, three salient points emerge. Firstly, for Artemio, as for other Piro people, Evangelical Christianity had to be a collective endeavour: as he said, 'To be an *evangelista*, you have to live in a village of Piro *evangelista* people.' Secondly, living as an *evangelista* is a life opposed to sexuality and to collective rituals based on fermented manioc beer: as he said, 'For young men who like having fun, it's much harder.' Thirdly, Artemio seems to have had little problem connecting these aspects of life as an *evangelista* to the Piro mythic narrative, 'The Ancient People who tried to enter the Sky', and to the general problem of shamanry in the Piro lived world.

Artemio, like most Piro people I talked to, made little distinction between the Adventism of Díaz and the Evangelical Protestantism he himself had tried to follow. Both were treated as variants of what I here term 'messianic Christianity'.[23] If a major contrast is drawn, it is that between Catholics and Protes-

---

[20] The Spanish term he used was *doctor*, a term used locally for those white people with great specialist knowledge. To my knowledge, the only *doctor* in this sense on the Bajo Urubamba area at this time was P. Ricardo Alvarez, who has a doctorate in anthropology from the Sorbonne.

[21] Here he pointed to a an old pan lid, strung on a piece of fibre, being used to keep rats away from maize cobs in the house.

[22] The reference to the worship of celestial bodies was presumably to contrast the ancient Piro people to the Incas, whose worship of the sun, moon, and stars forms part of general Peruvian popular knowledge, and of the school curriculum.

[23] I accept that the term 'messianic Christianity' is tautologous. I use it here only in deference to the wide diffusion of the term 'messianism' in anthropological literature.

tants. Even here, however, the differences are mainly seen to depend on minor variations in practice, and as Artemio pointed out, the major cause of dissension was laid at the door of the priests and Protestant preachers, not at differences in the personal beliefs of the followers. 'Messianic Christianity', whether Catholic or Protestant, Evangelical or Adventist, was primarily a collective project for Artemio, and minor differences led people to split up into small, mutually hostile villages. This hostility, however, need not be a negative phenomenon, from the Piro point of view: as I discussed in Chapter 6, such a multiplicity of villages is the pre-condition of Piro ritual life and the ongoing creation of affinity and kin ties.

As a collective project, 'messianic Christianity' meant that its adherents must follow it collectively, in a community of 'messianic Christians'. As such, 'messianic Christianity' is a solution to the problem of *gwashata*, 'living well'. But unlike everyday 'living well', 'messianic Christianity' implies an escape from mortality as the key feature of the Piro lived world. This aligns it with the collective shaman-becoming of the people in the mythic narrative, 'The Ancient People who tried to enter the Sky', who continually and collectively drink *ayahuasca* to gain sky-entry and consequent immortality.

'Messianic Christianity', like the actions of the ancient people in the myth, implied an end to Piro social life as the production of kinship relations and their ongoing transformation through ritual performance. Since they were to enter the sky and achieve Divinity, there was no more need for the girl's initiation ritual, for marriages, for manioc beer, etc. However, if the translation to the sky and consequent divinization failed, both 'messianic Christianity' and the collective drinking of *ayahuasca* would become unworkable, as time forced people to return to the modes of collective transformation implied in the consumption of fermented manioc beer and all that it entails.

This point is poignantly raised in 'The Ancient People who tried to enter the Sky'. In all the versions I know of, the 'bad people' fall into the lake because the chain or rope holding the plate breaks. Why did the chain or rope break? This is because those who should not have climbed on to the 'plate' did so. The versions vary as to the specific nature of the factor prohibiting them from doing so: an adulterous woman in Artemio's version; a menstruating woman in Alvarez's informant's version; and a menstruating woman, men who had recently had sexual intercourse, and an unmarried girl who had had sexual relationships in Sebastián's. It was, therefore, the sex lives of these people which caused them to crash out of the sky into the lake, where they are to this day. Menstruating women and people who have recently had sex should not drink *ayahuasca*, because their smell offends the powerful beings, who either refuse to come to them or send only terrifying visions.

So why did they get on to the 'plate'? Obviously, because they did not want to be left behind on earth without their kinspeople. Humanity, for Piro people, is a collective project. In Sebastián's version, it is stated:

the shaman, who had been to heaven, should have said, 'Those menstruating should wait a while before they go to heaven. Also those who have had sexual intercourse must wait, perhaps a month, until they have ceased to be guilty. Then they will be taken up,' should have been said by the shaman. But he did not say it. (Matteson 1965: 156–7)

This precaution would, of course, conflict radically with the very basis of 'living well', the co-residence of kinspeople. The 'guilty ones' had to get on to the plate with their kinspeople, and hence crash back to earth into a lake. Otherwise, the collective project of divinization would have resulted in the very thing it was seeking to prevent: the collapse of co-residence in one by one mortality. As I noted in Chapter 5, this is not a problem for individual shamans, for their project originates in an intense valorization of kin ties with dead children. A collective project of shaman-becoming, of divinization, cannot so side-step this issue, for it attacks the very *raison d'être* of that project.

The mythic narrative, 'The Ancient People who tried to enter the Sky', works both with and against the dynamics of 'messianic Christianity'. Temporally, it locates the origin of a specific set of entities, the people of the fierce lake, in a messianic moment which went wrong. All versions assert the continued existence of these people, and those of Sebastián and of Alvarez's informant continue with descriptions of recent personal experiences with the people who fell into the lake. These people are called *Giyakleshimane*, 'Miraculous Fish People' in the versions collected by Alvarez, and *Popragkalune*, 'Mist People', by Sebastián. They constitute a parallel humanity, neither solicitous of nor hostile to Piro people. The people of the wild lake are, from a Piro point of view, profoundly anti-historical. Firstly, as I discussed elsewhere, the upland lakes of the kind in which they dwell are the antithesis of riverine flow, and hence of the temporal dynamics which the river both effects and symbolizes (Gow 1991). Secondly, contacts between Piro people and these people of the fierce lake are slight and enigmatic. They stand in marked contrast to the kinds of people that Piro people know about and contact through the flow of the Urubamba.

These features of the mythic narrative, 'The Ancient People who tried to enter the Sky' explain why Artemio told it to me in the context of that conversation. Here, a failed messianic movement led to the creation of an 'anti-historical' alternative humanity, due to the sexuality of those people. As Artemio told me, only old men, those who have lost interest in sex, can easily follow the precepts of Adventism and Evangelism. For the rest of Piro people, sexuality, and the drinking of fermented manioc beer and the festivals that it entails, are necessary forms of ongoing social life. Hence the problem with which the conversation began, Ulises Díaz. This old Piro man, still clinging to a messianic expectation almost everyone else had long since abandoned, had nowhere to live. Because he refused to drink, he effectively refused to 'live well'. That is why nobody wanted him living in Santa Clara.

Artemio's narration of 'The Ancient People who tried to enter the Sky' also,

I think, goes some way to explaining why Piro people shifted allegiance from the Adventists to the SIL, and then away from the religious aspect of the SIL message. The Adventist period was characterized by a messianic expectation of imminent potential entry to the sky and consequent divinization. This would have connected up with the mythic narrative, 'The Ancient People who tried to enter the Sky', and held out the stark alternative of celestial divinization or permanent consignment to an anti-historical lake. The shift to the SIL would have extended this logic, but would also have begun a shift towards another vision of the relationship. The SIL missionaries' stress on the extended project of school foundation and on educating younger generations would have also engaged the logic of the mythic narrative, 'Tsla swallowed by a Giant Catfish', which asserts the ongoing potential of Piro social life. Through this mythic narrative, the specifically messianic features of relations to the Adventists and the SIL missionaries are neutralized and replaced by their insertion into Piro people's 'history', the successive arrival of new kinds of white people through whom Piro people find the means to 'live well'. This was, indeed, the meaning that SIL action had for most Piro people in the 1980s.

Perhaps the most interesting feature of the conversation in which Artemio told me 'The Ancient People who tried to enter The Sky' was the ease with which he was able to move from discussion of the dilemmas caused by the presence of an old Adventist to the difficulties of living as an Evangelical Christian, and then to his mother's stories of the 'ancient people', the 'ancient people's story' itself, and speculations on shamanry and the fate of the dead. Artemio was a man with a long-standing interest in Evangelical Christianity, and a prolonged and intense exposure to the teachings of missionaries. He cannot have been unaware of the status those missionaries accorded to Piro mythic narratives and to shamanry. Why then should he be able to move so easily between these issues? This was possible, I believe, because of a historical process of neutralization of the specifically messianic aspect of the Adventist and SIL messages by Piro people, of which Artemio's mythic narrative was both evidence and an ongoing part.

Evidence for this comes from a comparison of the three versions known to me of the mythic narrative, 'The Ancient People who tried to enter The Sky'. We can reasonably assume that Ricardo Alvarez's informant's version was told by someone with little contact with the SIL, for this person was presumably a resident of Sepahua. This person's version begins with an elaborate account of the genesis of the shaman's desire for collective sky-entry, in the death of the shaman's father, the subsequent contacts between living and dead, and the shaman's training for the translation to the sky. The 'god' who sends down the plate is the dead shaman himself. Sebastián's version, set in the village of Takila, simply states that these people constantly drank *ayahuasca*, 'in order to conjure a god' (Matteson 1965: 156–7). It is unclear from the context if Sebastián here meant one of the *goyakalune* or *Goyakalu*, and this lack of precision may well have been intentional. With Artemio's version, it is clear that the shaman is calling on *Dios*, *Goyakalu*, the Christian God. Across the three versions we see a progressive assimilation of this mythic narrative to a vision of messianic Christianity. Further evidence of this is that only Artemio's version specifies the 'sin' which leads the rope to break as a specifically Christian one, adultery, rather than the Piro vision of 'sin' as sexuality, and all the pleasures of life, in general.

The variations between these versions of this mythic narrative reveal, I think, a profound historical transformation in Piro people's cosmology. The Adventist/SIL period caused a major and definitive transformation in the conceptualization of the sky, and of the celestial deities. The divinities of an earlier cosmology, the multiple celestial *goyakalune*, had apparently disappeared or been demonized, to be replaced with the singular celestial *Goyakalu*, 'God'. As I noted above, this singular divinity was present in that earlier cosmology, as the celestial divinity *patutachri*, but it seems to be true that Piro people's responses to Adventist and SIL action effected the expansion of this one Divinity over the whole domain of celestial beings to become the unique Christian 'God'.

On the face of it, one might think that this was a pure effect of Adventist and SIL preaching, and its acceptance by Piro people. This would, indeed, explain the imprecision of Sebastián's version, given that he was talking to Matteson. However, I think it was also effected by another transformation, in shamanry. As I discussed in Chapter 5, the older Piro shamanry, focused on contact with the celestial divinities, was being replaced by down-river *ayahuasquero* shamanry, focused on the powerful beings of the forest and river. This latter shamanry was not incompatible with Christianity as understood by Piro people, for it had evolved in intimate association with that religion.

What was the relationship between the Adventist and SIL projects and Piro shamanry? Both Adventist and SIL missionaries were undoubtedly hostile to shamanry. As Artemio told me on the evening of 15 January 1981, 'In the Bible we are told that sorcery is wrong, and that sorcerers are sinners and will not get to Heaven.' In the same vein, Sebastián noted, of the 'present day lives of Piro people':

The spiritual life of the Piro people has also changed. Before, the shamans were feared and to children it was said, 'Watch out! Don't talk or laugh. Don't make fun of the shaman or he will ensorcell you, and you will die!' But now it isn't the shaman, but God who is feared and loved. Now only a few people fear shamans.

Neither are the demons feared, because we know God looks after us. He is great and made everything that exists. (Sebastián, Zumaeta, and Nies 1974: 180–1 and 184)

Also present in Sebastián's account is the reference to the learning about health care, which would replace the key role of shamans in curing illness. In this sense, 'messianic Christianity', in its Adventist and Evangelical forms, rendered shamanry obsolete by replacing it with a more powerful form of shamanry, collective divinization, where everyone has direct access to the technique of 'sky entry'.

This new 'shamanry' did not, however, deal well with the immediate problems that the older shamanry treated, the specific afflictions that people experience as a result of working in the forest and the river, and engaging in ongoing social life, with all of its jealousies and envies, and consequent sorcery. Piro people began to make a distinction between diseases, as Artemio told me:

I say this: there are illnesses sent by God to punish us for our sins, things like whooping cough, measles, tuberculosis. But there are other illnesses which cannot be cured by doctors or the medicines you buy—these are illnesses sent by demons. Some people are bad, and cause harm, and for these illnesses the hallucinogens are good. Such sick people will not be cured in a hospital, they need shamans.

These shamans were now, however, working in the new shamanic idiom, down-river *ayahuasquero* shamanry. This idiom deals exclusively with the harm that comes from the immediate lived world of Piro people, the river and the forest, and from each other.

Adventist and SIL missionary action among Piro people had, therefore, an ironic effect, for it facilitated their willingness to accept the down-river shamanry of the *moza gente*, 'the mixed blood people' of the Bajo Ucayali and Amazon areas. By drawing the celestial pole of an earlier shamanic cosmology into the domain of their own expertise, these missionaries did the groundwork for those later shamans to exploit. Once the missionaries had fully and definitively brought to Piro people knowledge of God and of the Word of God, they clarified the differences between a project of collective divinization through sky-entry and the everyday practices of shamans, in curing the ills of that everyday world.

Staying the Same

The dramatic transformations in the Piro lived world which occurred in the middle decades of the twentieth century, and which affected so many of the means by which Piro people projected their social world into the future, were undoubtedly due to the activities of Adventist, SIL, and Dominican missionaries, and owe much to these missionaries' ideological presumptions and to the actions that these entailed. However, these dramatic transformations owed even more to the intrinsically transformational nature of the Piro lived world. The SIL project which led to Sebastián's *genshinikanrewlu*, the 'New Life', the new way of thinking, was only possible because it made sense to Piro people as the solution to a specific crisis, 'How can we live well now?' Because that crisis was founded on Piro people's relations to white people, it necessarily had to take the form of a relationship with new white people, and to be formed in terms of the project of those new white people. From the point of view of Piro people, however, the project of those white people was to solve a Piro problem, and so necessarily had to be enacted in Piro people's own terms.

The problem here has been investigated by Viveiros de Castro in his discussion of the same historical reaction of the ancient Tupinambá of the Brazilian coast to early European missionaries (1993a). Noting the frustration of the missionaries at the Tupinambá's mix of enthusiasm and indifference in reaction to their message, Viveiros de Castro raises the analytical problems presented to anthropology of cultures marked by a profound 'desire to be the other, but on their own terms'. What can we make of Piro people's desire to have all the things of 'white people', in the familiar story of acculturation or culture-loss, but to desire them for specifically Piro reasons?

Viveiros de Castro, following the Jesuits themselves, has termed this problem the 'inconstancy of the savage soul'. There is plenty of evidence of such 'inconstancy' in Piro people's relationship to the specifically religious message of the SIL, as evidenced in the passages from Stoll quoted above, and in later hostility to the activities of the Swiss Mission. Stoll's conclusion echoes an earlier assessment of Piro people's interest in Christian missionaries. Commenting on the failure of P. Alemany's mission to Piro people in the early 1880s, in the light of the general failure of a long history of Franciscan missionary activity, Ortiz (1974: 427) reiterates an anonymous Franciscan writer's conclusion: 'The Piro in Cuzco, in Miariya, in Santa Rosa de Lima, in Buepoano and in the many other places he frequents is always the same, that is, self-interested, miscreant, shrewd and hypocritical.' The later problems of the SIL missionaries can thus be set within a much longer history of Piro people's 'inconstancy' in the face of Christian evangelization.

I think that both the anonymous Franciscan writer and Stoll were mistaken. Piro people were not 'the same' throughout the whole period of Franciscan missionary activity, for as we have seen, they had assimilated the Christian God into their shamanic cosmology. Nor did Piro people in the 1980s 'carry on as they had before salvation', for they had indeed, as they said, 'liberated themselves from slavery', and Sebastián, when he described the lives of Piro people in 1968, noted genuine and impressive transformations. When Sangama predicted the arrival of a teacher in an aeroplane, he was making a distinctly Piro prediction, and one which only really made sense within the Piro lived world. When the SIL missionaries appeared in apparent fulfilment of that prophecy, it is not too surprising that Piro people should react with both enthusiasm and indifference to what those missionaries themselves thought that they were up to.

It is perhaps possible to specify the precise content of Piro people's inconstancy in the face of missionary action in the twentieth century. Piro mythic narratives provide not one, but two ways of thinking about the relations between the immediate lived world and the sky. The first is present in the narrative, 'The Ancient People who tried to enter The Sky', and connects closely with the messianic moment of collective divinization. It asserts a radical end of the immediate lived world, and direct translation into the sky. The second is present in the narrative, 'Tsla swallowed by a Giant Catfish', and connects up with the temporal extension of the Piro lived world through constant transformations in relationships with new kinds of 'white people'. Through this second mythic narrative, Tsla's abandonment of the Piro lived world, marked as the 'land of death', is followed by the arrival of a succession of different kinds of *kajine*, 'white people'. These different kinds of 'white people' act for succeeding generations of Piro people as the Muchkajine, the 'Long Ago White People', acted for Tsla: they act as privileged companions. They make social life possible.

This perspective from Tsla mythology helps to explain a significant silence. Nowhere have I found any suggestion that the figure of Tsla was explicitly identified by Piro people with the Christian God of the missionaries. This is all the more surprising if we follow through the argument presented in the previous chapter, which suggested that earlier generations of Piro people located Tsla's destination in the sky. At most, we find a certain uneasiness with the figure of Tsla. Sebastián narrates no mythic narratives about Tsla in his 'history of the Piro people', *Gwacha Ginkakle*. The absence of any references to Tsla mythic narratives is remarkable here, for as I have argued, 'Tsla swallowed by a Giant Catfish' is the Piro 'myth of history'. Perhaps this silence reflects a SIL queasiness about the figure of Tsla, although there is very little evidence for this. At best, the *Diccionario Piro* rather bizarrely translates Tsla as 'Manco Capac' (Nies 1986: 305). While I can imagine a Piro person perhaps identifying this famous Inca with Tsla, I have never heard anyone do so, and it is hardly what the word 'Tsla' means to Piro people.[24]

I think that this silence about Tsla is real, and reflects something profound about Piro people's relationships with kinds of white people. The position of *kajine*, 'white people', as the successors to Tsla's Muchkajine, and the ignorance that Piro people express about the destination of Tsla, is a silent assertion of a much more profound point. Piro cosmology is not a fixed corpus of knowledge, but rather simply that which Piro people happen to know, and this

---

[24] Further weak evidence that Piro people may have identified Tsla and the Christian God is the following verb definition, from the *Diccionario Piro*,

royakawata (intr.) 1) to believe oneself to be a god. *Royakawata wa Tsla chinkaluru tsrunnini ginkak-leya*. In the myths of the ancient people Tsla believed himself to be a god. 2) to last a long time, to last for ever. (Nies 1986: 218)

Since there is nothing in the formation of the verb *royakawata* that hints at self-reference or epistemological status, I suspect that the verb actually means 'to last a long time, to last forever, to be divine'. I further suspect that this dictionary definition reflects a queasiness, on the part of either the compiler or of a converted informant, about the identification of Tsla with the Christian God, and an emphatic attempt to keep them apart.

knowledge is marked by an originary imbalance, due to Tsla's departure from the Piro lived world. As such, 'white people' and their forms of cosmological knowledge are necessary parts of fuller understandings of the cosmos. But the mythic narratives about Tsla and the Muchkajine, in the processes of doubling which prefigure the constant appearance of new kinds of 'white people', as discussed in the previous chapter, also imply that the cosmologies of different kinds of white people are themselves only parts of a potential totality. That totality does not lie with the Muchkajine or their successors in the different kinds of 'white people', but with the remote and silent figure of Tsla, that self-originated 'miraculous being'.

Tsla, as we saw in Chapter 4, has a significant feature: he is a miraculous speaker, who talked to his mother from within the womb. In this sense, he is opposed to humanity, i.e. Piro people, who must find their own knowledge through personal experiences and in carefully evaluating the speech of others. This helps to explain the peculiarly speculative cast of Piro people's knowledge of the cosmos, and the relentless manner in which they evaluate and re-evaluate what they are told by others and their own former states of knowledge. It is this feature that is the source of their 'inconstancy'. We have seen this speculative tone here at work in Dionisia García's story of the aeroplane, in Sebastián's accounts of God, and Artemio's discussions of religion. We found it also in the conversation of the evening of 15 January 1982, and in the discussion of the other versions of the 'ancient people's story' about the white-lipped peccaries. These form the subject of the next chapter.

9

The *Gringos* Rethought

Over the previous two chapters, I have traced out some of the connections between the transformations of transformations discussed in Part II and certain important historical events and processes in Piro people's lives over the hundred years from the 1880s. The specific modes in which Piro people envisioned and engaged with the *gringos*, the SIL missionaries, suggest strongly that the transformations of transformations were not simply affected by changing historical circumstances, but were produced by a system in a state of transformation. This system was connecting its internal transformations to certain types of historical events and processes, causing it to transform in certain directions: the system had unstable features which readily led Piro people to interpret certain practices of different kinds of white people as desirable, while ignoring or challenging others that conflicted with the more stable features of the system. The system endogenously generates such potential transformations, and projects them out into the world.

In this final chapter, I return at last to Artemio's story, 'A Man who went under the Earth', and the specific context of its telling. In Chapters 7 and 8, I was analysing events and processes that necessarily lay beyond my own lived experience of Piro people's lives, and I had to rely heavily on documentary evidence. My account of how mythic narratives operate within the system in a state of transformation was therefore rather diffuse, since the documentary archive gives us little access to how exactly Piro people were, in the past, making connections between specific versions of specific myths and the changes they were experiencing and effecting in the world. Here, through an analysis of the context of the telling of Artemio's story, 'A Man who went under the Earth', I seek to specify exactly how such connections are made, and therefore to show how the specific states of transformation in the system are played out. Further, following the account in Chapter 2 of the changes in the known versions of the myth of the white-lipped peccaries, I show how such transformations operate within the Piro lived world to obliterate time, and hence to project that lived world onwards into the future.

The Transformations of the Gringos

By the 1980s, the SIL missionaries had become a muted presence in the lives of Piro people. Their evangelical work was by then in the hands of the Swiss Mission, who maintained a much lower profile in the nominally Protestant communities than the SIL had done. Their work as teachers was taken over by

Piro teachers themselves in the affiliated communities, or by other local people in some cases (see Gow 1991: 230–1). The SIL missionaries' most significant role for Piro people in the 1980s lay in the courses they ran in their base in Yarinacocha for bilingual teachers, especially during the long rainy season school holidays. These courses resulted in a constant coming and going of teachers to the remote city of Pucallpa, often with several relatives in tow, in search of medical treatment or adventure. The SIL missionaries themselves, however, seldom appeared on the Bajo Urubamba.

The absence of SIL missionaries from the Bajo Urubamba reflected certain features of SIL policy, founded on the relationship of this organization to the Peruvian state. In 1971, faced with increased hostility from the revolutionary military government of Velasco, the SIL had signed a new contract, which demanded that their North American functionaries progressively withdraw from their bilingual education work, and be replaced by Peruvian nationals, with a view to total withdrawal in 1976 (Stoll 1982: 144–6). This withdrawal did not happen, but the new contract must undoubtedly have led them to reduce their local involvement with projects like that with Piro people: after three decades, they could not plausibly argue that they were still working on the language. Secondly, given their public claim that they were not a missionary organization (Stoll 1982: 110–12), the SIL increasingly shifted responsibility for religious affairs in the Bajo Urubamba area to the Swiss Mission. This organization concentrated its missionary efforts in the large Piro villages of Miaría, Puija, and Bufeo Pozo, and seldom came to the Santa Clara area.

How did Piro people experience this withdrawal of the SIL missionaries from the local world? As I discussed in the preceding chapter, the SIL missionaries had noted that Piro people were more enthusiastic about their religious message when they themselves were present (Stoll 1982: 125–6). As might be expected, it was the active co-residence of the *gringas* that mattered to Piro people, the potential of 'living well'. Instead of engaging in this project of 'living well', however, after many years they simply left, as people told me, 'to go to their own country perhaps, who knows where they went?' I was often asked if I knew them, and if I knew of their whereabouts. People seemed disappointed when I told them that I knew the answer to neither question.

This came out in an account of the *gringas* by Luisa Campos, Artemio's eldest sister. She told me:

It was good when the *gringas* lived here. They were good people, they were generous and happy all the time. We called them by Piro names because we liked them. Miss Esther we called *Giwno*, and Miss Joyce was *Chowretete*. We liked them because they were good people.

But they wouldn't drink manioc beer. And they didn't marry. They never had husbands that we ever saw. How might it have been? Perhaps they never knew what a man's fishhook is like!

A man's fishhook is, of course, his penis. For a Piro woman, this metaphor links sexual pleasure to the value of a man as provider of game, to 'eating real food'. Along with manioc-beer drunkenness, these are the things of the good life, of 'living well'. Living so long among Piro people, well-liked by them, learning to speak their language, and having helped them to a new way of 'living well', it seems that the SIL missionaries bemused them by then refusing to take part in the 'good life' they had helped to create.

In the specific case of Santa Clara, the *gringas* were replaced by the Catholic lay missionaries, and the Dominican priest of the penal colony at Sepa. The influence of this mission in the local area was undoubtedly important in transforming the attitudes of local Piro people to fermented manioc beer and to festivals. While critical of excessive drinking, the Catholic missionaries actively promoted the inter-village festivals. They were also always available for basic medical care and for advice, a situation which contrasted strongly with the now-remote SIL missionaries. Up-river, the mission of Sepahua played an even more important role in the local inter-village system.

More important than these religious aspects of the issue, Piro people's lives in the 1980s were marked by even more dramatic transformations, for they now had direct and overt contacts with powerful new outsiders, Peruvian state officials. Following the coup of 1968, the new left-wing military dictatorship under Velasco began to intervene much more directly in Piro people's lives than previous governments, by granting them legal title to their villages as *Comunidades Nativas* ('Native Communities') and by taking much more direct control over their schools (see Gow 1991 for more details). The *gringas*, the SIL missionary women, were thus progressively replaced by local state officials in the district capital of Atalaya, at the mouth of the Urubamba, and beyond them, *el gobierno*, 'the government', the Peruvian state.

The *gringos* had not, by that token, ceased to exist. Indeed, it seems likely that during the period of land titling of *Comunidades Nativas* by the officials of the agrarian reform agency SINAMOS (Sistema Nacional de Apoyo a la Mobilisación Social), they played an important symbolic role. The origins and history of the military dictatorship were marked by a heightened nationalism and overt hostility to the powers of imperialist foreigners in general, and to the United States of America in particular. The very process of registering 'Native Communities' was couched in the language of a new contract between the state and all Peruvians. This contract's inclusiveness at the national level was accompanied by hostility to *extranjeros*, 'foreigners'. The archetypical 'foreigners', in these discourses, were the imperialistic *gringos*, and especially those from the USA. There is little doubt that the functionaries of SINAMOS, in the process of land registration, brought such anti-*gringo* discourses to the Bajo Urubamba.[1]

---

[1] Two other elements were of significance in Piro people's transformed perceptions of *gringos* by the 1980s. As Brown and Fernandez 1991 have discussed in great detail, the areas immediately to the

During this period, certain new *gringos* were operating in the area. In the early seventies, the state petrol company Petro-Perú, along with the French oil company Total-Deminex, explored for oil in the Sepahua area and on the Inuya river. They had left by 1975, but in the early 1980s there were new rumours of future activity by Shell. These agents, however, tended not to be too strongly associated with *gringos*, but rather with a vague and generalized *compañía*, 'company', which was usually seen as an arm of 'the government'.

Whatever local people's actual experience of *gringos* during this period, the idea of *gringos* was insistently present in the very nature of the local economy. From the late 1940s onwards, the local commercial economy had been dominated by the extraction and export of tropical hardwoods. Most Piro men, and to a much lesser extent Piro women, were working in lumbering in order to acquire the goods they needed. Just as the lumber was going *afuera*, 'outside', to destinations and for purposes that Piro people did not know, so too were the *cosas finas*, the 'fine goods', coming in to the Bajo Urubamba from that outside, to satisfy local desires. As the true inhabitants of the 'outside', *gringos* were necessarily implicated in this commercial system. As I noted in Chapter 1, some Piro people understood that some of what they received in exchange for their work was the 'rubbish' of the *gringos*.

It was into this world that I arrived in late 1980, with the consequences I discussed in Chapter 1. I was a new co-resident *gringo*, and initially I was thought of by local people in terms of the now absent SIL missionaries. As I also discussed before, the people of Santa Clara asked me constantly for information about my country and the countries of other *gringos*, about our modes of living, and especially about the awesome technical powers of the *gringos* and about their factories and aeroplanes. These conversations were, however, only the overt side of local people's ideas about *gringos*, for I was also suspected of being a *pishtaco* or *sacacara*. It is to this hidden side of the local people's views of the *gringos* that I now turn.

Rumours about the Pishtaco *and the* Sacacara

My arrival in Santa Clara in December 1980 coincided exactly with the creation of Werner Herzog's film camp on the Camisea, a tributary of the

---

west of the Bajo Urubamba, the Tambo river and Gran Pajonal, had seen dramatic events involving *gringos* in one form or another. On the Tambo, the American David Pent had transformed from a missionary into a quasi-messianic *hacienda* owner, causing considerable unease among the local white bosses. My informants had vague memories of this man. More important in their memories were the events of the armed revolutionary activities of the MIR (Movimiento Izquierdista Revolucionario) in 1965, which was spreading a radical Guevarist anti-imperial message among Campa people. These events were remembered by my informants well if inchoately: they as frequently attributed the troubles to '*gringos*' as to '*comunistas*', 'Communists'. The tendency of local indigenous people to identify all apparently powerful strangers as *gringos* was a source of ceaseless irritation to middle-class coastal Peruvians in the area.

Urubamba far up-river from Santa Clara. Herzog's company began to hire local Machiguenga people as actors, and also to bring in contingents of Campa people from the Ene river to the west, and from the Gran Pajonal area, just west of Atalaya at the mouth of the Urubamba. My first actual contact with Herzog's project came on 20 February 1981, when I stood with a group of children on the banks of the Urubamba, watching the steamboat 'Huallaga', used in the filming, pass up river. It was an impressive sight, and caused a stir of excitement in the local villages.

Ten days later, as I related in Chapter 1, I heard the first of the *pishtaco* and *sacacara* rumours. Several children told me that a *pishtaco* or *sacacara* was coming from the Campa community of Ojeayo on the Inuya river, and that it cuts off the face and takes out the heart. They asked if I were a *sacacara*, and I solemnly told them that, no, I was a *gringo*. Two days later, Artemio's oldest sons, Denis and Artemio (thirteen and eleven years old respectively), told me that the *sacacara* was working in a co-operative up-river from Sepahua.[2] They said that it removed people's faces with a knife. Thinking they meant some kind of forest spirit, I asked them if it could not be killed. They told me that apparently it could be killed with a bow and arrows, like a human. They went on to say that it travels in a boat with a fast and silent engine, and that it had been sent by the government to take people's fat to make aeroplane fuel. These conversations ended there, for I left Santa Clara two days later to rest and reflect in Lima.

These stories raised troubling memories for me. My only overt contact with *pishtaco* rumours had been in the Andes near Huanta three years before. Travelling by truck at night, my fellow Andean travellers had told me, after we had stopped to drop a fellow Andean passenger off in a remote place at night, that this man was a *pishtaco*. They openly described his activities and their fear of him. Such confidences did not suggest that anyone might see me in this light. However, my reading in the literature told me that the opposite was entirely probable too. Some days later, wandering alone through the streets of Ayacucho, I was attacked and pursued by a stone-throwing crowd and had to take refuge in a church. I thus had some reason to fear *pishtaco* rumours, but the *sacacara* thing was a complete novelty. As I have said, I initially assumed that *sacacaras* were some kind of forest spirits.

All that changed when I returned to the Bajo Urubamba the following month. Disappointed with what I had found in Santa Clara, I had been persuaded by two Peruvian anthropologists, Carlos Montenegro and Alonso Zarzar, to try my luck in Sepahua. On my way, in the offices of an air transport company in Pucallpa, I was told by the daughter of an important white boss from the Tambo river of how the rumours were escalating, and how they

---

[2] This co-operative seems to have been the ranch 'Texas', just below Miaría village. The focus of a prolonged and violent land dispute, this ranch has proved a fertile source of the most diverse rumours over the 1980s and 1990s.

focused on Herzog's company. By the time I got to Sepahua, local indigenous
people's fear of *gringos* was palpable. I heard nothing much about *sacacaras*
there, for by then virtually no one would speak to me at all, other than the closest informants of Montenegro and Zarzar. By now, I was readily able to understand the nature of this silence, for I was clearly imagined to be part of
Herzog's project by local people. There was a constant traffic of light aircraft
to and from Herzog's base on the Camisea river, and I often met people from
there in the streets of Sepahua. I was guilty by association. Given the atmosphere in Sepahua, I decided to cut my losses and return to Santa Clara. When
I got back, however, I noticed an increase in the general air of hostility towards
me there too. Things looked bleak, and I wondered if I could continue the
fieldwork at all.

Luckily for me, one event had occurred in Sepahua which seemed to change
my position in the eyes of people in Santa Clara for the better. In Sepahua, I
had acquired a *compadre*, Julio Shahuano. This man, Cocama by birth but
married to a Piro woman, Elena Pacaya, had called me to cut the umbilical cord
of his new-born son Julio. He was probably inspired in his choice by the fact
that I knew his other *compadre*, Alonso Zarzar. The new light that this change
in my status shed on my motives undoubtedly transformed the ways people in
Santa Clara were willing to think about me. The mere fact of my return would
have suggested I wanted longer-term relations with them. I stayed on in Santa
Clara, and eventually was invited to become the *compadre* by baptism of three
men, Artemio Fasabi, Julian Miranda, and Antonio Zapata, which duly
occurred on 7 September 1981.

This transformation in my status, which I discussed in Chapter 1, led to
others. Because I now, as a *compadre* to local people, had a perfectly legitimate
reason to live in Santa Clara, it was more generally assumed I could not actually be a *sacacara*. Just the week before the baptism, during a festival, an old
Campa man, whom I did not know well, openly demanded to know if I was a
sacacara, and said he would kill me if I was. This man was reputed to have
killed several people in the past and was also very drunk at the time, so his
declaration genuinely frightened me. I went out of my way to assure him that
I was no *sacacara*. He then told me, as he calmed down, 'There were *sacacaras*
living in Betania on the Tambo when I lived there. They forbade the people to
drink manioc beer, to eat white-lipped peccary, collared peccary, and so on. But
why has God put these things in the world, if not for eating?' His reference to
the Adventist community of Betania specifies these '*sacacaras*' as Adventist
missionaries, and the fact that I clearly did drink manioc beer must have somewhat mollified him. At another festival, shortly after becoming *compadre* to the
three men, I was told by an old Piro man, Virgilio Gavino, that the *sacacaras*
were sent by the President of the Republic, Fernando Belaunde, to kill native
people. From the ease with which he told me this, I understood that I was no
longer so regarded myself.

By this time, Herzog and his company had left the Bajo Urubamba, thus removing the immediate cause of the rumours. I, young and indigent, was a much less plausible exemplar of the *gringo sacacara* than Herzog and his crew. And the story was changing too. Julio Urquía, Antonio's brother, visited Santa Clara in this period, and, as a former employee of Herzog's company, knew what had happened as personal experience. He said,

> That *sacacara* thing is just a lie. What would they do with human skin? It was all the fault of that white man, Juan Mengaño. The film company wanted three hundred Campa people, and made a contact with Mengaño to sell them. The Campa people felt mistreated, because Mengaño gave them no money to all. So, some fled back to their homes, and called the army to sort out the problem.

Here, the *sacacara* image was attributed to the ignorance and naïvety of the Campa workers, and to the well known financial treachery of the local bosses. When, in the middle of 1982, *sacacara* rumours began to spread again, it was certain local *mestizo* men who were their targets, and I was once even asked for a lift up the Urubamba by a man who told me, 'I am afraid to travel alone, they say that there is a *sacacara* about.' I was deeply grateful to him, for the evidence that the transformation of my status was now complete.[3]

The image of the *sacacara* circulated as rumour, and rumours have certain important qualities for Piro people. Rumours are necessarily narratives at second- or third-hand. It is never the direct witness who recounts them, but always someone who has heard it from someone else. In a community like Santa Clara, such rumours were circulated mainly by travellers, whether Piro or other indigenous people, or by white bosses. For Piro people, a particularly privileged source of rumours is other Piro villages, like Sepahua or Miaría. These 'other Piro villages' are inhabited by 'people like us', but people with whom one does not 'live well'. But they are connected to 'this village' by the endless to-ing and fro-ing of travellers. These visitors bring to the immediate village news of far-away events, what they have heard about in other villages. This sort of information is a privileged form of the outlandish: no matter how apparently implausible or grotesque, it has at least the virtue of being originally told by 'people like us'. A similar attitude is expressed towards rumours originating among indigenous peoples whom Piro people consider to be like themselves, such as locally resident Campa and Machiguenga, or known *mestizo* people. Other sources, such as the white bosses or more remote indigenous groups, are more suspect, coming as they do from people who are not 'people like us'.

---

[3] Contrary to what is often imagined, *pishtaco*-type imagery is not consistently applied to *gringos* (see Gose 1986). In 1988, *sacacara* rumours were unsurprisingly superseded by *terruco* ('terrorist') rumours, from which I was, on the whole, exempted. In 1999, I was subject to easy and freely-expressed *sacacara* joking (in its *pelacara* form) by people whom I had known as adolescents in the early 1980s.

Even rumours which originate among 'people like us', however, are deeply suspect, for Piro people know well that rumours are often simply lies, invented by their narrators with the specific intent of actively disrupting the *gwashata*, 'living well', of their listeners. It is something they may well have done themselves: for example, it is not unknown for visitors to tell their hosts, with an active desire to mislead, that the latter's kinspeople in distant communities have died.[4] This causes remarkable distress in the listeners, for the knowledge of death is compounded by the fact of separation during life. This is made all the worse because the listeners know well that the speakers may be lying, and hence their own uncertainty increases their sense of hopeless ignorance.

Much the same seems to have been true of the *sacacara* rumours. While people in Santa Clara could rely on their own experience that I was not a *sacacara*, or at least had spent a long time living there without giving any evidence of it, they were also subject to the opinions of their neighbours in nearby villages. As Artemio told me, later on, '*Compadre*, when I go to other villages, people say to me, 'What are you doing letting that *sacacara* live in your village?' I laugh and say, 'My *compadre* isn't a *sacacara*! He's just a young *gringo* who has come to keep us company, and to learn about us.' What liars those people are!' As with sorcery accusations, assessments of rumours force Piro people to choose between two views of their neighbours: are they simply benign 'people like us', or are they malign? Over time, it seems, the people of Santa Clara decided to trust to their own experiences of me, and decided that I was not, in fact, a *sacacara*.

Life in Herzog's Film Camps on the Camisea

The *sacacara* rumours were undoubtedly sustained, in the Santa Clara area, by my own presence and movements, but the main focus was on Herzog's film camps far up-river. I never visited Herzog's film camps on the Camisea, but judging by the evidence of Les Blank's and Maureen Gosling's film *The Burden of Dreams*, about the making of *Fitzcarraldo*, and the book of the same title edited by Blank and Bogan (1984), they formed a surreal social world, and a fertile ground for both benign and wilful misunderstandings. On the one hand, there were largely non-Spanish-speaking German and American filmmakers and actors, and on the other hand, the largely monolingual Campa and Machiguenga actors. In between were a broad range of multilingual potential interpreters, ranging from a Mexican film actor to a Piro man who dressed as a Campa man for the filming. Blank's and Gosling's film and the journals in Blank and Bogan's book make clear that life in these camps was tense and chaotic.

---

[4] This was one of the features of Piro people's behaviour that most shocked me by its apparent inhumanity.

Indeed, the film and journals record the following extraordinary conversation between Elia and Atalaina, two Campa women employed in Herzog's camp; Bruce Lane, interpreter and assistant to Blank; and Miguel Angel Fuentes, the Mexican actor, about *sacacaras*:

Lane: What did they say, then, that the *gringos* were going to take your face?

Elia: Yes, they're going to take faces, they're going to take out your fat for the aeroplane.

Fuentes: We're not like the Jivaros who shrink the head down like this.

Elia: I said to them, 'Better I go there to have my face taken than that my lovers see it,' I told them. I've come here almost every day. We came by here, and my friends arrived, those who came afraid, afraid when they saw the camps, terrified! I said to them, 'Don't be afraid!' 'There are lots of people who . . . like the rest!' . . . 'No, they're not waiting for you.' And they said to Atalaina that there is . . . with this . . . clinic . . . that they are going to put a syringe into your arm and it takes out your blood, they are putting . . . poison in your veins . . . and when you go back home, you will die! They are afraid. And, 'Don't eat so much when they invite you. They give a lot. Don't eat in case you get fat, so they may kill you!' (Blank and Bogan (1984: 38–40)[5]

According to Maureen Gosling's journal, this conversation took place on 22 April (Blank and Bogan 1984: 144), when the *sacacara* rumours were already well disseminated along the Urubamba.

In the beginning, I thought that the *sacacara* rumours reflected a misunderstanding of the process of filming *Fitzcarraldo*. Later, as I pursued my reflections on these matters, I was tempted to see the *sacacara* rumours as a potent indigenous critique of Herzog's project in filming *Fitzcarraldo*. The *sacacara*, as a taker of faces, would fit beautifully with a post-modern concern with the political economy of images, and their abuse. The taker of faces would be a taker of images. However, on further reflection, I came to realize that such a critique probably had little to do with the nature of these rumours on the Bajo Urubamba. Local indigenous people had relatively little experience of cinema at this period (see Gow 1995), and never seemed particularly exercised by potential misuses of photography or film. The rumours of *sacacara*, it seems to me now, reflected a genuine fear of the face-taking itself, rather than the film-making.

That said, it is likely that a variant of the politics of images was locally available, through the medium of SINAMOS and other political organizations. For SINAMOS officials, all *gringos* had been seen as imperialist exploiters, and this message was continued by such political organizations as the *Centro de Investigación y Promoción Amazónica* (CIPA), who worked with indigenous peoples in the region. In her diary, Maureen Gosling reports that CIPA were actively campaigning against Herzog's work in some Campa communities. She notes Campa people's suspicions about the film-making, reporting of the people in one community on the Ene river:

[5] My translation of the original Spanish text.

They had heard stories that people would be treated badly, that they would get killed, that they wouldn't get the money promised to them, if they joined the film company . . . Les [Blank] asked the leader if we could film the conversation . . . The leaders refused vehemently. They said they would do it only if we paid a million soles, since we were going to make millions of dollars with our film. (Blank and Bogan 1984: 168–9)

CIPA's actions here were stimulated by the hostility to the original filming by the Aguaruna people in northern Peruvian Amazonia, and the importance of the theme of money in the Campa leader's responses to Les Blank reflects CIPA's concern both to raise indigenous people's awareness of their exploitation and to strengthen their political organizations.

The connections that CIPA and others established between the situation of the Aguaruna people and local indigenous people may even, conceivably, have given stronger content to the *sacacara* rumours, by directly connecting the activities of Herzog's team to the ritual war complex of 'head-shrinking' by Jivaroan-speaking peoples such as the Aguaruna (see Harner 1972 and Descola 1996). This practice, attributed to the '*Jívaros*', was certainly known to indigenous people in the Bajo Urubamba area, for my informants described it to me, and the same was presumably true of Campa and Machiguenga people. And it is clear that Herzog's team had a considerable animus against the Aguaruna and, as seen in the conversation quoted before, the Mexican actor Miguel Angel Fuentes did not hesitate to raise the Jivaroan practice of 'head-shrinking' to defend the film crew against accusations of being *sacacaras*.

However, important as these connections probably were to the evolution of the *sacacara* rumours, I do not think that, of themselves, they could have stimulated those rumours to have had the energy they did in the Bajo Urubamba area. More would be necessary. In particular, the *sacacara* rumours, insofar as they were directed against *gringos* in general, rather than simply against Herzog and his team, would have to have made sense in terms of what local indigenous people knew and thought about *gringos* in general, and of the role that *gringos* had played in their recent history. Secondly, the *sacacara* rumours would have needed to connect up powerfully with local people's cosmological concerns to be rendered thinkable by them, and hence frightening to them. I discuss the *sacacara* rumours in relation to Piro people's history of relations with *gringos* in the next section, and here concentrate on their cosmological dimension.

In October of 1981, Teresa Barinesa told me the following story, which she had in turn been told by a Campa man who had run away from the Herzog's camp on the Camisea. She met this man in Atalaya, and intrigued by all the rumours, had asked him why he had fled.[6] He told her that, in the film camp, 'The workers were kept in compounds with high fences. Each day, those

---

[6] Teresa Barinesa did not speak Campa, but had worked for many years with Campa people, and may even have known these men personally.

chosen by the *gringos* were called out through the small gates and taken off to have their faces removed.' Teresa Barinesa, when she told me this, asked, 'What on earth can they have seen up there? These Campa men must have misunderstood some part of the filming, and run away in fear.' She also told me that she suspected the local lumber bosses of spreading the *sacacara* stories about to scare their indigenous workers. The film company was paying much higher wages than the local bosses, and the latter were afraid of being unable to work lumber that rainy season for lack of men.

Although Teresa Barinesa was baffled by the Campa actor's story, it would have had an immediate and powerful resonance for any Campa person. Weiss, in his study of Campa cosmology, reports the following, concerning the Perené area to the west of the Urubamba in the 1960s:

Peccaries, or wild pigs (*shintóri*), which are important game animals, are described as *ivíra Pává*, or *ivíra tasórentsi* (raised by god). According to the shaman Porekavánti, a single wild pig is released from its corral up in the mountains, and the swineherd, *tasórentsi*, pulls hairs out of its rump and blows them into the air, whereupon wild pigs multiply and descend to the waiting Campa hunters . . . it is the shaman's function to visit this supernatural swineherd in spirit and request that this be done. The releasing of the wild pigs is done on sufferance, and the Campa hunters are enjoined to kill these animals with a single shot, as the wounded animals return to the swineherd, who has the trouble of curing them, and will be reluctant to send them in the future. (1975: 264)[7]

It seems to me that the Campa actor's story originated in precisely this shamanic image, and it was an interpretation of his and his companions' situation in terms of this known economy of relations between humans, shamans, and white-lipped peccaries.

The connection between this image of the corrals of the white-lipped peccaries and Herzog's film camps is less outlandish than it might seem, for the Campa actor's story had some precise material referents. Maureen Gosling, co-director of the film, *Burden of Dreams*, noted in her journal:

As we approached our landing place, the pilot flew low to point out the important landmarks: the Pongo de Mainique—the rapids were Fitzcarraldo's ship would meet its fate, the 'Campo de los Artistas' (the artist's camp), the 'Campo de los Indios' (the Indians' camp), Camisea. All were reachable to each other only by boat . . .

A totally artificial situation had been created by bringing Campa men, women and children from three different areas, who barely knew each other, and settling them in a camp in Machiguenga territory in a housing situation totally unlike their own. They

---

[7] There is a problem with the translation of Campa–Asháninka terms for the two local species of peccary. The SIL missionary Kindberg translates *shintori* as collared peccary (Ucayali Spanish, *sajino*), and gives *piratsi* for the white-lipped peccary (Ucayali Spanish, *huangana*) (1980: 224, 244). My own informants did the same. Weiss (1975) and Bodley (1970), however, both translate *shintori* as 'white-lipped peccary'. In my interpretation of the data from Weiss and Bodley, I follow these authors' own translations.

live ordinarily in small extended family communities, or in conjunction with a mission, as in Obenteni. Here, barrack-like dormitories had been built for them; they had electricity, but the generator was noisy, being in the camp and not separated as it was in the Artists' Camp. In response to the strange conditions, they had built their own little shelters outside of the barracks for daytime cooking, socialising, making masato [manioc beer] . . . The camp included both people who were satisfied with their situation and those people who were unhappy and anxious, and wanted to leave. (Blank and Bogan 1984: 132, 135–6)

Herzog himself, when questioned about the separation of the indigenous people from the 'Artists', defended the structure of the camp as follows:

They should be among themselves and they . . . they, for example, wouldn't like our food and it would have caused problems and we didn't probably expect to eat their kind of food. So these two camps mark a very clear distinction that I never try to conceal. That there is a highly technical group of people here from a different continent, with a different history behind them, and another group of native Indians, who basically is living here in this environment, has its own way of life, its culture . . . (Blank and Bogan 1984: 41)

The careful separation of the dwelling spaces of the European and indigenous people was thus an intentional feature of the Camisea camps.

Aside from the general unrest and distrust of the Campa Pajonalino people in the Camisea film camp, there was a more specific reason for their anger and fear. I was told the following by a functionary of the Del Aguila air-taxi company, in Pucallpa on 14 March 1981:

The Campa people Herzog brought from Obenteni are causing trouble, because their relatives back in the Gran Pajonal think they've been killed to make their body fat into aeroplane fuel. So, they've threatened to kill the Municipal Agent of Obenteni unless they can have proof that their relatives are being well fed and paid. But the film company can't fly them back because of the bad weather, and they don't want to walk there.

The weather finally improved, and some Campa men were flown back to Obenteni. As they were leaving again by aeroplane, however, it seems that a bull wandered on to the airstrip. Herzog records the result in a letter to his partners, 'Our plane on permanent charter crashed on take-off in the Indian settlement of Obenteni from which we hired most of our Campa Indians. The pilot and five Indians survived, but all were badly injured' (Blank and Bogan 1984: 73). The injured men were flown to a hospital in the town of Satipo, on the colonization frontier to the west, thus taking them, once more, away from their kinspeople in the Gran Pajonal and on the Camisea. This event, occurring in this context, may well have helped to precipitate the flight of the men met by Teresa Barinesa in Atalaya. On 26 April 1981, Gosling saw a group of four men including a Piro man called Alfredo, leave for down-river, returning to their own villages (Blank and Bogan 1984: 148, 150). It seems very likely to me that it was one of these men Teresa Barinesa met in Atalaya, and that he was thus the Campa actor of the story.

The bizarre living arrangements in the Camisea film camp and the extreme anxieties caused by Herzog's methods would not, however, seem to have been enough to lead the Campa actors to interpret their circumstances as playing white-lipped peccaries to Herzog's *gringos*. Something more would be required for that. It seems likely that Teresa Barinesa was correct in her analysis, and that it was the very nature of the film-making which made the connection for these Campa men. Weiss records that Tambo Campa people say that jaguars see humans as white-lipped peccaries, and so hunt them. These man-eating jaguars are really themselves humans, for they are jaguar shamans (Weiss 1975: 289). It seems probable that the Pajonalino men understood the specific conditions of the film camp through that shift in perspective. Herzog's team, ostensibly so concerned with the well-being of their Campa actors, in fact saw them as game animals, white-lipped peccaries, just as human shamans see their fellows as these animals, and are in turn seen by them as jaguars. It is likely that the very nature of the filming and of their living conditions would have told these people that it was their visual appearance that mattered to the *gringos*.[8] Certainly, they had been carried far from their homeland to an unknown area, in order to engage in an activity totally alien to them.

Further, if Julio Urquía's story about the double-dealings of the boss Mengaño, is to be believed, it is possible that the Campa Pajonalino actors felt themselves to have been tricked by that man who, on the pretext of helping them to earn money, was in fact selling them to the *gringos*, much as the owner of the peccaries trades his pets with human shamans.[9] The Campa actors would be like the white-lipped peccaries whose owner, far from protecting them, was trading them with other powerful beings. This situation, where Campa people, 'die like white-lipped peccaries', would be a version of the messianic situation Bodley's informants described, as discussed in Chapter 8, where the unbelievers would die like these animals.[10] Led astray by the false promises of the boss (Mengaño) these people would suffer at the hands of the *gringos*, the fate they themselves mete out to the unfortunate white-lipped peccaries: violent death and subsequent consumption.

---

[8] I do not think that the Campa actor's story necessarily reflected a fear of the process of filming as such. Weiss, based on his work among Tambo and Perené river Campa people in the 1960s, found no worries about photography, other than a concern that the photographer pay the photographed (1975: 429). My sense is that the Campa actor thought the overt activity of filming was merely a pretext for the covert activity of 'face-taking'.

[9] The metaphor would have been a powerful one for Campa Pajonalino people, who had been heavily raided for slaves at least until the 1930s, and were a major source of children for the trade in 'servants' that continued into the 1980s.

[10] This suggests an alternative interpretation of Bodley's account. Possibly his informants meant that the unbelievers would die like white-lipped peccaries because, like these animals, they trust in untrustworthy shamans.

The Taker of Faces

It is certain that Piro people in Santa Clara like Artemio would have heard the Campa actor's story, whether by direct witness, for Teresa Barinesa must have gone to Atalaya with other people from Santa Clara who crewed the canoe, from Teresa Barinesa herself, or from other sources. As an actual personal experience narrative from a former resident of the Camisea film camp, it would have had added authority as a rumour, although still subject to scrutiny for its potential plausibility. The Campa actor's story would, by its imagery, have led to a much closer connection being made between the *sacacara* rumours and Piro people's ideas about white-lipped peccaries, and their relations with humans. Most importantly, it would have connected the issue of the white-lipped peccaries specifically to that of *gringos*, and hence to the long and intimate history of relations that Piro people had had with *gringos*.

In 1981, during Herzog's filming and the early months of my fieldwork on the Bajo Urubamba, the rumours of *sacacara* were strongly focused on *gringos* as a social category. They must have necessarily drawn much of their power for local people from the prime exemplars of such people, the SIL missionaries who had been so prominent in the recent history of the area. If, as I have been discussing over the last two chapters, the SIL missionaries derived much of their success among Piro people from their perceived origins far beyond the edges of the known world, and their association with powerful machines for journeyings from and back to that place, then the *sacacara* rumours articulated the darker side of Piro people's ideas about *gringos*. Instead of coming to help them to live new lives, the *gringos* were now perhaps coming to kill them.

The association of the *sacacara* image with SIL missionaries is found in the following story told to me by Artemio in 1982, and which presumably refers to the mid-1960s when he was training as a teacher in the SIL base at Yarinacocha. He told me, 'Down there in Yarinacocha, the *gringos* have a house full of machines. It is there that they kill the poor native people to steal their skins. It is said that they use these skins for . . . what do you call it? . . . Plastic surgery! Yes, they kill us native people to steal our skins!'

The school teacher, Teresa Barinesa, who reported a similar conversation to me, said that Artemio had told her that he had been shown a house made of glass by another man living in Yarinacocha, and had been told by this man that this was where the operations were performed.[11] She told me that she had remonstrated that the Peruvian government would have prevented such acts, to which Artemio pithily replied, 'What does the government care about what happens to poor native people like us?' Assuming that the SIL functionaries in

---

[11] I suspect that this was a reference to the famous *Hospital Amazónica* located in Yarinacocha near the SIL base.

this period were not actually engaged in the horrific activities Artemio attributed to them, what was the source of this strange rumour?

Unfortunately, there is no evidence available on the history of the key image of the *sacacara* in the Bajo Urubamba area. The linked *pishtaco* image was, it seems, available to people on the Bajo Urubamba from a much earlier period. Farabee reported a *pishtaco*-type story he was told by a Machiguenga youth on Alto Urubamba river in 1907 (1922: 38). Stoll, in his history of the SIL, notes that *pishtaco* rumours were circulating in the Iquitos area of northern Peruvian Amazonia in 1958–9, and were explicitly focused on the SIL base of Yarinacocha (1982: 131). Although I have been unable to find specific references in the literature, *pishtaco* rumours were almost certainly circulating on the Bajo Urubamba in the 1960s, for Weiss (1975: 292) reports them from his fieldwork at that period among Campa people to the west, as does Siskind for the same decade on the Purús river, far to the east (1973: 50–1). It is generally held that these *pishtaco* images are of Andean origin (see, for example, Weiss 1975 and Stoll 1982), but there is much that remains obscure about their Amazonian history.

If the *pishtaco* image was old by 1981, then the corresponding *sacacara* image seems to have been quite recent. Apart from my own fieldwork, the only other references to this image, in its *pelacara* form, were recorded by anthropologists conducting fieldwork in Jivaroan-speaking communities in the far north of Peruvian Amazonia, at this very same time (Seymour-Smith 1988, on the Shiwiar; Uriarte 1989, on the Peruvian Achuar). The extreme similarity of the two sets of rumours, reported from such widely separated areas and appearing simultaneously, suggests a common source for them. An obvious candidate would be the SIL base in Yarinacocha. Bilingual schoolteachers travelling to and from courses in Yarinacocha in early 1981, when the conflicts attending Herzog's filming of *Fitzcarraldo* in Aguaruna territory were being debated widely in Peru, could easily have brought the developed form of the rumours simultaneously to the Achuar–Shiwiar areas and to the Bajo Urubamba.[12] As Artemio's story about the 'plastic surgery' unit in Yarinacocha strongly suggests, the *sacacara/pelacara* image was already circulating in the SIL base a long time before, since it refers to the 1960s when he was training as a schoolteacher there. This in turn suggests that the *sacacara/pelacara* image was being developed among trainee schoolteachers and others in Yarinacocha out of the earlier *pishtaco* image.

If this history of the *sacacara* rumour is correct, I lack the data to interpret the evolution of this rumour in the social conditions of the SIL base in Yarinacocha in the 1960s and 1970s. However, some sense of the genesis and mean-

---

[12] In possible confirmation of this analysis, Philippe Descola (personal communication) told me he has never heard such rumours among Achuar in Ecuador, and that the whole complex of *pishtaco* rumours is of little importance in that country. This suggests that the *sacacara* rumours were circulating within an exclusively Peruvian institutional framework.

ing of the *sacacara* image can be gained by considering the progressive transformation of the image over time in early 1981 on the Bajo Urubamba.
Initially, in the account given by the children in Santa Clara, it was a *pishtaco*
or *sacacara* who cut off local people's faces and took out their hearts. Then,
Artemio's sons told me that the *sacacara* removed people's faces with a knife,
and took their body fat to make aeroplane fuel. After that, the image seems to
have stabilized and focused on the *sacacara* aspect, and the theft of facial skin.
It is as if the *pishtaco* aspect of the rumours was not sufficiently frightening in
itself, and the relative ease with which I was told about it suggested that local
people were confused by it, and uncommitted to it as an image of potential
danger. The *sacacara* image was much more powerful, to the point that it was
never discussed with me when people most insistently held me to be one, and
when this changed, I was only told of it in the most guarded terms.

My sense is that the *pishtaco* image, as long as it was tied to the theft of body
fat for technological purposes, did not make much sense to Piro or other
indigenous people of the Bajo Urubamba. In the Andes, *pishtaco* imagery feeds
into important schemes of ritual sacrifice, where body fat plays an important
role (Taussig 1980; Gose 1986; and Wachtel 1994). This image is much less
potent in the Bajo Urubamba context, for here the basic scheme of the cosmic
economy is not sacrificial (see Gow 1994 on this contrast). The body fat of
certain animals, such as jaguars and anacondas, is used by Piro people for various medicinal purposes, but the practice is far less elaborated than in the
Andes. As such, the *pishtaco* image seems to have been 'known about' on the
Bajo Urubamba, but not so much 'thought about'. On its own, the *pishtaco*
image could not crystallize Piro people's fears of Herzog's team and their activities. The *sacacara* image was necessary for that.

What power the *pishtaco* image had for Piro people seems to have been para-
sitic of the power of aeroplanes, which certainly did have a hold on Piro
people's imaginations. As we have seen throughout this study, Piro people had
had a long fascination with aeroplanes, and strongly associated them with both
the awesome technological knowledge of *gringos*, and with the possibility of the
gringos' arrival on the Bajo Urubamba. Aeroplanes were thought of as being
like river craft, but both more impressive and longer in their range. It will be
remembered that people in Santa Clara were disappointed to hear that it is
technically feasible to go to Europe or North America by boat. As such, aeroplanes were the technical means of journeys to and from the lands of the *gringos*. That these machines might require, in order to fly, some contribution from
Piro human substance would have been thinkable, if not very potent.

In Piro people's imagination, then, aeroplanes functioned as important
connectors in a global economy which they knew, from personal experience,
only in part. In the early 1980s, most local men worked in tropical hardwood
lumbering, which was the major source of income. The money men earned in
this way was spent on the *cosas finas*, 'fine things', all the things they needed

but did not know how to make, like salt, soap, and 'real clothing'. Piro people experienced this economy as the inequitable exchange of things they could produce locally from the forest for the 'fine things' made in factories. The most extreme forms of the factory, as I discussed before, were imagined to lie in the lands of the *gringos*, and these people were imagined as 'living just from machines'. It was, of course, to learn more about the world of the *gringos* that Artemio's mother, Clotilde Gordón, had asked me to return to Santa Clara.

If the *gringos* live 'just from machines', then they clearly do not engage in all the productive processes of local indigenous people. Indeed, that point had not been lost on Piro people, for they noted how *gringos* were often alone and unmarried, and often lacked children. How did they reproduce? Reports of their monstrous technical capabilities filtered on to the Bajo Urubamba in numerous ways, and the concept of 'plastic surgery' may well have provided an answer to that problem. *Gringos* do not need to reproduce, because they have a technique whereby they do not age. The logic of plastic surgery, of course, is to remain eternally youthful. So, the *gringos* arrive as *sacacaras* to kill and skin local indigenous people, in order to replace their own skins through the monstrous technique of plastic surgery. *Gringos*, in this image, really achieve what Artemio only dreamt of for Piro people when, as described in the previous chapter, he speculated, '. . . why can we not live forever, changing our skins like snakes and becoming young again? Snakes grow old, they shed their skins, and become young again.'

This formulation of the *sacacara* image, however apparently strange, would have connected with a practice with which Piro people were perfectly familiar themselves. This was the skinning of game animals to sell their skins to traders. The hunting of certain animals like jaguars and peccaries for their pelts had been a small but regular source of income for Piro men. The connection is made clearly in the following *sacacara* rumour, reported to me by the school-teacher, Teresa Barinesa, 'Some men who were coming down the Urubamba found a metal speedboat at the mouth of the Camisea river. As they searched it for the petrol and other valuables to steal, they found in its prow some plastic bags full of human skins.' This eerie image is made out of parts which would be perfectly familiar to Piro people. Travellers do regularly plunder unattended river craft for anything of value that the owner may have been foolish enough to have left there, while valuable items for trade, like animal skins, are usually kept in plastic bags. The horror, for Piro people, lies with the thieves' discovery that the skins are human skins, and hence that they, too, are potential victims of a murderous *sacacara*.

As victims of the *sacacara*, Piro and other indigenous people of the area would become the 'game animals' of the *gringos*. In everyday Piro life, game animals are hunted for food and, to a lesser extent, for their skins for sale. As food, game animals satisfy people's hunger for game, and their circulation generates and maintains kin relations. As skins for sale, game animals generate money, to satisfy desires for the 'fine things'. The *sacacara* image negates the former usage, for Piro people did not fear that they were going to be eaten, while intensifying the latter usage, for the *gringos* would evade mortality through purely commercial means and technological expertise. The *sacacara* economy of indigenous people's skins would be a monstrous inversion of the Piro lived world: a social world in which people escape mortality without producing kinship relations (see Gow 1995).

It is this feature of the *sacacara* image, the focus on the potential loss of facial skin, which made it so much more potent than the *pishtaco* image, which focuses on the loss of body fat or internal organs. The face is, for Piro people, the unmarked general grounding of *gwashata*, 'living well', as mutual availability between kinspeople.[13] It is on the face that the collapse or transformation of 'living well' appears most strongly. As I discussed in Chapter 4, the face is one of the key body parts transformed in ritual design painting, and face-painting is the most strongly marked mode of transformed appearance through design. Transforming the face renders the most important feature of everyday availability to others as unrecognizable and unknown. This is intentionally done when people take *toé*, as I discussed in Chapter 5. In this situation, the close kinspeople paint their faces black so that the drinkers cannot see or recognize them. In death, a person's face rots in the grave, becoming 'foamy' or 'blotchy', and we have seen how the mythic narratives about the moon deal with the transformation of facial appearance: in the variants of 'Klana Paints the Moon's Face', the celestial being ends up with the blotchy face of a corpse.

The victims of the *sacacara* would suffer a different fate to that of the moon or the ordinary dead. They would be instantly transformed into the image of a *gipnachri*, 'bone demon', the skeletal form of the dead as fully dead. A *sacacara* would kill people, but he would also render them instantly unrecognizable (see Gow 1991; 1995). He would, therefore, be peculiarly destructive of kinship, for no one would be able to recognize the dead (cf. Taylor 1993). Artemio told Teresa Barinesa that he feared that I would kill the people of Santa Clara *and* kidnap their children. This, of course, would be their total erasure. Their faces gone, they would be unrecognizable, and their children, raised by the *gringos*, would forget all about them, and become the *gringos'* children.

The *sacacara* image powerfully raises the basic uncertainties of Piro people's relationships with the *gringos*. If SIL missionary work was experienced by many Piro people as the arrival of powerful and distant white people who had come to teach them a 'new way of living', it necessarily raised the question of how Piro people and *gringos* stood in each other's regard. It seems that, during the period of intensive SIL activity on the Bajo Urubamba, Piro people had understood that the *gringas* wanted both to change Piro people and, at the same time, to become like Piro people through living with them. That is,

[13] See Munn (1986) and also Turner (1980; 1995).

the 'New Life' was a mutual 'coming to be human' between Piro and SIL peoples, as evidenced by the *gringas'* desire to learn the Piro language, and the affection in which they were held by its speakers. When the *gringas* left, and that co-residence was negated, it suggested that the *gringos* had ceased to see Piro people as 'humans', and had come to see them as something else. The *sacacara* image specifies what that 'something else' would be: *nikchi*, 'game animals'.

This sense that Piro people were now the potential 'game animals' of the *gringos* would have received powerful support from the Campa actor's story. As we have seen, it is with regard to the white-lipped peccaries that both Campa and Piro people have most elaborated the notion of a switch between points of view, between being seen as human and being seen as a game animal: Campa people through the eyes of the jaguar shaman, who sees fellow humans as white-lipped peccaries, and Piro people through the eyes of both white-lipped peccaries, who see themselves as human, and of humans, who see them as animals. By rendering the *sacacara* image in terms of such a commonplace piece of local knowledge, the Campa actor's story must have given powerful impetus to the fears this image generated. As I suggested above, this story would have first been heard in Santa Clara in late April or early May 1981, during my absence in Sepahua, and would have accounted for the palpable increase in local people's fear of me when I returned in July.

This transformation in the way in which *gringos* saw local indigenous people, from fellow humans among whom they wanted to live into game animals they sought to kill for their own purposes, would have had a potent meaning for Piro people. In whose eyes do white-lipped peccaries oscillate between human and game animal, according to Piro people? It is not, clearly, in the eyes of ordinary people, but in the eyes of shamans. This potential oscillation, between the mutual awareness of the humanity of others and its denial, is the very essence of shamanry, in the assertion that a non-human entity is 'human'; and of sorcery, where fellow humans are defined as 'game animals'. That *gringos* should be seen as a kind of shaman should hardly be surprising. As we have seen in Chapter 8, the Adventist and SIL missions were experienced as new kinds of shamanry. Similarly, the technological powers of the *gringos*, their mastery of aeroplanes and other marvels, are a form of the *giyak-lewata*, 'to miraculously create, to transform', such that *gringos* are like the hyper-shaman Tsla, in his status as *kgiyaklewakleru*, 'miraculous creator'. And the *sacacara* image attributes to the *gringos* remarkable powers of rejuvenation, in a form of technological divinization which parallels the achieved immortality of shamans.

However, as we have seen throughout this study, shamanry is simply one aspect of a more general concern for point of view in the Piro lived world. We have met the same concern with an oscillating point of view in the practices of design and the girl's initiation ritual, when humans appear to each other as jaguars. There it has a positive connotation, as these 'jaguars' transform over time into 'humans', so inverting the oscillations of shamanry, where shamans increasingly see their fellows as 'game animals'. But shifting points of view are also important in relations with 'white people', as we saw in Sangama's search for the 'very much other people', who would transform Piro people's relations with their bosses, and in the interest that Piro people had in living with the SIL missionaries.

These transformations of points of view in ritual action and in relations with 'white people' generate *gwashata*, 'living well', where co-residents manifest themselves towards each other in their everyday forms as fellow humans. It was this *gwashata*, 'living well', with Piro people that the SIL missionaries had apparently worked so hard to achieve. But then, it seemed, they had simply lost interest in the process and left. The *sacacara* rumours responded to that historical change with an explanation: the point of view of the *gringos* was shifting away from coming to see Piro people as fellow humans towards coming to see them as game animals.

From Different Points of View

If the Campa actor's story was crucial to the expansion of the *sacacara* rumours in Santa Clara, it would also have presented a problem to Piro people. The Campa actor's story arose from within Campa cosmological thought, where the relations between humans and white-lipped peccaries are primarily known through shamanic action. The Campa actor's story, in rendering the activities of the *sacacaras* potently meaningful by analogy to the transactions of human shamans and the owner of the white-lipped peccaries, would have evoked the general economy of shamanry in the cosmos. This would also have been true for Piro people, but with an additional inflection, for the Piro vision of white-lipped peccaries, while clearly connected to shamanry, is also tied to an 'ancient people's story', a specifically mythic narrative, the one I call here 'A Man who went under the Earth', and told to me by Artemio on the evening of 15 January 1982.[14]

The immediate cause of Artemio's story was my question about the *ayahuasca* vision I had had in a tiny village in the Gran Pajonal area some years before. Artemio and Julian had been discussing *ayahuasca*-taking, in the context of the moonlight of that evening. I had told them of my experience of flying under the earth, and seeing great cities lit up in the darkness below me,

---

[14] The only actual mythic narrative about white-lipped peccaries that I have found in the documentary corpus of Campa mythology is a Campa–Ashéninca myth, *Piratsi Ipoña Ashéninca*, 'The White-Lipped Peccaries And The Man' (Anderson 1986: 86–91). In this myth, a shaman out hunting sees these peccaries as people and invites them to his house to drink manioc beer. His wife and brother-in-law, however, continue to see them as game animals, and so proceed to kill and eat them. The shaman goes off with the survivors. It is thus an inversion of the Piro versions.

and I had asked them if there were people under the earth. Artemio told me that there indeed were such people, and that these people were the white-lipped peccaries.

Quite fortuitously, my account of my vision had evoked two features of the Campa actor's story and hence of the *sacacara* rumours, which may well have accounted for Artemio and Julian's wondering response to it. Firstly, it directly evoked the underworld home of the white-lipped peccaries, at least for Artemio, as revealed by the mythic narrative he then told me. It is possible that Julian had never heard this Piro mythic narrative, and so would have had to wait for Artemio's response to my question to make this connection. Secondly, my experience had occurred in the country, and among the kinspeople, of the Campa actor. Neither Artemio nor Julian had ever travelled in the Gran Pajonal, hidden behind the range of the mountains that looms up to the west of the town of Atalaya, and which is visible from the river-bank at Santa Clara. It was back into this remote and unknown world that the Campa actor was fleeing.

Artemio's response to my fortuitous evocation of the *sacacara* rumours was to tell me 'A Man who went under the Earth'. In Chapter 2, analysing the available variants of the Piro mythic narrative about the white-lipped peccaries, I argued that they provide a privileged point where Piro people can bring their own forms of knowledge into direct relationship with that of the *gringos*. It seems to be a myth, not about *gringos*, but for *gringos*, and especially for those *gringos* who come to stand towards the Piro speaker as listeners to the 'ancient people's stories', and towards whom the speaker, in turn, stands as a listener to '*gringo* people's stories'.

It is now possible to specify why this should be so. To do so we must return to another mythic narrative, 'Tsla Swallowed by a Giant Catfish', the Piro 'myth of history', the mythic narrative by which Piro people connect their history of relations with different kinds of white people to mythic narratives in general. As I discussed in Chapter 3, in 'Tsla Swallowed by a Giant Catfish', Tsla hears a bird calling, making an omen of death, and then calls on his brothers, the Muchkajine, the 'Long Ago White People', to follow him away, far down-river to an unknown destination. It is from this unknown destination down-river that successive waves of *kajine*, 'white people' have come. As I have shown, Piro people are reluctant to speculate on the nature of this unknown destination, and await information from those white people themselves.

There is, as I discussed in Chapter 7, one direct reference to the destination of Tsla in the literature on Piro mythic narratives, Zacarías Zumaeta's 'The World on the Other Side'. This mythic narrative unequivocally locates Tsla's destination in the sky. Logically, therefore, the different kinds of 'white people' are coming from the sky. But as I there argued, this mythic narrative was probably told under rather unusual circumstances, as a written commentary on the narrator's father Morán Zumaeta's 'Story of Sangama', a story about a man who could read, and who predicted the coming of the 'very much other people' from the 'far side' in a 'sky steamboat'. That is to say, he predicted the arrival of *gringos* from the sky in an aeroplane.

Artemio's story, 'A Man who went under the Earth', answered the same question, but in another form: that is, from the perspective of humanity, and the manner in which humanity is predicated on mortality. Above all, it answered this question in terms of the transformation of a point of view. What could the world Piro people inhabit look like to *gringos*? The world would necessarily have appeared to the *gringos* as the world of the white-lipped peccaries appeared to Piro people. That is, what look like game animals to us in this world, look like humans to each other down below in their world. This is as true of relations between *gringos* and Piro people as it is of the relations between Piro people and white-lipped peccaries. Similarly, our continuity as humans here in this world depends upon our refusal to see those who live below as people, for they are game animals to be killed and consumed. Here again, the valence of the relationships remains the same despite the shift in terms from *gringos* as subject and Piro people as object to Piro people as subject and white-lipped peccaries as object.

'A Man who went under the Earth' is, therefore, a mythic narrative which is profoundly compatible with the *sacacara* image. It responds to 'Tsla Swallowed by a Giant Catfish' by asserting that new kinds of 'white people', the *gringos*, come from the celestial destination of Tsla and the Muchkajine, and that they come to prey on Piro people. Artemio's story was unquestionably responding to the Campa actor's story, and to the way in which that story gave palpable and menacing meaning to the *sacacara* rumours. I think that Artemio was willing to tell me this story, in the specific form that he remembered it, because he had come to think of me as not being a 'real *gringo*', because I was only an *escocino* or *Giskosya gajeru*, a 'Scottish man', a *gringo* of the most deficient type, and I was also his *compadre*. As noted above, Artemio and other people in Santa Clara had not given up their fears of the *sacacara* activities. What had changed was that they no longer thought of *me* as a *sacacara*. And, of course, 'A Man who went under the Earth' congenially asserts that the 'man who was tired of living' put on the white-lipped peccary clothing and became a peccary, much as I was clearly becoming more like Piro people as I lived with them.

I suspect that both Artemio and Julian were aware of the *sacacara* aspect of 'A Man who went under the Earth' on that evening, but that they were less interested in it than, for obvious reasons, I was. They were much more interested in my *ayahuasca* vision. I had seen something, while in a little Campa village in the Gran Pajonal, that the old people said that the *cajunchis*, 'shamans', see when they take *ayahuasca*: the subterranean cities of the white-lipped peccaries in their human forms. This image, unexpectedly spoken forth by a young *gringo*, in turn raised a practical problem for people in Santa Clara. Why had the white-lipped peccaries disappeared, apparently for good?

This problem was real, and would have exercised such successful hunters as Artemio and Julian. A year before our conversation on 15 January 1982, Artemio's father, Don Mauricio, had told me, 'Before, there were many white-lipped peccaries here, but the *cajunchis* stopped that.' Baffled by this statement, I asked for clarification, and he continued, 'When the *cajunchis* take *ayahuasca*, they can find the hole in the forest through which the white-lipped peccaries enter, and hide it.'

What did Don Mauricio's enigmatic statement, made long before I was in any position to understand it, mean? Undoubtedly, it reflected a general anxiety about a perceived decline in game animals in the area, and hence in available food. As Don Mauricio also told me, 'Many people now hunt the game animals with shotguns. They pursue them too much.' This was also the height of the rainy season, and hence the time of scarce food and increased hunger. Perhaps, too, they felt unhappy about their inability to provide well for me.[15]

But there was clearly more here, for the specific issue of the white-lipped peccaries sparked off that dark statement about the '*cajunchis*'. Who were these *cajunchis*, 'shamans'? The reference was clearly not to shamans like Don Mauricio, who denied any knowledge of such things. The reference was, I suspect, to those few shamans, mainly old men and women, who continued to work in the older tradition of Piro shamanry, or who were suspected of doing so, people such as the jaguar shaman discussed in Chapter 4. As I discussed there and in Chapter 5, such shamanry is strongly associated with sorcery, the misuse of shamanic powers to kill, rather than cure, other people. A shaman who knew how to find and hide the hole of the white-lipped peccaries would do so from pure malice against his fellows, as part of a generalized aggression towards his fellow humans, whom he now sees as game animals. The act has a straightforward logic, since sorcerers treat humans as their game animals, they have no need for other game. As Don Mauricio said of one such man, 'That old man is a sorcerer, he's now turned into a demon. How many people might he have eaten already?'

That this issue was of concern to Artemio on that night is confirmed by his concluding question to me, when he asked my opinion of shamans. The Bible, he told me, forbids sorcery, and sorcerers will not get to Heaven. But, he said, the very existence of sorcery, the bad people who cause harm to others, justifies the existence of shamans, those who cure such illness. Here Artemio was seeking my approval, as a *gringo*, for a decision that he had already made, the decision to increase his involvement with shamanry and the consumption of hallucinogens. This involvement clearly conflicted with his earlier involvement with the SIL and the Swiss Mission, in his attempts to become a teacher and a preacher. But Artemio was in search of an accommodation between the knowledge of the

---

[15] Unlike the people of Huau, where I stayed briefly, the people in Santa Clara flatly refused my offers of money to pay for my keep.

gringos and the shamanry of his mother and father, and doing so in a characteristically Piro manner: the knowledge of the *gringos* is important, but there is
something missing from it, a gap to be filled from other sources.

This transformation in Artemio's ideas was attended by two other transformations. The first was the transformation in the traditions of shamanry
involved, from the older Piro celestial shamanry used by the malign *'cajunchis'*
to the newer, down-river tradition of *ayahuasquero* shamanry, used by his
father. For Artemio, this transformation could be rethought as a transformation away from sorcery towards Evangelical Christianity, and then towards the
curing shamanry of the *ayahuasquero* tradition. This transformation was facilitated by a second one, that in which the *gringos* transform from 'good people',
who come to bring the Word of God to Piro people, into *sacacaras*, who come
to kill Piro people for their facial skins. The two faces of the *gringos*, as teachers and as *sacacaras*, allowed Artemio to see the two faces of shamanry, as
sorcery and its cure.

This is, I think, why Artemio found this conversation so interesting, and
why he told me, 'A Man who went under the Earth'. In my account of my
ayahuasca vision, I had provided him with a key piece of evidence for this
transformation in his vision of the world. His *gringo* teachers and mentors were
ignorant of the potential of shamanry, which they said was wrong and false,
because they did not take hallucinogens. If they did, they would have literally
seen what it is all about. Knowing so little of what Piro people's recent history
meant to them, I could not see this. For me, Artemio's story re-invoked the
sacacara rumours, and set the curious episode of the Campa actor's story
within a wider frame. In so doing, Artemio's story raised the emotional stakes
for me, and undoubtedly rendered that evening of conversation both so memorable and so mysterious.

The Stars in their Courses

If the emotional stakes were raised for me in the conversation on that evening,
by the evocation of the former *sacacara* rumours, I think a parallel process was
occurring with Artemio. I had raised the emotional stakes for him, right at the
start, by asking him for the Piro name for the Southern Cross. It is likely that
my question reminded Artemio of some session of Piro language analysis with
the *lingüistas* long before, which he may have both found tedious and to fail to
answer his own questions. Perhaps, too, my question may have unsettled him
because he was unable to answer it, and this inability reminded him of the
accusation made against him by the other Piro schoolteachers, that he was not
un piro puro, 'a real Piro person', discussed in Chapter 1, an accusation that had
cost him his job. And he may well have often speculated about why *gringos*
should want to know such things.

In my asking Artemio for the Piro name of the Southern Cross, I had quite fortuitously stumbled on to a remarkable feature of the transformation of the Piro lived world since the middle decades of the twentieth century: the progressive disappearance of 'ancient Piro people's knowledge' about the sky. As I have been arguing throughout this study, knowledge about the sky is the area that has been jettisoned from the Piro lived world in order to allow the knowledge of different kinds of white people into it. I believe that this process has not been one of a conscious refusal to transmit this knowledge, but rather a gradual and sustained loss of interest in it. What the old time Piro people said about the sky is no longer interesting, because what the white peoples say about it is.

This process of lost interest can be tracked historically with some precision. Matteson, writing of the late 1940s and early 1950s, had noted a considerable elaboration of knowledge of the stars among Piro people. She wrote:

The heavens at night appear somewhat different to the Piro's eye than to ours. They see and name the dark spots in the milky way. A monkey has his head to the south, and there is a devil in the north. A number of strings of three or four faint stars each, east of the north end of the milky way, are named for a feature of the common geometrical design. The magellanic clouds are noticed and called 'the tomb'. There are also constellations named, but most of them do not coincide with the constellations we see. The Piro point to a cross in the north. It includes Denab, Sadr and two other stars of Cygnus. There is a very big constellation called the 'anteater' which sets in the southwest. Another combination of stars is the 'turtle coop'; another (including Altair) is the 'jaguar's paws'. The 'crocodile's chin' is a triangle including Markab (in Pegasus). The Pleiades are called kachkegirine; Arcturus, kolupa; and a morning star, gonsagi from gogi 'day' and sagi, a form word used of a ball or a large fruit. (1954: 64)

It was through reading Matteson's work that I was led to ask Artemio about the stars in the first place. I could never have imagined then that the issue was of such historical profundity to Piro people. Matteson had unquestionably met Piro people who were willing to talk about the stars, while I did not. Confirmation for this change comes from the SIL Piro–Spanish dictionary, *Diccionario Piro* (Nies 1986). Of the stars and constellations noted by Matteson, the only ones I have been able to find there are 'crocodile's chin' (*kshiyojrukota*, 'alligator's chin'), the Pleiades (*kachkegiri*), and *kolupa shkita*, 'fork of the tobacco snuff tube'.[16] This rather suggests that the Piro informants for the dictionary, one of whom was Artemio, were not that interested in the stars either.

In the 1980s, the only constellation name I was able to elicit was *kachkegirine*, 'the bunched-up ones', the Pleiades, and even that name elicited no further comment. I cannot be sure that the knowledge was disappearing

---

[16] This is an obsolete instrument, made of two bones in the form of a V, through which tobacco snuff was blown into the nose of one person by another. Its use must have been abandoned a long time ago (see illustration in Farabee 1922: 58).

totally, but it is certainly true that I could not elicit it. At best, I would be told
to ask Artemio's mother, old Clotilde, 'Go and ask the old woman, she will
know these things.' Unfortunately, Clotilde had very bad eyesight, and I had no
desire to irritate her with questions she would have found difficult to answer.
The only other reference was Antonio's brief comment, quoted before, 'My
grandparents said that the stars were people. So too was the moon.' This would
seem to have been the limit in Piro people's interest in what earlier generations
of Piro people had had to say about the stars of the night sky.

My question to Artemio about the Piro name for the Southern Cross led
him to question my interest in the subject, and then to ask a question of his
own, 'Is it true that Americans have been to the moon?' My reply and my
description of the moon as reported by the Americans led Artemio to question
the 'ancient people's story' about the moon told him by his mother, 'What of
that belief? Is it just a lie?' Artemio's statement of his ignorance, and the ignorance of earlier generations of Piro people, placed the burden of knowing
about the sky and celestial bodies on to me, in my privileged access to the
knowledge of the Americans. The status of Piro people's knowledge of such
things was being subjected by Artemio to doubt.

When the problem of doubt is raised in connection to 'ancient people's
stories', the story about the subterranean world of the white-lipped peccaries
inevitably springs to mind. These animals are images of doubt because of their
chancy distribution, now abundant, now totally absent.[17] No one knows for
sure why this is so, or where they go when they are absent. But the stories about
the white-lipped peccaries are hence easily accessed when doubt is raised about
mythic narratives, as we saw in Chapter 2. On the evening of 15 January 1982,
it was not just any doubt about mythic narratives that had been raised, but
doubt about the myth of the moon, which, as I discussed in Chapter 6 seems
to be 'dying'. Here the myth about the white-lipped peccaries can really get to
work, for it can explicate the 'death' of that other myth through its own form:
the Piro people's sky is the world of the *gringos*, much as Piro people's world is
the sky of the white-lipped peccaries. The ancient Piro people's story about the
subterranean home of the white-lipped peccaries validates the mythic system
in general precisely *because* it accepts that the weakest part of that system is in
flagrant contradiction to the knowledge of the *gringos*. The ancient people's
story about the moon, fragmenting for its own reasons and opening up new
potentials, posed a threat to the general system. The myth about the white-
lipped peccaries entered the breach.

---

[17] In 1995, Don Mauricio was telling me about Artemio's death, and then went on to discuss the
nature of life's uncertainties, and how it was impossible to tell what, in one's fortunes, was for good or
ill. Quite spontaneously, his talk then turned to the problem of the white-lipped peccaries, in a long
personal-experience narrative about a herd of these animals entering Santa Clara village on his birthday many years before.

Silent Changes

What did Artemio's telling of 'A Man who went under the Earth' do on the evening of 15 January 1982? It took all the problems of that conversation, about the names of stars and whether Americans had been to the moon, and all the wider problems raised by the *sacacara* rumours and my presence in Santa Clara, and reset them in the light of an 'ancient people's story'. The intellectual unease and existential anxiety raised by these specific novel problems were resolved by narrating how they were, in fact, old problems already known to the ancient Piro people. As with all myths, 'A Man who went under the Earth' solved these new problems by showing how they are analogous to other problems (Lévi-Strauss 1988: 171).

This is what all myths do, but there is clearly something special about the myth of the white-lipped peccaries, for we saw in Chapter 2 that this myth had been transforming rapidly over the three decades or so before the conversation of 15 January 1982. Can we specify exactly the historical events to which the rapid transformations in the myth about the white-lipped peccaries are responding? The obvious answer here is the set of events that made *gringos* into an important feature of Piro people's lives over the twentieth century. As I have discussed throughout Part III, these events were interpreted by Piro people as sufficient causes for many of the dramatic transformations of their lived world and its modes of projection into the future. In turn, as I have demonstrated, these transformations were thought through as dramatic transformations in Piro people's relations to the sky and to celestial beings. By dealing directly with the problem of relations between upper and lower worlds as a problem of point of view, through the switch provided by the white-lipped peccaries, this myth becomes the privileged place for absorbing these events into the mythic system through its rapid transformation.

This formulation, while certainly correct, remains insufficient for two reasons. Firstly, as we have seen, Piro people did not simply react to the appearance of the *gringos*, they seem to have anticipated it too: Sangama's account of the 'sky steamboat' and the 'very much other people' was formulated long before the SIL had any plans to evangelize Piro people. The transformations are, therefore, under-determined by the events. Secondly, as I have noted often before, the myth about the white-lipped peccaries is not simply about *gringos*, it is also in an important sense for *gringos*, for it seems to be told in situations of heightened interest in the relations between Piro people and *gringos*. The first of these points suggests that the historical events that the myth's transformations respond to are not simply those known features of the SIL mission and its consequences, but also an older set of events. This means that the myth was already transforming rapidly before it began the transformations recorded in Chapter 2. This would explain the second point. Because it was already transforming rapidly, Piro people could easily see its relevance to the conversations they might have with *gringos* about the relative statuses of their respective forms of knowledge.

Is there any evidence for such prior transformations? Clearly we will not find any evidence in the documentary archive, for, as I noted in the Introduction, 1947 is the earliest date at which anyone bothered to write down Piro myths. Nor would there be any point in asking Piro people themselves, for the myths they tell are, as far as they are concerned, *the* 'ancient people's story' about the white-lipped peccaries. The only recourse left is to look more closely at the myth itself, to see if any traces remain that would suggest its former state.

Sebastián's story 'The Sun' can, I think, plausibly be interpreted as a former Piro myth about the origin of the constellation of the Pleiades. The evidence for this claim lies in several features of this myth. Firstly, we have the curious episode of the main character's guts being removed by the wood storks, and then thrown, by the main character himself, into the river. Sebastián comments of the guts, as they lie spread out on the gunwales of the canoe, ¡*Kayonamole-taa ruchkapnitka!*, 'Such a design-covered mass his guts then formed!' This strange episode will be familiar to any reader of the *Mythologiques*. Lévi-Strauss there shows how, throughout the Americas, myths use this motif of eviscerated guts floating on water to explain the origin of the Pleiades (1970: 242–6). The Piro term for the Pleiades is *kachkegirine*, 'the bunched-up ones', which would correspond to Sebastián's description of the guts. The word root of the Piro name for the Pleiades, *-chke-* bears a marked assonance with the word root *-chka-* (root of *ruchkapnitka*, 'his guts then'). Such evidence is weak but suggestive, and the fact that this constellation name was the only one I could elicit in the 1980s suggests it may once have had an especial significance for Piro people.

Secondly, throughout indigenous Amazonian mythologies, the Pleiades are strongly associated with seasonal changes (Lévi-Strauss 1970: 216–27). As throughout southern Amazonia, the Pleiades disappear from the night sky over the Bajo Urubamba in mid-May, the beginning of the dry season, to reappear again in late June, at the very height of the dry season. As I noted in Chapter 2, Sebastián's 'The Sun' describes the subterranean world as one marked by migratory fish, which begin to appear in large numbers in mid to late June. It is thus possible that the man's sojourn in the underworld originally corresponded to the period in which the Pleiades, too, go under the earth. This suggests that the strong seasonality of Sebastián's first version was an echo of an older myth concerning the origins of a constellation which are associated with an important seasonal transition.[18]

---

[18] The neighbouring Campa people do tell a myth about the origin of the Pleiades. In the version published by Weiss (1975: 397–406), it bears no particular similarity to Sebastián's 'The Sun' except in one important feature: Mashiquinti (the Pleiades) is described as 'lazy'. The rest of this Campa myth corresponds closely to the Piro myth, 'The Ancient People Who tried to enter the Sky', discussed in Chapter 8.

It is precisely such seasonal changes, as I noted in Chapter 2, that are being lost to the complex of Piro myths about the white-lipped peccaries and the canoe journey of the sun. This suggests that the loss of interest in the stars may be connected with a specific loss of interest in the stars as seasonal phenomena. Unlike many other indigenous Amazonian peoples (see Lévi-Strauss 1970; S. Hugh-Jones 1979; Fabian 1992), I have never heard Piro people use astronomical observations for the prediction of seasonal processes. Consistently, they used a combination of the Roman calendar (especially the dates of religious or national holidays) and of observation of the state of the river, of flora and of fauna.[19] The Roman calendar must historically have replaced an earlier system of seasonal prediction, and the greater knowledge of the stars noted by Matteson would tend to suggest that such calculations used astronomical observations.

If this analysis is correct, it suggests that when Sebastián told Matteson his story in the earliest phase of SIL presence, this myth was already undergoing a rapid process of transformation, away from being a myth about the origin of the Pleiades towards a myth about a visit to the underworld. And it is further possible to speculate why this transformation was happening. This myth about the origin of a constellation which marks seasonality was transforming because Piro people were already taking on the Roman calendar and its series of religious festivals marking key moments of seasonal change (see Gow 1991: 221–2). Whether this was a consequence of life on the *haciendas*, with the rubber bosses, or through earlier contacts with Franciscan missionaries is not known, but it must certainly have happened.

My hypothesis is that, as the image of the man being gutted loses its anchorage in the origin of the Pleiades, the myth begins to search outwards for new meanings. In particular, it searches for new meanings in conversations with *gringos* about the nature of mythic knowledge. We already know, from the analysis of the present book, what the basic frames of such conversations are, for they are all the complex of ideas that Piro people in the second half of the twentieth century associated with *gringos*, such as journeying to the sky, and true knowledge of celestial beings and of immortality, and the parallel complex of ideas they associated with themselves, such as mortality, a true knowledge of the river and the forest, and of curing and killing shamanry. Throughout this study, I have pointed out many of these connections already, so in conclusion here I limit myself to elucidating how the transformations of this myth led to Artemio's own conclusion, that curing shamanry, although forbidden by the

---

[19] I was amazed to discover, during census-taking by a medical officer in 1995, that while Piro women showed consistent knowledge of their children's birthday dates and their ages, they could not reliably tell in what year they had been born. Identification of the birth-year involved recondite calculations based on the child's relative age during a known year. This suggests that days and months are most salient for Piro people as periods within an annual cycle, and hence are treated like cyclical star movements, rather than as part of a cumulative series of days, months, and years.

Evangelical Christianity he had professed, was both necessary and a potential future project.

If Sebastián's story 'The Sun' is a transformation of a former myth of origin of the Pleiades, it transforms that myth by inverting it to become a story about the genesis of a shaman. Where the former myth, we must assume, would have focused on the man's guts as the origin of a constellation, Sebastián's story, by losing that theme, is forced to focus on the man himself, and his subsequent adventures. From the man's point of view, the loss of the guts is a form of divinization, for like the immortal divinities, he has no longer any need for his guts. To be without guts replicates the position of the powerful shamans of the past described by Artemio, as discussed in Chapter 8, whose only work is the ingestion of *ayahuasca*. Indeed, the wood storks return the man to Kmaklewakleto explicitly because he is not a dead man. As we have seen, only shamans enter and leave the underworld and sky at will.

It can hardly have escaped Sebastián's notice that this story about a man who enters the underworld, is taken into the sky, divinized, then returns from the underworld to be with his own people, bore some interesting parallels to Matteson's own stories about Jesus. It was the cosmology implied by Matteson's stories that Sebastián was trying to assimilate, and in his narration of 'The Sun', he implicitly asks the key question of that cosmology, 'Where is it that the dead go?' The answer to that question would have been a key existential problem for Sebastián. As discussed in Chapter 8, Sebastián saw in Matteson's project the potential for a new way of 'living well' that would allow Piro people to escape the chaotic nature of their current lives. But accepting Matteson's project required abandoning Piro people's own knowledge of the fate of the dead gathered from shamanry and myth, for no SIL missionary would have been willing to negotiate on eschatology. Shamanic knowledge, therefore, had to go.

Sebastián's telling of 'The Sun' can, therefore, be read as a moment in the transformation of Piro shamanry discussed before, whereby the celestial axis of this shamanry was replaced by 'messianic Christianity'. Through telling this story, Sebastián was able to push the current practices of shamanic divinization back into the distant past of the 'ancient people', as something that had happened then, but happened no longer. Now Piro people were to follow the 'New Life', the true knowledge of God and of the sky brought by Matteson and her Bible translation work. As Sebastián himself put it later on, 'But now it isn't the shaman, but God who is feared and loved.' 'The Sun' allowed Sebastián to do the work of that assimilation by pushing shamanic cosmology backwards into the mythic past, and hence allowing Evangelical Christianity to become what Piro people thought now.

But the myth, while allowing Sebastián to integrate Matteson's new message to his own understanding of the world, did not thereby stop transforming. By the time of the telling of 'The Shallow River', the myth about the white-lipped peccaries has transformed from Sebastián's first version, losing its celestial dimension and focusing exclusively on the journey to the underworld home of the white-lipped peccaries. An echo of that lost dimension occurs elsewhere in *Gwacha Ginkakle*, in Sebastián's report of his father's continuing search for God, and his question, 'Where does God live, under the earth or in the sky?' By the time Sebastián tells 'The Shallow River', ideas about divinity and the sky have been fully assimilated to Evangelical Christian ideas of God and heaven, and the myth about the white-lipped peccaries can go on to do other things.

The loss of the celestial dimension from 'The Shallow River', as I noted in Chapter 2, results in a multiplication of the number of journeys to the underworld. There are now two different stories, about two different men who visit the home of the white-lipped peccaries. This doubling of the central character would seem to be a transformation of the shamanic/divine doubling of the central character in 'The Sun'. Having lost the original sense of that doubling as divinization, 'The Shallow River' responds by making the central character into two separate men. The doubling of 'The Shallow River' then feeds into Sebastián's following comments, when he asserts that these two stories accord well with his own knowledge of white-lipped peccary behaviour, and with the experiences of hunters. It is as if this multiplication of evidence is being brought to bear on the problematic assertion that the underworld is inhabited by the white-lipped peccaries. As such, 'The Shallow River' functions to guarantee the ongoing interest of the other myths in the face of their flagrant contradictions of Evangelical Christian cosmology.

Why should the myth about the white-lipped peccaries be an appropriate place for Sebastián to think through the veracity of myths in general? Firstly, this is so because the white-lipped peccaries are the mythic image of doubt, and hence they allow Sebastián to raise the question of doubt about the veracity of myths in the very form of a myth. The general problem of the ancient people's stories and their relationship to the knowledge of the SIL missionaries is given a specific mythic form, through the stories about the white-lipped peccaries. The myth about the white-lipped peccaries, therefore, becomes a buffer between the mythic system in general and the 'New Life'. It functioned to allow Sebastián to tell the 'ancient people's stories' in a book for schoolchildren, and to claim, in the same place, that those schoolchildren's lives are very different to those of the ancient people.

Secondly, this myth asserts the objective necessity of shamanry in general, and of sorcery in particular, for the white-lipped peccaries in 'The Shallow River' are the victims of sorcery, and their owner must cure them. This sorcery, of course, is the result of human predation, for the white-lipped peccaries are 'ensorcelled' with human hunting arrows. Therefore shamanry, even if abandoned as an overt practice in the new lives of Piro people, remains key to the general cosmic economy of those lives. Indeed, if this were not true, the ancient people's stories would not make much sense, for they treat of modes of transformation that are intrinsically shamanic. What has really changed with the 'New Life' is that Piro people do not, or at least should not, ensorcell *each other*.

But still the myth continued to transform. Artemio's version of 1982 retains the duplication of the central character of 'The Shallow River', but gives it a stronger content, for the two men are now a father–son pair. Secondly, the journey to the sky of 'The Sun' reappears, by viewing the man's return journey home from the white-lipped peccaries' point of view. And thirdly, 'A Man who went under the Earth' recovers some of the central narrative force of 'The Sun', for it, too, recounts the adventures of a man journeying out into the wider cosmos. But Artemio's version seems to complete the ongoing transformation identified between Sebastián's two versions. There is no hint here of a possible myth of origin of the Pleiades, for the man visits the sky as a white-lipped peccary, and the white-lipped peccaries' sky is this human world. And we know exactly what this story allowed Artemio to think next, for it allowed him to find the justification for the active pursuit of a shamanic career within his own knowledge of the world, including his knowledge of the Evangelical Christianity he had so long followed and preached.

In retrospect, what Artemio did in the conversation of the evening of 15 January 1982 was an astonishing intellectual feat, for he managed to transform his doubts about what the old-time Piro people had said about the moon into increasing certainty about becoming a shaman. He did this through reference to a remarkable technical achievement, the moon landing, by the very people who had told him that shamanry is forbidden by God. To get all the way from my story about the Americans visiting the moon to a justification of the desire to learn curing knowledge was, by any standards, an audacious piece of logical reasoning. It was possible for Artemio to do it because his chain of thought was made up of links already ordered in this way by the myth about the white-lipped peccaries. Mythic thought, admitting defeat on the topic of the moon, spotted certain victory on the field of the underworld, white-lipped peccaries, and shamanry.

Clearly, the three tellings of the myth about the white-lipped peccaries that I have analysed here are but a tiny part of all the thinking that Piro people were doing about their world over the period described. Even so, they do present us with snapshots of the wider processes of transformation in the Piro lived world over the later decades of the twentieth century. Sebastián was already an adult when the SIL missionaries arrived, and he told Matteson 'The Sun', which seems to be a former myth about the Pleiades, as part of his assimilation of the SIL message. Later, as an old man, he tells 'The Shallow River' to Piro children as part of a book explicitly directed at telling Piro people's history. Artemio, whose life had been coeval with the SIL project, then told 'A Man who went under the Earth' to me, a new kind of *gringo* who had appeared when the SIL project seemed to be over. It is through careful attention to the tellings of this myth that we gain unexpected access to how Piro people thought through and effected the transformations of their lives over this period.

If the various tellings of the myth about the white-lipped peccaries have allowed me to write a history of it, and hence of its tellers and of their world, this is not what the myth was doing for Sebastián or Artemio. For them, this myth clearly did not have such a history, for as they told it, they were telling *the* 'ancient people's story' about the white-lipped peccaries. Myths are the stories of the *tsrunni*, 'ancient people', and while living Piro people may experience themselves as being ignorant of them, as having forgotten them, or as having told them badly, they cannot experience themselves as having invented them. When Piro people tell myths, they experience themselves as profoundly passive in relation to the story, for they are simply repeating a story heard long ago in childhood, remembered, and now retold. The 'ancient people's stories' are the things that do not change. They are the oldest of the old.

From the analysis of this book, it might seem that Piro people are simply mistaken here. The myths are constantly transforming, silently keeping pace with the changes in the world, and with changes in Piro people's ideas about it. But if Piro people are deluded about the nature of their myths, it is the 'ancient people's stories' themselves which have tricked them. The transformations of the myth about the white-lipped peccaries were clearly happening in the minds of people like Sebastián and Artemio, but not by conscious thought. The myth was changing silently, stealthily refashioning itself in Piro people's thoughts such that, when a Piro person came to tell this ancient story, it entered the world already fully prepared for the new circumstance it found there.

The mythic system, threatened by the loss or forgetting of parts of its multiple connections to the world, transforms to cover the gaps which a changing world is opening up within it. It is as Lévi-Strauss said, the myths are causally related to history but, when threatened with historical events which would render them meaningless, they simply transform, in order to preserve themselves from such meaninglessness. Historical events, as Lévi-Strauss noted, are seldom strong enough to sweep them away for good. In this reaction to a changing world, myths obliterate time. The myths do the great work of oblivion. By obliterating time, the myths act to reset the temporal scale of the lived world, just as volcanic activity can reset the apparent age of the rocks it metamorphoses. It is the same with the myths. By endlessly resetting the apparent age of the Piro lived world, by obliterating the time that stretches out behind it, the ceaselessly changing 'ancient people's stories' allow it to go on, in its new modes, with its new sets of meaningful connections to be explored and lived.

Conclusion

This book began with the conversation on the evening of the 15 January 1982, and it has demonstrated that I had good reason to think, at the time, that this event was especially interesting. For there is indeed a link between Artemio's question about whether Americans had been to the moon, his mother's story about the moon, and his own subsequent telling of 'A Man who went under the Earth'. These things are connected by the logic of the way that Piro people like Artemio think about themselves and the world. That conversation, apparently progressing at random, was being guided by that logic. Further, that conversation was simply a brief fragment of a larger logic, the Piro lived world as I found it in the 1980s. And that lived world was simply the current state of a larger entity, a system in a state of transformation. As I have shown, many of the elements of this system appeared in that short conversation with Artemio on the evening of 15 January 1982.

The present study has demonstrated the potential for, and utility of, applying Lévi-Strauss's work on myth, and his proposals for a historical anthropology, to the kinds of data and insights collected by the Malinowskian project of extended fieldwork by participant observation. With Malinowski, we can thus look over the myth-maker's shoulder and watch the myths being made, and with Lévi-Strauss, we can begin to see all the other myth-makers who went before. By taking a myth told by one Piro man I knew well, and then comparing it to earlier versions collected by others, I was able to suggest that this myth has an intrinsic connection, for Piro people, with the social category to which I was assigned, *gringos*. And *gringos*, in the form of American missionaries, have had an important set of meanings for Piro people, long pre-dating any active and regular contacts. As we saw in the story of Sangama, the *gringos* were imagined by some Piro people, on the basis of what they knew about the world as it then was. Because of this, Piro people reacted to the arrival of the SIL missionaries in ways that made sense to them, even if it baffled those missionaries, and laid the grounding for the situation I found among them in the 1980s. It was not, as I originally thought, that Piro culture or society was falling apart: it was the system that orders the inner logic of how Piro people think that was impelling them towards certain kinds of changes, towards abandoning certain kinds of practices in favour of novel but analogous practices, and this was happening because that system is inherently transformational.

A System in a State of Transformation

These transformations would not make sense if we were to posit that there was, at some time in the past, a stable structure of Piro culture or society, geared to self-identical reproduction, which only began to transform due to outside interference. In the past, such a postulate seemed to be the price paid for the remarkable success of Malinowski's method. The sheer coherence that functionalists found in human lived worlds was imagined to be a *sui generis* feature of certain kinds of lived worlds, those Malinowski unashamedly called 'savage societies'. Because functionalism had ejected historical explanation from its project for anthropology as a science, the possibility that the coherence that ethnographers find in the lives of the people that they study might be a product of historical circumstances, and be inherently transformational, was not considered. Coherence was a product of social and cultural processes operating in the absence of historical change.

Lévi-Strauss's position is very different. Recognizing that indigenous American peoples must have had complex histories long before any Europeans ever saw the continent, and accepting that we unfortunately know little about those histories, he argues that the unity and solidity of the system of mythic transformations, which he has investigated by the technique of reiterated and expanding comparison of myths taken as synchronic, can only be explained diachronically. That unity and solidity, Lévi-Strauss argues, can only be explained as a historical phenomenon by rethinking the general history of indigenous American peoples (see Introduction). Here, I have sought to show this for one very small part of that greater system, in the historical processes which are leading the Piro myth of the moon to transform by 'dying', and the myth about the white-lipped peccaries to transform in step to maintain the general coherence of the wider system that Piro people call *tsrunnini ginkakle*, 'ancient people's stories'. This book is a monographic demonstration that myths are indeed instruments for the obliteration of time.

This position helps us to understand how it is that Piro people have been able to create the 'audacious innovation' over the past century. In an important sense, the 'audacious innovation' is not an innovation at all, for it is simply the current state of an ongoing transformational system, like the mythic system itself. If we consider the 'mission' witnessed by Marcoy in 1846, or the 'mass' witnessed by Sabaté in 1874, the 'audacious innovation' that I observed in the 1980s starts to look like what Piro people have always done, and it is likely that, were our historical knowledge greater, we could see this pattern stretching even further back into the past. Insofar as we can think of it as an innovation, it must be understood as the pathway that the transformation of the system happened to follow for historically contingent reasons. Had historical circumstances been different, we can hypothesize that it would still have transformed, but in different ways.

How is this system connected to myth? Clearly, this system is not coterminous with myths, for these form a distinct sub-system within the larger one. But the myths perform an important task within this larger system, that of obliterating awareness of aspects of the history of the system, and allowing it to retain its overall scale, even though the terms and the nature of the relations between the terms is changing. For example, as I have shown, the relations between Piro people and celestial beings has transformed rapidly over this century, and even many of the terms have changed. But the mythic narratives have kept pace with those changes, and hence obliterated the potential problem by removing their interest for Piro people, and so have allowed them, apparently seamlessly, to become interested in new terms, like Evangelical Protestant or Adventist Christianity, aeroplanes and *ayahuasquero* shamanry. The myths do the work of refiguring these changes to maintain the general scale of the system, such that it is subject to neither inflation nor deflation. Even where we might suspect deflation to be occurring, in features like the decline in design production or of the girl's initiation ritual, it is not, for as I have shown, these declines have been accompanied by an exactly corresponding rise in the importance of alphabetic writing, of schools, and of community festivals.

To understand how myths are able to do this, it is worth remembering the precise circumstances in which they are generally told and heard: they are primarily told by old people to their young grandchildren when there is little else to do, and they are told because they are interesting. They are thus told in the spatially most restricted aspect of kinship as a spatio-temporal system, within the intimacy of close kinspeople gathered in a house in the evening as people prepare for sleep. But they are also told in the maximal temporal extension of lived kinship: by grandparents to grandchildren. In their content, they speak of the maximal frames of Piro space-time, in the genesis of major features of that lived world. This, as I explained, is why they are so interesting to Piro people. The telling of the myths is located in the very heart of what most matters to Piro people, 'living well', and because of this the myths can get on with their work of obliterating history most effectively. And most impressively of all, the myths can do this without even having to be believed, which, as we have seen, they are not. All they have to do is to be interesting.

The potentially rapid transformations of the myths are, I suggested in Chapter 9, probably not subjectively available to Piro people. While I have never attempted the experiment, I strongly suspect that even were Piro people to be confronted by the evidence for this feature of myths, they would ignore it, deny it, or explain it away to their own satisfaction (see Lévi-Strauss 1970: 12–13; 1978: 34–43). It is the myths' potential for such rapid transformation that gives the system its extraordinary resilience in the face of what might otherwise look like overwhelming odds.

The myths also help to explain the curious features of the manner in which Piro people narrate their historical experiences, as I discussed in the Introduction. Myths form the most temporally distal pole of an axis that has personal-experience narratives as its most temporally proximal pole. Everything else must necessarily be located somewhere in between. As we move along that axis, away from the wealth and complexity of personal-experience narratives, we see a progressive reduction in the detail and vividness of these narratives, and a growth in their stereotypy. Piro historical narratives can be subjected to extreme summary without losing much of their force, which would not be true of either mythic narratives or personal-experience narratives: witness Moisés Miqueas's example in Chapter 3, when he said, 'After Tsla and the Muchkajine left, the white bosses came, then came the Spanish people, and then we made the *Comunidad Nativa* of Sepahua, and so that is how it came to be as it is today.' When we get to *tsrunni pirana*, the stories about the ancient people, they are reduced to extremely stereotyped and generalized statements about modes of action. But as we continue along this axis, we come to the 'ancient people's stories', where agent, event, and narrative complexity are suddenly and dramatically restored.

Piro historical narratives can be thought of as a mode of adequating the relationships along this axis of narratives from most proximal to most distal and vice versa. They function to mediate the myths and personal-experience narratives by progressively reducing the agent- and event-centredness of these genres, in both directions, and replacing these with general classes and processes. Tsla or the Kochmaloto Women at one end of the axis, and Artemio Fasabi or Clara Flores at the other end, are replaced in historical narratives with anonymous classes of agents, such as 'the ancient people' or 'the slaves of the haciendas'. Similarly, the eventfulness of Tsla's murder of his uncles, or of Clara Flores's encounter with a jaguar, is replaced with habitual actions, such as 'the bosses beat us with sticks', or with general processes, such as, 'the people of Huau began to leave to live elsewhere'. This stripping away of the specificity of both agents and events seems to me to be a very significant feature of Piro historical narratives.

These features are not especially surprising when we consider the actual modalities of the relationships involved. As I argued in *Of Mixed Blood*, kinship and history are identical for Piro people. The primary targets for almost all extended Piro narrative genres are other Piro people, that is, kinspeople, or other indigenous people defined as kinspeople. With a few significant exceptions, such as anthropologists or missionaries, Piro people do not direct such extended narrations towards powerful white people, because such white people would not be interested. For these latter, it is they who speak, and Piro people who listen. Because of this, all these Piro narrative genres circulate primarily in relationships of kin ties, and it is such kin ties which form their major subject matter, whether overtly in personal-experience narratives and in historical narratives (Gow 1990a; 1991; 1995), or covertly in mythic narratives (the present book and Gow 1997).

For Piro people, kin ties are made, not given. As Piro narrative genres move from the centrality of event and character in personal-experience narratives towards the stereotypy of historical narratives, they replay the move from the lived precision of the constitution and enactment of 'real kin' ties to the lived vagueness of the constitution and enactment of 'distant kin' ties. The distinction between 'real kin' and 'distant kin' is an existentially important feature of everyday social relations for Piro people (Gow 1990a; 1991). Like personal experience narratives, real kin ties are full of agents and events; like historical narratives, distant kin ties are evacuated of agents and events. The connection is hardly surprising, given that real kin ties are made in a ceaseless stream of everyday give and take, while distant kin ties are merely extrapolated from other people's use of kin terms (Gow 1991: 162–72).

The reappearance of actors and events in mythic narratives, noted above, is rather more surprising. It was unquestionably this feature of these narratives that helped me originally downplay their significance, as discussed in the Introduction. If Piro people's stories 'about ancient people' are stereotypical accounts of generalized actors going through generalized actions, why is it that these almost forgotten people's reported speech, the 'ancient people's stories', should be told in the form of these vivid stories? After all, in most of the circumstances in which Piro people could find themselves, the reported speech of people who are total strangers even to the speaker, let alone to the listeners, would be a working definition of extreme uncertainty. As I discussed in Chapter 3, this is, indeed, partly the case in relation to mythic narratives.

Here I think that, yet again, Lévi-Strauss was correct to term myths 'instruments for the obliteration of time'. Time, for Piro people, is primarily experienced as the making, living out, and unmaking of kinship. What they find interesting about the past is the remembering of how kin ties were made; what they find interesting about the present is the enactment and ongoing production of kin ties in 'living well' and its alternatives; and what they find interesting about the future is the potentials for the making of new kin ties and the dangers posed by the ontogenetic processes of mortality.

Now suppose that this time had not yet happened, what would the world look like then? It would look like the bizarre and alien world of the mythic narratives, a world in which an unborn child speaks from the womb, where women marry jaguars and have babies with anacondas, where people try to dam the Urubamba, and where men wander off into the underworld, to travel in the canoe of the sun or to become white-lipped peccaries. The 'ancient people's stories' tell of a world in which time, and hence history, and hence kinship, have yet to begin. As we have seen, time, history, and kinship began when Tsla told the Muchkajine, 'This is the land of death', and disappeared off downriver.

This perspective helps us to understand the otherwise bizarre genre convergence of personal-experience narratives and 'ancient people's stories'. The myths are the personal experience narratives of the mythic beings, but without the need for these beings to actually recount them or any requirement that any specific listener be posited. The mythic action is simply going on, oblivious as to how exactly this action could be memorialized (cf. Munn 1973: 112–18). To whom could the mythic agents have told these stories as personal-experience narratives? Speakers and listeners must be made in historical time, and historical time had not started when these events happened. This strange feature of mythic narratives, that they defy the basic properties by which Piro people understand states of knowledge to be validated, seems to me simply to add to, rather than detract from, their interest for Piro people. It is the insouciant weirdness of myths, in their absolute indifference to the epistemic scrutiny of their tellers or their listeners, that guarantees their interest for Piro people.

A social world that gives key epistemic value to personal experience, and which reiterates that value in the certainty of personal-experience narratives, finds its spectral image in the mythic narratives. These stories defy the value of personal experience and the certainty of its narration, and do so in the very form of a personal-experience narrative. The two extremes of Piro narrative form, personal-experience narratives and mythic narratives, unite lived time and 'a very long time ago, it is said', in a single form. And as Piro people know well, the 'ancient people's stories' exist nowhere else except in their being told and heard by living people. Piro people, therefore, know as lived experience what Lévi-Strauss aphorized, that a myth is 'a message that, properly speaking, is coming from nowhere' (1970: 18). Lévi-Strauss's analysis, often dismissed as excessively abstracted from lived human reality, has thus very precise phenomenal coordinates in the Piro lived world.

The Transformations of Sociological Method

Viewed thus, we can begin to see that Lévi-Strauss's project in the *Mythologiques* is far more than a study of myth, or even of history. Among many other things, it contains the project for a sociology capable of taking myth seriously.[1] Malinowski proposed his famous, and easily trounced, theory of myth as social charter, but, as I discussed in the Introduction, he went on to supplement it with a comment on myth as dealing with the 'unpleasant or negative truths'. We might legitimately wonder how these two accounts square, and ask what exactly Malinowski might have expected a functionalist account of the 'unpleasant or negative truths' to look like. My own sense is that a functionalist account of the 'unpleasant or negative truths' elaborated in myths would look like the *Mythologiques*, and that much of the unpleasantness and negativity of that work for so many commentators lies in Lévi-Strauss's resolute refusal to explain myths away or to dissolve the many troubling problems that they present to us by appending them to phenomena that we think that we understand better.

In the 'Overture' to the *Mythologiques*, Lévi-Strauss wrote:

Durkheim has said (p. 142) of the study of myths: 'It is a difficult problem which should be dealt with in itself, for itself, and according to its own particular method.' He

---

[1] I am very grateful to Eduardo Viveiros de Castro for pointing this out to me.

also suggested an explanation of this state of affairs when later (p. 190) he referred to the totemic myths, 'which no doubt explain nothing and merely shift the difficulty elsewhere, but at least, in so doing, appear to attenuate its crying illogicality.' This is a profound definition, which in my opinion can be extended to the entire field of mythological thought, if we give it a fuller meaning than the author himself would have agreed to. (1970: 5]][2]

For Lévi-Strauss, myth is not to be treated by a separate method, as Durkheim despairingly suggested, but by the very same methods that Durkheim used to explain suicide or religion, for it is through the engagement of those sociological methods in the study of mythology that they can be refined and extended.

If the *Mythologiques* is the project for a new mode of sociological thought, it is possible to specify what exactly is wrong with concepts like society or culture when they are thought of as transhistorical entities. The functionalist methods of research and analysis were brilliant at decoupling anthropological thought from its deadening legacy of bad historical explanations, but they did so at the price of decoupling the peoples studied from their own unknown histories. The heuristic device of eschewing groundless historical explanations slid easily into a proposition about the properties of the object studied: that culture and society were transhistorical objects which stood outside history. History, therefore, became something that could happen to cultures or societies, rather than being the very matrix within which they take form and exist. Leach was correct to note the slippage from 'Nuer society in 1935' to 'Nuer society' (1954: 7). The problem here, however, is that while the phrase 'English society in 1935' has a potentially specifiable content in relation to its well known anterior states, 'Nuer society in 1935' is a fairly lonely little temporal hook when we contemplate all the multitude of things that we do not know about the Nuer past, and probably never will.

As I noted in the Introduction, Leach's point can only be used to dodge the functionalist illusion if we have some independent sources on the anterior states of the system in question, which is often not the case. Further, the key problem with the development of structural-functionalism out of functionalism was not properly the issue of history, but the development of the metaphor of society as organism, and the consequent presumption that societies are systems geared to self-identical reproduction over time (Radcliffe-Brown 1952: 1–14). Once society had been imaged as an organism, it became necessary to imagine it reproducing, and to imagine how it did so. It then became possible to write things like the following, from Fortes's reflections on the reproduction of society:

A social system, by definition, has a life. It is a social system, that particular social system, only so long as its elements and components are maintained and adequately

[2] The page references in this quotation are to Durkheim's *Les formes élémentaires de la vie religieuse* (1925 edn.).

replaced; and the replacement process is the crucial one because the human organism has a limited life span. (1958: 1)

It was this metaphorical extension of life to social systems, and the corresponding imaging of human lives as their component parts, which led anthropologists to imagine the extension of social systems in time as reproduction and to imagine that extension to be analogous and parallel to human reproduction, rather than identical with it.

Once societies were imagined to reproduce, it was virtually inevitable that an interest in historical analysis would start to focus on that problem. Leach himself avoided the problem by virtue of an unappealing and unsatisfactory theory of maximizing individuals, but the problem has dogged many attempts to historicize anthropological analysis. Sahlins, who proclaims his intent to make structuralism historical, states in the introduction to *Historical Metaphors and Mythical Realities* that 'the great challenge to a historical anthropology' is to know how 'the reproduction of a structure becomes its transformation' (1981: 8). By the conclusion, the tone has changed,

'Reproduction' has become a fashionable term these days, rather taking the theoretical place of, or specifying, the notion of 'function'. But one may question whether the continuity of a system ever occurs without its alteration, or alteration without continuity. Even the apparently extreme processes of culture-in-history we have been discussing, reproduction and transformation, are they truly—i.e. phenomenally— distinct? Clearly, they are analytically distinct. (1981: 67)

Sahlins is correct here, but it strikes me that the problem that he sets up, the issue of the phenomenal nature of the distinction between reproduction and transformation, is a pure artefact of thinking about 'culture-in-history'. If, as I have argued following Lévi-Strauss, there is nowhere else that culture could be other than 'in history', the question about the continuity of the system evaporates, as does the analytical distinction between reproduction and transformation.

Sahlins's position comes perilously close to the one for which Lévi-Strauss criticized Sartre, that of imagining that history, as a method, has a distinct object. For Sahlins, that distinct object would be the continuity of the system in time. This is simply to mistake methods of analysis for properties of the object analysed. Lévi-Strauss's distinction between synchronic and diachronic analyses does not refer to the difference between the analysis of phenomena belonging to one moment in history and the analysis of phenomena belonging to different points in history. It refers to the difference between modes of analyses in which temporal sequence can be ignored because it is irrelevant to the features of the phenomena under consideration, and modes of analyses in which temporal sequence is being used to explain features of the phenomena under consideration. In Chapter 2 in this book I engaged in a synchronic analysis of a set of Piro myths, while in Chapter 9 I engaged in a diachronic

analysis of the same myths. The latter analysis has no inherent virtue, or intellectual priority, over the former. Indeed, the latter would have been impossible
without the former.

For all the criticisms of Lévi-Strauss and structuralism, the various advo-
cates of an anti-Lévi-Straussian historical anthropology regularly smuggle
synchronic analysis back into their work in disguised form. Usually, this takes
the form of a concern for 'contact'. By positing a unique moment in which two
formerly separate social systems or cultures came into contact, anthropologists
are able to specify a base-line period (and preferably date) from which reproduction becomes potential transformation. I noted in the Introduction that
such situations tend to be the ones about which historical data are likely to be
scantiest and most imponderable. But such contact analyses also tend to imply
a point at which history starts. In the Introduction, I quoted the celebrated
statement by Wolf, 'The global processes set in motion by European expansion
constitute *their* history as well. There are thus no 'contemporary ancestors', no
people without history, no peoples—to use Lévi-Strauss's phrase—whose
histories have remained cold' (1982: 385). Close reading and, in particular,
careful attention to the tense of that 'have remained', reveal that Wolf's claim
here implies that there were, indeed, once people without history, peoples
whose histories had remained cold, and that this was before the global
processes set in motion by European expansion. And readers of the second
chapter of Wolf's book, 'The World in 1400', are entertained to a broad-brush
portrait of the world in that year, devoid of any serious discussion of the status
of this historical knowledge or of how it was acquired, and quite silent on the
evident disparities in our knowledge of what was happening in London, Rome,
and Paris in that year when compared to parallel events on the Bajo Urubamba,
in Cuzco or in Ipanema.

This point is important, for as Lévi-Strauss noted, anthropological analysis
faces a real danger if anthropologists begin to imagine that history, as a method,
has a distinct object. Strathern has given that danger a fitting name, 'presentism'. Responding to criticisms of her rethinking of Melanesian ethnography
in *The Gender of the Gift* (1988), she remarks, 'The great trap of historical
analysis is presentism: the assumption that what goes on in the postwar, paci-
fied Highlands, for example, can be put down to the fact that it is a period of
postwar pacification' (P. Brown *et al.*, 1992: 152). Presentism is simply the
gratuitous illusion of the functionalists under a new guise. Presentist historical
analysis certainly rejects any notion of the lived world studied as an isolated
and self-contained totality, but it does so at the price of asserting another mode
of totalizing functional integration, that between the lived world studied and
whatever it is that its analysts assume to be the most important features of its
present historical circumstances. For example, my fieldwork on the Bajo
Urubamba occurred during an unprecedented increase in global Cold War
tensions, which badly scared many millions of Europeans and others and

whose distant echoes were felt by Piro people. Had those tensions got out of hand, they would indeed have had major implications for Piro people. But this does not mean that very much of what I saw on the Bajo Urubamba during the 1980s could be explained by late Cold War insanity. The fact that both were going on in the 1980s did not mean that they were necessarily causally connected.

If Sahlins is right to see function hidden under the concern for reproduction, and if Strathern is right to see presentism as the danger of historical analysis, then much of what is taken to be historically-minded anthropological analysis is simply presentist functionalism. The gratuitous illusion of the functionalists survives, masquerading now as historical analysis. Here we might ask an obvious question. Why it is that the illusion of the functionalists has been both so seductive and so productive within anthropology?

The answer must be that the sheer coherence and dense meaningfulness that is found by ethnographers working by participant observation is not illusory. It is real, but it is not the product of the seamless, self-identical reproduction of a social system over time. Instead, it is the result of people attributing meaningfulness and coherence to the world around them, adapting and transforming their thoughts about the world in order to make sense both of that world and of themselves. The great power of the Malinowskian method of fieldwork lies in the uncovering of just how impressive such processes of making meaning are, in the dense interconnections that people make between different areas of their lives. Its danger lies in attributing this coherence and meaningfulness to something that lies outside the processes by which people make sense of their lives, to things of the order of a society or a culture conceived of as a transhistorical entity ideally geared to self-identical reproduction.

In a series of important ethnographic and theoretical studies, Toren has developed an approach to this problem which allows us to understand how this process occurs without recourse to concepts of society or culture as transhistorical entities (1990; 1993; 1999). Starting from an adaptation of Piagetian developmental psychology to Malinowskian ethnographic investigation, Toren argues that while children enter a world that is given to them, they must necessarily make sense of that world for themselves, and that they make sense of it in relation to the senses that others have made of it. A child growing up in a Fijian village will necessarily come to make sense of the world in a manner that is recognizably Fijian, by dint of dense interactions with other Fijian villagers. However, the fact that all the people in this Fijian village make sense of the world in ways that are manifestly versions of each other does not require us to posit a common culture or society into which they have all been 'enculturated' or 'socialized'. Instead, we can see such commonalities as the effect of how these various people have come to constitute themselves over time, and as the grounding for the specific social lives they engage in.

Toren's work has two important implications for the present work. Firstly, because she argues that children necessarily make sense of the world through their own unique experiences of it, nothing guarantees that they all make sense of it in exactly the same way. Indeed, everything suggests that the senses made are going to be unique. Such internal variation in turn strongly suggests the potential for endogenous transformation of meaning over time, and Toren argues that this is, indeed, what happens. Her account is homologous to the analysis of the present book, based on different materials, and it suggests the mechanism that may underlie mythopoesis in the Piro case. Piro children will necessarily understand myths in ways unique to themselves, and then, as old adults, tell these myths mediated by all their unique intervening experiences and by the current states of the world. All mythic narratives are thus subject to variation.

Secondly, Toren's approach points us away from strictly theoretical postulates towards empirical data and, in particular, to the curious and unexpected features of that data. When Toren discovered that, in Fiji, younger children, older children, and adults produce descriptions of ritual gatherings that are totally and systematically at odds with each other, the problem was not to decide which descriptions best corresponded to reality, but to ask why this should be so. The answer reveals the actual ontogenetic processes by which Fijians, as they grow up, come to make sense of these ritual gatherings, and in the process, come to experience rituals as an objectively necessary feature of their lived world. But it is the curious divergences of the descriptions that reveal that this making sense is a micro-historical process, inherent in Fijian people's ontogenies, rather than a generalized feature of a Fijian culture or society construed as a totality of linked and shared meanings.

It is such curious and unexpected features of known lived worlds, the strange foldings and doublings back in what seem to be seamless systems, that lead us inevitably to historical investigations (see Lévi-Strauss 1963: 101–19; and Gould 1987: 60–97 for geology). The present book grew out of just such an odd feature, the apparent ease with which Artemio could question one Piro myth on the basis of my account of Americans going to the moon, and then tell 'A Man who went under the Earth' on the basis of my account of my vision of the underworld. If, as I originally thought, Piro mythic knowledge was disappearing, why was Artemio's story about the man who became a white-lipped peccary so vibrant? But if this suggested that Piro mythic knowledge was alive and well, how then could Artemio have questioned the story about the moon? The answer, of course, is that Piro mythic knowledge is a complex object, one whose interior coherence is constantly being generated by transformation in the ontogenies of Piro people in historical enacted time.

The approach taken by Toren has a further advantage, for by being explicitly rooted in biological thinking, and hence in the actual nature of human life, it allows us finally to rid ourselves of the organismic metaphor of society. The sense that people make of their lives and of the world occurs in the specific nature of human ontogeny and as a result of it. It is, therefore, unnecessary to postulate social systems as living and reproductive entities of a distinct order to organic human being. Social systems are simply what humans necessarily make as they live. This shifts the problem away from that of how social systems reproduce or transform, to the problems of the specific historical conditions of how any given people come to live the lives that they do.

The problems that Toren has addressed in the ontogenies of Fijian children's understandings of ritual life, or that I have addressed here for a short period of the history of a Piro myth, differ markedly in scale from Lévi-Strauss's grand project in the *Mythologiques* and its successor volumes, but I do not think that they differ in intent. What unites them is a common concern with the historical conditions of the human mind, whether those conditions are to be scaled in the years of a child's growing, in the decades of a community's memories, or in the millennia of a continent's peopling. The sense that anthropologists find in the lives of the people they study is always referable to the nature of the human mind, rather than to any functionalist appeal to needs, whether biological, cultural or social. Because this is so, the specific nature of the sense that is found becomes a historical problem, for it raises questions about the contingent nature of the world that lay to hand when any given human mind was making sense within it.

This appeal to place historical problems at the heart of the anthropological endeavour would seem to lead directly to a serious danger, for does it not simply relocate into the centre of our task all the imponderability of historical evidence, discussed so extensively in the present work? Is the cost of resolving the gratuitous illusion of the functionalists to be that of rendering the whole anthropological endeavour either methodologically impossible or a minor and problematic sub-discipline of history?

This problem, of how to recognize ethnographic data as historical objects, receives its most extensive discussion, to my knowledge, in Lévi-Strauss's *The Way of Masks* (1983). There, the author starts with a stylistic problem, the apparent anomaly of the Salish *xwexwe* mask within the known corpus of Northwest Coast plastic arts. Tracing out the career of this mask as it moved north to the Kwakiutl people, Lévi-Strauss reveals a much bigger system of transformations, stretching over many centuries and over a large area of western North America and beyond, wherein specific mask forms are revealed to be the concrete instantiations of structural potentialities of this wider system, actualized in specific times and places in response to immediate relations with neighbouring communities.

Lévi-Strauss there reiterates his criticisms of the shortcomings of functionalist methods, discussed in the Introduction:

One of the most pernicious notions bequeathed to us by functionalism, and which still keeps so many anthropologists under its rule, is that of isolated tribes, enclosed within themselves, each living on its own account a peculiar experience of an aesthetic, mystical or ritual order. Thus, it is not recognised that before the colonial era and the centuries of destructive action ... these populations, being more numerous, were also elbow to elbow. With few exceptions, nothing that happened in one was unknown to its neighbours, and the modalities according to which each explained the world and represented the universe to itself were elaborated in an unceasing and vigorous dialogue. (1983: 144–5)

Where the functionalists would have been content to fully elucidate problems like the Salish *xwexwe* mask within its immediate context in space and time, Lévi-Strauss insists that we should search for how this immediate local context is being made in space and time as part of a much wider system.

What, then, do such concepts as society look like from the perspective developed by Lévi-Strauss, and the position defended here? Lévi-Strauss's account points towards a much more complex understanding of the indigenous American communities that ethnographers have studied. It suggests that what ethnographers study, by participant observation, in the 'convenient community' that Radcliffe-Brown advocated, are the temporally and spatially limited nodes of what Lévi-Strauss termed 'larger entities' (1981: 609). These larger entities are no mere theoretical postulates, but can be uncovered by synchronic and diachronic analysis, and unquestionably reflect genuine social processes occurring between their component communities over time and space. As Lévi-Strauss pointed out, such processes are unlikely to be observable by methods of participant observation, and they are still less likely to be recorded in the documentary archive. But they can be seen in curious and unexpected features of ethnographically known lived worlds, such as the extreme differences between the Salish and Kwakiutl versions of what both peoples claim to be the same mask, which forms the point of departure of *The Way of Masks* (1983), or in the curious conjunction of a question about Americans going to the moon and a story about a man who became a white-lipped peccary discussed in the present work.

Connections

Lévi-Strauss concludes *The Way of Masks* with a striking image:

By gathering scattered threads, I have only tried to reconstruct the backdrop for a stage some two thousand kilometres wide and perhaps three to four hundred kilometres deep, along whose entire stretch the actors of a play for which we do not have the script have left their footprints. (1983: 228)

The present work has not followed Lévi-Strauss's lead, for it has not shown how the evening of 15 January 1982 fits on to such a broader stage. But the existence of this larger stage can be glimpsed in sets of connections of which I have been conscious throughout the writing of it, and further sets of connections brought to my attention by others.

As I tell 'A Man who went under the Earth' to Bruna Franchetto, who worked with the Kuikuro of Central Brazil, she says, 'I know this story, it is the story of the Yamurikumã Women,' the mythic originators of an important Kuikuro ceremony. Stephen Hugh-Jones, who worked with the Barasana of southeastern Colombia, remarks of Sebastián's 'The Sun' that it is the story of Manioc Stick Anaconda, the mythic ancestor of those people. Eduardo Viveiros de Castro, when I ask him about a small detail of that story, tells me, 'It's actually in the key myth to the *Mythologiques*, read Lévi-Strauss.' And, far away from the metropolitan settings of those conversations, I am sitting in the Panará village of Nansepotiti in Central Brazil when Sokriti spontaneously tells his version of 'The Birth of Tsla' to Elizabeth Ewart, who then tells it to me. Such connections could be multiplied almost indefinitely, but what do they mean?

Readers familiar with the *Mythologiques* already know the answer. In the extraordinary space that Lévi-Strauss generates in his analysis, all the myths come to be connected by more or less direct links. As readers enter fully into the sheer scale of Lévi-Strauss's project on myth, they come to appreciate the ways in which the 'key myth', the Bororo story, 'The Macaws and Their Nests', echoes forth across the vast landscape of indigenous American mythologies, in the process of the ramifying complexity of this 'one myth only'. As a reader of the *Mythologiques* I was thus only transiently surprised when, reading Nimuendajú one day, I found the following story:

Once a woman was pregnant with white-lipped peccaries, which belonged to the sun. The moon wanted to practise his archery; he got ready with his bow and arrow, and ordered the woman to let out one peccary after another. He missed them all, and they ran far away, because there was no water nearby. When the sun, who was at that moment cooking a deer in a pot, saw that his peccaries had fled, he became furious and threw the boiling water at the moon's face, leading to the marks there. (1987: 125)

To find the main outlines of my analysis in this book subjected to excellent summary in an myth of the Ofaié people of Southern Brazil pleases me greatly, but it would surprise no reader of the *Mythologiques*.

Recent ethnographers of indigenous Amazonian peoples do not yet know what to make of such connections outside of the uniquely Lévi-Straussian space of the *Mythologiques*. Our work has been done, in large part, within explicitly Malinowskian protocols of fieldwork by participant observation, the pre-condition for the believability of our accounts. Apparently we have not been entirely successful, for to our anthropological colleagues we are the objects of a certain incredulity, which is at once dismissive and intrigued. This reception of our ethnographic accounts has been well described by Seeger:

Joanna [Overing] Kaplan, in her call for papers for the Forty-Second Congress of the Americanists in 1976, noted that South Americanists are often accused of being ideal-ist by their more 'empirically' minded or materialist Africanist or Southeast Asianist colleagues. A similar accusation of creating perfect structures whose existence is not quite believable has been levelled at Lévi-Strauss on more than one occasion (Geertz 1973, p.18). (1981: 240–1)

It is doubtless true that, in order to minimize the genuine unfamiliarity of our ethnographies, many of the recent ethnographers of Amazonia have tended to inhabit fully the gratuitous illusion of the functionalists, and to avoid all of the even more outlandish issues raised by the wider stage of indigenous Amazonian ethnographies.

That said, the problems raised by Lévi-Strauss in the *Mythologiques* replicate themselves within this ethnographic project. As our knowledge of indigenous Amazonian peoples has grown (see Descola and Taylor 1993; Viveiros de Castro 1996), so, too, have attempts at synthetic overviews, and it is increasingly obvious that, at some level, the socio-cosmological systems of all indigenous Amazonian peoples are topological transformations of each other in ways that are neither trivial nor over-generalized. Whether analysts start from personhood (Seeger, Da Matta and Viveiros de Castro 1979), labour control (Turner 1979; Rivière 1984), reciprocity (Overing 1981), kinship structures (Gow 1991; Dreyfus 1993; Rivière 1993; Viveiros de Castro 1993) or cosmology (Descola 1992), indigenous Amazonian peoples reveal themselves to be transformed versions of a single social logic distinctive to the region.

These synthetic overviews do not look like comparisons in the sense that this term implied within the structural-functionalist frame, where the reiteration of instances was intended to bring us ever closer to some important underlying principle which would explain such similarities. Indeed, what is most interesting about the synthetic overviews mentioned above is their concern for the diversity of the concrete instantiations of the single social logic which is being intimated. After all, the Piaroa are like the Trio, who are like the Barasana, who are in turn like the Achuar, who are like the Araweté, who are like the Kayapó, who are like the Piro, and so on, but in each case the likeness is only partial. In each case, the likeness comes along with a string of systematic differences. There is no sense, in either the overviews or in the specific ethnographic projects on which they build, of the identification of extra-social factors which might lead a common social logic to express itself in *this* way in *this* case. The differences are understood to be irreducible, and the extreme variety of the cases is not taken as a mere product of the extension of the ethnographic project, but as a *sui generis* feature of the region described.

But what, in turn, could such variety mean? Perhaps here the ethnographers of indigenous Amazonian peoples might take heart from Melanesian studies. For Amazonianists, Melanesianists function as a kind of disciplinary twin, one where the substance of Malinowski's ideas looms far larger than his methodology, and where Lévi-Strauss is treated more as a methodologist than as a participant in a debate. At the end of *The Gender of the Gift*, Marilyn Strathern notes how her reanalysis of Melanesian ethnography, which is rooted in comparison,

> . . . underlines the failure of a comparative method whose persuasion rests in elucidating a repetition of instances. That arithmetic—based on the plurality of units—has disappeared. Here we have varieties of or versions of a 'single' instance. These societies hold their conventions in common. I would draw an analogy. In the same way that one might wish to comprehend capitalist organization as it developed historically in Europe, so one needs to inject a real history into our comprehension of Melanesian gift economies. The history itself may be irrecoverable, but we surely know enough about historical processes to recognize a series of connected events. (1988: 341)

An anthropologist reflecting on the lives of peoples living on the far side of the world, studying problems different from those that concern Amazonianists, and making no reference to the *Mythologiques*, reaches an identical conclusion to its author: there is only one example, and what comparison studies is the ramifying versions of that single example as it plays itself out in real time.

And what, in turn, can we make of such a conclusion? Firstly, Strathern's conclusion can be used to precipitate an important point from the *Mythologiques* for recent Amazonianist ethnographies. Lévi-Strauss is clear that myths, however novel in their adaptation to the specific events of their telling, are always made out of other myths. Because of this, the connections that we, following Lévi-Strauss, find between myths are always real connections, for they form a series of connected events. Strathern helps us to see a further implication of this, for it is logically also true of lived worlds (or cultures or societies, if these terms are preferred): lived worlds can only be made out of other lived worlds. This was a point that the structural functionalists considered to be trivial, for the fact that people are made out of people was simply 'biological reproduction'. But if people must be made out of people, and lived worlds out of lived worlds, then the connections that can be found between the recent ethnographies of indigenous Amazonian people turn out to be real connections, for they form a series of connected events.

This, in turn, suggests that the attempts at comparison of indigenous Amazonian peoples noted above are, like the *Mythologiques*, histories. They are histories insofar as they trace out the similarities and differences between radiating versions of a single case. The similarities and differences between the Achuar, the Piaroa, and the Piro are systematic evidence of historical processes. We do not know what these processes might have been, and in most cases probably could never know, but we do have, in these recent ethnographies, a knowledge of their historical products. And the sheer diversity of those products supports the conclusions of Lévi-Strauss and of this book: indigenous Amazonian lived worlds are not characterized by self-identical reproduction, but by their transformational exuberance.

Thirdly, it may even be possible to connect the recent ethnographies to real histories. While some archaeologists have cautioned against finding continuities between prehistoric Amazonian cultures and contemporary indigenous peoples (Roosevelt 1993), others have long argued that much of what we see in contemporary Amazonia is the product of very long-term historical processes. Long ago, Lathrap argued that certain cultural processes in the Ucayali valley in the latter half of the twentieth century, which might initially look like historically recent phenomena, are actually patterns several millennia old (1970: 17–21). This project has been followed up with others (Lathrap, Gebhart-Sayer and Mester 1985; DeBoer and Raymond 1987; Lathrap, Gebhart-Sayer, Mester and Myers 1987; Roe 1988; Heckenberger 1996; Basso 1995) which show real promise of linking the ethnographies of contemporary peoples to long-term historical processes. A parallel project can be found in linguistics (Urban 1992; 1996a; 1996b). The outlines of a debate are there, even if it has seldom been engaged in (see Lévi-Strauss 1993). At the very least, archaeology and historical linguistics have forcefully brought back to our notice that the peoples of Amazonia were not asleep until European colonization woke them up to history. Much was happening.

Tsla and his Brothers

This discussion of the wider spatial and temporal settings of the Piro lived world that I studied in the 1980s corresponds to Lévi-Strauss's insistence on the identification of larger entities than functionalist methods of research and analysis would allow (1981: 609). By arguing that indigenous Amazonian peoples have complex histories which may have little to do with the ongoing consequences of European colonial expansion, we are able to see how *that* larger entity, which some anthropologists have imagined to be coterminous with history in general, is just one among many. And we can use what we know or can reasonably assume about those other larger entities to gain a better perspective on it. In particular, we can begin to understand how indigenous Amazonian peoples made the ongoing consequences of European colonial expansion take the form that they did by linking them in specific ways to their own ongoing projects.

My analysis in this book has shown some of the ongoing consequences of European colonial expansion in negative outline, so to speak, as they connected with the ongoing consequences of Piro people living their lives in historical, enacted time. My refusal to integrate the known logic of that expansive dynamic with my account of those Piro people's lives has been quite deliberate, for my task here has been to find the ongoing consequences of Piro people living their lives as an object of enquiry in its own right, which is a much harder task for historical study than the already well-known consequences of European colonial expansion. Much has been said about those consequences already, for they are relatively easy to study because they are often well documented, even if deeper historical analysis remains lacking for important aspects of them.

The present study would have achieved little if all it said was that what Piro people have done, historically, is react to those features of the ongoing consequences of European colonial expansion that have impinged upon them. Instead, it is necessary to demonstrate that the specific form of successive colonial situations arose from within the ways Piro people set about constituting them. This is so not because, in the sentimental language of resistance theories, Piro people are not passive victims but active agents. For much of their recent history, Piro people have indeed been victims of exploitation, brutality, and injustice, in situations where they had no say and few means to fight back, and it would be grotesque for me to pretend that things had been otherwise. Instead, the reason why it is necessary to demonstrate that the specific form of successive colonial situations arose from the ways Piro people set about constituting them is because Piro people are made by other Piro people, and have no choice but to constitute the world around them in ways that are intrinsically meaningful to them. And, sad though it is to say, this is true even of how they have had to live as passive victims of exploitation, brutality, and injustice. As Marx said, 'Men make their own history, but they do not make it as they please; they do not make it under self-selected circumstances, but under circumstances existing already, given and transmitted from the past' (1969: 398).

This is where the problem of historical analysis for anthropologists really starts, for we have very limited access indeed to the 'circumstances existing already, given and transmitted from the past' for cases like that of Piro people. In view of this problem, and in the light of the analysis of the present book, the place to start such an analysis would be with mythic narratives. This is obviously not because I think that such narratives preserve details of ancient cultural patterns nor that they have been preserved unchanged through the generations and hence give us access to how ancestral Piro people thought. Instead, following Lévi-Strauss, it is because I think that myths are themselves historical products, and ones which carry within themselves the traces of that which they seek to erase, their own former states.

How do the Piro mythic narratives collected in the latter half of the twentieth century set the stage for our understanding of the interactions between Piro people and the ongoing consequences of European colonial expansion? As we have seen, they do this most overtly through what I have called the Piro 'myth of history', wherein Tsla and his brothers, the Muchkajine, depart down-river to their remote and unknown destination, and from which successive waves of white people have come. This mythic narrative develops from another, 'The Birth of Tsla', where the Muchkajine, the 'Long Ago White People', originate in the excessive twinning of Tsla. The 'Long Ago White People' are Tsla's 'twin', and are themselves twins (or triplets) to each other. This process of twinning extends into Piro historical narratives where, as I have shown, kinds of white people are characterized by a process of doubling,

in the form of successive waves of new forms of white people arriving to interact with Piro people.

The Piro case conforms well to Lévi-Strauss's analysis in *The Story of Lynx*
(1995). There, as I noted in Chapter 7, he argued that the speed with which so
many indigenous American peoples were able to integrate the entirely unexpected appearance of Europeans into their mythologies can only be explained
by the existence of a 'hollow space' in such mythic thought, and that this
hollow space is generated by indigenous American peoples' ideas about twins.
Of these latter, Lévi-Strauss writes:

> What these myths implicitly state is that the poles between which natural phenomena
> and social life are organized—such as sky and earth, fire and water, above and below,
> Indians and non-Indians, fellow citizens and strangers—could never be twins. The
> mind attempts to join them without ever succeeding in establishing parity between
> them. This is because it is these cascading distinctive features, such as mythical thought
> conceives them, that set in motion the machine of the universe. (1995: 63)

Characters who start out as twins in indigenous American mythic thought
become increasingly differentiated into the generators of the universe.

What Lévi-Strauss demonstrates in *The Story of Lynx* is the historical lability of the mythologies of indigenous American peoples, rather than a sociological principle operant in the historical actions of such peoples. Nothing
would guarantee that myths recorded in the late twentieth century could elucidate Piro people's actions in earlier periods. That said, the presence of this
connection between twinning and the origin of white people in the mythologies of indigenous American peoples suggests that it may also be a genuine
sociological principle too. Lévi-Strauss notes that many indigenous American
peoples, 'have chosen to explain the world on the model of a dualism in perpetual disequilibrium, whose successive states are embedded into one another—a
dualism that is expressed coherently at times in mythology, at times in social
organisation, and at times in both' (1995: 239). This statement, by providing a
movement between mythology and social organization, suggests the potential
for a corresponding movement towards historical enacted time. The task,
therefore, becomes finding a sociological equivalent for the dynamic disequilibrium Lévi-Strauss identifies in indigenous American mythic thought, and
one that would both be directly operant in relations between such indigenous
peoples and their colonizers, and visible in the documentary archive. Such a
sociological feature would be the sociological equivalent of the 'hollow space'
Lévi-Strauss identified in the corresponding systems of mythic thought.

A potential candidate, in the Piro case, has been supplied by Ricardo
Alvarez. Basing himself on Piro oral history, he argues that the Piro word
kajitu, which currently means 'white man', originally referred to Inca state
officials who organized the up-river trade at the Pongo de Mainique (1984: 35),
a trade described in the literature, and one that continued in modified form

after the Conquest until the late nineteenth century. While Alvarez's account is entirely plausible, it is possible that the term *kajitu* may have also been applied to other distant trading partners, for the archive also shows a consistent pattern of sustained trading relations between Piro people and their neighbours down-river to the north, including peoples along the Central Amazon (Myers 1983). This historical evidence suggests that *kajine*, a term that currently means 'white people', may have been a central category of Piro thought, and a crucial point of view for the creation of Piro social life, for a very long time indeed, and in all probability from well before 1492.

Alvarez, in the text cited above, translates the word *kajitu* as 'the one who has objects', a translation that was presumably made by a Piro informant.[3] While such *post hoc* translations are necessarily suspect as historical data, this one does conform closely with the known historical interest of earlier generations of Piro people in the goods of their neighbours, and with current Piro conceptualizations of white people, as discussed in this book. If Alvarez is correct, this suggests that Piro people have, over time, consistently shifted their category of *kajitu* on to that group of people within their known world who best exemplify the 'possessor of objects' function.

Stephen Hugh-Jones has noted that while indigenous Amazonian peoples' desire for their colonizers' goods appears again and again in the ethnographic literature, and indeed in the documentary archive, it has received little profound analysis (1992). Doubtless because most anthropologists who have studied these peoples necessarily come from highly industrialized social milieux, such desires have seemed to them both self-evident and sociologically trivial. Because things are so manifestly important to people like us, we look at indigenous Amazonian peoples and note how few they have, and are hardly surprised by their desires for more. Hugh-Jones, however, points out that, ever since Mauss, anthropologists should have been alerted to the possibility that a desire for things might be a desire for the social relationships that those things embody, rather than the utility of the things themselves. As I have discussed throughout this study, for the Piro case, such relationships with white people, and the wealth they procure thereby, are experienced as necessary for the ongoing projection of the Piro lived world into the future. But, as will be clear by now, Piro people's desire for relations with white people is not characterized by any one kind of relationship with one kind of white people, nor by some notionally achievable 'shopping list' of goods desired, but rather by the sort of dynamic disequilibrium noted by Lévi-Strauss in indigenous American mythic thought.

The Piro case discussed here suggests an added complexity to Hugh-Jones's

---

[3] The etymology would seem in fact to be *ka+gaji+tu*, (*gaji-*, 'heart') 'supernaturally powerful possessor of a heart', which may be linked to the episode of the hearts in the mythic narrative, 'The Birth of Tsla' (see Ch. 4).

account. It is not simply that Piro people want relations with the 'possessors of objects', and hence their goods. They seem also to posit such peoples, and hence relations with them through goods, entirely in the abstract. My analysis of 'The Story of Sangama', in Chapter 7, showed how Sangama posited the existence of the *paneneko*, the 'very much other people', and the potential for contact with them and the acquisition of their goods. Sangama's alluring account of the 'sky steamboat' did not depend, as Hugh-Jones's account might imply, on actual contact with the 'very much other people', and hence on the establishment of an object-mediated relationship with them. Instead, it lay in the imagined actualization of a relation which was then purely virtual. How can we account for this virtual relation, which clearly intrigued Sangama's audience?

A model here is provided by Viveiros de Castro's concept of potential affinity. Starting from certain odd features of indigenous Amazonian kinship systems, Viveiros de Castro argues that the essence of affinity for these peoples lies not with real immediate affines, who are in fact consistently assimilated to kin, but rather with the figure of the potential affine. The potential affine is almost never transformed into a real affine, but is rather the object of warfare or other relationships which negate the values associated with affinity in everyday life. Commenting on Tupinambá cannibalism, Viveiros de Castro notes:

The relationship to the enemy is anterior and superior to society's relationship to itself, rescuing it from an indifferent and natural self-identity—one where others would be mirrors and reflect back the image of a Subject posited in advance as *telos* . . . Free and fierce, the Tupinambá were servants of warfare: this pushed them into the future. Inhabitants of a society without corporations—incorporal, so to speak—and cannibal (thus incorporating), its being was time. (1992: 301)

It is, therefore, the potential affine, the enemy, who allows social life to exist, rather than the real affine, who simply replays, in domesticated form at the intimate level of daily life, the function of the enemy.

Viveiros de Castro's account derives from analyses of warfare, and from indigenous Amazonian communities in which warfare with other peoples was a dominant social value. His analysis would, at first sight, seem difficult to extend to Piro people, who habitually emphasized trading relations with other peoples over warfare.[4] However, ever since Lévi-Strauss's famous article (1976b), from which I extracted the notion of the 'audacious innovation', we have known that, in indigenous Amazonian contexts, warfare and trade are the two faces of the same relation with the other. Might it, therefore, be possible to

---

[4] Piro people did not tell me much about warfare with other indigenous peoples and, at most, presented themselves as victims of the violence of 'wild Indian' peoples. That said, the documentary archive reveals a long history of raiding by Piro people against their neighbours, many of whom genuinely feared the military capacities of these people (Camino 1977; Roe 1982: 82). However, I came across no evidence of Piro people ever revelling in their bellicosity.

translate Viveiros de Castro's account of the Tupinambá into a Piro idiom? Could the relationship to the possessor of objects be anterior and superior to Piro people's relationship to each other? Could Piro people be servants of a trade which propels them into the future?

To explore this possibility, we might ask what it is that Piro people say that they do with their relations with white people. Piro people say that they make kinship. The object-mediated relation with white people, the possessors of objects, becomes here the model of relationship in general. As I have discussed at length elsewhere (1991; 1993) and reiterated in the Introduction, Piro people in the 1980s narrated their recent history as the process by which contemporary kin ties were generated. In particular, as I noted before, they told me that before the enslavement of the ancient people by the rubber bosses, there was no kinship, 'The ancient people had no villages, they lived fighting and hating each other in the forest.' It was thus the rubber bosses who brought to the ancient Piro people the form, enslavement, and forced intermixture, in which the latter could make social lives. And subsequent kinds of white people have brought new social forms, the *hacienda*, the 'New Life', and the *Comunidad Nativa*, in which subsequent generations of Piro people made and extended kinship. White people are, therefore, imagined by Piro people as objectively necessary for their existence as humans.

Following Viveiros de Castro, therefore, we can agree that, for Piro people in the 1980s, the relationship to white people, the possessors of objects, was anterior and superior to Piro people's relationship to each other. But following Viveiros de Castro's formulation also helps to explain an odd feature of Piro people's formulation, for if kinship is made in relation to white people, it is not necessarily made with them. White people remain, on the whole, potential affines, not real ones. In marked contrast, the hostile and endogamous groups of ancient people, as well as other indigenous peoples, made kinship by intermarrying, and becoming real affines. Such real affinity, operating in everyday life, generated real kin ties, in an ongoing process that leads Piro people to assert of themselves, 'We are mixed people, we are people of mixed blood.' The kinds of white people, by contrast, have not on the whole realized their potential affinity as real affinity, and hence remain potential affines.

To further the comparison with Viveiros de Castro's analysis of the Tupinambá, is time the being of Piro people? This is clearly true, if we consider Piro people's historical narratives. As I have noted before, the condition of the enslavement of the ancient people was their seduction by the goods of the rubber bosses. It was their desire for goods that led them to enter into the oppressive debt-relations with their bosses. And it was the desires of subsequent generations for goods at less cost in terms of oppression and suffering that led Piro people to constantly transform their lives, in the long process that they called 'becoming civilized'.

Of course, it would clearly be very risky indeed to project accounts of social life recorded among Piro people in the late twentieth century far back into the past, but I think that we have no choice but to do so judiciously. If Piro people's accounts of their social life appear as a transformed variant of the ritual cannibalism of the sixteenth-century Tupinambá of the Brazilian coast, this is very unlikely to be a product of the respective colonial histories of either people. It is far more likely to be a product of the ways in which indigenous Amazonian peoples have always thought about social life as an ongoing temporal process, and consequently of how they enact it in historical time.

Thinking of Piro people as the servants of trade as a temporal project helps us to understand why they so rapidly shifted allegiance from the Franciscan priests to the traders-cum-rubber bosses in the 1880s, in the fateful move that was to lead them to lose their considerable military and political independence. My suggestion is that Piro people in the 1880s saw in the rubber traders a new and better kind of white people than the Franciscan priests, ones far better suited to fill the 'possessor of objects' function for them. Experience would have been a reasonable guide here, for trading expeditions to the Bajo Ucayali and beyond would have given them a sense of the conflicts between the Franciscans and civil Republican authorities (see Gow 1991: 35–7). And beyond them, they would have heard of, and had some contacts with, Brazilians. But I doubt that the knowledge and experience of this multiplicity would have meant so much to Piro people were they not already attributing some kind of ongoing doubling to the *kajine*.

To make this argument, it is not necessary to posit that Piro people in the late nineteenth century were telling Tsla mythology in the form in which it is known from a century later, nor that such myths provided the template for Piro people's reception of the traders. In the absence of any positive evidence, and in the light both of Lévi-Strauss's theory of myth and the analysis of this book, such an assumption would trade all the advances made in the analysis of myth as a historical object for the very dubious advantage of a 'just so story' about how Piro people came to be how they were in the 1980s. The Tsla mythology recorded in the latter half of the twentieth century is just as much a product of historical transformations as are Piro people's ideas of the origins of their social lives or the specific content of those social lives. It is conceivable that Piro people in the late nineteenth century were telling Tsla mythology in much the same form that their descendants were telling it a century later, and just about conceivable that such myths informed their actions with regard to the rubber bosses. But even if this were true, we have no evidence for it, and so any claim that those Piro people were thinking of their circumstances through Tsla mythology can never go beyond hypothesis or prejudice.

Instead, all that is necessary for my argument here are two more plausible and stronger claims to historical continuity: firstly, an enduring expulsion of twinning from the Piro lived world on to a distant other; and secondly, an enduring identification of that distant other with the 'possessor of objects' function. To claim that Piro people in past generations found coexistent twins as logically impossible as they did in the 1980s is not likely to generate much controversy, at least within Americanist circles. Equally, to claim that Piro people in past generations, like their descendants in the 1980s, posited the existence of other, better, 'possessors of objects' beyond their current *kajitu* trade partners seems as uncontroversial (see Helms 1988). But if these two simple claims are accepted, they have major consequences, for these enduring relations would have led Piro people consistently to respond to the crises of their lived worlds by searching out new and better trade partners on the edges of the known. This radical consequence of accepting two simple claims would in turn radically transform our understanding of the colonial history of Peruvian Amazonia. Now, far from being the privileged moment of the rupture of otherness into the region, the first Europeans to meet Piro people would become simply another form of others to enter a lived world richly provided with the means for exploring their potential.

We are here faced with a very unfamiliar form of continuity. What does it mean to say that Piro people have, over the centuries, shifted from one other to the next, and in the process constantly re-fashioned themselves in the eyes of the others, and in their own? What kind of continuity inheres in such ceaseless change? A model here lies in my account of transformations of transformations. The shifts I have discussed in styles of clothing, shamanry or ritual life over the twentieth century are genuine changes, and must be understood as such by the analyst. They are understood to be so by Piro people. But they do not raise, for Piro people, the problem of continuity and change, for Piro people know that they are transformations of transformations. For example, 'ancient people's clothing' and 'white people's clothing' are certainly different, but they are transformational versions of the same transformation that all clothing effects.

For people who live in a cosmos where men can put on white-lipped peccary clothing, or jaguars can dress like humans, the decision 'to look like white people' is not as dramatic, nor as catastrophic, an act as it has struck many outsiders. If there is here a major difference between coming to 'look like' white-lipped peccaries and jaguars and coming to 'look like' white people, it is that anthropologists and other foreign visitors to the area have imagined themselves to be white people, and hence to have known more than Piro people about what that term might mean. They have seldom tried to do what I have attempted here, that is, imagine what white people look like from Piro people's point of view.

The problem of the dramatic transformation in Piro people's lives over the century from the 1880s turns out to be less a problem in the continuity of the Piro lived world, and more a problem in the way in which anthropologists and other foreign visitors to Amazonia habitually think about the indigenous peoples of the region. A certain under-analysed way of thinking about indigenous

Amazonian peoples assumes that their ideas about the world, all those stories about men who become white-lipped peccaries and all those thoughts about clothing, are intrinsically fragile when confronted by historical change. Such ideas cannot, we imagine, long survive contact with the harsh realities of the world as it truly is. This leads outside observers and analysts to search for evidence of change, and to attribute to all the changes that they do find a portentous historical significance that these probably do not have for indigenous Amazonian peoples. Because we assume their ideas to be so fragile, we do not bother to enquire into their historical trajectories, or even to ask seriously about their real world meanings. We therefore miss out on how such ideas might actually inform the ways in which indigenous Amazonian people live the lives they do, and on the potentially profound continuities hidden within their mercurial transformations.

Hot and Cold Societies Meet

At the end of this long book devoted to radical changes, we are led to consider long-term continuities. Space does not permit any in-depth investigation of such continuities here, but even the restricted historical analysis presented in this study raises an important point about them. If we consider the recent history of Piro people, we are forced to see it as an ongoing struggle to live at a certain scale. Against often great odds, Piro people over the past hundred years or so have tried to imagine, and to put into effect, modes of living well, ways of living in egalitarian communities marked by high levels of tranquillity and generosity between kinspeople.[5] For these people, the desire to live well, and to live well in this specific way, has been a potent one, and one they seek to effect in their lives, through the making of villages. As I described in Chapter 1, the very fact of the existence of Santa Clara village, in 1980 when I first saw it, was the product of the collective desire of its inhabitants to live in a certain way, to live well.

In their concern to maintain egalitarian relations and a high degree of unanimity in their values, the Piro communities that I got to know in the early 1980s corresponded closely to Lévi-Strauss's definition of a 'cold society' (see Charbonnier 1969: 32–42). In the Introduction, I discussed how Lévi-Strauss's distinction between cold and hot societies has often been interpreted by other anthropologists as the refusal, on the part of that author, to attribute a history to certain kinds of people. This is of course untrue, for Lévi-Strauss is clear that all societies have histories, and his distinction refers to the specific mode by which different societies imagine themselves in relation to the past. But another, and perhaps more important point has been lost in this debate, which

---

[5] Of course, some Piro people refuse the whole thing, and have left the Bajo Urubamba for long periods or permanently, to seek other fortunes elsewhere. Their notions of 'living well' must necessarily be very different to anything I ever learned in Santa Clara.

is the extremely strong negative connotation that Lévi-Strauss gives to 'hot societies', with their generation of extreme social inequalities as their primary dynamic.

As is clear from this book, Piro people have, throughout the past century and more, been engaged with various kinds of people who are clearly from 'hot societies', people who have inserted Piro people into a variety of social hierarchies. These people, from rubber bosses through missionaries to anthropologists, voice their own activities as historically meaningful, dedicated to the progressive transformation of the world and the genesis of new values. Of course, the transformations sought and the values generated vary greatly as we pass from one category of such people to another, but these differences cannot mask the underlying commonality to the 'heat' with which they are attributed, the singular concern on the part of all of those white people with 'progress', an attribute to be passed from themselves to Piro people. In these circumstances, it is hardly surprising that Piro people should have come to adopt a variant of such images of the past themselves, and that they, too, recount their past in progressive ways, as when they told me in the 1980s that they had become 'civilized'.

As I said in the Introduction, I found Piro people's images of their past deeply rebarbative, and I could not imagine why anyone would choose to present themselves in such a clearly unflattering light. In the course of writing this book, however, certain features of those historical narratives have begun to appear more significant to me, and to take on a different meaning. If we look at Piro people's accounts of their history, one feature above all stands out: initiating action is consistently attributed to the various different kinds of white people, while succeeding generations of Piro people react to those actions. In these narratives, white people are marked by their agency, while Piro people are patient. As we have seen throughout this study, these narratives are false on this point, for Piro people throughout the recent past have actively formulated visions of the future and initiated interactions with outsiders. So, if Piro people wanted to present themselves as initiatory agents in their past, they do not lack for the materials with which to do so. But they do not.

The analysis of the present book suggests a reason why this might be so. In order to retain the scale of their lives, Piro people in their historical narratives actively expel initiatory agency outwards from themselves. Radical historical transformation is not, these stories endlessly stress, a mode of action proper to Piro people. It is attributed to others, to non-Piro people, with all of its 'heat', its dangerous implications of social differentiation and inequality. Luckily, the different kinds of white people lie immediately to hand for this task, and they are usually perfectly flattered by these stories, which they take as compliments. On the whole, these white people like progress, and to have their self-evident differences to Piro people read as inequalities. It is only the occasional romantic anthropologist like myself who finds Piro people's historical narratives so unattractive, and who consequently ponders them more deeply. Only such a person would notice the sting they carry, the way in which Piro people continue to attribute to all kinds of white people social values and sets of action they themselves despise and fear: a love of social inequalities and a pridefulness in world transformational action. White people, as Piro people say, are not very thoughtful about social life.

What Piro people gain by such attributions is living well as both a value and as a fact. They are able to live in those villages filled with people much like themselves, constantly sharing food with each other, visiting and being visited, and talking over all the minor events of the day. Nothing much ever happens, and I, used to a more rapid pace of life and with the short attention span of my 'hot society', was initially often very bored living there. As the new pace of life grew on me, I began to notice its virtues, in the easy companionship, the minute attention to shifting moods that are subtly expressed, and all the time and space needed to attend to a natural world of such beauty and variety, where the river, the forest, and the sky are ceaselessly changing. When the time came to return, I did so with genuine regret at having to leave these people, and I felt strongly the justice of their reproach, 'Why go back to your land? Stay here. Here we live well.'

For a long time, I imagined that the interest Piro people showed in my tales about the ways of the *gringos* lay in their sense that they had come to inhabit a new and threatening world, in which the ideas and values of their ancestors could be no guide for them. This was true, in part, for Piro people do, indeed, believe that white people have important knowledge. It has taken me much longer to understand the interest that they take in their ancestors' knowledge, the 'ancient people's stories', those myths that they listen to and tell, over and over again in the long quiet evenings on the Urubamba. My late *compadre* Artemio's story about that man who went under the earth and became a white-lipped peccary, told to me in a conversation that seemed to deny the meaning of such myths, began the process of change. Insistent within my thoughts, this story demanded of me that I seek to understand it, and in so doing, it has led me to a new understanding of Piro people's lives.

When I first heard 'A Man who went under the Earth', I took it to be a metaphor for my condition, but that story had other ideas. It always pointed away from myself towards the lives of Piro people, to what interests them, and to their attention to the things around them. And so tonight, as I turn into my street, tired and troubled from the day's work, I see Orion, gleaming majestic in the winter sky over Walthamstow. In wonder, I follow the line of Orion's Belt and find the dimly shimmering Pleiades. Artemio's story, and all the thinking it has made me do, reminds me of that evening in my childhood when my father first taught me how to navigate from the Great Bear to the Pole Star. This use of our senses, so easily lost in a world of strong streetlights and strong egos, is restored to me now by a Piro myth.

APPENDIX

Myth Texts

1: Myths of the Sun And Peccaries

'The King Vultures who carry the Sun', by Roselia Pacaya García (Nies 1972: 108–13).
Date unknown.

Now I am going to tell about the sun. It is said that the king vultures carried the sun in a canoe. Some of them steered the canoe from the poop, while others would pole the canoe. In the morning it was cool, but as the sun rose higher, it got hotter and hotter. As they got further up, the heat was terrible. Nobody could stand it.

The sun travelled along seated in the middle of the canoe, shining fiercely. When the sun got to the position of three o'clock, the heat was going down. When it was late and the sun was about to set, it no longer was hot.

It is said that day after day the king vultures carried the sun like this. When it was midday exactly, the king vultures returned to their houses to eat, after resting a little. In the morning, before it was too hot, the king vultures gave food to the sun, and he also ate. But in the intense heat of midday, nobody could bear him. Thus, the king vultures carried the sun, sitting in the canoe, to wherever they wanted to go. How hard was the work of carrying the sun!

They say that when the canoe reached that point, they left the sun and each went to his own house. The king vulture is the chief of the vultures, and so he went where he wanted, to his own house.

Just so, this finishes the story about the king vultures who carried the sun.

'The Canoe of the Sun', by an unknown teller (Ricardo Alvarez 1960: 50–1). Date
unknown.

For the Piro, the sun is a celestial body which moves in rotation around the earth in the span of a day and a night.

The sun has some auxiliary satellites: these are the *tuyuyos* (*shajmegirí*), large and blackened birds discoloured by the burning sun, in an infinite number. These animals, such tireless paddlers, pole without cease to take the sun from one end to the other of the earth. At midday the sun, from the highest point of the sky, stops a short while to make his food and that of his paddlers. On the best beach, fifty *tuyuyos* stop the canoe and leave the sun. Ten search for firewood, ten bring water, ten make food for the polers, and twenty cook for the sun. The sun needs more cooks because he eats a lot: while each paddler eats a plate of food, the sun eats a pot full of food and drinks a huge quantity of *chicha*.

Again they continue on their trajectory, poling without stopping. At nightfall they arrive at the opposite edge of the earth. Then they pole faster to be able to go underground through a narrow canyon or *pongo*, without going too far. If it should happen that one day they fail to go through the *pongo*, the sun will be smashed to pieces and darkness will cover the earth.

Below the earth the sun travels on to rise at dawn the next day in the same place from where it started: and thus, without stopping until midday, he continues his journey day after day until he fails to enter the *pongo*.

That is the life of the sun and his satellites. He lights the world because he travels across it. At night, he does not light it because he is journeying below it. The sun will go out for good when his satellites or polers are careless and hit the rocks at the mouth of the *pongo*.

'The Shallow River', by Juan Sebastián Pérez Etene (Sebastián, Zumaeta, and Nies 1974: 90–7), Date 1968.

Now I am going to tell you about the shallow river. You young people will have to listen carefully to discover if these stories are true or not.

According to the ancient people, it is said that there is another world below this one which is called 'the shallow river'. There are two different stories.

According to the first story, the first person who got there was guided by the white-lipped peccaries, which he had followed by entering their hole, down into the other world. There he saw a shallow river, where there were all kinds of fish, among them the *kolyo*. There lived there a woman called Kmaklewakleto, who raised the white-lipped peccaries as pets.

There lived there a great number of white-lipped peccaries of every kind: fat, thin, big, and small. There was one kind called *koshichineru*, which had white cheeks, and another kind called *manxineru*.

The man who discovered this world, lived there a little time and then when he came back here, he told that he had found a world beneath the earth, that one which had the shallow river.

In the second story, the shallow river was discovered by another man who wounded some white-lipped peccaries with his arrows. The white-lipped peccaries then fled from there to their hole, which they went down.

The man followed them, tracking them by the blood they had spilt. Then, when he got to the hole they had gone down, he heard a noise like a river.

Then the man entered the hole, and going forward little by little, arrived in the other world, where he saw again the blood of the white-lipped peccaries. Crossing the river, he arrived at the place where the woman called Kmaklewakleto lived.

This one, on seeing her injured white-lipped peccaries, cried out, 'Ay! What has happened to you this time? Have they shot you again?'. Then, as she cured them, pulling out the splinters of the arrows that had stuck into their bodies, she continued complaining, 'That's why I don't like letting my pets out, because people mistreat them.'

Thus we have these two stories of the existence of a world below this one, that which is known by the name of 'The Shallow River'. In this generation, nobody has entered this place, but the white-lipped peccaries do have their holes by which they enter and leave.

But the truth is that the white-lipped peccaries disappear from time to time and are no longer seen, then after a few years they reappear everywhere in the forest and along the rivers. Also, some hunters tell that the white-lipped peccaries have their hole where they go in and come out, and from the hole you can hear the noise of the herd that goes about beneath the earth.

For this reason, the ancient people said that there was a world below the earth where the white-lipped peccaries were raised, and that world was called 'The Shallow River'.

Because of this, on hearing this story, think about whether it is true or not.

'The Mother of the White-Lipped Peccaries', by an unknown teller (Ricardo Alvarez 1960: 152–3). Date unknown.

Long ago only the species of white-lipped peccaries known in the forest were those which the Piro classified as of the families of the Koshichinari and the Manchinari. But they were wild animals and they destroyed the gardens of manioc and maize, and the plantain gardens, and caused other troubles to the villagers, with the particular problem that nobody could kill them with arrows, for, as soon as they scented people, they would flee inside the earth to hide themselves.

The damage was such that the Piro decided to seek the advice of shamans [orig. *brujos*] to exterminate them. In the meeting it was decided to give the shaman with most prestige the task.

This shaman went down under the earth, following the tracks of the white-lipped peccaries, walking for five days and nights. At the end of this period, he found the great city of the white-lipped peccaries, set out in lots separated by wide streets. Each lot was fenced in with *pona* (palm bark) to the height of two metres. In the centre of the city was the palace of the 'Mother of the White-Lipped Peccaries'.

The shaman went to talk to the mother of the white-lipped peccaries, who received him with solicitude and courtesy. Afterwards, she took him around all the farms [orig. *estancias*], explaining to him the distinct characteristics of the white-lipped peccaries. There were peccaries of the Koshichinari family, black and small, which went up to the earth; others of the Payoneri, round and fat; of the Manchineri, with white feet; of the Kakoaleneri, fat and reddish; of the Gimekaneri, which are the biggest; and of the Hahamlineri, which are very wild, and jump at their fence to escape to the earth.

The mother of the peccaries also told the Piro shaman that all the peccaries obey her call and they never flee from her presence. She showed him the trumpets with which she called each family to shut them up in their appropriate pen.

The Piro man was amazed by the fabulous numbers of peccaries that there were there, and thought that they would be an excellent meat for the men of the earth.

The mother of the peccaries invited the shaman to sleep there that night. The Piro man happily agreed. But when the mother of the peccaries was snoring, the shaman stole the trumpets with which she called her children, and fled back to the earth. When he had walked several hours, although it was still night, he played the trumpets and the peccaries jumped and broke their pens, and ran one after the other towards the sound of the trumpets.

When the mother woke up she discovered her peccaries gone. She went to find her trumpets and found them missing too. Then she cursed the Piro man, but without effect, for the Piro man was a great shaman, of greater power than the mother of the peccaries.

Since then the forest is populated with white-lipped peccaries, which are a tasty and abundant food, thanks to the Piro *kahonchi*, 'shaman', who knew how to snatch them away from the mother would kept them under the earth.

2: Myths of the Moon

'Klana, the discontented woman', by an unknown teller (Ricardo Alvarez 1960: 98–9). Date unknown.

Klana was a woman who had several husbands, and still wanted more. She wanted to marry the moon and she even stretched out her hand for him to grab her and take her with him. But the moon did not want her, for one of Klana's husbands was the moon's brother. Due to this rejection, Klana fled into the forest, and went to the house of the little bird Komshi to help her make clay pots, for that was the work of Komshi.

But the youngest brother of the moon, who did not have a wife, wanted Klana. But when he realized that, Klana had already fled. But the youth, called Kamayaka, ran after Klana in the company of the owl, who was his friend. The two searched for Klana day and night without rest. Several days passed and they did not find her. Finally they came to Komshi's house and asked her if she had seen Klana go by. Komshi said that she had passed by five rainy seasons before. Kamayaka did not believe Komshi.

Kamayaka wanted to look under the clay pots to see if she was hidden there, but Komshi threatened him with a stick to not touch the pots because, she said, they were unfired and could break. Kamayaka and Komshi argued for a long time, and they were at the point of fighting.

While they were involved in the discussion, the owl raise a pot and Klana was there. The owl said, 'Kamayaka, here is Klana.' Kamayaka went to see her, he greeted her and asked, 'Why did you run away?' Klana replied, 'Because I have no husband.' Kamayaka said, 'I will be your husband.' Klana said, 'Take me with you.'

Kamayaka took Klana to his house, which was the house of the moon. But Klana still wanted to go on looking for other husbands and every so often she would run off to find them and she always did.

Among the Piro people, the name Klana is a symbol of a woman of the festive life.

'The Moon's Festival', by an unknown teller (Ricardo Alvarez 1960: 76–9). Date unknown.

A young Piro man was promised in marriage to a young girl, also Piro, who was an orphan and who had been raised by the youth's parents. But before the performance of her initiation ritual and the marriage of the girl, the young man died. The girl and his mother cried inconsolably at the youth's death.

The young man's mother watched over the girl day and night so that no other man could make love to her. She told her she would be beaten to death if she abandoned them to follow another husband. But the girl behaved well, remaining faithful to her parents-in-law, worked hard and did not leave the house.

One night the dead man came to the house and entered the hammock in which the girl slept. The mother-in-law saw someone get in, and picked up a burning piece of wood from the fire to see who it was. She saw nobody. She woke up the girl, and asked about her vision, but the girl knew nothing either, only that she had seen her dead husband-to-be in a dream, and that perhaps this vision had been real for the mother.

The old woman believed this too. Because of this she cried without out cease both day and night.

The next day, the uncles and other kinspeople of the dead man went fishing in the small streams. They set off in several canoes. One of these was crewed by a lame uncle, who was not well suited to steer the canoe because of the defect in one of his legs. Thus, while the rest of the people were returning from the fishing, the lame man had not yet reached the stream, but he would not return home without having fished. He continued going up-river all alone and saw watermelons and peanuts on a beach. He stopped to eat some of these fruit. There he saw a man with a black cotton robe and with his eyes covered, picking up the watermelons with his toes, passing them to his hands, and studying them beneath the cloth which covered his head. He looked like the dead nephew, because when they laid him out, they had covered his eye. But the uncle did not dare to speak to him. But when the unknown man noticed that someone was nearby, he raised the cloth and recognized his uncle. 'How are you, uncle?' he said to him. The uncle wept from emotion. The dead man said, 'Don't weep, uncle, because I am alive and well. Before, my body hurt, but now nothing pains me, I am happy'. The uncle continued to weep. The dead man went on, 'Uncle, go to my mother's house and tell them to make lots of maize and manioc beer, because in five days I will go there to perform the initiation ritual and marry. But nobody else must know this but you and my mother.'

The lame man went home, leaving off fishing, and ran to tell his sister what he had seen. The sister did not believe him, but she cried at the memory he brought her of her son. That same day at sunset, when the woman went to the river to fetch water, her son arrived and said, 'Mother, make manioc beer, maize beer and peanut beer because my wife will perform initiation ritual.' The old mother believed him because she could see him. And so she did as he said. She told the other women so that they might help her make manioc and maize beer. All were willing and made an abundance of beer, without knowing what festival they were to celebrate.

Five days later the beer was ready. At nightfall, the dead man came down from the sky. Everyone saw him and recognized him. They cried with emotion. He told them, 'Don't cry, are you sad because I have come back to life and returned to my house?' More people arrived from the sky, until the plaza was full. They began to drink manioc beer, to dance and to sing. Now there were no living or dead people, everyone was equally happy. There were no strangers, all treated each other as kinspeople.

At midnight, when everyone was already drunk, the moon descended with a large bunch of people. The wife that the man had in the after life came as well, as did her parents. They came to celebrate the initiation ritual on earth to join the Piro man. They brought manioc beer, a thick and white manioc beer with a gelatinous substance that looked like worms. The moon invited the earth people to drink his manioc beer but it revolted them because it looked like worms. The earth people invited the moon's people to drink their manioc beer, but in turn they refused because they had brought their own beer. Only those who were performing the initiation ritual drank the manioc beer of the sky even although it looked like worms. It made them strong and agile. Because of this, they invited their kinspeople to drink it. The moon's people insistently invited the earth people to drink, saying, 'Our manioc beer gives strength and life, one who drinks it will never die, he will never become old and he will change his skin.' But nobody wanted to drink it.

The festival continued animatedly. They played the drums and the flutes, everyone dancing. The moon was drunk, dancing and singing without remembering that he had to leave the earth before the sun rose. Because the moon was drunk, his companions did not want to tell that dawn was close, for they wanted the festival to go on for days, until the beer was finished. Neither did the earth people want to warn the moon, for they wanted to celebrate with the moon's people.

But in that village was a boy of the Machiguenga people called, 'Yopokapige', who was a servant of the Piros. He was also drunk. At the first light of dawn, he shouted, 'It's about to be morning, the sun is going to rise!' The moon heard him, took the beer, and set off for the sky. His people followed him as well as those who had come before them, along with the dead Piro man and his wife from the after-life. They all left drunk, singing and playing the drum and flute.

The earth people wept from sorrow. But they beat the boy who told the moon about the dawn to death. They continued to drink until the beer ran out.

The dead man came every week to visit his wife. After a year, he took his wife and his mother to the sky, and none of them ever returned.

3: The birth of Tsla

'The Birth of Tsla', by Antonio Urquía, Santa Clara village. Date 8 January 1982.

Tsla was a small man, stunted, but he was powerful. He could change anything. My grandmother told me that Tsla was building his house at the Pongo de Mainique. He was like Inca, he had workers who served him. One of these was Kamayaka. He was sent down to fetch water. A *saltón* (a giant catfish: Piro, *katsalo*; Lat. *Brachyplatystoma filamentosum*) swallowed him and he was taken off down-river.

Tsla waited and waited, but Kamayaka didn't appear. So Tsla and the Muchkajine, who were also his workers, went to follow the *saltón*. They followed it and caught it at the mouth of the Mishahua river. They took Kamayaka from the belly of the fish. There Kamayaka made his house. There is a huge cliff there. But a little bird sang there, and on account of this, Kamayaka went down-river, no one knows where.

The mother of Tsla was a human and she wandered in the forest, looking for flowers. One she put on her belly and from inside Tsla told her to stop it.

Her husbands were a herd of jaguars, but at that time, they were men. Her mother-in-law told the woman to remove their lice. All the jaguars were seated in a circle, and she went round delousing them. But their lice were big fleas, and she choked. The jaguars leapt on her and ate her.

The mother of the jaguars took the womb, saying that this was her piece and she hung it on a achiote bush. Then three *maracanitos* (parrot sp.; Piro, *saweto*) came out. These were Tsla and his brothers the Muchkajine. One of these was Kamayaka. I don't know the name of the other.

Soon, they grew. The Muchkajine were normal sized, but Tsla was small, but powerful. Tsla always cried for his mother.

One day, Tsla decided to avenge his mother. With his brothers, he went to a lake where they put spikes of bamboo (Ucayali Spanish, *paca*) in the water at the bank.

A jaguar came along and said, 'What are you doing?' 'We're playing,' they said. Tsla dived into the water, then the Muchkajine, but because of Tsla's powers, they were unharmed. The jaguar jumped in and stuck to the bamboo spikes. Tsla cut out his heart and put it in a pot to cook. Then another jaguar came along, and they did the same to him. Thus were they getting rid of the jaguars. The last was suspicious, but they got him to dive in.

Tsla had the task of cutting out their hearts and putting them in the pot. Along came the grandmother, who was called Yompichkajru.[1] She asked him what he was cooking, and he told her that the hearts in the pot were pigeons. But she suspected the truth, and fled into the forest. Because she was pregnant at the time, there are now jaguars in the forest. If Tsla had been able to kill her, there would no longer be jaguars. It is from her that the jaguars of today come.

Tsla and the Muchkajine went into the forest. There they met a monster, the spirit of the forest (orig.: *un monstruo, el duende del monte*]. They fought with him. He beat the Muchkajine, but Tsla beat him. He ate people, this monster.

They married his daughter, Eriana. They lived in his house, which seemed to be a good house, but it was only made of feathers. The wind blew it away.

Tsla went into the forest and climbed a tree to capture parrots. He found three little parrots in the nest. He threw one down to the monster, who kissed it. He threw the second one down, and again the monster kissed it. Tsla told the last one to peck the monster when he tried to kiss him. So, he threw it down. The monster made to kiss it, and the little parrot pecked his mouth. So, it remained crooked.

---

[1] Matteson gives this name as Yomchikgigojre (1951: 43) while Antonio's later version called her Yompichgojru (see Chapter 4).

REFERENCES

ALVAREZ, FRANCISCO. (1951). La vieja a quien se escapó el alma. *Misiones Dominicanas* 32: 101–3.

ALVAREZ, RICARDO. (1959). Galería de Piros ilustres: Manuel Saavedra. *Misiones Dominicanas* 40: 41–52.

——(1960). *Los Piros*. Lima: Litografía Universo.

——(1962). Ritos piros de la Iniciación 1. *Misiones Dominicanas* 43: 35–9.

——(1963). Ritos piros de la Iniciación 2. *Misiones Dominicanas* 44: 8–13.

——(1970). *Los Piros: Hijos de Dioses*. Lima: Heraclio Fournier S.A.

——(1984). *Tsla: Estudio Etno-histórico del Urubamba y Alto-Ucayali*. Salamanca: Editorial San Esteban.

AMICH, J. (1975). *Historia de las Misiones del Convento de Santa Rosa de Ocopa*. Lima: Editorial Milla Bastres.

ANDERSON, R. J. (ed). (1986). *Cuentos Folklóricos de los Asheninca*. Vol. 2. Yarinacocha: Instituto Lingüístico de Verano.

BAER, G. (1974). The Pahotko-masks of the Piro (Eastern Peru). *Bulletin de la Société Suisse des Américanistes*, 38: 7–16.

——(1976-7). Masken der Piro, Shipibo und Matsigenka (Ost-Peru). *Verhandlungen der Naturforschenden Gesellschaft in Basel*, 87/88: 101–15.

——(1994). *Cosmologia y Shamanismo de los Matsiguenga (Perú Oriental)*. Quito: Ediciones Abya-Yala.

BASSO, E. (1985). *A Musical View of the Universe: Kalapalo Myth and Ritual Performance*. Philadelphia: Univerity of Pennsylvania Press.

——(1987). *In Favor of Deceit: A Study of Tricksters in an Amazonian Society*. Tucson: The University of Arizona Press.

——(1995). *The Last Cannibals: A South American Oral History*. Austin: University of Texas Press.

BERTRAND-ROUSSEAU, P. (1983). De como los Shipibo y otras Tribus aprendieron a hacer los Dibujos (tipicos) y a adonarse. *Amazonía Peruana*, 9: 79–85.

BIEDMA, M. (1981). *La Conquista Franciscana del Alto Ucayali* [Introduction and Annotations by Antonino Tibesar]. Lima: Editorial Milla Bastres.

BLANK, L. and J. BOGAN (eds.). (1984). *Burden of Dreams: Screenplay, Journals, Reviews, Photographs*. Berkeley, Calif.: North Atlantic Books.

BOAS, F. (n.d.). *Introduction to the Handbook of American Indian Languages*. Washington D.C.: Georgetown University School of Languages and Linguistics.

BODLEY, J. H. (1970). 'Campa Socio-Economic Adaptation' (unpublished manuscript). Ann Arbor, Mich.

——(1982). *Victims of Progress*. 2nd edn. Menlo Park, Calif.: Benjamin/pummings Publishing Company, Inc.

BROWN, M. F. and E. FERNANDEZ. (1991). *War of Shadows: The Struggle for Utopia in the Peruvian Amazon*. Berkeley, Los Angeles, and Oxford: University of California Press.

CAMINO, A. (1977). Trueque, Correrías e Intercambios entre los Quechuas Andinos y los Piro y Machiguenga de la Montaña Amazonía Peruana. *Amazonia Peruana*, 1(2): 123–42.

BROWN, P. *et al.* (1992). Book Review Forum: M. Strathern, *The Gender of the Gift*. *Pacific Studies* 15(1): 123–59.

CHAPMAN, A. (1982). *Drama and Power in a Hunting Society: The Selk'nam of Tierra del Fuego*. Cambridge: Cambridge University Press.

CHARBONNIER, G. (1969). *Conversations with Claude Lévi-Strauss*. London: Jonathan Cape.

CHAUMEIL, J.-P. (1988). 'Le Huambisa défenseur: La figure de l'Indien dans la chamanisme populaire (région d'Iquitos, Pérou)'. *Recherches Amérindiennes au Québec*, 18(2–3): 115–26.

DA MATTA, R. (1971). Myth and anti-myth among the Timbira. In P. and E. Maranda (eds.), *Structural Analysis of Oral Tradition*. Philadelphia: University of Pennsylvania Press.

D'ANS, A.-M. (1982). *L'Amazonie péruvienne indigéne*. Paris: Payot.

DEBOER, W. and J. S. RAYMOND. (1987). Roots Revisited: the Origins of the Shipibo Art Style. *Journal of Latin American Lore* 13(1): 115–32.

DESCOLA, P. (1994). *In the Society of Nature: A Native Ecology in Amazonia*. Cambridge: Cambridge University Press.

——(1992). Societies of Nature and the Nature of Society. In Adam Kuper (ed.) *Conceptualizing Society*. London: Routledge.

——(1996). *The Spears of Twilight: Life and Death in the Amazon Jungle*. London: HarperCollins.

——(1998). Estrutura ou Sentimento: A relação com o Animal na Amazônia. *Mana* 4(1): 23–45.

——and A. C. TAYLOR. (1993). Introduction à *La remontée de l'Amazone*. *L'Homme* 126–8: 13–24.

DREYFUS, S. (1993). Systèmes dravidiens à filiations cognatiques en Amazonie. *L'Homme* 126–28: 121–40.

EMMONS, L. H. (1997). *Neotropical Rainforest Mammals: A Field Guide*. Chicago and London: University of Chicago Press.

ERIKSON, P. (1987). De l'apprivoisement à l'apprivoisionnement: chasse, alliance et familiarisation en Amazonie amérindienne. *Technique et Culture* 9: 105–40.

FABIAN, S. M. (1992). *Space-Time of the Bororo of Brazil*. Gainsville: University Press of Florida.

FARABEE, W. C. (1922). *Indian Tribes of Eastern Peru*. Papers of the Peabody Museum of Archaeology and Ethnology, Harvard University, 10. Cambridge Mass.: Harvard University Press.

FIEDLER, A. (1951). *The River of the Singing Fish*. London: Readers Union with Hodder and Stoughton.

FOUCAULT, M. (1970). *The Order of Things*. London: Tavistock.

FORTES, M. (1958). Introduction. In J. R. Goody (ed.), *The Developmental Cycle of Domestic Groups*. Cambridge: Cambridge University Press.

FRY, C. (1889). *La gran region de los bosques; o, ríos peruanos navegables: Urubamba, Ucayali, Amazonas, Pachitea y Palcazú. Diario de viajes y exploraciones . . . 1886, 1887 y 1880*. 2 vols. Lima: Imprenta de B. Gil.

GADE, D. W. (1972). Comercio y Colonización en la Zona de Contacto entre la Sierra y las Tierras Bajas del Valle del Urubamba en el Peru. *Actas y Memorias del XXXIX Congreso Internacional de Americanistas* 4: 207–21.

GEBHART-SAYER, A. (1984). *The Cosmos Encoiled: Indian Art of the Peruvian Amazon.* New York: Center for InterAmerican Relations.

——(1985). The Geometric Designs of the Shipibo-Conibo in Ritual Context. *Journal of Latin American Lore* 11(2): 145–75.

GEERTZ, C. (1973). *The Interpretation of Cultures.* New York: Basic Books.

GINZBURG, C. (1989). *Clues, Myths, and the Historical Method.* Baltimore, Md.: Johns Hopkins University Press.

——(1992a). *Extasies: Deciphering the Witches' Sabbath.* London: Penguin.

——(1992b). *The Cheese and the Worms: The Cosmos of a Sixteenth-Century Miller.* London: Penguin.

GOODY, J. (1987). *The Interface Between the Written and the Oral.* Cambridge: Cambridge University Press.

GOSE, P. (1986). Sacrifice and the commodity form in the Andes. *Man* (n.s.) 21: 296–310.

GOULD, S. J. (1987). *Time's Arrow, Time's Cycle: Myth and Metaphor in the Discovery of Geological Time.* Cambridge, Mass. and London: Harvard University Press.

GOW, P. (1987). La Vida Monstruosa de las Plantas. *Amazonía Peruana* 14: 115–22.

——(1989). The Perverse Child: Desire in a Native Amazonian Subsistence Economy. Man (n.s.) 24: 299–314.

——(1989). Visual Compulsion: Design and Image in Western Amazonia. *Revindi* 2: 19–32.

——(1990a). Aprendiendo a defenderse': La Historia Oral y el Parentesco en el Bajo Urubamba. *Amazonía Indígena* 11: 10–16.

——(1990b). Could Sangama Read? The Origin of Writing among the Piro of Eastern Peru. *History and Anthropology* 5: 87–103.

——(1991). *Of Mixed Blood: Kinship and History in Peruvian Amazonia.* Oxford Studies in Social and Cultural Anthropology. Oxford: Oxford University Press.

——(1993). Gringos and Wild Indians: Images of History in Western Amazonian Cultures. *L'Homme* 126–28: 331–51.

——(1994). River People: Shamanism and History in Western Amazonia. In C. Humphrey and N. Thomas (eds.) *Shamanism, History and the State.* Ann Arbor: University of Michigan Press.

——(1995a) Land, People and Paper in Western Amazonia. In Eric Hirsch and Michael O'Hanlon (eds.), *The Anthropology of Landscape: Perspectives on Place and Space.* Oxford: Clarendon Press.

——(1995b). Cinema da Floresta: Filme, Alucinação e Sonho na Amazônia Peruana. *Revista de Antropologia* 38(2): 37–54.

——(1996). ¿Podía leer Sangama?: Sistemas graficas, Lenguaje y Shamanismo entre los Piro (Perú Oriental). In Fernando Santos Granero (ed.), *Globalización y Cambio en la Amazonía Indígena.* Vol. 1: Quito: FLACSO and Ediciones Abya Yala.

——(1997). O Parentesco como Consciência Humana: O Caso dos Piro. *Mana* 3(2): 39–65.

——(1999a). Piro Designs: Painting as Meaningful Action in an Amazonian Lived World. *Journal of the Royal Anthropological Institute (n.s.)* 5: 229–46.

——(1999b). A Geometria do Corpo. In Adauto Novaes (ed.), *A Outra Margem do Ocidente,* Sao Paulo: MINC-FUNARTE/pompanhia Das Letras.

GRAHAM, L. (1995). *Performing Dreams: Discourses of Immortality among the Xavante of Central Brazil.* Austin: University of Texas Press.

GREGOR, T (1977). *Mehinaku: The Drama of Daily Life in a Brazilian Indian Village.* Chicago and London: University of Chicago Press.

——(1985). *Anxious Pleasures: The Sexual Lives of Amazonian People.* Chicago and London: University of Chicago Press.

HARNER, M. (1972). *The Jívaro: People of the Sacred Waterfalls.* London: Robert Hale and Company

HEATH, C. (1980). 'El Tiempo nos venció: La situación actual de los Shipibos del Rio Ucayali. *Boletín de Lima* 5: 3–14.

HECKENBERGER, M. (1996). War and Peace in the Shadow of Empire: Sociopolitical change in the Upper Xingú of Southeastern Amazonia, A.D. 1400–2000. Unpublished Ph. D., University of Pittsburgh, Penn.

HELMS, M. (1988). *Ulysses' Sail: An Ethnographic Odyssey of Power, Knowledge and Geographical Distance.* Princeton, NJ: Princeton University Press.

HILL, J. D. (1993). *Keepers of the Sacred Chants: The Poetics of Ritual Power in an Amazonian Society.* Tucson and London: University of Arizona Press.

——(ed.). (1988). *Rethinking History and Myth: Indigenous South American Perspectives on the Past.* Urbana and Chicago: University of Illinois Press.

HUGH-JONES, C. (1979). *From the Milk River: Spatial and Temporal Processes in Northwest Amazonia.* Cambridge: Cambridge University Press.

HUGH-JONES, S. (1979). *The Palm and the Pleiades: Initiation and Cosmology in Northwest Amazonia.* Cambridge: Cambridge University Press.

——(1988). The Gun and the Bow: Myths of White Men and Indians. *L'Homme* 106–7: 138–55.

——(1992). Yesterday's Luxuries, Tomorrow's Necessities; Business and Barter in Northwest Amazonia. In Caroline Humphrey and Stephen Hugh-Jones (eds.), *Barter, Exchange and Value: An anthropological approach.* Cambridge: Cambridge University Press.

HUXLEY, M. and C. CAPA. (1965). *Farewell to Eden.* London: Chatto and Windus.

INGOLD, T. (1986). *The Evolution of Social Life.* Cambridge: Cambridge University Press.

IRELAND, E. (1988). Cerebral Savage: The Whitemen as Symbol of Cleverness and Savagery in Waurá Myth. In J. Hill (ed.).

KENSINGER, K. M., et al. (1975). *The Cashinahua of Eastern Peru.* Boston: Haffenreffer Museum of Anthropology.

KINDBERG, L. (comp.). (1980). *Diccionario Ashaninca.* Yarinacocha: Instituto Lingüístico de Verano.

KUECHLER, S. (1987). Malanggan: Art and Memory in a Melanesian Society. *Man* (n.s.), 22: 238–55.

KULICK, D. (1998). *Travestí: Sex, Gender and Culture among Brazilian Transgendered Prostitutes.* Chicago and London: University of Chicago Press.

LATHRAP, D. W. (1970). *The Upper Amazon.* London: Thames and Hudson.

——(1976). Shipibo Tourist Art. In N. H. Graburn (ed.), *Ethnic and Tourist Arts: Cultural Expressions from the Fourth World.* Berkeley, Calif.: University of California Press.

——A. Gebhart-Sayer and A. Mester. (1985). The Roots of the Shipibo Art Style: Three Waves on Imiriacocha or there were 'Incas' before the Incas. *Journal of Latin American Lore* 11(1): 31–120.

——T. Myers, A. Gebhart-Sayer, and A. Mester. (1987). Further Discussion of the Roots of the Shipibo Art Style: A Rejoinder to DeBoer and Raymond. *Journal of Latin American Lore* 13(2): 225–72.

Leach, E. R. (1954). *The Political Systems of Highland Burma*. London: Bell.

——(1961). *Rethinking Anthropology*. London: Athlone Press.

Lévi-Strauss, C. (1963). *Structural Anthropology*. New York and London: Basic Books, Inc.

——(1966). *The Savage Mind*. London: Weidenfeld and Nicholson.

——(1970). *The Raw and the Cooked*. London: Jonathan Cape.

——(1973). *From Honey to Ashes*. London: Jonathan Cape.

——(1976a). *Tristes Tropiques*. London: Penguin Books.

——(1976b [1942]). Guerra e comércio entre os índios da América do Sul. In E. Schaden (ed.), *Leituras de Etnologia Brasileira*. São Paulo: Nacional.

——(1977). *Structural Anthropology II*. London: Allen Lane.

——(1978). *The Origin of Table Manners*. London: Jonathan Cape.

——(1981). *The Naked Man*. London: Jonathan Cape.

——(1983). *The Way of Masks*. London: Jonathan Cape.

——(1988). *The Jealous Potter*. Chicago and London: University of Chicago Press.

——(1993). Un autre regard. *L'Homme* 126–8: 7–10.

——(1995). *The Story of Lynx*. Chicago and London: University of Chicago Press.

——(1997). *Look, Listen, Read*. New York: Basic Books.

——(1998). Lévi-Strauss nos 90: A Antropologia de Cabeça para Baixo' [interview with Eduardo Viveiros de Castro]. *Mana*, 4(2): 119–26.

Lima, T. S. (1999). The two and its Many: Reflections on Perspectivism in a Tupi Cosmology. *Ethnos* 64(1): 107–31.

McCallum, C. (1989). *Gender, personhood and social organization amongst the Cashinahua of Western Amazonia*. Doctoral Thesis, The Univerity of London.

Malinowski, B. (1948). *Magic, Science and Religion and Other Essays*. Boston and Glencoe: Beacon Press and Free Press.

——(1968). *A Diary in the Strict Sense of the Term*. New York: Harcourt, Brace and World Inc.

Marcoy, P. (1869). *Voyages à travers l'Amérique du Sud de l'Océan Pacifique à l'Océan Atlantique*. Paris: Hachette.

Marx, K. (1969). The Eighteenth Brumaire of Louis Napoleon. In Karl Marx and Friedrich Engels, *Selected Works*, Vol. 1. Moscow: Progress Publishers.

Matteson, E. (1951). Piro Myths. *Kroeber Anthropological Society Papers* 4 : 37–87.

——(1953). *Pero Chijne Ginkakle (Resumen de la Historia del Perú)*. Lima: Ministerio de Educación Pública.

——(1954). The Piro of the Urubamba. *Kroeber Anthropological Society Papers* 10: 25–99.

——(1955). Sketch of Piro ethnography based on an analyzed text. *Anais do XXXI Congreso Internacional de Americanistas*, 1: 55–62. São Paulo, Brazil.

——(1965). *The Piro (Arawakan) Language*. Berkeley and Los Angeles: University of California Press.

MATTHIESSEN, P. (1962). *The Cloud Forest: A Chronicle of the South American Wilderness*. London: André Deutsch.

Maybury-Lewis, D. (ed.). (1979). *Dialectical Societies: The Gê and the Bororo of Central Brazil*. Cambridge, Mass.: Harvard University Press.

MENTORE, G. (1993). Tempering the Social Self: Body Adornment, Vital Substance and Knowledge among the Waiwai. *Journal of Archaeology and Anthropology*, 9: 22–34.

MIMICA, J. (1988). *Intimations of Infinity: The Mythopoeia of the Iqwaye Counting System and Number*. Oxford, New York, and Hamburg: Berg.

MUNN, N. D. (1973). *Walbiri Iconography: Graphic Representation and Cultural Symbolism in a Central Australian Society*. Ithaca, NY: Cornell University Press.

——(1977). The spatiotemporal transformations of Gawa canoes. *Journal de la Société des Océanistes* 33: 39–54.

——(1983). Gawan Kula: Spatiotemporal Control and the Symbolism of Influence. In J. W. Leach and E. R. Leach, *The Kula*. Cambridge: Cambridge University Press.

——(1986). *The Fame of Gawa: A Symbolic Study of Value Transformation in a Massim (Papua New Guinea) Society*. Cambridge: Cambridge University Press.

MYERS, T. P. (1974). Spanish Contacts and Social Change on the Ucayali River, Peru. *Ethnohistory* 21(2): 135–59.

——(1983). Redes de Intercambio Tempranas en la Hoya Amazónica. *Amazonía Peruana* 4(8): 61–76.

NIMUENDAJÚ, C. (1987). *As Lendas da Criação e Destruição do Mundo como Fundamentos da Religião dos Apapocúva-Guarani*. São Paulo: HUCITEC, Editora da Universidade de São Paulo.

NIES, J. (1972). *Muchikawa Kewenni Pirana ga wa Pimri Ginkaklukaka (Los Antiguos Perros y otros Cuentos: Cartilla de lectura 10)*. Lima: Ministerio de Educación.

——(comp.). (1986). *Diccionario Piro (Tokanchi Gikshijikowaka-steno)*. Serie Lingüística Peruana 22. Yarinacocha: Ministerio de Educación and Instituto Lingüístico de Verano.

OBEYESEKERE, G. (1992). *The Apotheosis of Captain Cook: European Mythmaking in the Pacific*. Princeton, NJ: Princeton University Press.

ORTIZ, D. (1974). *Alto Ucayali y Pachitea: Visión Historica de dos Importantes Regiones de la Selva Peruana*. 2 vols. Lima: San Antonio.

OVERING [KAPLAN], J. (1975). [KAPLAN, J.]. *The Piaroa: A people of the Orinoco Basin*. Oxford: Clarendon Press.

——(1977). [KAPLAN, J.] Commentary. In Social Time and Social Space in Lowland South American Societies, J. Kaplan (org.), *Actes du XLIIe Congrès International des Americanistes*. Vol. 2. Paris.

——(1981). Review Article: Amazonian Anthropology. *Journal of Latin American Studies* 13(1): 151–64.

——(1989). The Aesthetics of Production: The Sense of Community among the Cubeo and Piaroa. *Dialectical Anthropology*, 14: 159–75.

——(1995). O Mito como Histório: Un problema de Tempo, Realidade e outras Questôes. *Mana* 1(1): 107–40.

——(1999). Elogio do Cotidiano: A Cofiança e a Arte da Vida Social em uma Communidade Amazonica. *Mana* 5(1): 81–107.

——and M. KAPLAN. (1987). Los Wóthuha (Piaroa). In W. Coppens with B. Escalente (eds.), *Los Aborígenes de Venezuela, Volumen III: Etnología Contemporanea*. Caracas: Fundación La Salle.

PÉREZ MARCIO, M. F (1953). *Los Hijos de la Selva*. Buenos Aires: Casa Editora Sudamericana.

POLLOCK, D. (1992). Culina Shamanism: Gender, Power, and Knowledge. In E. J. Matteson Langdon and G. Baer (eds.), *Portals of Power: Shamanism in South America*. Albuquerque: University of New Mexico Press.

RADCLIFFE-BROWN, A. R. (1952). *Structure and Function in Primitive Society*. London: Routledge and Kegan Paul.

RENARD-CASEVITZ, F.-M. (1992). História Kampa, Memória Ashaninca. In M. Carneiro da Cunha (ed.), *História dos Indios no Brasil*. São Paulo: Companhia das letras.

——(1993). Guerriers du sel, suniers de la paix. *L'Homme* 126–8: 25–43.

REEVE, M.-E. (1988). Cauchu Uras: Lowland Quichua Histories of the Amazon Rubber Boom. In J. Hill (ed.), *Rethinking History and Myth*.

RIBEIRO, D. (1980). Kadiwéu: Ensaios Etnológicos sobre o Saber, o Azar e a Beleza. Petrópolis: Editora Vozes.

RIVIÈRE, P. (1969). *Marriage among the Trio*. Oxford: Oxford University Press.

——(1984). Individual and Society in Guiana: *A Comparative Study of Amerindian Social Organization*. Cambridge: Cambridge University Press.

——(1993). The Amerindianization of Descent and Affinity. *L'Homme*, 126–28: 507–16.

ROE, P. G. (1982). *The Cosmic Zygote: Cosmology in the Amazon Basin*. New Brunswick, NJ: Rutgers University Press.

——(1988). The Josho Nahuanbo are all Wet and Undercooked: Shipibo Views of the Whiteman and the Incas in Myth, Legend and History. In Hill (ed.), *Rethinking History and Myth*.

ROMAN, L. (1985). 'Etica y Estética en el Arte Piro. *Antropologica* 3: 125–33.

——(1986). Pendencias y dependencias en la Amazonía sur del Perú. *Antropologica* 4: 7–38.

ROMAN, L. and A. ZARZAR (1983). *Relaciones Intertribales en el Bajo Urubamba y Alto Ucayali*. Lima: CIPA.

ROOSEVELT, A. C. (1993). The Rise and Fall of the Amazon Chiefdoms. *L'Homme*, 126–28: 255–83.

SABATÉ, L. (1925). Viaje de los Misioneros del Convento del Cuzco a las Tribues Selvajes de los Campas, Piros, Cunibos y Shipibos por el P. Fr. Luis Sabaté en el año de 1874. In P. F. Bernardino Izaguirre (ed.), *Historia de las Misiones Franciscanas y Narración de los Progresos de la Geografia en el Oriente del Perú, Relatos Originales y Producciones en Lenguas Indigenas de various Misioneros 1691–1921*. Vol. 10: 7–317, Lima. Talleres tipográficos de la Penitenciaría.

SAHLINS, M. (1981). *Historical Metaphors and Mythical Realities: Structure in the Early History of the Sandwich Islands Kingdom*. Ann Arbor: University of Michigan Press.

——(1995). *How 'Natives' Think: About Captain Cook, for example*. Chicago and London: University of Chicago Press.

SAMANEZ Y OCAMPO, J. B. (1980). *Exploración de los Ríos Peruanos, Apurímac, Eni, Ucayali y Urubamba, hecho por Samanez y Ocampo en 1883 y 1884*. Lima: privately printed.

SANTOS GRANERO, F. (1988). Avances y Limitaciones de la Historiografía Amazónica: 1950–1988. In F. Santos (ed.), *1 Seminario de Investigaciones Sociales en la Amazonía*. Iquitos: CETA.

——(1991). *The Power of Love: The Moral Uses of Knowledge amongst the Amuesha of Central Peru*. London and Atlantic Highlands, NJ: Athlone Press.

SCHOLTE, B. (1970). Epistemic Paradigms: Some Problems in Cross-cultural Research on Social Anthropological History and Theory. In E. N. Hayes and T. Hayes (eds.), *Claude Lévi-Strauss: The Anthropologist as Hero*. Cambridge, Mass. and London: MIT Press.

SCHREMPP, G. (1992). *Magical Arrows: The Maori, the Greeks and the Folklore of the Universe*. Madison, Wisc. and London: University of Wisconsin Press.

SEBASTIÁN, J., M. ZUMAETA, and J. NIES. (1974). *Yine pirana 12: Gwacha Ginkakle (Cartilla de lectura 12: Historia de los piros)*. Lima: Ministerio de Educación.

SEEGER, A. (1981). *Nature and Society in Central Brazil: The Suyá Indians of Mato Grosso*. Cambridge, Mass.: Harvard University Press.

——(1987). *Why Suyá Sing: A Musical Anthropology of an Amazonian People*. Cambridge: Cambridge University Press.

SEEGER, A., R. DA MATTA and E. VIVEIROS DE CASTRO (1979). A Construção da Pessoa nas Sociedades Indígenas Brasileiras. *Boletim do Museo Nacional* (n.s.) 32: 2–19.

SEYMOUR-SMITH, C. (1988). *Shiwiar: Identidad Étnica y Cambio en el río Corrientes*. Quito and Lima: Ediciones ABYA-YALA and CAAAP.

SICK, H. (1993). *Birds in Brazil: A Natural History*. Princeton, NJ: Princeton University Press.

SIQUIERA Jr., J. G. (1992). A Iconografia Kadiwéu atual. In L. Vidal (ed), *Grafismo indígena: Estudos de Antropôlogia Estéticas*. São Paulo: Studio Nobel, FAPESP and Edusp.

SISKIND, J. (1973). *To Hunt in the Morning*, London, Oxford and New York: Oxford University Press.

STOLL, D. (1982). *Fishers of Men or Founders of Empire?: The Wycliffe Bible Translators in Latin America*. London and Cambridge, Mass.: Zed Books.

STRATHERN, M. (1988). *The Gender of the Gift: Problems with Women and Problems with Society in Melanesia*. Berkeley, Los Angeles and London: University of California Press.

TAUSSIG, M. (1980). *The Devil and Commodity Fetishism in South America*. Chapel Hill: University of North Carolina Press.

TAYLOR, A.-C. (1993). Remembering to Forget: identity, memory and mourning among the Jivaro. *Man* (n.s.) 28: 653–78.

——(1996). The soul's body and its states: an Amazonian perspective on the nature of being human. *Journal of the Royal Anthropoligical Institute*, 2: 201–15.

THOMPSON, D. W. (1942). *Of Growth and Form*. Cambridge: Cambridge University Press.

TIBESAR, A. (1950). The salt trade among the montaña Indians of the Tarma areas of Eastern Peru. *Primitive Man* 23: 103–8.

TOREN, C. (1990). *Making Sense of Hierarchy: Cognition as Social Process in Fiji*. London and Atlantic Highlands, NJ: Athlone Press.

——(1993). Making History: The Significance of Childhood Cognition for a Comparative Anthropology of Mind. *Man* (n.s.) 28: 461–78.

——(1999). *Mind, Materiality and History: Explorations in Fijian Ethnography*. London and New York: Routledge.

TOWNSLEY, G. (1993). Song Paths: The Ways and Means of Yaminahua Shamanic Knowledge. *L'Homme*, 126–8: 449–68.

TURNER, T. S. (1979). The Ge and Bororo Societies as Dialectical Systems: A General Model. In D. Maybury-Lewis (ed.).

——(1980). The Social Skin. In J. Cherfas (ed.), *Not Work Alone*. London: Temple Smith.

——(1985). Animal Symbolism, Totemism and the Structure of Myth. In G. Urton (ed.), *Animal Myths and Metaphors in South America*. Salt Lake City: University of Utah Press.

——(1988). History, Myth and Social Consciousness among the Kayapó of Central Brazil . In J. Hill (ed.), *Rethinking History and Myth*, 235–81.

——(1992). Os Mebengokre Kayapó: História e Mudança Social de Comunidades Autônomas para a Coexistência Interétnica. In M. Carneiro da Cunha (ed.), *História dos Indios no Brasil*, São Paulo: Companhia das letras.

——(1993). De Cosmologia a História: Resistência, Adaptação e Consiência Social entre os Kayapó. In E. Viveiros de Castro and M. Carneiro da Cunha (eds.), *Amazônia: Etnologia e História Indigena*, São Paulo: FAPESP.

——(1995). Social Body and Embodied Subject: Bodiliness, Subjectivity and Sociality among the Kayapo. *Cultural Anthropology* 10(2): 143–70.

——(n.d.). The Fire of the Jaguar: Myth and Social Organization among the Northern Kayapó of Central Brazil. Unpublished manuscript.

URBAN, G. (1991). *A Discourse-Centred Approach to Culture: Native South American Myths and Rituals*. Austin: University of Texas Press.

——(1992). A História da Cultura Brasileira segundo as Línguas Nativas. In M. Carneiro da Cunha (ed.), *História dos Indios no Brasil*, São Paulo: Companhia das Letras.

——(1996a). *Metaphysical Community: The Interplay of the Senses and the Intellect*. Austin, Tex.: University of Texas Press.

——(1996b). On the Geographical Origins and Dispersions of Tupian Languages. *Revista de Antropologia* 39(2): 61–104.

URIARTE, L. M. (1989). Native Blowguns and National Guns: The Achuar Jiaveroans and the Dialectics of Power in the Peruvian Amazon. Unpublished Ph.D., University of Illinois at Urbana-Champaign.

URTON, G. (1981). *At the Crossroads of the Earth and Sky: An Andean Cosmology*. Austin, Tex.: University of Texas Press.

VARESE, S. (1972). Interethnic Relations in the Selva of Peru. In R. Dostal (ed.), *The Situation of the Indian in South America*. Geneva: World Council of Churches.

——(1973 [1968]). *La Sal de Los Cerros (Una Aproximacion al Mundo Campa)*. Lima: Retablo de Papel Ediciones.

VEBER, H. (1996). External Inducement and Non-Westernization in the Uses of the Ashéninka Cushma. *Journal of Material Culture* 1(2): 155–82.

VILAÇA, A. (1992). *Comendo como Gente: Formas de Canibalismo Wari'*. Rio de Janeiro: Editora Universidad Federal do Rio de Janeiro.

——(1996). Quem somos nós: Questões da alteridade no encontro dos Wari' com os brancos. Unpublished Ph.d., Museu Nacional/Programa de Pós-Gradução em Antropologica Social, Universidad Federal do Rio de Janeiro.

VILAÇA, A. (1997). Christians without faith. *Ethnos*, 62(1–2): 91–115.

VILLAREJO, Av. (1979). *Así es la Selva: Estudio Mongráfico de la Amazonía Peruana.* Iquitos: CETA.

VIVEIROS DE CASTRO, E. (1977). *Indivíduo e Sociedade no Alto-Xingu: Os Yawalapíti.* Master's Thesis, Museu Nacional da Universidade Federal do Rio de Janeiro.

——(1978). A Fabricação do Corpo na Sociedade Xinguana. *Boletim do Museu Nacional* (n.s.) 32: 40–9.

——(1992). *From the Enemy's Point of View: Humanity and Divinity in an Amazonian Society.* Chicago: University of Chicago Press.

——(1993a). Le Marbre et le Myrte: De l'inconstance de le âme sauvage. In A. Becquelin and A. Molinié (eds.), *Mémoire de la tradition*, Nanterre: Société d'Ethnologie, 365–431.

——(1993b). Algums Aspetos da Afinidade no Dravidianato Amazônico. In E. Viveiros de Castro and M. Carneiro da Cunha (eds.), *Amazônia: Etnologia e Histório Indigena*, São Paulo: FAPESP.

——(1996). Images of Nature and Society in Amazonian Ethnology. In *Annual Reviews in Anthropology*, 25: 179–200.

——(1998). Cosmological Deixis and Amerindian Perspectivism. *Journal of the Royal Anthropological Institute* (n.s.) 4: 469–88.

WACHTEL, N. (1994). *Gods and Vampires: Return to Chipaya.* Chicago and London: University of Chicago Press.

Wallis, E. E. (1961). *The Dayuma Story: Life Under Auca Spears.* London: Hodder and Stoughton.

——(1966). *Tariri: My Story, from Jungle Killer to Christian Missionary.* London: Hodder and Stoughton.

WEISS, G. (1975). *Campa Cosmology: The World of a Forest Tribe in South America.* New York: American Museum of Natural History.

WELTFISCH, G. (1971). *The Lost Universe: The Way of Life of The Pawnee.* New York: Ballantine Books Inc.

WOLF, E. (1982). *Europe and the People without History.* Berkeley, Calif.: University of California Press.

WRIGHT, R. M. (1998). *Cosmos, Self and History in Baniwa Religion: For Those Unborn.* Austin, Tex.: University of Texas Press.

ZUIDEMA, T. (1985). The Lion in the City: Royal Symbols of Transition in Cuzco. In G. Urton (ed) *Animal Myths and Metaphors in South America.* Salt Lake City, Ut.: University of Utah Press.

INDEX